DARK VICTORY

DARK VICTORY

DAVID MARR AND MARIAN WILKINSON

First published in 2003

Copyright © David Marr and Marian Wilkinson 2003

All rights reserved. No part of this book may be reproduced or transmitted in any form or by any means, electronic or mechanical, including photocopying, recording or by any information storage and retrieval system, without prior permission in writing from the publisher. The *Australian Copyright Act 1968* (the Act) allows a maximum of one chapter or 10 per cent of this book, whichever is the greater, to be photocopied by any educational institution for its educational purposes provided that the educational institution (or body that administers it) has given a remuneration notice to Copyright Agency Limited (CAL) under the Act.

Allen & Unwin
83 Alexander Street
Crows Nest NSW 2065
Australia
Phone: (61 2) 8425 0100
Fax: (61 2) 9906 2218
Email: info@allenandunwin.com
Web: www.allenandunwin.com

National Library of Australia
Cataloguing-in-Publication entry:

Marr, David, 1947- .
    Dark victory

    Includes index.
    ISBN 1 86508 939 7.

    1. Australia. Parliament - Elections, 2001.
    2. Political campaigns - Australia.
    3. Howard, John, 1939- . 4. Liberal Party of Australia.
    5. Illegal aliens - Australia. 6. Refugees - Government policy - Australia. 7. Tampa (Ship). 8. Australia - Armed Forces - Political activity. I. Wilkinson, Marian, 1954- . II. Title.

Text design by Bookhouse, Sydney
Set in 10.25/14 pt Caslon 540 by Bookhouse, Sydney
Printed by Griffin Press, Adelaide

10 9 8 7 6 5

for
JOHN IREMONGER
of course

Contents

1 **Full up** 1
    August 23 to 26

2 **Sea rescue** 14
    August 26

3 **Australia v. the boat people** 30

4 **Canberra scrambles** 48
    August 27

5 **Pan Pan** 62
    August 28

6 **Boarding party** 75
    August 29

7 **Labor cornered** 89
    To August 31

8 **Pacific Solution** 102
    August 30 & 31

9 **The rule of law** 110
    August 29 to September 3

10	**The thick grey line** September 3 to 10	129
11	**The shadow of the Twin Towers** September 11 to 19	142
12	**The voyage of the *Manoora*** September 3 to October 8	158
13	**Launching the campaign** To October 8	172
14	**Orders from the top** October 6 to 9	181
15	**Truth overboard** October 9 to 12	194
16	**A military campaign** October 14 to 23	211
17	**The boat that sank** October 17 to 28	224
18	**The worst of times** October 23 to November 4	239
19	**The navy leaks** November 4 to 8	252
20	**The burning issue** November 8 and 9	266
21	**Victory party** November 10	277

Aftermath 287
Notes 294
Glossary and abbreviations 322
Acknowledgements 327
Index 333

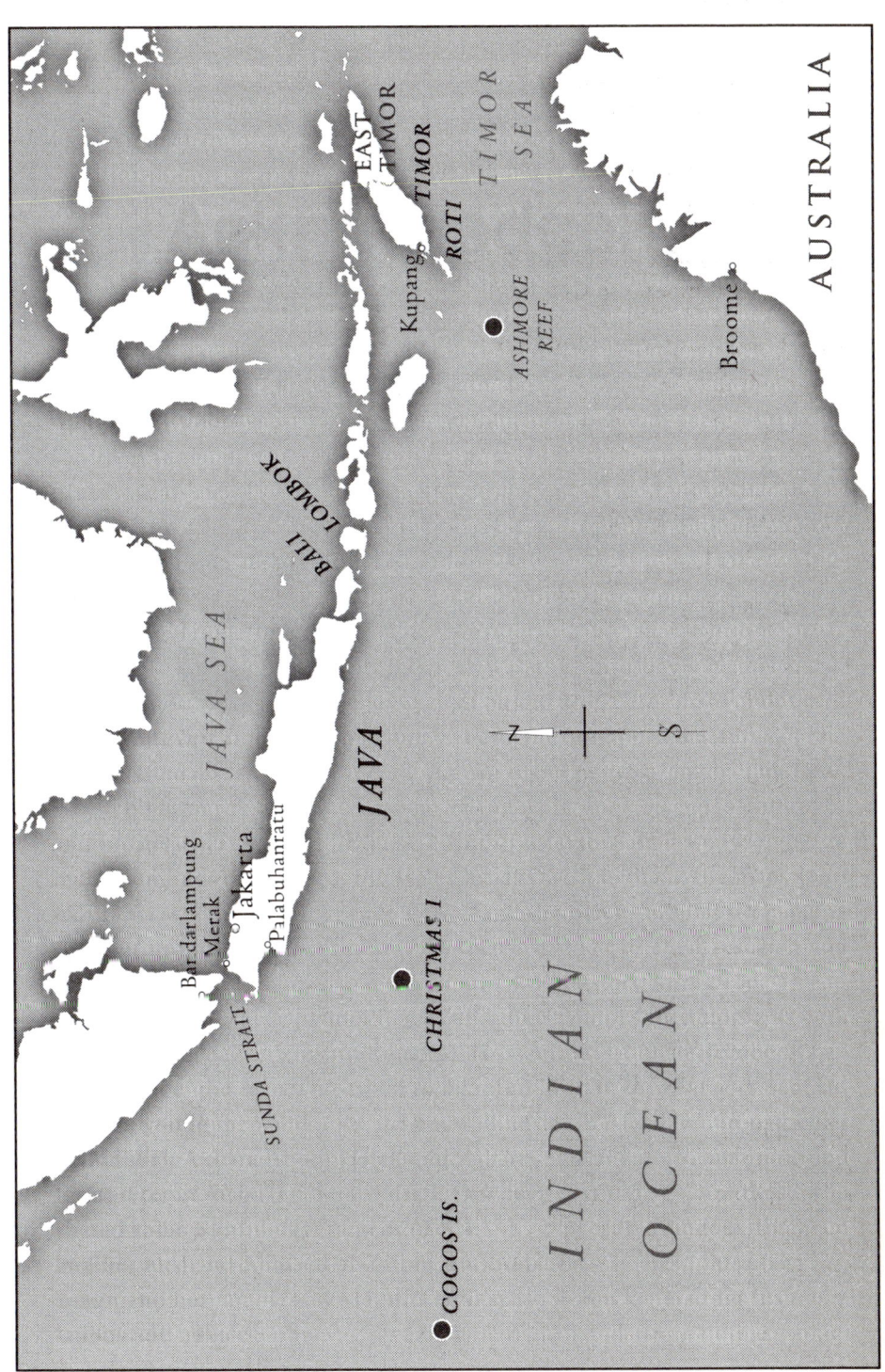

ONE
Full up

AUGUST 23 TO 26

When the red dot first appeared on the horizon, no one stirred. They had been disappointed too often in the days since their engine failed to be roused by the sight of a ship in the distance. One boat had already sailed by, ignoring them. Australian planes had circled overhead but left them to wallow in the sea. The shape they saw on the horizon was so small some of those on the KM *Palapa 1* thought it might be another boat like theirs, crammed full of people making for Christmas Island. But when that small red dot turned into a cargo ship, people climbed onto the roof to wave and shout. Khodadad Sarwari said: 'There was nothing left for us in this world if the ship goes past.'[1]

Sarwari, a teacher, sat jammed between his wife, their three children and his brother on the boat's flimsy upper deck. The family was fleeing the Taliban. So were most of the people on the *Palapa*. By now they were exhausted, ill and thirsty. Most had spent the last few days vomiting. They had faced death the previous night in a violent storm which they believed they had survived only by a miracle. Now a cargo boat was bearing down on them. 'We were telling the children there is hope because we didn't want them to give up, to collapse. We were praying God would save us.

Then when it was getting closer we saw it was huge and there was a big sign on it written: *Tampa*.'[2]

The great hull slid past. 'All of a sudden people were screaming that they are not going to rescue us', said Sarwari. 'We were extremely hopeless.' These were the worst moments of their whole ordeal on the ocean. 'Now we were not thinking about this world but preparing ourselves for the other world. The most terrifying thing for us was to see our children, at their age, dying. But after ten minutes the boys were saying it's getting closer and again there was hope.' The cargo boat had stopped and was edging back towards them, sheltering the *Palapa* in the lee of its enormous hull. When a long metal stair was lowered, the people on the *Palapa* finally knew they were saved.

Rajab Ali Merzaee, an Afghan medical student, watched two sailors come down to the foot of the stairs. 'They were two very strong men. Very lovely, very good persons.'[3] The sailors called out to them to leave their belongings behind and allow women and children to cross first. Men who tried to disobey the order where thrown back onto the *Palapa*'s deck. Any luggage they had in their hands was thrown back, too. The *Palapa* was rising and falling on the swell. Already battered by the storm, the boat began losing chunks of deck and railing as it slammed into the *Tampa*'s hull. The lines kept breaking. The sailors on the stair timed their moves, reaching over to pluck one or two survivors from the deck each time the *Palapa* rose on the swell. This went on for two and a half hours.

Sailors carried little children, the sick and terrified up the long metal stair. The rest formed a long, slow queue. When these filthy men and women reached the *Tampa*'s deck, they were searched very thoroughly, counted twice and had a number written on their arms with a black marker pen. One of the sailors told Rajab Ali Hossaini they had been expecting to take about eighty survivors on board. 'When people were coming eighty, one hundred, two hundred, three hundred, they were wide-eyed looking: what is going on, what sort of boat is this with people just coming up?'[4] Even the survivors were amazed that so many had been packed onto the boat. 'That's bloody smugglers: even the smallest space, they used that one for the sake of profit', said Hamid from Kabul who was one of the last men to leave the *Palapa*. 'They play with human lives. They don't care about human lives. They care about their money.'[5]

Up on the deck of the *Tampa* the survivors were praying, crying and laughing. They had a future. They would reach Australia. They would see their children grow up. Several times on the *Palapa* over the last three days they had given themselves up for dead. 'Now we were smiling, we were telling stories, we were thanking God we were saved', said Merzaee. But there were those among the survivors who wondered why they had been put through the ordeal of the last days. Why were they left to drift? Why were they not saved once those Australian planes saw them? Why were they made to endure that terrible storm? Sarwari asked himself, 'Why people were so heartless not to rescue us?'

Australia had known for days the 20-metre Indonesian fishing boat with an ancient engine, a rickety upper deck and an incompetent crew was on its way. The *Palapa* was bringing the biggest load of asylum seekers ever to set out for Christmas Island, Australia's tiny territory sitting below Java in the Indian Ocean. The island was crowded with people who had arrived on boats in the weeks before. There had never been such a crush of asylum seekers. More were on the way. Over on the mainland, Australia's immigration prisons were full. So when the *Palapa* got into trouble on the crossing, some ruthless Australian bureaucrats took it as a godsend. Somehow, these people could now be sent back to Indonesia. For over twenty hours, rescue authorities in Australia did nothing effective to help the people on the *Palapa* except harass the Indonesians to take responsibility for the problem. That delay put the lives of 438 people in terrible danger. In the end, Australian rescue authorities had no choice but to put out a call for the *Palapa*'s rescue. The *Tampa* answered. But Australia was still determined these people would go back to Indonesia. What followed was a crisis which for a time engaged the attention of the world.

I

Assadullah Rezaee had hesitated when he arrived at the wharf with his wife and three children at about 2 am on Thursday August 23. There were six buses ahead of them and more kept arriving. 'When I saw the boat and when I looked at the people I thought I better turn back. But other friends told me, it doesn't matter whether I go now or stay behind and try again, the agents won't have a better boat for you. It will probably be worse than this.'[6] Rezaee, a farmer from the Afghan province of Ghazni, had paid US$11 500 to get his family to Australia and had been promised something better than a fishing boat. Rezaee showed his chit and was told to take his family to the crude upper deck. They couldn't stand. The roof there was only a metre or so above the deck. As people poured on to the *Palapa*, they couldn't move at all but sat, squashed together, with their knees under their chins.

Hamid had travelled from Jakarta with two Indonesian soldiers on board his bus. More men in uniform were waiting at the wharf. 'The smugglers and the police officers or the soldiers were rushing around and trying to offload us as quickly as possible and putting us in those boats because they were saying that the guards or the security that they were dealing with, their shift would change when the sun rises.' He had watched officials giving the smugglers a hand all the way from Kabul. At Jakarta airport, the smuggler guiding Hamid's party had not even taken them through immigration. 'It looked like all the Indonesian police and military were co-operating with him because they took us outside the terminal and there were Datsun vehicles already available for us.' For a month Hamid had waited with thirty Afghans in a villa in the Jakarta suburbs. Around them were other villas where asylum seekers were waiting, like them, for boats. One night they were moved to a hotel where the smugglers took the last of his money and put him on a bus with a ticket, a bottle of water and some biscuits. He had no other food. 'I was told the destination is very close and we would get there very quickly.'[7]

The buses brought them all to Pantau, a little port near the surfing resort of Pelabuhan Ratu on the south western coast of Java. Hamid climbed aboard the first boat he had ever been on in his life. 'I saw boats on television or in movies but in Afghanistan it's a landlocked country. It doesn't have boat or ship.' Like nearly everyone on the *Palapa*, Hamid could not swim. By torchlight, he discovered he was on an old, wooden tub. Someone was working on the engine and there was an ominous sound of hammering from beneath the deck. This was not the modern ship with individual cabins he had been told to expect. He assumed the *Palapa* was taking the people still pouring on board out to the real ship waiting somewhere in deeper water. Then he overheard one of the smugglers talking to the Indonesian captain who was holding a box—in fact, a compass—in his hand. The smuggler said: 'You going straight ahead and there's no other island in front of you; any island comes in front of you, that would be Christmas Island.'[8]

The last buses arrived. As people climbed on board they were handed flimsy life jackets, bottles of water and bags of sliced bread. Many had brought supplies of their own: biscuits, water, dried and fresh fruit. Twenty-one families with 43 children plus luggage were eventually packed onto the temporary upper deck. The youngest child was one. On the main deck below were 350 men travelling alone, many far younger than they pretended to be. A couple of dozen were only boys. At about 4 am the smugglers drove off in a car, the crew kicked the motor into life and the *Palapa* headed out to sea. The boat rolled in the chop. The crowded decks filled with diesel fumes. People were soon vomiting.

For as many as three hundred of the people on the *Palapa*, this was a second attempt to reach Christmas Island. They had set out a month earlier from the same port on a voyage that should have taken only 36 hours. Four days later they were still searching for Christmas Island. The captain had only a compass to steer by. He was blind in one eye. The seas were very rough. They gave up and headed north, running aground a couple of days later on a muddy beach at Bandar Lampung on the tip of Sumatra. Tired and sick, they were taken by ferry across the Sunda Strait—as it happens through the port of Merak—and by bus back to cheap hotels in Jakarta. Many had picked up scabies on the boat. Some gave up at this point and disappeared. The rest had returned in the curtained buses guarded by uniformed Indonesians to take a second chance on an even more crowded boat, the *Palapa*.

Captain Bastian Disun stayed at the wheel all day. The weather was good. They expected to arrive at Christmas Island the following afternoon. Few had much of an idea of what to find when they got there. They knew Australia was a prosperous western democracy. 'I also knew about the Queen', said Khodadad Sarwari. 'And that most people were from a European background and the language they spoke was English.'[9] They could not be blamed for having a vague idea that Australia was deeply committed to human rights. Years of hard diplomatic effort had gone into selling that message to the world. For decades, Australia had positioned itself as a leader of United Nations' campaigns against racism, poverty and oppression. 'They were telling the world they are helping the humanitarian work and helping the refugees and accepting the refugees and that a lot of refugees and migrants they are coming to Australia', said Wahidullah Akbari, the son of a Kandahar shopkeeper who set out alone at the age of sixteen to make his way to this safe haven. 'We thought we would receive the same treatment.'[10]

Some were already on the road when smugglers sold them the idea of Australia, a more reliable and less expensive destination than Europe or North America. They could, of course, have stayed in Indonesia or the camps of Pakistan and been safe from the Taliban. But in Australia they could begin new lives. So trucks, shops, fields, gold and carpets were sold to raise the US$5000 or so to deliver these farmers, teachers, students and labourers to Australia. Little children were cheaper. The smugglers extorted what they could—the last few dollars—to give children a place on the boats.

At the end of the journey they knew there was a camp where they would be held for a time. The smugglers had told them this but the prospect of three or four months' detention was no deterrent for those who believed Australia would accept them as refugees. Even if that process stretched into years, it would be worth it in the end. 'Our future would be secure, would be better. It doesn't matter how bad it is, it would be better than the war in Afghanistan', said Rajab Ali Merzaee. He had the high cheekbones and oriental eyes of the Hazara people, the underdogs of every Afghan regime. The province of Ghazni was his home but he had studied medicine for four years in the more peaceful north. He spoke a little English. His family had a small shop which barely made them a living but his father had a patch of land he sold to pay the smugglers. Merzaee said that had he known what his father was planning, he would have refused to go. But the deal was done before he knew of it. Merzaee and his wife crossed the border, waited in Karachi for about a month, then flew to Jakarta. By the time they boarded the *Palapa*, they had been travelling for two months.

Everyone on board the *Palapa* claimed to be Afghan apart from six Sri Lankans and three men who admitted they were Pakistani. As many as a hundred of the passengers may also have been Pakistanis posing as Afghans. This was a common problem in the refugee world: they speak almost the same language and look very much alike but Pakistanis have very little claim to be accepted as refugees. They were trying to rort the system in order to emigrate. But the three hundred or so genuine Afghans on the *Palapa* had every reason to believe that at the end of this journey Australia would welcome them. They were on the run from one of the world's worst regimes. As that overloaded fishing boat chugged south, there was no end in sight to the Taliban. The World Trade Centre was still standing; the war against terror was months away. These people were, indeed, refugees who had, according to the Universal Declaration of Human Rights, 'the right to seek and to enjoy in other countries asylum from persecution'.[11]

I

At about 9 pm, Disun handed the wheel to one of the three crew and went to sleep on the floor of the wheelhouse. Merzaee noticed the boat was being pushed harder. 'He tried to move the boat faster and he wasn't controlling it. The sea was rough and he wasn't taking that into account.' Twice before dawn the engine stopped but the crew got it going again. 'Everyone was asleep when they heard a big noise, a banging, then after that the engine stopped.' When the crew went to look, they found the engine had worked loose on its mounting and, falling sideways, sheared the gears inside their casing.[12] The crew could do nothing. Two mechanics among the refugees climbed down into the bilge to look at the problem. The engine still turned over—that would keep the pumps running to the end—but there was no power to the propeller. It was hopeless. 'The engine was from the time of Hitler', said Hamid and there were no tools on board to do repairs.[13] At dawn on August 24, after travelling for a little over 24 hours, the *Palapa* was dead in the water.

Everyone was now awake. There was pandemonium on the boat. 'Everybody was crying and shouting and yelling.' The captain burst into tears. 'We all were crying. The rest of the people worried and we would expect that death would come any minute.'[14] After a time they calmed down. They prayed. When a ship appeared a few hours later, it seemed their ordeal was over. 'We were screaming and whistling', said Khodadad Sarwari. They climbed onto the *Palapa*'s flimsy roof to wave their orange life jackets in the air and hold up their children so the sailors on the ship could see there were families on board. There was no doubt the *Palapa* had been seen, the cargo boat flashed a light as it passed, but it kept on sailing. The master of that ship had left hundreds of human beings to their fate, but saved himself and his shipping line an awful lot of trouble.

The *Palapa*'s captain assured them they were already in Australian waters so they tore planks from the flooring of the upper deck and began to paddle. Four teams of five or six people paddled all afternoon. 'I knew it was not moving the boat anywhere, but simply to give people a bit of hope', said Khodadad Sarwari. Soon after dark they heard a plane overhead.

They flashed the lights of the boat but the plane flew on. In the morning, a couple of teams started paddling again. Then a few minutes before 10 am, a plane appeared. 'We took all the children and women to the top of the boat and then we were waving for the plane', said Rajab Ali Hossaini. The plane flew into the distance, turned and passed low over the *Palapa*. By this time, the roof was jammed with people waving their life jackets in the air and shouting for help.

❙

Barry Spencer, commander of the Surveillance Australia mission, ordered the de Havilland Dash-8 to make several 'overflies' of the little boat which he assessed to be a Suspect Illegal Entry Vessel (SIEV). Spencer 'had a look at it both visually and with the television camera and took photography of it, still photography. There were approximately eighty people on the deck, waving their hands and waving bits of material. The vessel was dead in the water, not moving at all, no mode of power'.[15] He radioed a report to the Canberra headquarters of Coastwatch, the civil agency that co-ordinates surveillance of the seas around Australia.

Though it was a Saturday afternoon in the national capital, the information flowed deep into the bureaucracy. It went to the National Surveillance Centre at Coastwatch headquarters for analysis. The sighting of every fresh SIEV was also reported directly to Jenny Bryant, a senior bureaucrat in the Department of Prime Minister and Cabinet which had, at its head, the mandarin most concerned with boats and refugees, Max Moore-Wilton.[16] The sighting of the *Palapa* was also reported to the Department of Immigration and Multicultural Affairs (DIMA) whose minister was the whey-faced and stubborn Philip Ruddock. The news came as no surprise to DIMA: the department had known the *Palapa* was on its way for almost 24 hours.

Immigration was extremely concerned that there would be nowhere to put these people when they arrived at Christmas Island. 'On 22 August we had the largest arrival ever of 359', said Ruddock. 'That had followed closely behind a boat that had arrived on Christmas Island with 345 and that was on the 16th August. We were moving people off as quickly as possible but we were looking at possibly as many as 900 people. And the occupation levels at immigration detention centres were close to full capacity. We had 3600 people in detention at that time at the end of August.'[17]

News of the *Palapa* did not reach the Rescue Coordination Centre (RCC) at the Australian Maritime Safety Authority (AMSA) for two hours. 'Coastwatch advised sighting of vessel 55 nautical miles west north-west of Christmas Island. Vessel appeared to have in excess of 80 people on board and seemed to be "dead in the water".'[18] A boat dead in the water does not necessarily need rescue. Perhaps the engines are being repaired. Perhaps the boat will soon be under way again. Calling on all shipping to go to the aid of a stricken vessel is a dramatic gesture. It's not done lightly. Were this an Australian fishing boat being paddled by its crew or a lone round the world yachtswoman with an oar over the side, an immediate rescue might well have been called. But in the bureaucratic world of sea rescue, waiting to see what happened to the *Palapa* that afternoon was perfectly routine.

Four hours after his first observation, Barry Spencer was back over the *Palapa* in the Coastwatch de Havilland. The boat had drifted west and away from Christmas Island. Otherwise nothing much had changed: people were still rowing and jumping up and down on the roof waving life jackets. He stayed over the *Palapa* for at least half an hour, videoing the scene and taking more photographs. Spencer could see there were far more people than he first thought on board. He now put the number at '200 plus'. He also tried, without success, to raise the boat on the radio. But the *Palapa* had no radio, indeed no communication equipment of any kind. Spencer was running out of fuel and returned to his base on Christmas Island.

The *Palapa* was clearly in grave difficulties: drifting helplessly on the Indian Ocean with a very large number of people on board. A second Coastwatch report on the boat reached the rescue authority in Canberra, RCC Australia, early in the evening. It was a decisive moment but no text of this report has ever surfaced. One summary read: 'Report from Coastwatch indicating vessel appears to be in distress.' That would seem to require an immediate call to shipping to go to the *Palapa*'s rescue. A less urgent version of the same report was later supplied to the Senate: the *Palapa* only 'appeared to require assistance'.[19] Either way, RCC Australia was worried enough to ring Coastwatch to discuss the *Palapa*'s predicament. Again, no notes of this conversation have ever been produced. The summary reads: 'Coastwatch advised . . . the vessel did not indicate distress.'[20] In a very formal sense, that was true: there was no MAYDAY, no SOS. But this was not a vessel operating under the ordinary rules of commercial shipping. It was a smugglers' hulk with no engine, crammed full of human beings.

Australia put out no call to shipping that night, but did inform the Indonesian rescue authority BASARNAS that there was a vessel requiring assistance in its rescue zone. In 1990, Australia and Indonesia drew a line east–west across the Indian Ocean dividing it into zones of responsibility. Christmas Island lay inside the Indonesian zone. The boundary simply recognised that Indonesia was 'best placed' to respond to emergencies in its zone. That's about all. The agreement is a very slender document. Contrary to all that would be said over the next days and weeks by Australia's leaders, the 1990 arrangement does not oblige Indonesia to carry out every rescue in its zone.[21] Sea rescue does not work that way. What matters first and foremost is saving lives, not which country takes charge of the rescue or looks after the survivors. Clive Davidson, chief executive officer of AMSA, explained: 'The responsibility on all search and rescue agencies around the world is to respond comprehensively and completely to every search and rescue event, wherever they may be.'[22]

Insted of seeing to the rescue itself, RCC Australia concentrated its efforts on trying to whip BASARNAS into action. The last time it had gone to such lengths to pass responsibility for a rescue to the Indonesians was two years earlier for a fishing boat with only half a dozen lives at stake. RCC Australia knew only too well that BASARNAS, responsible for a huge archipelago full of fishing boats and ferries, was under-resourced and overwhelmed. RCC officers joke that BASARNAS 'is great, one time in ten'. Their boss Clive Davidson has to be more diplomatic but admitted that when Australian rescue authorities call their counterparts in Jakarta, 'it would be common for them not to respond'.[23] Indeed, that is what happened on the night of August 25. The fax sent to BASARNAS alerting it to the *Palapa* ended, 'Please confirm receipt of this fax by return fax'. BASARNAS did not respond. At some point in the evening someone at RCC Australia rang the BASARNAS headquarters in Jakarta. Davidson said: 'When we called the Indonesian search and rescue agency there was nobody that competently spoke English to talk to.'[24] Canberra had no idea what, if anything, BASARNAS was doing about the *Palapa* that night and took no further action itself.

FULL UP | 11

1

'Dark came again and we were alone', said Khodadad Sarwari. 'The plane did not come back. Then we lost hope. That was the hardest night we had on board because there were glimpses of hope and they disappeared.'[25] The sea had been rising all day. Video taken of the *Palapa* in the afternoon showed it already wallowing in a deep swell. Towards nightfall the weather turned nasty and at about midnight the *Palapa* was hit by a violent storm. Waves began crashing across the lower deck. It was extremely dangerous. As the boat rolled, people scrambled to the high side of the deck which then plunged the boat even deeper as it rolled to the other side. Everyone was urged to sit still. They tied themselves and their children to the boat with their clothes but the waves still threw them around the deck. 'The skin was torn from our backs and arms', said Sarwari. 'There was blood everywhere.' Strangely, in all this turmoil, some continued to sleep, only waking to grab at something to stop themselves being washed overboard.

On the lower deck, the men tried to form a human wall in a futile attempt to keep out the waves. A hole opened in the hull. It was stuffed with plastic and someone sat on this crude bung all night to keep it in place. There were no buckets to bail with. The pumps were just able to cope but needed all the power the generator could produce. There was nothing left to run the lights so all this horror took place in pitch dark. They could hear the storm above them, the boat groaning as the waves hit and, from both decks, shouts, cries and prayers. Hamid said: 'We were expecting that any moment the sharks come and eat us piece by piece.'[26]

The upper deck was working loose. 'The nails were coming out that held the top deck in place', said Assadullah Rezaee. 'The deck was moving and we thought it might fall from the boat. It was coming loose. The posts were held only by nails, no bolts or screws, only nails.' Women and children tried to move down to the deck below but there was no room for them there. They had no choice but to stay as the flimsy structure plunged from side to side. Someone below found a lump of metal and bashed the nails back into place all through the night.

The Indonesian crew retreated to the wheelhouse. They had abandoned responsibility for the boat. Three or four times during the storm the young mechanics stopped the engine for a while to let it cool down. For a horrifying half hour it would not restart but the men got it going again. Without the pumps they knew there was no hope. In the wild emotions of those hours, these people of deep faith took the presence of children on the boat to be a sign that the *Palapa* might last the night. 'Sometime my wife said it was so frightening and so difficult I would like to die', said Rajab Ali Merzaee. 'But I said no. We understand if God wants to take the adults because we have done something wrong, but the children haven't done anything. He might show them mercy.'

As the sun rose the storm died. The refugees had faced death in that storm and feared the boat could not survive another night like that. They asked the captain where they were. He looked at his box compass and wept. He had no idea. They were furious with him for the deal he had done with the smugglers, for the shoddy state of the boat, for sailing with a wrecked engine. But what was the use? They would share the same fate. 'The water does not make this judgement whether you are Afghan or Indonesian. The water will kill anybody. Indiscriminate.'[27]

I

Canberra's priority that Sunday morning was to bully BASARNAS into action. It was still very early in Jakarta but a little after 8 am over there, the Australian embassy sent the naval attaché David Ramsay around to BASARNAS to ask firmly that the agency get moving. This had no result except to put a number of Indonesian noses out of joint and make Australia's dealings with Indonesia even more difficult over the next few days.

Barry Spencer took off at about 7 am Christmas Island time. Part of his mission that morning was 'to relocate' the *Palapa* and 'advise Canberra of its position'. Though the stricken vessel was only 85 nautical miles from the island, it was two hours before the de Havilland was once more over the boat. The asylum seekers had used that time well. They had begun to wonder if the Australians did not realise they needed rescue. Perhaps it was not a failure of heart. Perhaps the Australians didn't know they were in trouble. They searched the boat for writing materials and something to write on. In the end they used engine oil on scarves. One of the English-speakers traced out the words and a man with a bit of sign-writing experience in Kabul finished the job. The banners were just ready when the plane appeared. One read SOS and the other HELP. 'The plane went far and come back, far and come back', said Rajab Ali Hossaini. But then it left and again they were plunged into despair.

Australia could not delay a rescue any longer once those words appeared. Spencer saw 'the people on board the vessel were holding up flags that read "SOS" "Help" and were waving orange rags . . . it then became a marine search and rescue operation which was then handed over to the pilot'.[28] RCC Australia got the news ten minutes later, then spent another twenty hectic minutes trying to pressure BASARNAS, first by fax and then through the defence attaché in Jakarta, calling him once again 'to assist obtaining response from Indonesian search and rescue authority to coordinate response to incident'.[29] At this moment, DIMA made an unprecedented attempt to interfere in a search and rescue operation with a call to RCC Australia 'asking if vessels that respond to Australian search and rescue broadcast can tow the stranded vessel to Indonesia'.[30]

The call to shipping that might have been issued 18 hours earlier finally went out at 12.48 pm Canberra time: 'Subject: Distress Relay. A 35-metre Indonesian type vessel with 80 plus persons on board adrift in vicinity of 09.32.5 south 104.44 east . . . vessel has SOS and HELP written on the roof. Vessels within 10 hours report best ETA and intentions to this station.'[31]

TWO
Sea rescue

AUGUST 26

Arne Rinnan's response was automatic. He plotted a fresh course for the *Tampa* and calculated it would take four hours at full sea speed, 21 knots, to reach the Indonesian boat's position. Then he acknowledged the Mayday. 'We are on a voyage from Fremantle to Singapore via Sunda Strait', he told RCC Australia. 'We have changed course and are headed for position of distress . . . Please advise further course of action. A Rinnan, Master.'[1]

Rinnan was a salt-dried sailor with a sharp eye and a cocky sense of humour. At 61 he still cut a bit of a dash in a stiff white shirt and epaulettes. His bony Scandinavian face with a potato nose and a sweep of silver hair would soon be known around the world. So would his practical, fractured English. But the recognition and honours coming his way so late in his career were not because Arne Rinnan was an absolutely exceptional mariner. He was a good man and a good sailor who had been a long time at sea driving cargo ships. He knew the rules and was not going to be bullied into breaking them. Rinnan was also backed by a determined company for whom he had worked nearly all his career since joining the Wilhelmsen Line's *Tennessee* as a deck hand in 1958.

Rinnan's career was steady and unremarkable. He was one of the last of his kind to rise through the ranks, all the way from deckhand to captain. His first command, back in 1975, was the old *Taronga* named after the zoo on Sydney Harbour. The ship he commanded now was not named after a remote fjord or an obscure Norse god but the port in Florida. After this voyage Rinnan had only one more lap of the world and then retirement.

His ship was a 44 000-tonne floating warehouse three city blocks long with rust red containers stacked six high on its weather deck. When the call from RCC Australia came, the *Tampa* was on a voyage through the East to China and Japan, on to North America and eventually home to Norway. On board was a crew of 27—Scandinavian officers and Filipino men—and a cargo of steel pipes, dried milk, food, timber and second-hand earth-moving equipment worth about $20 million.

The *Tampa* was not just a passing Norwegian cargo boat. The Wilhelmsen Line had been a presence in Australia since the 1890s when its ships began carrying wool to Europe. Its links with Australia were old and intimate. For most of the next century the Norwegian line was the third biggest shipper of Australian goods to Europe. The wool connection drew the line deep into the Australian Establishment and to keep its position on routes dominated by a cartel of British shipping lines, the Norwegian company had become a very skilled lobbyist of Australian industry and government. In some moods the line spoke of itself as 'a true Australian company' but that was taking it too far.[2] Oslo called the shots and the ethic of the company was distinctly Scandinavian. David Playfair, a meat baron who chaired the local Wilhelmsen board for fifteen years, described the Norwegians he worked with as 'gentlemen to a man, but they were businessmen first. Hard headed shipowners. Not romantics. The Norwegians had one outstanding quality in common. They were always fair. Hard but fair'.[3]

A complex company structure lay behind the *Tampa*. While the ship was owned by Wilh. Wilhelmsen ASA—the oldest and biggest shipping line in Norway—it was operated by a new partnership between Wilhelmsen and Sweden's powerful Wallenius Line. This Wallenius Wilhelmsen consortium was only set up in 1999 but already operated one of the world's largest fleets of roll-on roll-off container ships with revenues of roughly $US1.3 billion a year. Australia was about to tangle with a consortium of two of the biggest, richest, toughest shipping lines in the business.

Rinnan did not seek permission from his owners before changing course. He knew he was doing what the line expected, Norwegian law demanded and Australian rescue authorities requested: steaming to the aid of a vessel in distress. After an hour, he received a rather odd direction from RCC Australia: 'Please note that Indonesian search and rescue authorities have accepted co-ordination of this incident.'[4] He tried and failed to get through to BASARNAS but this was clearly still an Australian operation because over an hour later a Coastwatch de Havilland Dash-8 appeared to guide the *Tampa* to the vessel which still lay out of sight over the horizon.

I

Standing empty on that early Sunday morning in Oslo was a plain room on the fourth floor of the Wilhelmsen Line's headquarters in the suburb of Lysaker. A big table stood at the centre of the 'contingency' room; TV monitors hung from the walls. To hand were charts, a tracking system to pin-point the position of the company's ships and a formidable range of communications systems. Outside the door was a row of offices set up for specialist teams to deal with the medical, insurance, personnel and media problems Wilhelmsen ships might face everywhere on the globe.

It was 8.25 in Oslo when the shipping line heard from Rinnan that he was on his way to a rescue. Key executives began to head for Lysaker following procedures laid down some fifteen years before and followed many times since. They and their deputies would continuously occupy the contingency room for the next eight days. The shipping line's canny owner, Wilh Wilhelmsen, decreed that in emergencies like this everyone must have a deputy 'because if it takes time you have to sleep, otherwise you may not make decisions in a very professional manner. That was one of the challenges: to make people go home and sleep because they all had this feel of responsibility and didn't really want to leave the job until it was done and we had to order them home to sleep'.[5]

Wilhelmsen is small and dour with nothing of the tycoon about him. He dresses simply, wears his wealth lightly, speaks softly and expects to be obeyed. The leader of the fourth generation of the family dynasty, Wilhelmsen knows Australia well. It was his grandfather who shipped the first wool in the 1890s. Wilhelmsen, himself, spent an apprenticeship year in Sydney. His son had done the same thing. He had close Australian friends, visited most years and knew the lie of the political land. He would insist on the rights of the line but not put at risk the long-term prospects of his company in the kerfuffle over the *Tampa*. Wilhelmsen once wrote that shipping 'requires a long term strategic approach. If you are not prepared to be there for a hundred years, you should not be there in the first place. It means taking a view that goes well beyond your own generation'.[6]

Wilhelmsen came to the *Tampa* crisis with memories of the years after the Vietnam War, when his ships rescued nearly 1000 boat people from the South China Sea. Back in those days, he said, 'the boat people issue had been on the schedule for a long time. We, as an industry, were aware this was going to be an issue, so we were quite well prepared'.[7] The problem was to find somewhere to land large numbers of people who didn't want to go home. International law had not—and still has not—solved this problem. Thailand, Malaysia, Indonesia and Singapore refused to allow the Vietnamese refugees ashore. Reports came in of thousands being left to drown by passing ships. Survivors rescued by the Wilhelmsen Line in the 1980s spoke of up to fifty ships ignoring them before the Scandinavians came to their rescue.[8]

Temporary United Nations arrangements for the resettlement of rescued boat people saved tens of thousands of lives in the 1980s. But these voluntary arrangements had long since expired.[9] No similar plans had been made to safeguard boat people heading for Australia in the 1990s. Ship owners were left to bank on the civilised commitment of Australia to the rules of sea rescue codified in the United Nations Convention for the Law of the Sea (UNCLOS) and embedded in the law of both Australia and Norway. UNCLOS obliges every ship's master 'in so far as he can do so without serious danger to the ship, the crew or the passengers, to render assistance to any person found at sea in danger of being lost' and 'to proceed with all possible speed to the rescue of persons in distress'.[10]

I

Arne Rinnan was still half an hour away from the *Palapa* when he saw a mirror flashing an SOS. The Coastwatch plane guiding the *Tampa* was now running low on fuel and radioed that it was returning to Christmas Island. Where should he land the survivors, Rinnan asked? The officer said he didn't know and the plane disappeared over the horizon.[11]

The *Tampa* slid alongside the *Palapa* at about 2 pm. From the bridge Rinnan looked down on a '20 metre, grey coloured, wooden vessel in poor condition with damage to stern and superstructure'.[12] The upper deck was crowded with people. Some were throwing documents into the sea. Rinnan positioned his ship to shelter the *Palapa* from a fresh breeze and a 2-metre swell. He would remain on the bridge all afternoon manoeuvring the *Tampa* with its thrusters to try to keep the two boats together. Complicating the rescue was the need to keep the *Tampa*'s aluminium 'accommodation ladder' well above the *Palapa* to stop it being smashed to pieces as the little boat rose on the swell. The survivors would all have to be lifted to safety. In charge of the operation was the first officer, Christian Maltau, a bluff, young Norwegian with a short, blond beard. With him at the foot of the ladder was a very strong young engineer, Kai Nolte, who lifted the first survivor—a child—to safety at 2.30 pm. The rescue continued all afternoon to the rhythm of the swell. Nolte said after a while, 'This is just like fishing'.[13]

The survivors had to leave everything behind. 'It would slow the rescue operation if everyone was going to bring their bags and suitcases and plastic bags and whatever, and also we were afraid of pirates and concealed weapons.' Anything they brought to the foot of the stair was thrown back into the boat. A third sailor came down to join Maltau and Nolte so one could rest while two lifted. 'The whole operation went very smooth', said Maltau. 'No one was injured.'[14]

When lines to the *Palapa* kept breaking, Maltau jumped across and coiled ropes around the whole wheelhouse to secure the boat. He had a look around. The *Palapa* was disintegrating and what he saw left him with profound contempt for the smugglers. The cheap Chinese life jackets the adults were wearing had no whistles, no lights and would not keep an unconscious person's head out of the water. There were none for children. There was no galley, just a few scraps of food in plastic bags. From the wheelhouse he souvenired an old box compass. Apart from that there was no navigational equipment at all. 'No sextant, no log, no charts, no nautical publications, no electronic navigation devices, no GPS. They didn't have communication equipment, no radio, no nothing. So finding Christmas Island from their position—which actually was pretty close—would be like finding the famous needle in the haystack, considering also the strong westerly monsoon current.' The smugglers wouldn't even invest in a global positioning satellite (GPS) system to get their passengers to the island. 'You can go to Radio Shack and buy a $150 GPS receiver this big and that's all it takes.'[15]

As the tally of survivors kept rising, Oslo upgraded the rescue operation from 'fairly substantial' to 'major' and Wilh Wilhelmsen made his way into the contingency room. No Wilhelmsen ship had ever been involved in a rescue on this scale before. By the time the last person left the *Palapa* at 5 pm, the fishing boat had disgorged 26 females (two pregnant), 43 children (the youngest about one year old) and 369 men. Total: 438. Maltau judged the hulk impossible to tow so it would have to be abandoned with all the luggage. The survivors would be left with literally nothing but the clothes on their backs. Lost on the *Palapa* were boxes, bags, backpacks, medicines, documents, toys, clothes and shoes. Pacing hot decks under the tropical sun over the next few weeks, the survivors particularly regretted those lost shoes.

They were led to an empty area of the weather deck immediately below the bridge. Except for a short gap along the port railing where they could look out to sea, the survivors found themselves walled in by containers on three sides. The bridge towered above them as high as a city building. Rinnan looked down from that perch as his deck filled with people. He would come down to the deck only once while they were on his ship. The survivors' image of him was a head up in the sky with silver hair and binoculars keeping an eye on them. Maltau commanded the deck and in preparation for the rescue, he had directed the crew to open five empty containers: three for shelter and two, rigged with buckets and plastic bags, as latrines. Water lines had been brought up to the deck and the cook had been working for hours preparing bread and chicken soup for eighty or so survivors. The crew apologised there was not enough food and promised more soup was on its way. The survivors were eating, laughing and celebrating on their patch of deck. Some knelt to pray. Some were rehashing the horrors of the past days. Many were in a bad way. Between a dozen and twenty adults had collapsed unconscious on the deck.[16]

The survivors learnt the *Tampa* was bound for Singapore and were pleading with the crew not to be taken there. They believed the sailors were on their side and Khodadad Sarwari said they were encouraged to take the issue up with the captain. When the last survivor was on board and the *Palapa* had been cast loose, Christian Maltau appeared. They remember a courtly exchange. 'We said he was very fortunate that God had given him the ability to rescue the lives of so many people. Then he said: "Our direction is towards Singapore. Can you go with us to Singapore?" Everybody called out, "We're not going to Singapore". He asked if we had some other request. Then we said, "We are only going to Christmas. Take us to Christmas Island. You help us, you rescue us and now the only thing you could do is take us to Christmas Island".' Maltau remembers a much more prosaic exchange in which he asked for a spokesman, rapidly realised the man did not represent the survivors, then called for more. Five men came forward and asked to see the captain. Maltau radioed the bridge. Rinnan invited the delegation up. At about 5.15 pm, Maltau took them through the security net, into the main companionway and up many flights of stairs to the bridge. The Norwegians would come to call these men, 'The tour operators'.[17]

I

Arne Rinnan's first impulse had been to take the survivors to the nearest port, Christmas Island, which he could reach in four hours. But while the survivors were still being lifted from the *Palapa*, Rinnan heard at last from BASARNAS. Nineteen hours of badgering Jakarta had finally paid off for Canberra. But the Norwegian master also found dealing with the Indonesians difficult. 'We got one telephone call from the rescue centre in Indonesia. That is correct. But when we asked for later instruction, we never received it and then we tried to call them back, there was no response.' That one call from Jakarta advised Rinnan to disembark the survivors at the ferry port of Merak as he made his way to Singapore through the Sunda Strait. It was a destination many of the survivors knew only too well from their first failed attempt to reach Christmas Island. Rinnan was a little surprised by all this but when everyone from the *Palapa* was safely on board his ship, he set course for Merak twelve hours away.[18]

That would ordinarily have been the end of the responsibilities of the Australian rescue authorities. 'For all intents and purposes the issue was over', said AMSA's chief Clive Davidson. But not in this case. Philip Ruddock's Department of Immigration and Multicultural Affairs had made an extraordinary request that RCC Australia continue to 'monitor the progress' of the Norwegian ship. Davidson could not recall such a request ever being made before. 'I suspect it was new ground.'[19] For professional mariners, one of the most deeply troubling aspects of the *Tampa* story was the willingness of a rescue authority to facilitate what was esentially a political operation.

By the time the delegation reached the bridge, the *Tampa* had only been underway for about half an hour. 'A group of five men from among the survivors escorted to the bridge to talk to the Master', said the ship's log. 'They claimed they were from Afghanistan, Pakistan, Sri Lanka and Indonesia. The following is what they said. "Thank you for saving our lives. We have two priorities, either take us to Christmas Island or any western country. We have left behind everything we have. The situation is very bad at home we do not want to go to Singapore or Indonesia, remember we have nothing to lose captain."' One of the delegation, a scholar from Afghanistan, said the survivors 'were very much distressed. Some of them they threatened if we are going to be returned to Indonesia we will jump from the boat and die'.[20]

The five men were highly excited, perhaps even hysterical. 'They were behaving in a very aggravated excited manner, the body language was all in my face', reported Rinnan. And they made threats. 'We were all threatened. There was a tense moment up there.' Rinnan believed there might be 'dire consequences for safety of ship, crew and passengers' if he did not heed what the survivors were saying. But he was never personally intimidated. 'Not blackmailed, no.' What Rinnan had to consider was the safety of a very large number of people. From Maltau he knew that however tense things were on the bridge, the real danger was down on the deck where the survivors, most of them adult men, outnumbered his crew sixteen to one. Rinnan had no firearms on board. Even if he had, the owners would not have allowed the situation to deteriorate into violent confrontation.[21]

Rinnan was angry and would give graphic accounts of this ugly incident on the bridge. But despite this ragged, aggressive behaviour, Rinnan clearly understood and in part sympathised with the plight of the people he had just rescued. 'First when we picked them up they were people in distress and obviously there were people running out of Afghanistan. These were not Taliban. They told us that. These were people running away from the

Taliban government . . . They are human beings as the rest of us, and unfortunately these people are from Afghanistan.'[22]

By chance, RCC Australia called the ship in the middle of the confrontation between the captain and the survivors. It was 5.43 pm. The call was part of the strange watching brief DIMA had given the rescue authority which now learnt '*Tampa* had been given an ultimatum that survivors wished to go to Christmas Island'. Rinnan had a question. 'The captain wants to know whether if we are pressured whether we can proceed to Christmas Island?' The RCC officer replied: 'That's a question, sir, that I'd say is up to the captain. I can't answer that for him. Yes, it's a decision that he has to come to on his own merits.' That anonymous officer of RCC Australia was giving the traditional answer. It is one of the fundamental principles of the sea that the master of a vessel must judge what is best for his crew, his passengers and his ship. That can't be second-guessed by a rescue authority—or a government—thousands of kilometres away. The chief executive of Australia's rescue authority, Clive Davidson, agreed that it was the master's call. 'Custom and practice is that the master would assess the situation and would proceed on his voyage and deliver the rescued people to a convenient place.' Many months after these events, the authority of the master in this predicament was publicly backed by an assistant secretary in the Attorney General's department, Mark Zanker. 'It is difficult to see that the master had any choice but to change course as he did towards Christmas Island.'[23]

Rinnan sent the delegation back to the deck with the promise that they would see the lights of the island about midnight. News spread fast among the survivors. Those who were not already sleeping found what shelter they could from the wind and settled down. Khodadad Sarwari was very pleased. 'A peaceful solution was found.'

Rinnan turned the *Tampa* about at 6.10 pm. When he advised RCC Australia, he was told: 'It is entirely your decision as to where to proceed.' But the rescue authority was alarmed. Had the ship been hijacked? Was it in the hands of pirates? 'It was unclear as to the nature of the threats that were being made to the master and the crew', said Davidson. He couldn't even tell if Rinnan was free to speak. 'There was grave concern about the safety of the crew.' The ship's radio officer, Ramesh Iyengar, was warned 'if vessel goes to Christmas Island under duress to offload survivors, this will be an act of piracy with serious consequences for the offenders'. And

Iyengar was quizzed: 'Is it against your will to go to Christmas Island?' He replied: 'Yes, most definitely.' But as that message was passed by Chinese whispers through the bureaucracy, the radio operator's remark was attributed to Rinnan and, for a time, taken to mean that the ship and its crew had been completely overborne.[24]

For about an hour and a half, Canberra believed the *Tampa* might have been hijacked, but it was known before midnight that this wasn't so. Rinnan was at all times in complete control of his ship. It suited the Australian government to exaggerate the real threats of violence on the ship in order to tell the world that once the *Tampa* turned for Christmas Island it was no longer on a rescue mission. The official diplomatic line would be that the ship changed course 'for reasons unrelated to the distress for which assistance was rendered'.[25] The Australian government would say the 'rescue situation' was over and the 'hijack' situation has now begun. Nations owe nothing to hijackers. They must not be allowed to achieve their objective: landing in Australia. And if that meant the innocent crew of the *Tampa* was to be exposed once again to the very dangers that persuaded Rinnan to change course in the first place, then the Australian government would show no sign that it cared.

I

In Newport, a suburb on Sydney's northern beaches, James Neill had turned in early that Sunday. Neill is a big, casual bloke with a sharp, practical mind. He owns Aus Ship P & I, an Australian offshoot of an international network of lawyers, insurers and trouble shooters who look after the problems of international shipping lines. These protection and indemnity (P & I) clubs handle the crises while the ships sail on. Already sitting in the contingency room in Lysaker were representatives of the Scandinavian P & I club Gard used by the Wilhelmsen Line. Neill was the Australian 'correspondent' for Gard which is why Rinnan rang and woke him to make arrangements to land the 438 survivors on Christmas Island. Neill climbed out of bed to begin a very long night's work.

First he rang Neville Nixon, the DIMA 'ports officer' on duty that night. Nixon was the man he always rang when stowaways were found on his ships, a good man to deal with. He had not heard of the *Tampa*'s troubles. They spoke briefly. A little later Nixon rang back asking for the *Tampa*'s number. He told Neill: 'There's been a bit of a stink and there might be a few problems with this one.' At 7.10 Nixon rang Rinnan who made it absolutely clear that the *Tampa* had not been hijacked. 'The captain admitted that the situation on board was not so serious that he did not have control of the vessel.'[26] Rinnan also explained to the DIMA officer his reasons for proceeding to Christmas Island.

Clearly there was trouble in the wind. Rinnan sought Neill's advice. The lawyer told him he could not go wrong 'if the decision he made was genuinely based on consideration for the safety of the crew and the survivors'. They went through the issues together. The primary consideration was transit time. Rinnan wanted the quickest possible journey with these extra 438 people on board. Christmas Island was six or seven hours closer than Merak. Second was safety: though the *Tampa* was a big ship, there was only safety equipment for sixty and these people exposed on the deck would be at risk if the *Tampa* were hit by one of the Indian Ocean's sudden, violent tropical storms. Third, there was always a risk that Indonesia might change its mind by the time the *Tampa* reached Merak. If the Indonesians refused to let the people disembark, the ship would be in an impossible situation. There would be no prospect of unloading them elsewhere in Southeast Asia but equally no prospect, either, of them staying on the *Tampa* all the way back to Norway.[27]

James Neill's advice was to keep heading for Christmas Island. Whatever trouble was brewing there, Australia would eventually heed international pressure and take responsibility for the survivors. Indonesia might do nothing but Australia would do something. Neill told Rinnan: 'I think it might take eight or ten days, but you will eventually get them off.'[28]

Half an hour after his first call to the ship, DIMA's Neville Nixon was back on the line to declare the *Tampa* could not enter Australian waters. Rinnan could hardly believe his ears.[29] Closing territorial waters to a ship is a grave step at the best of times; closing them in the aftermath of a mass rescue—which Australia had asked the ship to undertake—was surely unprecedented. Nixon told him he must head back to Merak. 'We will not be in Merak for the next day or so', said Rinnan. 'What will happen when the people on the deck don't see the lights of Christmas Island around midnight?' Nixon was unmoved. He assured Rinnan it was possible to change course without the survivors realising. 'Smooth-talking Neville' said he had 'long experience in this situation. If you just take a slow turn to port then you can turn back to Merak. Nobody will recognise that on the deck'.[30]

Events took a yet more bizarre turn a few minutes later when Nixon came back on the line to deliver to Arne Rinnan the sort of warnings DIMA issues to the crews of rotten little Indonesian fishing boats ferrying asylum seekers to Australia. Rinnan was threatened with the very heavy penalties for people smuggling set out in the Migration Act if he disobeyed the order to turn back to Indonesia. The shipping line's chronology reads: 'Advised if the vessel enters Australian territorial waters it would be breaking the migration law and will be subject to prosecution and fines up to A$110 000 and jail.'

Rinnan was amazed, surprised and disappointed but put up no fight. He faxed RCC Australia that he had spoken to Nixon. 'Vessel is not allowed to enter Christmas Island therefore am turning round, slowly, don't want rescued people to know, will [illegible]track to Indonesia for landing.' Rinnan was not proud of this. 'I was a little bit confusing in that few hours. He said he had a long experience to do these things and I was well, stupid enough to listen to it, I tried to do the best thing out of it.'[31]

|

The decision to stop the *Tampa* was taken by John Howard. Portly Max Moore-Wilton, the nation's most powerful bureaucrat, was on deck all night and appeared to be the architect of these unfolding events. He says the 'government decision' to turn the *Tampa* around was taken higher up the line than him.[32] Senior bureaucrats involved in the operation believe the Prime Minister approved a strategy devised by Moore-Wilton to send the ship away by issuing those threats to its master. Philip Ruddock was barely in the loop. He spent the night at his Canberra flat preparing for the following morning's Cabinet and taking calls from DIMA bureaucrats about the *Tampa* operation. 'I was certainly receiving those calls. I endorsed the advice that had been proffered by officers.'[33]

Moore-Wilton was a radical, hard-nosed operator whose reach extended over all government departments. As secretary of the Department of Prime Minister and Cabinet, he had been driving Canberra's efforts for the previous two years to crack down on boat people and people smuggling. His closest colleague in that task was his deputy, Jane Halton, but she had taken a break that weekend in the snow. Moore-Wilton rang her all through the night and next morning as she drove back to Canberra from Thredbo. Breaking traditional constraints was Moore-Wilton's hallmark. So was outrageous bluff. That it began as a game of bluff is underscored by the fact that no legal advice appears to have been sought at a senior level before Australian authorities questioned the master of the *Tampa*'s judgement and then threatened him with prosecution as a people smuggler. Senior officers of the Attorney General's Department only learnt of this later—with dismay.[34]

Mobilised to execute the strategy that night were two senior DIMA bureaucrats. Philippa Godwin, head of the department's division of unauthorised arrivals and detention, was in frequent contact with RCC Australia, gathering and exchanging information. Also involved was the deputy secretary of the department, Andrew Metcalfe. Finally there was the man who made the extraordinary threatening calls to Rinnan, Neville Nixon. The calls seemed to work. By about 10 pm it seemed that Canberra's unprecedented efforts over the last couple of days—to see the asylum seekers on the *Palapa* sent back to Indonesia—had been crowned with a most unexpected success. Not for long.

The *Tampa*'s second attempt to sail for Merak lasted about half an hour. The survivors began to stir as the ship made its slow turn. Though they came from a landlocked country, they could tell the wind was shifting and see from the stars that the ship was changing course. Maltau radioed the bridge. 'They were saying that as long as the captain sailed the ship towards Christmas Island they would behave as one group. United. They would stay calm. But if the ship would turn around and sail north, they couldn't guarantee how they would react and that that might cause a lot of trouble on board and people would then start to jump overboard. They couldn't guarantee they would any longer act as one group.'[35]

Rinnan looked down on the deck. 'You could see it from the bridge, they started to be restless, started looking at the stars, the wind direction changed, everything changed.' He was not sure the survivors would carry out their threats of suicide but wasn't going to test the point. 'I'm not a big gambler and I do not like to have a lot of people in the water around the ship if I headed for Merak. So I decided to go to Christmas Island.' He set course for the island once more at 8.28 pm.[36]

When Moore-Wilton learnt the *Tampa* was heading south again, he directed it be ordered to turn around once more. This time Rinnan found

Neville Nixon aggressive and agitated but he told the man from DIMA: 'We are heading for Christmas Island for the safety of ship and the crew and everybody on board because there was 438 of them and 27 of us.' The captain asked to speak to Nixon's superior and a little later Andrew Metcalfe rang the ship. 'He told me exactly the same as Neville.' But Rinnan held his course and at 10.40 pm faxed the Australian rescue centre that he expected to reach Christmas Island by midnight. 'Vessel will drift 5 nautical miles off the island until daybreak.'[37]

Wilh Wilhelmsen sat in the contingency room watching in disbelief events unfold on the far side of the world. 'But I guess we have also been out in many rainy days. Many surprises happen to us as a shipping line and as a business person. So you may be taken by surprise for a while and then you sit down and become rational about it.' Wilhelmsen's rational view was that Australia would come to its senses once the government had some skilled advice on shipping law: the Australians were making mistakes so obvious that they would realise this for themselves and change tack. So the contingency room did not take seriously threats to fine and jail Rinnan this night. 'I don't think we really spent much time on that threat', said Wilhelmsen. 'We felt that as events would unfold it would go away.'[38]

Australia was violating the shipping world's understanding of how the *Tampa* should be treated in the aftermath of the rescue, but the Wilhelmsen Line knew that Australia was not compelled by law to land the *Palapa* survivors. No nation was. This is the gap in international law that led so many skippers to ignore the plight of boat people in the South China Sea after the Vietnam War. Why rescue them if you can't land them? Ever since the stop-gaps of those years had expired, shipping companies had been lobbying to find some permanent solution to this problem. United Nations' attempts to write a binding convention had failed. James Neill put his client's position bluntly. 'There is no law that says where the survivors should be put ashore. There is maritime convention but no law. Nothing that can be enforced.'[39]

The traditional obligations already ignored by Canberra that night made a formidable list: The obligation to respect the decision of the master, to support a ship carrying out a rescue off your coast, to alleviate the distress of those who have been rescued and to assist the *Tampa* now that it had become a ship in distress itself with 438 fractious people on board.[40] Other obligations would arise and be finessed as the crisis continued. None could be enforced in an Australian court. These rules operate not by force of law but by good sense and civilised expectation. Untouched by these obligations is the right of any nation to close its borders against unwanted incursion. It may provoke the ridicule and disapproval of the world, but a sovereign nation can always close its doors to a boatload of shipwrecked refugees.

The shipping line made a crucial decision: it would only treat the 438 people on the *Tampa* as survivors of a sea rescue. As such, they were owed the decent, conventional right of disembarkation at the nearest port. And the *Tampa* had the right to clear its decks of them and get on with its voyage. That those people might want asylum in Australia was not going to be the shipping line's concern. It was already perfectly clear to Oslo that the asylum issue was driving Australia's repeated orders that the *Tampa* take the survivors to Indonesia. Wilh Wilhelmsen said, 'That was when this turned from a large, routine rescue operation into a political roller coaster'. He did not want his company involved in the politics. 'That's not our business.'[41]

Around midnight—3 am in Canberra—the *Tampa* was approaching the edge of Australia's territorial waters. Rinnan had conflicting orders here. The federal police on the island had told him to bring the *Tampa* close to shore and drift there till daylight but Neville Nixon had insisted that Australia's waters were closed to the ship. To cross the line in the face of such a direction was a serious matter. Theoretically it could lead to the seizure of this $100 million vessel by Australia. James Neil explained: 'It was a big call.'[42]

Max Moore-Wilton had not given up. He tracked down Peter Dexter, chief of the shipping line's Australian operations, at a hotel in Queensland. The men knew each other well. Both had served terms as chief of the government-owned Australian National Line. Later Dexter's employers would praise the role he was able to play in the crisis 'because of his highly placed political contacts'. But on the night it all broke, Dexter was holidaying with his wife at Port Douglas after a stint in Japan. He knew the *Tampa* had been diverted to assist a boat in distress with asylum seekers on board but when Moore-Wilton's call came through at about 3 am he learnt what was happening out on the Indian Ocean. Moore-Wilton made it clear to Dexter, 'There was no desire to see the ship coming any further.'[43]

As Rinnan approached the line, he made the usual report to the island's harbourmaster, who asked him to wait outside territorial waters. Rinnan saw nothing particularly significant in this. On directions from Canberra, the harbourmaster seemed to be suggesting a sensible arrangement to give the authorities time to deal with the ship and the survivors in the morning. Rinnan recorded in his log: 'Master advises position and requested to stay outside 12 nm.' James Neill regrets his client did not consult him before pausing here. So much of the mess that lay ahead might have been avoided had the *Tampa* steamed straight in. 'Rinnan was essentially tricked.'[44]

The night was windy but clear. The survivors had settled down. 'They saw the lights of Christmas Island and was really surprised, really relaxed', said Rinnan. He hoped this 'should be the end of the story' and that help would come out in the morning just as he had been promised. Maltau reported from the deck that 'as long as they could see Christmas Island, they were quite happy'.[45]

THREE
Australia v. the boat people

For months, Canberra had been in a panic about boat people pouring down from Indonesia. A few hundred had arrived each year since the late 1970s, but now a few thousand were turning up at Christmas Island and Ashmore Reef in overloaded, rotten boats. The numbers were tiny compared to the flood of asylum seekers reaching Europe, but Australians have a long antipathy to boat people and are uncomfortable with *any* arriving on their shores. That the latest boats were carrying refugees fleeing persecution in Iraq and Afghanistan made no difference. Australians saw them as 'illegals' for having no visas; 'queue jumpers' for making their own way to Australia; and rich for paying people smugglers for the journey. The fresh strategies John Howard's government had tried for the past two years to stem the flow seemed to be failing. Canberra was in a mood for radical action.

Some weeks before the confrontation with the *Tampa*, Philip Ruddock had flown quietly to Jakarta. His plane was due in before midnight on June 12 and briefed to meet him was Australia's ambassador to Indonesia, Ric Smith. The problem of boat people was already a top priority at the embassy, but Ruddock was there to see what more could be done—by the embassy and by the Indonesians. Ruddock was known in the embassy as a difficult minister. He had earned the nickname 'The Minister with No Ears' for his habit of lecturing Indonesian officials. His chief topic was the need for Indonesia to set up a big detention camp on one of its islands to keep asylum seekers from making their way down to Australia. The Indonesians, who faced international criticism for similar camps during the Indo-Chinese refugee crisis in the 1970s, refused. Even so, the Indonesian police had been happy to work with Australian agents on the ground 'disrupting' people-smuggling syndicates. Exploring radical new ideas for this work was on the minister's agenda in Jakarta.

Philip Ruddock was a man who found himself, unexpectedly, at the centre of the political action and liked it there. In 1996, after waiting over twenty years in parliament, he achieved his modest ambition, becoming Minister for Immigration. Then the boats started coming and immigration became a hot issue. Ruddock's handling of the challenge pleased the Howard government. He was ice-cold and never conceded ground. Following Howard's second election victory in 1998, Ruddock was promoted to the inner Cabinet and the more the boats came down, the more important his portfolio became. But those who knew him well wondered what price he had paid to find himself among the hard men at the heart of the Howard government. Had he left himself behind somewhere along the way?

Ruddock was a member of Amnesty International and still wore its badge in his button hole. In 1988 he had voted against his own leader, John Howard, for wanting to put a brake on Asian immigration. Another Liberal who put his career on the line that day was Ian Macphee. 'I cannot square his beliefs and convictions of those days with his actions of today', said Macphee in the aftermath of the *Tampa* crisis. He blamed Ruddock's climb to power. 'You could see him being converted from someone with a social conscience into somebody who was determined above all to hang onto his job and gain the respect of his ministerial colleagues.'[1]

Working on Ruddock was the overpowering ethos of the immigration bureaucracy. DIMA offers fine people new lives in Australia. But the department deals, day to day, with bogus claims, desperate individuals, dud lawyers, sleazy immigration agents, fake marriages, importuning politicians, cruel people smugglers and corruption that can run deep into the Australian community. In 1983, it was revealed that the High Court judge Lionel

Murphy had been trying to protect a solicitor 'mate' facing charges over the illegal entry of Korean kitchen hands. The result of this pressure from all directions on DIMA was an ethos of embattlement and cynicism—and a policy of total control. Almost at any cost. It would take more strength of character than Ruddock has to see beyond the horizon of his bureaucrats and follow a course of effective but compassionate policing.

Ruddock has, in any case, the soul of a great bureaucrat. He is a lawyer, an Anglican and a stamp collector. He puts his faith in systems. 'Integrity' is a key Ruddock word. Talking to the Canberra Press Club in 1998 he declared: 'As well as our determination to safeguard the integrity of our immigration program we are also determined to safeguard the integrity of the nation's borders.' Thousands of times since, Ruddock has said the same thing. When grim measures are taken to hold the system together—such as imprisoning children in desert camps—they apparently raise no doubts in Ruddock about the system itself. As the stop-gaps became more extreme, more dangerous, Ruddock continued to defend the 'integrity' of the system with cool and absolute conviction. What 'integrity' really meant was total control of the process by DIMA.

The result was a fundamental contest between the department and the courts. Ruddock became a bitter public critic of the judiciary and advocate of the strange—but in time very familiar—argument that immigration decisions should be beyond the reach of the courts. Ruddock's language was extreme. The courts, he said, were responsible for 'the most corrosive actions against an effective and fair immigration program'. They rarely, in fact, overturned the decisions of immigration and refugee tribunals but when they did, Ruddock took it as much more than a setback for DIMA. It was an affront to democracy. 'The courts have reinterpreted and re-written Australian law, ignoring the sovereignty of Parliament and the will of the Australian people.' The minister was not alone in these attacks. Under John Howard, Australia saw the most prolonged campaign ever mounted by a government against the judiciary—mostly over decisions involving race: native title and refugees.[2]

The political impact of these attacks was profound. The idea grew up that Australia could not really protect itself against boat people while judges had a say in the matter. The law was part of the problem, a barrier to effective action. If asylum seekers were to be kept out of Australia, they had first to be kept out of the Australian legal system. This was not a time for legal niceties. The problem was too big, too urgent for that. Ruddock's knockout blow to his critics was always the apocalyptic vision of Australia overrun by 20 million refugees in the world looking for a home. 'Maybe you can accommodate a few hundred, a thousand, 12 000, 20 000, 100 000, 200 000, a million. I mean, when does it become an issue about where you actually exercise some control to ensure you are able to manage the process?'³

That brought Ruddock to Jakarta in June 2001. At 8 am the morning after his arrival, he met all the key players on the embassy's People Smuggling Group. He was in a provocative mood. Around the table were officers of DIMA and the Department of Foreign Affairs plus military attachés and Australian police. Leigh Dixon of the Australian Federal Police (AFP) gave a run down of Australian work with the Indonesian National Police to attack the syndicates with varying degrees of success. Out of the blue, Ruddock began asking Dixon and the others about pirates: why were boat loads of asylum seekers who often carried money and jewellery not attacked by pirates active in waters around the archipelago? Dixon was upset and concerned about the direction of the conversation. Was Ruddock thinking of some covert action involving pirates? Dixon became increasingly frustrated: the minister did not seem to be interested in the police strategies he was outlining to combat people smuggling. When Ruddock persisted in questioning Dixon about the possibilities of pirates attacking the boats, he cut the minister off, saying he didn't know about the actions of pirates because he was 'just a simple policeman and not a politician'.⁴

Dixon did not tell his police commissioner, Mick Keelty, about this worrying exchange at the time, though Keelty did learn of it from Dixon much later and expressed concern. Ruddock has refused to comment on his discussions in the embassy that morning in June 2001. However, on the issue of pirates he said, 'There had been a great deal of public comment on that topic around the time of the several meetings I had during visits to Indonesia'. He provided a copy of an article from the *Economist* of July 2001 focusing on the difficulties of establishing an international legal regime to prosecute pirates in Southeast Asia.⁵

Rumours of Ruddock's discussions at this and other meetings soon rocketed around the mission. One consistent rumour was that Ruddock had also raised the issue of sabotage. According to an official present, discussions between key players on the People Smuggling Group became very tense when the minister asked whether the smugglers' boats could be stopped by physically interfering with them. 'Essentially, the minister put it over jokingly—"well could we interfere with the boats?"' said this official. 'No minister I know, in a conference room with that particular group of people, puts anything like that with humour.' Several officials apparently baulked at the idea. According to one of them, the police representative reproached Ruddock. 'Leigh Dixon reminded the minister of Australian law, he took an ethical and moral stance and at the end of it, Ruddock laughed it off, and said it was just a concept in the air.'[6] Dixon would later tell his commissioner he could not recall Ruddock talking about interfering with asylum boats—pirates but not sabotage.

Philip Ruddock—former national president of the Young Liberals, a suburban solicitor sitting in parliament even before the first boat people reached Australia, a decent politician who put his career on the line defending non-racist immigration—was now an essential figure in the Howard government and minister responsible for refugees, slipping into Jakarta to plug a few gaps in the system. He and Australia had come a long way together.

I

The first boat people arrived on a wooden fishing vessel, the *Kein Giang*, which dropped anchor off the Darwin suburb of Nightcliff on the evening of 28 April 1976. The leader of the five men on board greeted immigration officials the next morning: 'Welcome to my boat. My name is Lam Binh and these are my friends from South Vietnam and we would like permission to stay in Australia.' Saigon had fallen a year before and the South China Sea had been full of refugee boats ever since. The *Kein Giang* had been shunted round Singapore and Malaysia for two months. Overwhelmed by tens of thousands of refugees, these countries were provisioning boats, refuelling them and forcing them to keep going. In the jargon of the refugee world, the boats were being 'pushed off'. Navigating with the help of a page torn from a school atlas, Lam Binh and his friends headed south and Australia found itself with refugees knocking on its door. 'They simply turned up, uninvited, asking for refuge', wrote the former diplomat Bruce Grant. 'For Australia, history and geography had merged, causing a shiver of apprehension.'[7]

Australia has never seen itself as a haven for people fleeing persecution and poverty as Britain and America have. At the far end of the earth,

Australia set out to build a new, white nation. The fear of being swamped by Chinese helped draw the colonies together into a federation and this new Australia became a pioneer of immigration restrictions. They were always popular. The attitude to the Chinese in the 1880s and the Afghans in the 1990s was much the same: do what it takes to keep them out. No questions asked. Most Australians have never really wanted to know what is done to protect the nation from its great fear: invasion by migration.

After World War II, the word 'refugee' took on a particular meaning for Australians which it has never lost. In Europe, Indo-China and Africa refugees just arrive. They present themselves at the border asking for protection. But after the war, when Australia was opening itself to a vast influx of white migrants, officials were sent to Europe to *choose* suitable, white refugees. Australian officials were in complete control of the process and they chose with care. Ever since then, in Australian eyes, 'genuine' refugees are people who wait patiently in camps far away for us to come and select them.

The removal of the last shreds of the White Australia Policy in 1973—'To turn a decent face to the world', said Gough Whitlam—was made politically possible by two understandings. First, that Canberra's politicians would not play the race card even though they knew there was still widespread fear of coloured immigrants in Australia. The second understanding was that these very new Australians—non-white and perhaps non-Christian—would be chosen with great care. This was very clear to immigration officers of the time. Moving from a European to an Asian posting in the 1970s, Wayne Gibbons found 'the contrast between the work style, the work ethic in those two areas was quite dramatic. In one you were out to approve anyone who popped their hand up and said they wanted to come to Australia and the other, there was a question of trying to keep as many from getting in as possible'.[8] Control, selection, choice were still everything.

The *Kein Giang* arrived in Darwin only three years after the burial of White Australia. Australia's generosity in those years to the refugees pouring out of Vietnam was absolutely in line with the underlying objective of tight control. Australia took large numbers of Vietnamese but *chose* them from holding camps in Thailand, Malaysia and Indonesia. Australia was very keen to make sure the boats landed their cargoes of people up there, not down here. Australia pressured those countries to let boat people land and was a harsh public critic of 'pushing off'. Gibbons escorted the international press through Malaysia at one stage to show them local police at work forcing boats back out to sea. His colleague Hec McMillan said, 'The purpose for taking journalists was to help create international pressure on Malaysia by depicting the distress of incoming refugees'.[9]

Australian immigration officials confessed to sabotaging boats. 'If the boat was un-seaworthy, the Malaysians were very sympathetic and they'd allow them to land and go into a camp', said Greg Humphries, another old immigration hand. 'But if the boat was seaworthy, they'd say, "On your way we've had enough . . . we've got enough." Some of our fellows would take the police inspector or the sergeant or the police away, divert his attention, and a couple of hours later there'd be great excitement. The boat had sunk. How did it sink? Well, we knew how it'd sunk because the boys had pulled the plug out or bored a hole in it. But it left the Malaysian authorities scratching their heads on many occasions, how these boats are suddenly sunk.'[10]

The policy of forward selection was a great success. In the decade after the fall of Saigon, Australia took 95 000 Vietnamese refugees but less than 5000 of these made the journey all the way under their own steam. A handful of opinion polls showed how unsympathetic Australians were to these boat arrivals. Thirty per cent of those questioned in 1979 said Australia should take none of them at all; a bare majority said Australia should take some; only 8 per cent thought all the boat people who arrive should be allowed to settle in Australia. This response was even more hostile than it at first appears for in those years all the Vietnamese fleeing their country were deemed to be genuine refugees.[11]

Shipwreck survivors weren't any more welcome. On a voyage to Darwin in December 1979, the Shell tanker *Entalina* plucked 150 refugees from a sinking boat in the Java Sea. After twice being robbed and raped by Thai pirates, the survivors drifted for sixteen days while their pleas for help were ignored by a couple of dozen passing ships. Captain Sloan of the *Entalina* expected political problems would follow the rescue, 'but we couldn't leave them to die'.[12] Australia refused to accept the survivors when the tanker reached Darwin, saying it was a British ship and Britain must take responsibility for these people. Britain insisted Australia must allow the refugees to land because Darwin was the *Entalina*'s next port of call. The wharfies threatened to black ban the ship if the survivors were taken ashore. But the sick were transferred to a Darwin hospital and the rest of the survivors housed in a quarantine station while newspapers thundered about Britain's legal duties and Australia's moral responsibility. Eventually, the mess was sorted out by the United Nations High Commission for Refugees (UNHCR).

No boat people reached Australia for most of the 1980s and when they reappeared their numbers were tiny: about 220 each year. But such were the passions they aroused that the Labor government legislated in 1992 to lock them all in remote holding camps. The system Australia put in place was almost unprecedented in the western world. Most countries detain asylum seekers briefly for health, identity and security checks. But Australia now held them in detention for the entire time it took to process their refugee claims. This was in breach of a number of United Nations conventions: on refugees, on civil and political rights and the rights of children.[13] But mandatory detention was instantly popular in Australia and has remained so ever since. A poll taken in 1993 showed almost complete community support for the policy, while 44 per cent of those questioned at that time wanted to see *all* boat people barred from settling in Australia.[14]

Party pollsters knew these figures and knew there was a big constituency for shutting the door on boat people. But only out on the loony fringe of politics, in the world of crazy tax schemes and anti-Semitic newsletters was such a policy advocated in the 1990s. Although the Liberal and Labor parties did not campaign on the issue, their leaders did nothing to calm the fears those polling figures revealed. The level of fear was extraordinary. A poll in 1998 showed the average Australian overestimated by 70 times the number of boat people arriving each year in the country.[15] Politicians across the spectrum joined in persistent, low level abuse of boat people as 'queue jumpers' for not waiting in foreign camps and 'illegals' for arriving without the proper papers.

Australia has always been a stickler for papers. Sovereign nations decide not only who crosses their borders, but what formalities are required. Australia has a tough border regime requiring visas for almost all non citizens. Like most refugees at any time anywhere in the world, boat people arrive without papers. Australia undertook not to punish them for this when it signed the Refugee Convention. But Australia took to branding them as 'illegals' for arriving without visas. By the late 1990s this had become an even more effective term of abuse than 'queue jumper'. How safe could

Australia be if these dark skinned, mostly Muslim 'illegals' were allowed loose in the community?

The problem for boat people was always the boat: the symbol of Australia's old fears of invasion. People worried far less—indeed, hardly at all—about asylum seekers arriving by air, even though they were jumping the same queue, there were far more of them and they were about half as likely as those who came by sea to be genuine refugees. Air arrivals were released into the community and though their numbers rose through the 1990s, this was not seen as evidence that Australia was failing to police its borders. The arrival of boats was. Not without reason: by the end of the decade, boat landings had become almost a joke.

On a wet March morning in 1999, a rusting 30-metre fishing boat came aground on Holloway Beach near Cairns and residents were reporting Chinese running into the cane fields. Twenty-six men were arrested and Canberra ordered an immediate inquiry. A month later, while this was underway, a 40-metre tugboat landed even further south, at Scotts Head in NSW. The boat had been sighted at various points as it made its way down the coast, but never stopped. The 59 Chinese who came ashore had no idea where to go and kept turning up to be arrested for days. 'They stand out', Kempsey patrol supervisor Wal Trees explained. 'Although they are dressed in good suits, they're not Western-style suits. They don't fit into Kempsey, I can tell you.'[16]

I

John Howard wanted something done about the boats and gave Max Moore-Wilton the job. He had brought Moore-Wilton down from Sydney in 1996 with a brief to shake up the nation's bureaucracy, slash its ranks and bring the ethos of the commercial world into the public service. He was not starting from scratch. Under Labor, the old British ethos of the bureaucracy had begun to give way to a more American approach, but with Moore-Wilton in charge Canberra had rapidly become Washminster on the Molonglo. The upper reaches of the service were purged. The mandarins lost their security of tenure. Cabinet took an interest in the political colour of appointments way down the line. The result was a public service more politicised, more compliant and less able to offer 'frank and fearless' advice to ministers. Moore-Wilton was unrepentant. 'Frank and fearless seems to have been given some sort of particular status, a bit like Frank N. Furter. I think frank and fearless in some people is a sign of hubris and stupidity . . . and there are a number of people who have confused frank and fearless with just being a bloody nuisance.'[17]

This forceful, brash, often entertaining figure became Howard's closest adviser. There was a very particular chemistry between them: the tearaway bureaucrat would pick the fights the two men then fought together. Both of them revelled in these stoushes, fighting side by side, their backs to the wall. Moore-Wilton had taken a few tumbles in his career. In Sydney he'd failed in the perhaps impossible task of making the Australian national shipping line, ANL, a paying concern. He knew a bit about the shipping world. He had earned the nickname Max the Axe for shedding jobs by the tens of thousands. He was a can-do man, quick on his feet, hard to corner and deliberately provocative. Moore-Wilton encouraged the notion that there were no limits to what he might do, which made him a formidable presence among his more conventional colleagues. He could dazzle, inspire, bully and frighten grown men and women. He stood at the centre of the *Tampa* story and its political aftermath.

After those rusting boats came down the East Coast in early 1999, Moore-Wilton assembled a coastal surveillance taskforce bringing together all the bureaucrats who had—or should have had—a role in policing asylum seekers and patrolling the nation's coastline. The agencies were rather laid back about this work. Little was being done on the ground by the Federal police and neither the military nor the intelligence analysts of the Office of National Assessment (ONA) regarded boat people and people smuggling as security issues. Moore-Wilton bashed bureaucratic heads together and found $124 million to fund a new 'whole of government' operation for four years with more planes, more intelligence gathering and sharing, more agents checking papers at foreign airports, more DIMA 'compliance officers' out in the field, fresh attempts to broker deals with Indonesia, and vastly tougher penalties for people smuggling including the massive fines later used to threaten Arne Rinnan.[18]

Moore-Wilton was bubbling over with radical ideas. Asylum seekers were beginning to turn up at the barren and deserted Ashmore Reef south of Timor. The reef is an Australian National Nature Reserve and a boat was stationed there most of the year to see that Indonesian fishermen didn't plunder the last stocks of trochus and trepang. The boat was the asylum seekers' lifeline. 'It was a dysfunctional policy', said Moore-Wilton. 'There was a fisheries issue that was having a completely bizarre outcome. I simply asked, was it our responsibility to establish a reception point for illegal immigration?' He proposed removing the boat. Bureaucrats were horrified. Moore-Wilton admitted the plan was 'potentially hazardous' but pushed it at a number of meetings. Solid opposition from police, government lawyers and the officers of Environment Australia—concerned for the trochus and trepang—killed the idea.[19]

He had also wanted to use the navy to blockade the boats. The military compiled a big report on this but Admiral Chris Barrie, the new commander of the defence forces, said, 'No one at that stage thought it was worth the candle'. A handful of Australian ships deployed in the Indian Ocean weren't going to guarantee results. 'You say you're going to mount this wonderful naval operation, but the boat still gets through. You all look like a bunch of dills.' The navy made it clear it would not finesse the rules protecting the safety of lives at sea. 'In the public service you do have a problem of understanding just what the limits on the use of force are', explained Barrie. 'We are not there to use force [but] to make absolutely sure this never happens. We are there to exercise our rights and responsibilities, and the first premise is that no one loses their life.'[20]

The new border protection regime installed in 1999 remained civilian— with tougher penalties, more money, better co-ordination and more intelligence from abroad. Supervising this reinvigorated operation was Jane Halton, a protégé of Moore-Wilton's in the Prime Minister's department. The two became a kind of double act over the next few years fighting the boats. Halton was very attuned to the new ethos of the service under her boss. She was tart, forceful, hardworking and combative. Her Unauthorised Arrivals Taskforce would oversee the murky business of 'working with other countries to disrupt people smugglers'.[21]

But as the new team in Canberra set to work, relations between Australia and Indonesia sank to rock bottom over East Timor. However, the police of both countries—the AFP and the Indonesian National Police (INP)— continued to work together through this diplomatic hiatus. It was a triumph of Australian tact, money and schmoozing. The AFP's chief liaison officer, Leigh Dixon, had spent time on secondment to the INP in Jakarta. Senior

Indonesian police were guests of the AFP at the Sydney Olympics. On the opening day of the games, September 15, a 'specific protocol' was agreed between the two forces 'to target people smuggling syndicates operating out of Indonesia'. The terms of this protocol, eventually set aside by the Indonesians in the aftermath of the *Tampa* crisis, have never been revealed. But its purpose was: 'To prevent the departure of a vessel either by the arrest of individuals or by the detention of individuals, or by ensuring that the individuals don't reach the point of embarkation.'[22]

Australian police could only 'task' the Indonesians to do this work. They could not operate in the field themselves. They paid the INP in vehicles, radios and other equipment plus travelling expenses in hard currency. It would be expected in Indonesia that the men would share these crucial cash 'expenses' with their INP superiors. The scene was messy: while the two national police forces co-operated to bust smugglers, corrupt local police, immigration officials and soldiers were working with the smugglers to keep the trade moving.

Indonesia is a poor and corrupt state spread across a vast archipelago with no laws against people smuggling. The INP knew who the smugglers were but could do very little to touch them. So the five INP 'strike teams' funded and directed by the AFP to 'disrupt and dismantle' the syndicates followed the passengers, keeping an eye on the cheap hotels where they lived and the ports where they searched for boats. At AFP direction, the Indonesians attached tracking devices to many of the boats before they set out for Australia. Success in these disruption operations depended on recruiting spies among the crews and customers. 'What it boils down to is how much money you want to spend on intelligence', said an AFP/INP agent who recruited spies. 'Everyone is poor, everyone wants to put food in their belly, money is what makes it all turn around. There's no loyalties.'[23]

Kevin John Enniss was one of the most notorious of these agents. An Australian in the fishing boat business, he had been arrested in West Timor by local police on fraud charges in 1999. When he was released on bail, he became a principal source of information for the AFP and also had some contact with the INP. Enniss set up operations in the West Timor port of Kupang, the start of the smuggling route that ran down to Roti Island and on to Ashmore Reef, the quickest and safest route to Australia. According to the AFP, Enniss was paid 'expenses' to travel around West

Timor buying information on passengers which the INP then used to arrest them on minor visa and passport charges.[24] Enniss also robbed asylum seekers by promoting himself as a people smuggler and taking their money which, according to the police, he then handed to the INP.[25] What happened to the cash after it went to the Indonesian police was of no concern to the AFP. There was just one less boat person who could use his life savings to get to Australia.

Enniss also boasted to Ross Coulthart and the producer of Channel 9's *Sunday* that he and two confederates 'had paid Indonesian locals on four or five occasions to scuttle people smuggling boats with passengers on them. When the two journalists reacted with horror, 'he was unrepentant saying the boats were sunk close to land so everyone got off safely'. Enniss has since denied to the AFP ever organising sabotage. But informants close to the smuggling trade talk of crews bribed to wreck engines, particularly at changeover points like Roti Island where an experienced crew hands over to fishermen for the last leg to Ashmore Reef. 'It normally happens when they're in port . . . they just chuck a handful of something in the engine so that it doesn't work properly.' They say to the smugglers: 'We've done our bit, where's our money, we couldn't help if the boat broke down.'[26]

Commissioner Keelty has insisted the AFP has never been involved, directly or indirectly, in the sabotage of vessels. But he has conceded that by the time the AFP's directions to the INP were interpreted down at the ports, it was impossible to police Australian demands that nothing illegal be done in these operations. 'If we became aware that they were doing something illegal or something that was unhumanitarian, then it would be brought to our notice and we would ask that they not do it that way. The difficulty is once we ask them to do it, we have to largely leave it in their hands as how they best do it.'[27]

An Indonesian intelligence officer told a local journalist of an operation where boats were disabled to prevent them getting far from port. According to the journalist's notes of this conversation, operatives would damage fuel tanks or engines while trying to ensure the boats broke down within reach of land. 'If we could not make the syndicates refrain from sending people illegally overseas or stop the people from paying the syndicates to enter other countries illegally, then this is the only way to stop them.' The officer would not discuss whether these operations were known to be Australian.

He did say, 'The Australian government has been so desperate in trying to stop the flow of those illegal migrants'.[28]

The voyage to Australia was becoming more dangerous. As controls tightened at airports in the region, more asylum seekers began making their way to Australia by sea. As it became harder for smugglers to get their boats away, vessels were leaving port more heavily overloaded. As Australia denied family reunion to refugees, the boats began filling with women and children. To avoid being tracked by Australian signals interception, the smugglers were sending their boats to sea without radios. Once Indonesian sailors began risking long jail terms in Australia, the smugglers used more incompetent crews, men and boys with barely any training. And there was also the possibility of sabotage to explain, how the engines of boats such as the *Palapa* failed far out to sea.

No one knows how many lives have been lost on these voyages. Philip Ruddock has campaigned for years to make people aware how hazardous these seas are. He claims a third of the boats that set out for Ashmore never arrived. Some turned back, lost. Some sank. About 160 people drowned in December 2000 when their boat went down on its way to Ashmore. After more drownings a few weeks later, Ruddock lashed out at the families of the dead. 'These are treacherous waters and some of the boats are not seaworthy. Given the dangers, I find it very difficult to comprehend that Australians would willingly break the law to help their relatives—often young children—embark on such a dangerous and ill-advised journey. Nevertheless it has become obvious that relatives in Australia know the route, the boat, the date and time of departure from Indonesia and the estimated time of arrival at Ashmore Islands or other destinations. They are knowingly taking part in illegal operations, breaking Australian law and putting their relatives at risk.'[29] All true. But it was no time for Australia to think of finessing sea rescue in the Indian Ocean.

By grim coincidence, no sooner had Canberra started seriously tackling the problem of people smuggling, than the numbers of boats reaching Australia rose very sharply. The mandatory detention system, able to cope with two or three hundred boat people a year, was suddenly faced in 1999 with the arrival of 3274 people in shabby boats at Ashmore and Christmas Island. Most were now Afghans and Iraqis. The next year, 2937 turned up. Media coverage of this upsurge in human traffic was dramatic. Both sides of politics talked of a national emergency. The fear and irritation these arrivals provoked was not in any way mollified—rather the reverse—by the discovery that most of them had valid claims for refugee protection. They had fled religious, racial and political persecution in their homelands of Iraq, Iran and Afghanistan.[30] Criminals delivered them to Australia, but their claims for protection were real.

Between January and May 2001, seventeen more boats landed 1640 would-be refugees mainly on Ashmore Reef. By the standards of Germany or Britain, these numbers were almost trivial but that was never the point: Australians wanted no boat people at all. Even mainstream politicians began talking about closing the door on them—while repeating the mantra that: 'After Canada, Australia is the second most generous nation on earth to refugees.' That was true only in the Australian meaning of the word. Like Canada, Australia has a fine record for resettling 'offshore' refugees from UNHCR camps in distant countries. But Australia's overall record— 'offshore' plus those 'onshore' refugees who come by boat and plane—was not so wonderful. Peter Mares wrote in his book *Borderline* that 'Australia actually takes in far fewer refugees per capita than Denmark, Sweden, Norway and Canada'.[31]

Adding to the growing political panic in Australia was the state of the detention camps, by this time bursting at the seams and frequently violent. Three days of demonstrations in the remote desert camp at Woomera in June 2000 ended in a mass break out. Escapes followed from the camp in Port Hedland in Western Australia and demonstrations erupted in the Sydney camp at Villawood. Most camps saw hunger strikes with inmates sewing up their lips. A nasty riot at Port Hedland during the Western Australian election campaign had seen police attacked with bricks, steel pipes and gardening tools. In April, tear gas was used at the Curtin camp in Western Australia to put down yet another riot. The Human Rights and Equal Opportunities Commission claimed chemical restraints— non-consensual intra-muscular sedation—were also being used to control prisoners.[32] This violence did not win the asylum seekers any general sympathy. Most Australians took it as further proof that such people had no place in their country.

By the time Ruddock flew to Jakarta in June 2001, the Indonesian government was showing signs of becoming hostile to Australian operations on its soil. This got worse in the aftermath of his visit. Immigration and police officials in West Timor had contacted the Australian embassy in Jakarta claiming Kevin Enniss was actually a people smuggler himself.[33] Local immigration authorities raided his house and a nasty internal dispute erupted between the rival police and immigration officials in West Timor over Enniss' role. Suddenly, difficult questions about the Australian operation were being asked at senior levels of the Indonesian Foreign Ministry and the Immigration department. These included questions about Enniss, about Australia's aid to selected Indonesian police officials and the conduct of the disruption program. It emerged that senior levels of the Indonesian government did not know about the disruption operation and moved to block it. When Enniss left West Timor in August, local immigration officials cancelled his visa and refused to allow him to return. Australia's operations up there were threatening to fall apart.

I

Pauline Hanson, fresh from a triumphant showing in Western Australia, launched her party's Queensland campaign in February by demanding Australia start turning the boats away. 'We go out, we meet them, we fill them up with fuel, fill them up with food, give them medical supplies and we say, "Go that way".' Hanson warned in both campaigns that boat people were a sore point for supporters of One Nation. 'They don't see them as refugees. They are queue jumpers . . . they're coming in by the thousands, it's beyond a joke and people are saying "We've had enough".' Australia must send them packing. 'The clear message is, they don't want them here, they want the government to turn the boats around and say go back where they come from.'[34]

Hanson, a Lazarus with flaming red hair, was back from the political dead. She had worked her peculiar charm in Western Australia to win 9.6 per cent of a poll that crushed the conservative government of Richard Court. A week later in Queensland, she won 20 per cent of the vote across the 39 seats her party contested in an election that delivered Labor its best result in that State for over sixty years. The political fortunes of John Howard's Liberal Party had sunk very low. Labor now had excellent prospects of winning the federal election to be held towards the end of the year. But the primary vote of both parties was soft. The Greens to the Left and One Nation to the Right were cutting into the base of both big parties.

Howard could not rely on One Nation's preferences flowing back to him. They were all over the shop. The government's best hope in the election ahead was to somehow win back the *primary* votes of One Nation followers. Without them, John Howard looked a dead duck. But what issue could work this electoral miracle?

For two years, the now-defeated Richard Court had been calling on Canberra to send the boats back to where they came from. Sources within the Liberal Party say both Court and Ruddock were trying, from early 2001, to interest John Howard in taking more vigorous initiatives against the asylum seekers. He was showing little interest. The Prime Minister seemed not yet convinced that military action against boat people was the answer to either of the problems facing him that year: bringing people smuggling under control and winning the election that would have to be held before Christmas.

Max Moore-Wilton had never abandoned his idea of using the navy to blockade the boats and the new Minister for Defence, Peter Reith, was game. Reith was one of the hard men of the government, a man with a track record for taking on high risk, confrontational strategies. At the August 8 meeting of the National Security Committee (NSC) of Cabinet, Howard asked Admiral Chris Barrie what the military could do. The question was exploratory. There was a conversation in very general terms about a show of force by the navy to send a message to the smugglers. The military was asked to prepare some proposals for laying a 'thick grey line' across the Indian Ocean.

Howard was in Jakarta in mid-August to pay his respects to the new president of Indonesia, Megawati Sukarnoputri, and spoke to a number of her ministers about the problem of boat people. 'I put a proposition to the Indonesian government that we would pay for the construction of a very large detention centre in Indonesia so that the Indonesian government would hold people there rather than allowing them to leave and come to Australia on boats.'[35] But Indonesia rebuffed this Australian plan once again.

The Prime Minister returned to find the situation at home had moved to a new level of farce, tragedy and confusion. Two daring escapes had taken place from Villawood: 23 men dug a tunnel from the camp mosque to the outside world and a few days later another 23 made off by cutting through the razor wire. The ABC's *Four Corners* had also broadcast the story of a six-year-old Iranian boy in Villawood, Shayan Bedraie, who was so traumatised he was refusing to eat and had spent seven stints in a Sydney children's hospital. This was one of the rare press reports that penetrated the indifference of Australians to the predicament of asylum seekers. *Four Corners* was savagely attacked by newspaper columnists briefed, apparently by DIMA, with intimate details of the Bedraie family. Meanwhile another heavily overloaded boat had arrived at Christmas Island with 348 men, women and children on board.

'What do you do now?' Neil Mitchell of 3AW asked the Prime Minister. 'It is a huge problem', Howard replied. 'We are a humanitarian country. We don't turn people back into the sea, we don't turn unseaworthy boats which are likely to capsize and the people on them be drowned. We can't behave in that manner. People say well send them back from where they came, the country from which they came won't have them back. Many of them are frightened to go back to those countries and we are faced with this awful dilemma of on the one hand trying to behave like a humanitarian decent country, on the other hand making certain that we don't become just an easy touch for illegal immigrants.'

'The strategies are not working are they?' said Mitchell.

'Well when you say the strategies are not working what is the alternative? You see the only alternative strategy I hear is really the strategy of using our armed forces to stop the people coming and turning them back. Now for a humanitarian nation that really is not an option.'

John Howard is a master of ambiguity. His words must always be read with care. He was not absolutely ruling out the use of the military but he had clearly not yet made up his mind—ten days after the NSC meeting—to blockade the Indian Ocean. He said: 'I believe the government has got the balance about as correct as it can in current circumstances.'

The *Tampa* changed those circumstances. Suddenly here was an opportunity for Howard to show Canberra was in control. The camps were bursting and there was no room for another 400 behind the wire. So Rinnan was told to take the survivors to Indonesia. The Norwegian master knew it would be difficult to land these people. But in the face of the survivors' anger and despair, for the safety of his crew and the survivors themselves, for the most humane outcome after their ordeal and for the best prospects of resuming his ship's voyage, Arne Rinnan eventually ignored Australia's threats and headed for Christmas Island. Canberra's dramatic gesture had backfired.

FOUR
Canberra scrambles

AUGUST 27

The sun came up on the miserable sight of the survivors on the deck of the ship. As first officer of the *Tampa*, Christian Maltau was responsible for the health of 438 people who had spent several days at sea under great stress, with little food, and who now crowded the open deck of his ship. A hot day lay ahead. Maltau had been moving among these people since first light. Some were unconscious, some were hysterical and dozens had diarrhoea. There was already a stench from the latrines. As the survivors stirred they asked why they had not yet reached the island. 'Take us to Christmas Island', they told the crew. 'We can't stay here for ever.'[1] The crew made light of the delay and told them they were just waiting for permission to take them ashore. They were given a breakfast of boiled eggs and bread.

The police on Christmas Island had contacted Rinnan while it was still barely light to say the Australian government was meeting and the ship was to wait instructions. Half an hour later, DIMA's Neville Nixon was back on the line to tell the master 'the Australian government at the highest level formally requests that you not approach Christmas Island and that you stand off at a distance at least equal to your current position'. Rinnan agreed to keep the *Tampa* outside Australia's territorial waters until he heard from Canberra.²

In Canberra, Max Moore-Wilton had gathered a group of high officials to prepare 'very quick oral advice to ministers' before Cabinet met.³ Moore-Wilton was not a man to take the *Tampa*'s defiance lightly. Nor was John Howard. That Rinnan had ignored their orders would soon be known. The first sketchy press reports had already appeared of that strange night on the Indian Ocean. Politically, it was much too late for this mass rescue to take its normal course. According to government sources, officials were not asked what should be done at this point—the rights and wrongs of the situation were not the issue—but how to enforce the direction already given to the *Tampa* to leave and take the survivors to Indonesia.

Cabinet began at 9 am. Howard had already met a number of bureaucrats and Admiral Chris Barrie, chief of the Defence Force. Over the next couple of hours, officials went in and out of the Cabinet room. Howard said, 'We had available to us the advice of our law officers, the advice of customs, the advice of the Defence Force and the advice of the Department of Foreign Affairs and Trade'.⁴ In the middle of the meeting, a direction was sent to the administrator of Christmas Island, Bill Taylor, to 'take all steps necessary' to ensure no boats could go out to the Norwegian ship. Flying Fish Cove, the island's only port, was closed indefinitely. Cabinet also instructed the Department of Foreign Affairs and Trade (DFAT) to let Norway and Indonesia know that the *Tampa* was their problem.

The cherry and white Coastwatch de Havilland appeared above the *Tampa* to radio Cabinet's verdict. It was 8.45 am on the island and 11.45 am in Canberra. Rinnan was told the ship did not have permission to enter Australian territorial waters, nor would it be given permission to land the survivors in Australia or any Australian territory. The question of where they would be disembarked was to be resolved by the governments of Indonesia and Norway. The Wilhelmsen Line recorded: 'Captain Rinnan received this shocking news with stoic calm.' He radioed back that he was not budging and added that he had people on board dehydrated and sick. Coastwatch replied that he was to await further instructions from the Department of Prime Minister and Cabinet. Down on the deck, the survivors were assured the captain was still determined to land them all on the island and that talks were continuing. The survivors were calm but Rajab Ali Merzaee said, 'The crew were very, very angry'.[5]

Neither the Wilhelmsen Line nor Rinnan believed Australia had made a considered and final decision. The lack of courtesy and breaches of convention were so gross that the crisis must surely be resolved once the government had the expert advice it needed. The company recorded that Rinnan, 'expected the Australians to change their decision once they had a little more time to consider the situation. So he decided to give them that time'.[6]

The line's lawyer, James Neill, rang Philippa Godwin at DIMA to deliver Maltau's first report on the survivors' health a little later in the morning. 'The medical situation on board is critical. If it is not addressed immediately people will die shortly. At this time, four people on board are unconscious, one broken leg and three women are pregnant. Additionally diarrhoea is severe and a number of people are in a dangerously dehydrated condition.' The lawyer made the first of many demands for medical help, demands that would be repeated fruitlessly for the next 50 hours. 'It is a simple matter to send a boat from shore to collect the sickest people, supply food and medical assistance. It could be along side in 30 minutes.' He ended by jogging Godwin's memory. 'I remind you that this vessel has interrupted its commercial activities to save life pursuant to International Conventions—Australia also has obligations in this respect. You need to do something urgently. We require hearing from you by 5 pm.'[7]

I

John Howard faced the press in Canberra at 1 pm with Philip Ruddock at his side. The Prime Minister goes to great pains to present himself as the authentic representative of ordinary Australia. His clothes are dull, his tastes are dull, his speeches are dull. He is never funny, never surprising, rarely moving. Yet Howard is the least dull politician. He came to office playing on his country's fear of difference and change, yet when he reached the top he proved the most radical leader his party had known for half a century. Slow to make up his mind and cautious to enter a fight, Howard is most alive in a brawl with his back against the wall. Crises turn him to steel. The deliberate plainness of the man hides a politician of extraordinary capability. Howard is the most professional leader Australia has seen since the heyday of Robert Menzies—not original or inspiring but professional.

Though never eloquent, he is a master of political speech. He can spin, block, prevaricate, sidestep, confound and just keep talking through everything. His very muscular jaw has been working hard all his life. Above all, Howard is a master of the political art of deceiving without lying.

The press conference was not frenzied. News of the *Tampa* was breaking everywhere and Rinnan had already been on radio giving a spare account of the night but journalists were deeply puzzled. Mass sea rescues of refugees had not been on the news agenda in Australia for over twenty years. The press and the country were both predisposed to accept the Prime Minister's claim that this was not Australia's problem. Howard was absolutely resolute: these people would not come to Australia. 'The vessel took on board several hundred people as a result of the vessel on which they had been travelling being becalmed, in circumstances where there was a clear obligation under international law for those people to be taken to the nearest feasible port of disembarkation which we are informed was an Indonesian port called, I think, Merak . . . it is our view that as a matter of international law this matter is something that must be resolved between the government of Indonesia and the government of Norway.'

Howard put all his great skill into the choice of those words. What did 'becalmed' or 'feasible' mean? For days he would insist it wasn't 'feasible' to disembark so many people from such a big ship in the tiny Christmas Island port of Flying Fish Cove. The operation would certainly have been easier and safer in Merak but, as events proved, it was always feasible at the destination the *Tampa* had now reached. With great subtlety, Howard suggested that the *Tampa* had chosen the longer journey in order to bring the survivors to an Australian port. 'The Indonesian port was as close if not closer than Christmas Island', Ruddock told the journalists. That was simply not true, but from this press conference forward it was generally believed to be so.

Howard's lawyers could *not* have told Cabinet the crisis was one for Indonesia and Norway to resolve. He took this position with the press with absolute confidence—and was believed—but it was impossible for him to have been given such advice. The gap in international law here is notorious. For over thirty years, nations and shipping lines have been trying to resolve the question of who takes responsibility for asylum seekers rescued at sea. The United Nations High Commission for Refugees has spent years on the problem and has failed to find a lasting answer. Maritime law experts know the problem intimately. Ernst Willheim, former head of the office of international law in the Federal Attorney General's Department put it this way: 'Although the master's duty to render assistance is clear, the law relating to subsequent rights and responsibilities, including disembarkation of those who have been rescued, is sadly lacking in clarity.' Australia had argued against fixing any clear-cut formula, preferring to leave each situation 'to be worked out in the context of international solidarity and against the background of humanitarian principles'.[8]

Indonesia and Norway were certainly on a list of countries which might have to take responsibility for the people on the *Tampa*. But so was Australia because Australia was the 'coastal state' nearest the scene of the rescue. This view was all the more compelling because the *Tampa* was now waiting outside an Australian port. On another view, responsibility for the survivors lay with the distant flag state of the ship, Norway. The notion of carting those people across the world to Oslo was, to say the least, impractical. A third argument was that Singapore should take the survivors because Singapore was the *Tampa*'s next port of call. At no stage in the crisis did Howard point in that direction. He knew Singapore would refuse and Singapore was not a country Australia could risk alienating over a little question like this. That left Indonesia.

Ruddock was particularly blunt about this. His reason was simple: they had to go there because the *Palapa* went down 'in the sea rescue area that is normally supervised by Indonesia'. Throughout the crisis, Canberra's mantra would be that the rescue took place in the Indonesian zone, so Indonesia was obliged to take the survivors ashore. The Opposition attacked Indonesia's failure to live up to its responsibilities here just as confidently as the government did. Neither had the backing of high-level legal advice on the point that morning, or at any time during the crisis. What an international lawyer would have told them was that nothing in international law or the 1990 sea rescue agreement between Australia and its neighbour imposed any such obligation on Indonesia. Yet from the first day of the crisis, there arose an unshakeable belief that Canberra was doing no more than asking Indonesia to do its duty. The *Tampa* must go to Merak and disembark its passengers there.

'Are you concerned that you may be putting the Norwegian captain and his crew at risk through this measure?', asked pugnacious Andrew Clennell of the *Sydney Morning Herald*. The Prime Minister was not. Howard had nothing to offer Rinnan to help him survive the inevitable difficulties he would face if the ship set off once again for Merak. Howard vaguely thought there must be guns on the *Tampa*. 'I guess on any vessel there would be a limited number of personal firearms available. I think the captain always has something. But I just don't know.' Howard seemed unperturbed by the possibility that his orders might put lives at risk on the *Tampa*—the lives of the crew as well as the asylum seekers. The ship simply had to sail and the rest was Rinnan's problem.

Clennell had a second difficult question: 'How are you going to stop them coming in to Christmas Island? If they say "bugger you, we'll keep going" what are you going to do? Draw guns on them?' This was a question that did bother Howard and he had his bureaucrats working frantically on it. Meanwhile, he fobbed Clennell off with the formula that became familiar as the really difficult issues loomed in Howard's path over the next extraordinary week. 'I don't want to start dealing in hypothetical situations.'

Australia would deny aid to the survivors of a shipwreck and close its border to refugees. That this might set the country on a collision course with Indonesia, Norway, the United Nations, a great shipping line and the opinion of the maritime world did not deflect Howard from his decision to send this message: 'We simply cannot allow a situation to develop where Australia is seen around the world as a country of easy destination, irrespective of the circumstances, irrespective of the obligations of others under international law and irrespective of the legal status of the people who would seek to come to Australia ... we believe the stance taken by the Australian government is the only one appropriate in the circumstances.'

❙

The Canberra bureaucracy was in shock. What began that day and continued for the next two months was a can-do exercise essentially run out of the Prime Minister's department by Max Moore-Wilton. His daily challenge to the bureaucrats was: Find a Way. They had no illusions about the political dimensions of this exercise. Some of them wondered if, somewhere ahead, there would be lines they were unwilling to cross. The military found those lines. The civilians never did. The work was distasteful but they were caught up in the same atmosphere of crisis that dazzled politicians and the press. The bureaucrats felt professionally obliged to deliver what the Prime Minister and the government wanted; not frank and fearless advice but solutions to 'the predicament Rinnan has put us in'. They were expected to 'leave their baggage'—their personal values—'at the door'. They did.[9]

Moore-Wilton's number two, Jane Halton, was back from the snow. She convened a 'high level group' of very senior bureaucrats from the departments of Prime Minister and Cabinet, Immigration, Defence, Foreign Affairs, Transport and Attorney General. Clive Davidson, chief of AMSA/RCC, the head of Coastwatch and senior Australian Federal Police were also in the group. Others came and went as needed.[10] After a time the group became known as the People Smuggling Taskforce. It met—at first almost daily—in Conference Room 3 in the Prime Minister's department. The style was freewheeling. The meetings were not run in the traditional public service way. Notes were only intermittently taken. The members didn't often see minutes. Halton spent a great deal of the time on her mobile talking to Howard, Reith, Ruddock or the Prime Minister's adviser Miles Jordana, while the high officials around the table sat twiddling their thumbs. Security was tight. There were no leaks. The existence of the taskforce was largely unknown.

The riding instructions were that no survivors would come ashore—including, if at all possible, the sick—and the *Tampa* was to be sent away without causing a diplomatic row with Norway. The response of Indonesia was not, it seems, crucial to the shaping of the strategy. Halton's taskforce was meeting by early afternoon on August 27 to prepare material for the National Security Committee of Cabinet later that day. The key issues were: 'the impact if any of safety regulations; the likely attitude of the Norwegians; how to handle the possible health and related issues.' The taskforce decided medical teams could not go onto the *Tampa* without security backing 'given the risk of hostage taking'.[11] That attitude meant the response to the *Tampa*'s pleas for medical assistance could not be swift.

Looming over them was the possibility that the *Tampa* would disobey Canberra and bring the survivors into Flying Fish Cove. 'What options were there to handle the situation?' asked the minutes of this first meeting. 'What logistical capacity did we have, could it be moved/people transferred etc?' The problem was that once the ship brought the survivors into territorial waters, the machinery of the Migration Act would deliver them to the mainland. The law was designed to hoover boat people up as they approached Australia for fear they might otherwise slip ashore and disappear into the hinterland. Nothing in the legislation allowed Canberra to send boat people away. Once the *Tampa* sailed into Australia's territorial waters and DIMA officers suspected—as they already did—that the survivors wanted to enter Australia, then the Migration Act required them to be brought exactly where they wanted to go: into detention in Australia.[12]

The stop-gap solution was to make sure DIMA officers were kept away from the operation. None were to be allowed anywhere near the *Tampa*. Some naval personnel also had the status of immigration officer under the Act. Cancellation of that status was gazetted by Ruddock. To give DIMA a fighting chance in court, officers of the department would have to be able to pretend they never suspected the survivors wanted to come ashore. This fiction meant no civilians—such as doctors and nurses—could be allowed out to the ship. They would inevitably report what was already obvious, that these people wanted to enter Australia. Above all, Canberra had to see there was no contact between the survivors and lawyers: no face-to-face meetings, no messages, no instructions. The greatest danger the *Tampa* strategy faced was a lawyer finding a client on the deck of the ship and taking the matter to court. If the *Tampa* entered territorial waters, the only sure way to keep the survivors out of Australia would be to keep them out of the courts. By force if necessary.

I

The Australian embassy in Jakarta was scrambling to get on top of the situation. Some advance warning had been delivered to the Indonesian government even while Cabinet was still meeting, but any slim chance of persuading the Indonesians to co-operate with Australia on the *Tampa* was lost once Howard went into his 1 pm press conference. Howard's complaints and demands were laid out in public before the Indonesian government could absorb them or begin to explore with its leaders the possibility of co-operation. It didn't help Australia's cause that both the Foreign Minister, Hassan Wirajuda, and President Megawati Sukarnoputri were away on a goodwill tour of Southeast Asia. The impulse of the officials left behind in Jakarta was to say no to the *Tampa*. After the loss of East Timor, the instinct of Indonesia's political leadership was to say no to any request from Australia.

Alexander Downer later claimed he knew from the start that Indonesia would refuse to take the *Tampa* survivors back. 'My judgement was they would stick to their time-worn policy, which is a . . . not to take illegals full stop. Once these people had left Indonesian waters they were going to take the view that they'd come to Indonesia illegally and they wouldn't take them back. I mean obviously we would have liked them to take them back but it would have constituted a very significant change in policy that they've had for a long time.'[13] Nevertheless, he and his diplomats set out that afternoon to do all they could to change Indonesia's mind.

They failed. From the outset the Indonesian officials 'expressed reluctance to receive illegal immigrants from third countries. Indonesia's view was the *Tampa* passengers were illegal in Indonesia too'.[14] Jakarta shared the commonsense verdict of the rest of the world that wherever these people *should* have gone, they had now reached Australia and were Australia's problem. Canberra would continue to pressure Jakarta in the faint hope of reversing this verdict, but Downer understood 'perfectly clearly' on this first afternoon of the crisis that the Indonesians would not take back the *Tampa* survivors. [15]

Yet Australia would continue to tell Rinnan, Norway and the shipping line that the *Tampa* had to sail for Merak. Not only was that port closed, but no other port in Asia would take the survivors. Australia knew—and Norway soon realised—that if the *Tampa* left Christmas Island, no one could tell where its human cargo could disembark. The Australian government didn't care. The *Tampa*'s destination was a mere detail. It simply wanted the boat and those people gone.

I

The Royal Ministry of Foreign Affairs is a fusty apartment block on a narrow street in Oslo. Ibsen's old flat is preserved there and unhappy memories still linger over the building's use as the local Gestapo headquarters during the Second World War. On this Monday morning, the *Tampa* crisis landed on the desk of Hans Wilhelm Longva, director general of the Ministry's Department of Legal Affairs.

The Norwegian embassy in Canberra had worked swiftly after being first alerted at 10 am, while Cabinet was still meeting, that there was a 'situation developing'. The ambassador was at home in Norway on holidays, so Lars Alsaker, the first secretary, contacted the Australian search and rescue authorities and was given a candid and very detailed briefing on the adventures of the *Tampa* during the night. Alsaker sent this material through to Longva with the formal notification which arrived from the Department of Foreign Affairs early in the Canberra afternoon that Australia considered the *Tampa* problem was one for Norway and Indonesia to solve between themselves. Norway was never persuaded of this. Longva said, 'We had no contact with Indonesia, it was completely irrelevant'.[16]

Longva is no dry lawyer but an experienced diplomatic troubleshooter who had served in Beirut during the civil war in Lebanon and in Kuwait during the Iraqi invasion. He is an open, sharp man in his mid-fifties with a ruddy, well-worn face and an easy laugh. His confident, dismissive charm is oddly like Max Moore-Wilton's. But there the resemblance between the bureaucratic adversaries ends. Longva is a traditionalist. He argued for the old rules and old understandings that obligations of rescue are owed to anyone in distress. All that mattered was that there were lives that needed to be saved. 'To us it was very, very important that these people were dealt with as shipwreck people and rescuees. These were the only parts of international law which we felt concerned us as Norway. The obligations of the Australian government towards shipwrecked people, towards rescuees are not modified by any assumption that they may want to apply for asylum.'

Longva began what fell into a strange routine over the next few days: he was up for sunrise on Christmas Island—1.30 am in Oslo—and had his first conversation of the day with Australia's ambassador to Norway, Malcolm Leader. 'He was an important point of contact.' Longva worked at home for the next few hours before leaving for a 7.30 am meeting each morning with the head of the ministry, Bjarne Lindstrøm. Wilh Wilhelmsen attended several of these meetings. 'The Foreign Office wanted to talk to us about the condition of the vessel and ask what they could do to assist us. And they were the proper channel to talk to their counterparts in Australia. We were not the proper channel to do that.' Longva had continuous access to the *Tampa*'s log and to the shipping line's contingency room. Both Longva and Wilhelmsen assumed Australia was listening to all communications with the ship. Both claim to be unworried by this. Longva said, 'We had a very open attitude in the negotiations, so there was nothing we were trying to hide. I don't think there was anything they would have intercepted that they wouldn't have got from us'. Longva laughed as he explained: 'Throughout this story every day had its surprises, our perception of Australia also changed every day.'

Working with Longva was Rolf Fife. A lawyer descended from a long line of mariners, Fife feared Australia's treatment of Rinnan was exactly the sort of behaviour that would encourage other ships' masters to shirk their responsibilities. 'We fear the long-term consequences of letting the performance of the duty to render assistance to persons in distress be influenced by any later legal status of such persons, including any complications that could arise with his employer or with immigration authorities. The master's absolute obligation to carry out rescues would be fatally undermined if he in fact should become motivated to avert his eyes in cases of distress. Whether a ship's master is alert, dedicated and motivated to shift his course to make sure whether he has seen a human being on the horizon or just a reflection on the waves—that is what at some point really makes the difference.' The ministry checked Rinnan out to see if they had a ship's master who was trustworthy. They were satisfied. 'We felt there was a rock solid case for going wherever the ship master felt was necessary under the prevailing conditions.'[17]

Wilh Wilhelmsen joined Longva and his team that first morning of the crisis. They all shared the feeling that the *Tampa* problem would be smoothed over easily once Australia was reminded of the principles at stake. However, the ambassador to Australia, Ove Thorsheim, who found his summer holiday at home abruptly ended, was directed to fly at once to Christmas Island. Longva and a team of in-house lawyers drafted an immediate message of protest to Australia. It went off that day. 'We instructed our embassy in Canberra to immediately approach the Australian Foreign Ministry pointing out that in our view we felt they had an obligation to receive [the people on the *Tampa*] and to request that Australia conform with their obligations in international law and receive them.' This was ignored.

I

On a hot day in the tropics, the patch of deck between the containers became an oven. People were unconscious, in pain and in distress. The children were hard hit by diarrhoea. As the buckets in the latrines filled they were carried out of the containers and emptied over the side of the ship. The hotter the day grew, the more agitated the survivors became. They wanted to know what was happening. 'We had a hard time explaining the situation on board to them, and that we could not be blamed for not setting them ashore', said Able Seaman Noel Lapuz. 'To be honest, there were times when I was not particularly happy to be among them.'[18]

Christian Maltau continued his medical round. Maltau had grown up in a medical family, was trained in first aid and was in radio contact with Haukeland Hospital in Bergen, which specialises in rescue emergencies. He told Bergen the medical situation was growing worse. The Norwegian doctors were most concerned about the cases of dehydration and the predicament of a pregnant woman in pain whom the male crew could not examine. The Haukeland Hospital directed treatment, as best it could, using the basic medical supplies on board. These were running out, fast. The Bergen doctors had Maltau check the unconscious were not faking their symptoms by lifting their eyelids and shining lights in their eyes. That afternoon, Maltau shaved the children's heads to treat their lice and scabs.

A little before midday, island time, RCC Australia faxed Rinnan. 'The Australian government has offered to provide all necessary humanitarian assistance to MV *Tampa* for looking after survivors from KM *Palapa* 1.' Rinnan was asked about food, water, weapons and if a helicopter could land on the ship. The rescue authority was concerned that any attempt to take off sick survivors by boat 'would provoke a mass attempt to embark the rescue craft'. Rinnan replied: 'We now have four unconscious survivors (vital signs OK), many others with diarrhoea. We estimate we have enough food and water for perhaps a week. There are no weapons on board. A helicopter will not be able to land on board. We suggest a suitable winching area on the swimming pool deck ... Please urgently advise when we can expect medical help for these survivors.'[19]

RCC Australia began a fruitless search for a helicopter. While that was underway, a call came to the Canberra rescue centre from an officer of BASARNAS who was rather behind the game. He wondered why the *Tampa* had not yet arrived in Merak. After a long conversation which 'he appeared to understand', RCC sent Rinnan another order to sail north. 'Indonesian SAR authorities have offered medical assistance and advise your vessel proceed directly to Merak ... Please advise your intentions.' Rinnan did not reply.[20]

A bizarre idea had reached the rescue centre from the Department of Prime Minister and Cabinet: the Indonesians might be persuaded to come south and winch the sick off the Norwegian ship themselves. BASARNAS was asked 'if they have any warships with helicopters on board which may be able to provide medivac assistance to MV *Tampa*'.[21] But Clive Davidson warned whoever had had this bright idea, 'In practical terms, if medivac is necessary . . . we fully expect [BASARNAS] would request us to co-ordinate because of the proximity to Christmas Island and we would have no choice but to organise this.'[22] The idea died.

Late in the afternoon, a ragged hunger strike began. The crew was perplexed. Khodadad Sarwari said, 'The crew came down to the people and said what is it, what is it? What is your objection to us? This is our food and we haven't done anything. The people said it is not about objection to you. Everyone was thankful to them. But they wanted to make the point that Australia shut their door on them'. 'It was done especially to get the sick and the women and children out of this situation', Assadullah Rezaee said. 'These people need to be treated. There were a lot of people sick.' Rinnan sent a message to the deck, asking the survivors, as a personal favour to him, to allow the children to eat. They agreed.

With sunset approaching, the crew began to prepare the survivors for another night on the deck. The children were given milk and chocolate, much of it snatched away by adults. The crew brought a few dozen blankets and from below deck fetched 300 cardboard cartons that were then squashed flat to make rough mattresses. 'The fact that we never received any adequate supplies of medicines, food, blankets and other things that could have relieved the human suffering on board was perhaps what upset us most during the whole incident', said Maltau. 'We were close enough to shore to see the buildings, even the hospital, but no help arrived.'[23]

As it was getting dark, Rinnan had a call from RCC Australia. Another garbled conversation with BASARNAS had led the Australian rescue authorities to believe the *Tampa* was now on its way to Merak. Rinnan doused these hopes. 'We are not heading any place just yet, drifting outside Christmas Island.'

'What is your intention?' RCC asked.

'To stay drifting. I have been instructed by my company to stay drifting. We were expecting some help to come on board today but no one came.' Rinnan asked if they had been speaking to BASARNAS.

'They in fact advised us you were underway towards Merak.'

'I have never said that', Rinnan replied. 'For your information the people stopped eating at 1800 today. Hunger strike and not taking no fresh water. They let the children eat a little bit. This is turning into some situation. The next time you send out request for assistance I will overlook it.'[24]

FIVE
Pan Pan

AUGUST 28

Early next morning, Dr Peter Schuller came on duty at the Cairns base of the Royal Flying Doctor Service (RFDS) at the start of a 48-hour shift. Celebrated in films and novels for its work in the outback, the RFDS is also the medical arm of Australia's sea rescue authority. Its mission is to look after the health of people in Australia's far-flung places, in the deserts or on the high seas. The particular skill of men like Schuller is to assess, by radio or telephone, when people need to be collected and taken to hospital. When in doubt, they fly out the sick. Schuller's experience of Australian maritime search and rescue operations was that 'the moment someone sneezes, they are evacuated'.[1]

Somehow the drama of the *Tampa*, everywhere on television the previous night and all over the papers that morning, had passed Schuller by. He discovered it in the notes of his colleague, Dr Walter Dietz, who had managed to have one conversation the evening before with Christian Maltau. Dietz noted: four women in late pregnancy; one unconscious male around 38–40 years who had had a fit and could not be roused, and four others initially unconscious who had come around. He also noted that Maltau was 'not panicking'. Dietz assessed there was no immediate danger out there but he was concerned for the health of the survivors if the situation on the *Tampa* continued. He wanted to stay in contact with the ship all night, particularly to check on the unconscious man: 'this sounds a bit suspicious'. Dietz found for some reason that he was not able to get through to Maltau again.[2]

Schuller shared Dietz's concern. He tried to ring the ship but he, too, found he could not get through. Nevertheless, the RFDS doctor was not worried: given the situation on board, the numbers involved, and the level of medical problems already evident, he took it for granted that medical assistance would be provided to the ship as soon as possible and the man still unconscious would be evacuated.[3] That was not the case. No arrangements were being made to get civilian doctors and nurses from Christmas Island out to the *Tampa*. To the great surprise of AMSA officers, an order had come down from the Department of Prime Minister and Cabinet that the usual procedures were not to be followed on this one. Though AMSA is an independent authority, the order from above was obeyed.

The government had decided the only medical team to go out to the ship would be military. Three tactical reasons lay behind this. First, a military operation would not engage the machinery of the Migration Act and compel the government to bring the asylum seekers ashore. Second, soldiers may be needed to handle the security problems inevitable once the asylum seekers realised they were not going to be allowed to land. Not just any military team was to be sent, but a detachment of the army's elite anti-terrorist Special Air Service (SAS). This would have a third advantage: SAS operations were always surrounded by a very high level of secrecy. But such a military response would take time to mount in this very far flung outpost of Australia. Three Hercules loaded with military personnel were on their way. The last would be on the island by midday. A helicopter would not arrive until some time next day. Meanwhile, the survivors on the *Tampa* would just have to wait.

What was he doing about the sick, Howard was asked? How long would he leave them untreated on the *Tampa*? Did he care if they died? Was he worried by the hunger strike? Was he indifferent to threats of suicide? The Prime Minister replied: 'We are a humane people. Others know that and they sometimes try and intimidate us with our own decency. On the other hand, we cannot surrender our right as a sovereign country our right to control our borders and we cannot have a situation where people can come to this country when they choose.' What mattered here was not the suffering of the survivors on the *Tampa* but control of the borders. 'Every situation has its 450 souls, every situation has stories of hunger strikes, every situation has the threat of people doing self-damage and jumping overboard and even suggestions of throwing children overboard. All of those things are talked about in a situation like this, but on the other hand, I have to worry and my colleagues have to worry about a situation where we appear to be losing control of the flow of people coming into this country. Now, we have decided in relation to this particular vessel to take a stand.'[4]

I

Alexander Downer is not a man endowed by nature to perform diplomatic miracles yet nothing less was expected of him now. The latest product of a political dynasty and one of the last Anglo-Australians left in politics, he has a taste for pin stripes and an edge to his voice that does not sit easily with the brutal diplomatic objectives he was pursuing now. Downer is one of those fussy men who insist on their dignity; someone who gives the disturbing impression of having learnt the hard way how to bully. Not a rogue, but weak. In tight corners he grows shrill. He had to persuade the Norwegians to order the *Tampa* to sail to Indonesia and the Indonesians—despite their clear refusal—to take these people back.

Howard was not making Downer's task any easier. The Prime Minister was hectoring the Indonesians on radio: the *Palapa* was their boat, manned by their crew, sailing from one of their ports, rescued in their rescue zone and 'the first intention of the ship's master' had been to take the survivors to an Indonesian port. 'When you add all of those things together there's a very strong case, not only morally but also in international law, for Indonesia to take these people back.' All that had been said, more politely, the day before but Howard on morning radio now delivered a blunt reproach to the Indonesians. 'Until there's a message sent to the world that you can no longer pass with ease through Indonesia and come to Australia, until that message is sent to the world we're going to continue to have an enormous problem and we're going to continue to have our refugee programme undermined... the key is really ending the flow and the flow is through Indonesia.'[5]

Downer got nowhere with Indonesia's man in Canberra, Arizal Effendi. The ambassador told the minister his country's position had not changed:

the asylum seekers were now in Australia and would not be taken back by Indonesia. All Downer could bring parliament a few hours later was an assurance that Australia was continuing 'to seek the assistance of the Norwegian and Indonesian governments to secure an acceptable solution for all concerned'. Howard announced he would speak to President Megawati Sukarnoputri. There was a vague hope that Indonesia might shift its position once she and her foreign minister, Hassan Wirajuda, returned to Jakarta that night from their goodwill tour of Southeast Asia.

Jane Halton's taskforce was in almost continuous session. Apart from overseeing the despatch of soldiers, police and immigration officials to the island, hunting for a helicopter and drawing up lists of medical supplies, the taskforce was preparing briefings for a second meeting of the National Security Committee of Cabinet (NSC) due that afternoon. The senior bureaucrats were also turning their minds to what Australia could do if Rinnan decided to take his ship into Flying Fish Cove. The frigate HMAS *Arunta* would leave base that day for Christmas Island but was not due there until the end of the week. The scrappy taskforce minutes read: 'The group considered several scenarios... captain decides to go to CI (do we impound vessel, detain rescuees??), passengers start jumping and have to be rescued (minimise risk by keeping vessels away until *Arunta* arrives), *Tampa* hijacked and runs aground or headed to mainland Aust (can master disable to prevent damage???).'

Government lawyers had swiftly concluded there was no legislative basis for expelling the *Tampa* and its passengers if they reached Australian waters. Mark Zanker of the Attorney General's Department commented: 'There was certainly nothing in the [Migration] Act that provided for the giving of instructions to vessels not to land persons who would be unauthorized arrivals, and no power on the part of officials to do other than to take the arrivals into detention—not to remove them to another place or country outside Australia.'[6] Theoretically there was an ancient prerogative power of the Crown to repel anyone trying to cross the border, but the lawyers' view at this time was that this could not be relied on. There would have to be fresh legislation.

The taskforce decided there would be total control of information about the *Tampa* operation by the government through ministerial offices. None of the officials involved in Canberra or on Christmas Island would be allowed to talk to the press. 'All agencies advised that no one aside from

Ministers and their offices are to make public comment. Defence has been advised to ensure there is no film footage from the HMAS *Arunta*.'

I

A naval blockade of the Indian Ocean was now being championed by the Prime Minister. The National Security Committee of Cabinet met at 4.30 that afternoon to consider, for the second time in two days, a military option to stop the boats. The NSC brings together the key ministers of Defence, Foreign Affairs, Treasury, Finance, the Deputy Prime Minister and, on this occasion, Philip Ruddock. The ministers sit on one side of the table with department heads and senior military chiefs on the other. Howard runs the meetings in an informal, free-flowing way. Max Moore-Wilton is his right-hand-man at NSC. The decisions of the committee stand without needing to be endorsed by Cabinet.

Admiral Chris Barrie, chief of the Defence Force, was asked what the military could do by way of an operation. 'I sketched out a "what is possible". That is to say, if you combine an aerial surveillance with a surface response, then this is the sort of thing that you can do. We also went through the international law aspect, and then we sort of described, if you like, the broad, strategic framework for the operation.' The military resources that could be brought to bear were not infinite. In Barrie's view they didn't have to be. 'Your real kick is getting a surface response vessel to [the target] vessel at a point where you can exercise your rights under international law.'[7]

The NSC directed Barrie to issue a 'warning order' to the commander of the Australian Theatre, Rear Admiral Chris Ritchie, to prepare 'a maritime control and response plan to detect and intercept and warn vessels carrying unauthorised arrivals for the purpose of deterring SIEVs from entering Australian territorial waters'. Ritchie would have extraordinarily little time for this complex task. The naval plan for Operation Trump—later rechristened Operation Relex—was to be presented to a further NSC meeting the following afternoon at 4 pm. The plan would cover the Indian Ocean between Indonesia and the Australian outposts of Christmas Island and Ashmore Reef. 'Expect initial Operation Trump duration twelve weeks from execution. Commitment will then be reviewed.'[8] That would take the blockade right up to the national election.

At some point on August 28, the Howard government made another radical decision: to task Australia's overseas intelligence service, ASIS, to run a disruption operation against people smugglers in Indonesia. For months ASIS had been pushing to get involved. According to one political source, some ASIS officers had considered the possibility of interfering with people smuggling boats in Indonesian ports. The ideas being kicked around were to sink boats while they were still tied up, sabotaging their engines and even burning them to the waterline. The idea was to disable the boats before anyone got onboard.

Just what the government authorised ASIS to do on August 28 is unclear. ASIS officials met with Jane Halton soon after the decision, according to one person who attended the meeting to discuss disruption. Both AFP and Defence sources say ASIS did become involved in a covert operation against people smugglers in Indonesia and was told to concentrate on particular smuggling rings.

According to one source, its role did involve physical interference with people smuggling boats while they were in port. The minister responsible for ASIS, Alexander Downer, would not answer questions about the nature of the ASIS disruption operation in Indonesia. He is adamant 'the Australian government did not sabotage any boats . . . nor were any boats sabotaged and sunk on the instructions of the Australian government'. His office pointed out that ASIS is prohibited from undertaking paramilitary activities or using violence or weapons. 'There is a clear distinction between deterrence and disruption on one hand and sabotage on the other', said his spokesperson, and the government 'would not condone any action that would endanger lives at sea'. Beyond that, 'it is not government policy to discuss the operational details of the government's disruption efforts'.[9]

Giving ASIS the green light to join the disruption operation in Indonesia caused some worries inside the Australian Federal Police. According to one senior public servant, neither the head of the AFP, Mick Keelty, nor the secretary of DIMA, Bill Farmer, were present at the meeting that decided to give ASIS a role in the disruption operation. This development would inevitably put the AFP in an awkward position. The police already had a disruption operation underway in Indonesia, working with the Indonesian National Police and informants. Admittedly, its operation had run into trouble over its informant Kevin Enniss and there were objections at the top of the Indonesian government about its activities. But the AFP at least had clear operational guidelines—it could not break the law and it could only operate through the Indonesian police. ASIS had far more latitude to act in Indonesia.

As the day grew hotter, the crew of the *Tampa* rigged three large tarpaulins to shade the deck. 'The atmosphere had become very agitated on the weather deck', the company reported. 'The crew had their hands more than full with ensuring a minimum of sanitation and help to the increasing number of sick people. At least 100 of the refugees were suffering from diarrhoea. More than 10 were unconscious at any one time.'[10] The health situation was deteriorating. The hunger strike was exacerbating general levels of agitation and distress. But the immediate challenge facing Maltau was a growing list of survivors whose medical problems were beyond the reach of the chief officer's first aid skills. Medical supplies were also running low. The ship's store of intravenous fluid was gone.

Unable to get the help he needed from the Haukeland Hospital in Bergen—'The process was rather time consuming and there was a new doctor on duty every time I called them up'—Maltau turned to his father for advice. Jan Martin Maltau was professor of anaesthesia at the medical school at Tromsø University. He and his colleagues now advised on treatment but as the day went on it became more difficult for Maltau Jnr to reach them on the ship's satellite phone. Maltau said, 'I have been using these things for fifteen years. It was not busy, it was jammed. You couldn't get the handshake'.[11]

Schuller at the Cairns base of the Flying Doctor Service had still not been able to get through to the ship. In the mid afternoon RCC Australia directed him to phone an army doctor who was somewhere in the air off the coast of Western Australia. He was to tell no one of the conversation. Schuller had not much to say to Dr Graeme Hammond because 'we haven't liaised with the ship since last night' but in his view there were four people 'in some degree of unconscious state' who required medical assessment. That detail was not noted when Schuller reported the conversation to RCC Australia a little later in the afternoon. Their records say: 'We don't believe there is any real medical problems at this stage.' Their records do note an exchange with Schuller over the role of the military in assessing the medical situation on the *Tampa*. But Schuller was still not worried because

Hammond had assured him he would soon be landing on the *Tampa* to co-ordinate a response.[12]

The military airlift had already taken a medical team to Christmas Island and RCC Australia was trying to persuade Defence authorities to send one of these doctors out to the ship. To no avail. Defence would not move without orders from its own command. RCC telephoned someone at the Flying Doctor Service—evidently not Schuller—'and informed doctor that process is in abeyance'.[13]

Four conditions had been laid down by the shipping line's lawyer James Neill before the *Tampa* even considered departing: immediate medical assistance; armed security for the crew; safety equipment for the 438 new passengers such as life jackets, life rafts, etc; and a country where these people could be landed. 'There must be certainty of entry before the ship sails.' Neill was also trying to assist the government by sourcing a helicopter but by midday he had given up on that and was insisting Canberra send out a doctor to the ship straightaway or people might begin to die.[14] Philippa Godwin at DIMA replied insisting no one was in danger on the ship because the Flying Doctor Service said so. That was now the previous night's assessment.

As the afternoon wore on with no help in sight, Rinnan put his case to the world. A press strategy had been developed by the shipping line in consultation with its P & I club, Gard. 'Owners deliberately avoided any direct conflict with the Australian government', reported *Gard News*. 'Attention was always focused on health and safety issues rather than monetary loss.' Rinnan, Wilh Wilhelmsen and the local head of the shipping line, Peter Dexter, would all use the same careful form of words when invited to condemn they were merely 'surprised and disappointed' by Canberra.[15] But Rinnan was free to speak frankly about conditions on the ship. That kept the pressure on Howard. Several graphic accounts were published in the press of the state of the *Tampa* that day. Rinnan spoke to the *Australian*, which reported: 'The situation on his vessel was deteriorating, and tensions were growing the longer the ship was forced to wait outside Australian waters. He said any movement away from the island could prompt his passengers to jump overboard. One of the asylum-seekers, Mohammed Wali, confirmed to the media the hunger strikers would take drastic action, such as jumping overboard, if pressured. Captain Rinnan also warned against the presence of military personnel on board, fearing they could destabilise the asylum-seekers. "I don't want the military on board", he said. "If they start to get nervous I think there might be violence." The ship was running out of medical supplies and blankets, he said. Everyone except pregnant women and children were refusing to eat.'[16]

The impact of these stories was immensely increased by the release of half a dozen photographs taken by the chief engineer of the *Tampa*, Frank Nordheim, on his brand new digital camera. But for this move by the shipping line, the Australian government might have been able to prevent the public ever seeing what was actually happening on the *Tampa*'s deck. Nordheim's photographs of four hundred people huddled under great red walls of containers would appear in newspapers and on television around the world.

Meanwhile, Howard was on Channel Nine denying there were any medical problems at all on the ship. 'A doctor from the Royal Flying Doctor Service was in radio contact with the vessel either this morning or yesterday afternoon and ascertained, for example, that four of the illnesses were not as represented. One of them was completely feigned. The other three were completely mild.' The report was stale and, what's more, Schuller and his colleagues deny ever reporting illnesses on board were being feigned. Howard was openly suggesting the shipping line was engaged in a deception.[17]

I

The Wilhelmsen Line was preparing to take the *Tampa* into Flying Fish Cove. To defy Canberra and cross into Australia's territorial sea would be a momentous step. Theoretically the line could lose its ship. 'We are thinking about that all the time', said Rinnan. 'You are breaking Australian law so it was a serious thing to do.' But the line was backed by Norway's Ministry of Foreign Affairs and the Norwegian Maritime Directorate. The official view in Oslo was that the *Tampa*, having carried out a mass rescue at Australia's request, was now itself a ship in distress. 'In the Norwegian view Australia's rescue responsibilities . . . clearly include an obligation to allow the rescuees into the nearest harbour, which is in the Australian Territory of Christmas Island. Such an obligation follows from rules of customary international law concerning access to port for ships and persons in distress as well as generally accepted international humanitarian standards.'[18]

PAN PAN | 71

The Oslo view of the situation was backed by high level lawyers in the Attorney General's Department in Canberra. They believed it was impossible to claim the *Tampa* was not a ship in distress. First, it was grossly overloaded, the crew was vastly outnumbered and threats to the safety of both crew and survivors could not be dismissed. Second, it was Rinnan's view that he had a medical crisis on his hands. Rinnan was not a doctor but he was on the spot and the best—indeed, the only—person capable of judging the situation. One of those Canberra lawyers, Mark Zanker commented: 'I think common sense dictates that it must be for the master to determine whether their vessel is in distress, and the circumstances in which that judgement could be called into question must be very circumscribed.'[19]

It was now night in Canberra. A very blunt message arrived from the Norwegian search and rescue centre at Stavanger demanding RCC Australia send help to the *Tampa*. 'Norwegian radio-medico has recently been in contact with the ship. The situation is deteriorating. The ship is in urgent need of medical assistance. The priority of the assistance is as follows: (a) medical doctor on board (b) supply of medicines (c) blankets (d) intravenous liquid. Ten of the persons are unconscious with spasms. Forty six children on board. Two pregnant women. One broken leg and several are suffering from hypothermia. All adults are on hunger strike.'[20]

Fifteen minutes later, Rinnan broadcast a Pan Pan: an urgent message concerning the safety of a vessel and those on board. 'Request urgent medical assistance. We have explained the condition of the survivors on board the Tampa to the Norwegian radio-medico who have described the situation as a mass situation medical crisis.' To the list of problems sent by Stavanger, Rinnan added: 'Major outbreak of skin disease, and most of the people suffer from fatigue and exhaustion. Many complaining of stomach cramps. Many showing highly agitated and nervous behaviour. We request urgent medical supplies/assistance.'[21] RCC Australia did not acknowledge the Pan Pan.

When Schuller received a copy of the message a little later, he realised for the first time that 'The normal process of all systems go was not happening'. He rang the ship and this time got through. While he was speaking to Maltau, Rinnan came on the line to emphasise the seriousness of the situation: there were now fifteen unconscious, there were not enough toilets, the hunger strike was continuing, there were only forty blankets for

438 people and the nights were cool. Rinnan was particularly worried about the fate of the very young children over the next 24 to 36 hours if the situation was not resolved.[22]

Now very concerned, Schuller rang the desk officer at RCC Australia who told him 'there is political pressure from the top' and suggested the doctor speak to the Prime Minister's department. Schuller asked him to hunt down the number and ring back but when the phone rang half an hour later, it was the AMSA chief Clive Davidson on the line. Schuller recalls him saying: 'I am in contact with the Prime Minister's department. Why do you want to talk with them?' The doctor explained he was concerned the medical situation on the *Tampa* was becoming serious and that nothing was being done about it. Davidson ended the conversation by assuring Schuller his advice was being sent through the appropriate channels.[23] Later that night Schuller put his concerns in a fax to the rescue centre. 'There certainly appears to be a substantial deterioration in the last 24 hours. I can only confirm that there is indeed a "mass situation medical crisis" as described in their telex message and that this can only worsen. They are requesting a medical doctor on board with medicines, blankets and i.v. fluids. I have no doubt that this is urgently needed.'[24] He never had a reply.

It was nearly midnight in Canberra and the Pan Pan had still not been acknowledged. Rinnan now demanded to know when he could expect medical assistance. He was told a doctor on Christmas Island would ring him. A few minutes later, the mysterious Dr Hammond was on the line. Both Rinnan and Maltau had the impression that this was a civilian doctor who worked on Christmas Island. They explained the medical situation on board in detail. Maltau says he twice told Hammond that there were people unconscious and that the ship was out of intravenous fluid. Hammond assured Rinnan the 'authorities were investigating options' and he would come on board as soon as possible but he didn't have a helicopter. Rinnan said, 'If you have no transportation I can send one of my boats and pick you up but I cannot do that from 12 nautical miles, I have to get closer to the coast'. Hammond said that was not possible. Canberra would not even allow one of Rinnan's boats to go in and get 'medical supplies and a doctor'. All RCC Australia could say was that such a request would 'be given urgent consideration by Australian authorities'. Rinnan's view was unchanged: it was 'not safe to launch a boat that distance from Christmas Island at night'.[25]

Hammond reported to RCC Australia at nearly three in the morning that: 'Doctor felt that while situation was hard to assess, should be able to wait.'[26]

I

Alexander Downer was now provoked to do what he could have done at any time in the last 48 hours: ring his Norwegian counterpart, Thorbjoern Jagland. The Norwegian government was also about to face an election on 20 November. The problem of asylum seekers was a live political issue in Norway, indeed a factor in the government's defeat would be a feeling that it was too soft on the issue. But there was no political advantage whatever for Jagland to make life difficult for the nation's biggest shipping line and to be seen to be finessing the international rules of sea rescue by which Norway set such store.

When Downer got hold of Jagland in Helsinki, he asked him to order the *Tampa* to sail for Indonesia. 'I was very astonished when I was approached by the Foreign Minister and asked to intervene in this situation. I didn't believe it. I couldn't believe it, that a nation like Australia could do that. But after a while I realised that this was serious.' Downer was undiplomatically aggressive. Jagland was particularly surprised to hear the foreign minister of a 'seafaring nation' that had 'ratified all these conventions' argue the way Downer was arguing. 'He wanted me to take a political decision and overrule the captain.'[27]

Jagland tried to explain to the Australian that he had no authority under Norwegian law to do this. 'I don't know if he didn't see it, but he didn't accept it. So maybe he was under such pressure that he couldn't.' As far as Jagland was concerned, Downer's request was both legally and politically impossible. 'The rules of the sea are so important for us as a seafaring nation. You can imagine if something had happened with the boat on the way to Indonesia and I had taken the decision that this boat should go there, I would be responsible for everything. I couldn't do that. And I am also convinced that the captain would never have accepted it. So I was not in a position to get him to do it.'

Jagland defended Rinnan's authority to make the decisions he had. 'The boat could only carry forty or sixty and it now carried four hundred. He said he couldn't go over the ocean and people were sick. So he decided to go to the nearest harbour and I could only say that he had the full right to do so, according to international law.' Jagland could not and would not overrule him. 'He was responsible for the ship. I couldn't take over this responsibility.' But Downer was unconvinced. 'He continued to urge me to do something to intervene and stop the boat.' Jagland continued to refuse.

The crisis had moved to an entirely new plane. Canberra was now brawling with both a great maritime power and its most sensitive neighbour, Indonesia. In a single day, Alexander Downer had been snubbed by both the Norwegian foreign minister and the Indonesian ambassador. By this time, President Megawati and her foreign minister, Hassan Wirajuda, had returned to Jakarta, conferred with ministers and 'reaffirmed their position that it was not Indonesia's problem'.[28] This final verdict reached the Australian embassy in Jakarta that night and was on Downer's desk next morning. August 29 was to be one of the most bizarre days in Australia's history and everything done that day to force the *Tampa* out to sea was done in the certain knowledge that Indonesia would not take the asylum seekers back. The *Tampa* would be on a voyage to nowhere.

SIX
Boarding party

AUGUST 29

Soon after dawn, Rinnan took the grave step of issuing a MAYDAY: 'Subject: Immediate medical assistance. We refer to your replies to our PAN PAN message of yesterday. As suggested by you we have been in contact with Dr Hammond and pressed for urgent assistance. His conclusion however is that he is unable to get on board such a big vessel in its present position although we have offered full assistance. The situation on board is deteriorating even further, and it is getting out of hand. On this background, I have no alternative but to declare a distress situation which can only be solved by approaching closest shore to find shelter so that medical assistance can be rendered. Best regards, A Rinnan.'[1]

RRC Australia shot back a reply not only forbidding the *Tampa* to enter territorial waters but taking the unheard of step of questioning Rinnan's judgement. 'You have no basis for calling the distress. Please provide evidence of "grave and imminent danger" to persons on board or your vessel. If you proceed Australia will take full action to protect the integrity of Australia's territorial rights.' Again, a helicopter was promised sometime that day to bring medical help to the ship. At almost exactly the same time, BASARNAS told the Australian search and rescue authorities the *Tampa* could not unload the survivors at any Indonesian port. 'We're sorry to tell you that BASARNAS can't take any action on the refugees on the MV *Tampa* . . . for our government doesn't give permission to the ship to enter our territory. Thank you for your good coordination.'[2]

Rinnan's MAYDAY was on the Cabinet table within a few minutes. Sitting with the Prime Minister were his deputy John Anderson, Downer, Ruddock, Reith, Moore-Wilton, Barrie, the Treasurer Peter Costello and the Attorney General Daryl Williams. Downer left the room to call the Norwegian foreign minister again. Jagland was still in Helsinki where it was a few minutes before 2 am. The conversation that followed left Jagland 'in shock'.[3]

A blustering, emotional Downer demanded that the Norwegian minister order the *Tampa* to stay away. Jagland pointed out, once again, that he had no authority to do so. Once more the Australian minister swept the point aside. Jagland was astonished that Downer would challenge Rinnan's assessment of the situation on the ship. 'I asked him where he had this information from but he didn't say.' As far as Jagland was concerned it didn't matter on what grounds the Australian government disputed Rinnan's decision. 'I had to stick to the principle that the captain had the right to make the judgement.' Downer now told Jagland that if the *Tampa* entered Australian territorial waters, it would be boarded by military force. 'I could only reiterate what I said all the time, that this was against international law but that we couldn't do anything about this. We are a tiny nation far away. We couldn't intervene in it but I can only maintain the principles.'[4]

Now that there were threats of military action in the air, Jagland wanted John Howard to speak to the Norwegian Prime Minister, Jens Stoltenberg. He alerted Stoltenberg's chief of staff Jonas Gahr Støre who was 'utterly disgusted' to hear that Downer was questioning Rinnan's assessment of the crisis on the *Tampa*. 'It seems that people would have to die in order to persuade Australian authorities that this was a health issue. These people have been without proper food and medication for a week, so who are we or anyone in Australia to make judgements about that? I am a former naval officer myself and in a situation like that there is nobody but the captain who can make decisions, this is so written into every code of conduct.'[5] Støre rang Howard's office and left a message asking him to ring Stoltenberg in Oslo.

Jagland briefed Stoltenberg, who then rang the Foreign Ministry for 'a crash course in the law of the sea' given by its legal chief, Hans Wilhelm

Longva. He was in no doubt that Rinnan's assessment of the situation on the *Tampa* gave 'a solid basis in international law' for the ship to seek help and shelter inside Australian waters. Whether Rinnan's medical judgement was right or wrong was irrelevant. 'This is a person with a relatively sophisticated and advanced education but not an expert in medicine', said Longva. In his view, Australian authorities had to defer to the master's assessment. 'It is the only way this can function.' The issue of the MAYDAY had created new obligations for Australia. 'In our view, Australia had a clear obligation to receive the ship and provide assistance. We felt it was an appalling decision to use military force against a ship in this situation.'[6]

While Longva was coaching Stoltenberg, Canberra was talking to the Wilhelmsen Line. Once again there were threats of fines and talk of Rinnan being imprisoned. In Oslo, Støre heard 'the company itself, Wilhelmsen, got some kind of threat in terms of their own business opportunities in Australia'. Howard denies this. 'The shipping line was, in fact, assured that the particular nature of this incident would *not* compromise its longer term commercial interests in this country.' Peter Dexter said he was asked 'to request the ship to remain outside Australian waters. Obviously we took that on board'. The line agreed to give Australia three more hours but Rinnan conceded none of his authority. 'It is my prerogative in my sole judgment based on present position to declare distress. It is still my firm judgment that survivors on board are in "imminent danger" therefore I maintain my MAYDAY.' Rinnan added that if help did not arrive by 2 pm Canberra time, he would have 'no alternative but to approach sheltered position, where a transfer by boat can take place before the end of daylight today'. Howard is reported to have rung and thanked Dexter.[7]

Howard now rang the Norwegian Prime Minister. This was 'one of the more peculiar exchanges he had had as Prime Minister', Stoltenberg later told his chief of staff. 'At that stage Prime Minister Howard was very, very upset and he was demanding that the Norwegian Prime Minister intervene and stop the ship from entering Australian waters, saying that it would lead to legal consequences for the captain and that Australia would not hesitate in using military means in keeping that ship out of its waters.' Howard insisted the asylum seekers were the responsibility of Indonesia first and Norway second. The *Tampa* had to go to Merak. Stoltenberg replied that he had 'no means or mandate to command a captain on what was best for the people on board, so there was no way he could or would intervene and urged the PM to let the ship enter and get the people off the boat'. The Norwegian Prime Minister pledged his country's willingness to help Australia, 'but it was no option to keep those people on the ship for cargo, so let's do first things first'.[8]

After only half an hour, Rinnan and the shipping line were having second thoughts about their deal with Canberra. According to Rinnan, one of the leaders of the survivors, Mohammad Wali, had warned of fresh threats of suicides if medical help did not arrive quickly. A deadline Wali set earlier that morning had passed without incident, but Rinnan and the shipping line were worried. Wilh Wilhelmsen was now particularly concerned for the safety of the crew if the restlessness of the people on the deck turned to anger. 'These were people from a warrior nation, from a culture that Captain Rinnan didn't know too well. He had been a master for a long time but I don't think he knew very much about Afghans except they had been fighting for twenty years. If they were going to take action, what sort of action would they take? It wouldn't help them to kill the crew. They could certainly force them to steer the vessel onto the beach or something like that.'[9]

The decision was made: the *Tampa* would cross the line. The survivors were asked to remain calm and not to try swimming ashore when the ship came close to the island. The crew then retreated to the accommodation section of the boat and all the doors were secured. In the contingency room in Oslo, Wilh Wilhelmsen felt 'the pulse rate was very high and tension at breaking point'. This was the most stressful moment of the entire crisis. Marianne Fosaas sat across the table from the owner of the line. 'We were looking at each other, all of us with the same question: what will happen next?'[10]

Howard was hardly off the phone to Stoltenberg when he heard the *Tampa* was about to move. RCC Australia issued last frantic threats: 'What *Tampa* was proposing is a flagrant breach of Australian law and that the Australian government is now initiating necessary actions to board the vessel under appropriate legal powers, including those under the Migration Act 1958.' Reference to the act was legal shorthand for fines, seizures and imprisonment. But Rinnan was already over the line. He told RCC Australia that at 11.39 am Canberra time 'the *Tampa* entered Australian territorial waters with the intention of approaching sheltered waters within two nautical miles of Flying Fish Cove'.¹¹

Howard was informed at once and Admiral Barrie issued the order for the SAS to head out to the ship. Rinnan knew nothing of this. He alerted Don O'Donnell, the harbourmaster at Flying Fish Cove. 'Good morning. Please be advised that we are approaching Christmas Island to take shelter to be able to effect transfer of medical assistance to your Dr Hammond.'

'If you get too near the island and people start jumping ship, it will be on your full responsibilities', warned O'Donnell.

'I have told the people that there are sharks in the water and a lot of current there', replied Rinnan. 'It's the only way we can see to get medical supplies on board.'

O'Donnell signed off. A few minutes later he was back on the line with news that amazed Rinnan: no doctor called Hammond worked on Christmas Island. By now the *Tampa* was only four miles off Flying Fish Cove. 'You are not, I repeat, not, to come closer than two miles, do you understand?'¹²

Rinnan asked if he could send a boat ashore. 'Negative, captain. You will hold position with your thrusters and your engines and will not come any closer than two miles. And you are not to send anybody off the ship to come ashore.'

Rinnan asked what time a doctor could come on board. O'Donnell was unable to say. 'I can't tell you that. I'm just telling you to hold your position at no more than two miles and make sure no one, that no one, comes off the ship in any shape, manner or form.' Again Rinnan agreed. 'People are coming out to you now. Please take your vessel four miles offshore, four miles offshore. People are coming out to you now.'¹³

I

Christmas Island is a plateau of almost exhausted guano fields sticking out of the Indian Ocean. When this rock was of no further use to the British Empire, it was handed to Australia in 1958. The people are mostly Chinese and Malays. Buddhism is the principal religion. There is one town, for which time has furnished no better name than The Settlement. The little port of Flying Fish Cove is one of the few breaks in the cliffs that fringe the island. Behind the town is an airport where private jets once brought high-rolling Indonesians to play in the island's casino. Oddly enough,

Christmas Island was one corner of Australia that could be entered without a visa—if you were a rich Asian gambler travelling on a whim. But the casino failed in the economic meltdown of the late 1990s and the island was left to live on the last of the phosphate mines, lots of money from Canberra and tourists who come for fishing and the famous annual migration of red crabs.

Until now, the processing of boat people had been a fairly relaxed affair. Islanders helped bring in the boats. Three or four AFP officers handled the paper work. There was no secure detention and contact between islanders and asylum seekers was easy and friendly. The hospital looked after medical problems and new arrivals were welcome to use the phone at the visitors' centre. Sometimes calls came from the mainland. 'Is my brother on the island?' a heavily accented voice would ask. 'His boat should have arrived by now.'

The arrival of the *Tampa* had seen the island transformed into an armed camp. The army's Hercules transports brought medical and food supplies, ocean-going inflatable zodiacs, an Iroquois helicopter (in pieces) and 120 SAS soldiers to the island. Canberra's determination that medical help to the ship could only be delivered by helicopter—and then not being able to find one—had shaped the crisis. On radio that morning, Howard admitted 'we've been working furiously over the last 36 hours to get helicopters to Christmas Island and to be in a position to provide this emergency relief'.[14] Despite fresh promises in the last few hours to Rinnan, Dexter and the shipping line, it would be a further day before a helicopter was in the air at Christmas Island. By then it was too late.

Canberra had gagged local officials and closed Flying Fish Cove. Journalists now pouring into The Settlement on flights from Jakarta and Perth found it impossible to take a boat out to the *Tampa*. Once the SAS was on board, Canberra would decree anything to do with the *Tampa* involved 'operational security' and declare a 'no-fly' zone around the ship. No one on board was to be allowed ashore and civilians on the island—especially doctors, lawyers and journalists—were not to be allowed out to the ship. No cameraman would get close enough to the *Tampa* to put a human face on this story. The icon of the scandal was to be a red-hulled ship on a blue sea photographed through heat haze by a very long lens.

Dozens of islanders stood about the shore of Flying Fish Cove watching the SAS prepare to invade the *Tampa*. 'I think it's a joke', said stevedore Johari Sukaimi. 'Nobody's armed on there. Why are they sending over the army?' The unhappy locals issued a statement deploring all this and giving Arne Rinnan their enthusiastic backing. 'We call on the Prime Minister to order the opening of our port to the Norwegian vessel to allow the asylum seekers to land on our island ... We applaud the captain of the *Tampa* for his correct application of humanitarian principles, and the law, in taking on to his ship these refugees. We believe it is our humanitarian duty to assist the captain and crew and the asylum seekers by accepting these people on to Christmas Island.' The statement was signed by the shire council, the Union of Christmas Island Workers, the Chinese Literary Association, the Islamic Council and the Christmas Island Women's Association.[15]

The SAS was armed with exquisitely careful legal advice. Under the Migration Act, DIMA can send soldiers out to board and search foreign ships at sea in order to hunt down asylum seekers, bring them ashore and put them in detention. This was the last thing Canberra wanted to happen on the *Tampa*. Already, unprecedented steps had been taken to keep DIMA out of this operation. The secretary of the department, Bill Farmer, had ordered his own officers to keep clear of the ship and made sure DIMA gave no directions to the SAS.[16] One last bizarre precaution was needed to make sure the soldiers could not be deemed to be agents of the department. The powers of the Migration Act can only be exercised at sea by military parties using 'Commonwealth vessels'. By law, a Commonwealth vessel must fly the Commonwealth ensign. So at 9 am island time, when the first zodiac carrying sixteen fully-armed SAS troops in full camouflage set out for the *Tampa*, there was no flag flying.

I

Christian Maltau was standing at the pilot door to greet the doctor he and Rinnan believed was now coming out to the ship. The ladder rattled down the hull as the zodiac came around the *Tampa*'s stern. Maltau was suddenly radioed from the bridge: get the ladder in, soldiers are coming. The chief officer was too late. Troops were already on the ladder. They swarmed aboard and ran past Maltau to 'secure' the asylum seekers on the weather deck. It was a grim sight for them. 'From the guns in Afghanistan we had bad memories', said Assadullah Rezaee. 'That was not a good thing to see.

Probably they thought this was a serious situation and we were dangerous people.'

Maltau escorted the troops' commander, Major Vance Khan, to the bridge. The exchanges between Rinnan and Khan were stiff and polite. The captain warned Khan that everything said on the bridge could be heard on an open line to Oslo. The master protested the presence of troops on his ship. He had asked for medical assistance, not soldiers. The SAS officer assured the master he was not taking command of the ship. His men were only there to protect the medical personnel now arriving on a second zodiac. But Khan said they would not begin treating the sick until the *Tampa* was once again outside territorial waters. 'They said all the responsibility for the welfare of the shipwreck people is on my shoulder. I had the responsibility for the welfare of the people.' But Rinnan refused to sail. 'I told him I will not do it. I am now inside. I will not go outside again.' Khan repeated the threat. 'So I told him we will be sitting here waiting further negotiations on shore.'[17]

Rinnan was in a strong position. The *Tampa* was not seaworthy and could not lawfully sail. A ship licensed to carry only forty people could not leave port with over ten times that number on board. That is the view of nearly every legal commentator on this crisis. One senior law officer in the Attorney General's Department, Mark Zanker, believed that it was 'highly doubtful' even equipping the ship with life jackets and life rafts for everyone on board would make it seaworthy 'given that the master of the *Tampa* had declared a distress situation'. For the *Tampa* to sail unseaworthy from Christmas Island would break both Australian and Norwegian laws. The harbourmaster at Flying Fish Cove was obliged to take all necessary steps—even the use of force—to see the ship did *not* sail. To depart while unseaworthy would also breach the shipping line's contracts with its insurers. The *Tampa* would have no cover for its hull, its cargo and the people on board. Canberra was not only demanding its own laws be flouted, but was telling the Wilhelmsen Line to put at risk a ship with a replacement value of about $150 million, cargo worth about $20 million and over 450 lives.[18] It was a big ask and the answer was no.

Rinnan was in an even stronger position than he knew. The SAS had boarded the ship at about 12.30 pm Canberra time. At 2 pm the Prime Minister would be on his feet giving parliament the dramatic news from Christmas Island. He needed some sort of report on the medical situation and time was running out. The standoff between Rinnan and Khan lasted about 12 minutes, then the medical assessment began. The SAS commander accepted a cup of coffee. He was under orders to keep the pressure on Rinnan to sail. The Norwegian continued to refuse.[19]

Oslo's response to the arrival of the SAS was mixed. 'Whilst it appeared to be very threatening when they came, my feeling was very quickly a feeling of relief', said Wilh Wilhelmsen. The boarding of the ship was 'not according to code' but 'it certainly made me feel much more comfortable for the life and safety of that crew'. Very weary by this time, the crew could hand over to the soldiers responsibility for the health of the survivors, for feeding them—only thirty or forty were still on hunger strike—and for cleaning the crowded deck and putrid latrines where all the crew's efforts had managed to keep sanitation only at a level Rinnan called 'bad but acceptable'. This mixture of affront and relief was also shared by the Norwegian government. 'The ship is now subject to full territorial jurisdiction of Australia', said the Foreign Minister Thorbjoern Jagland. 'This is illustrated by the fact that Australian military personnel is on board of this vessel. So, the people on board, the refugees also, are under full Australian territorial jurisdiction, which means this is in the hands of Australia fully.' The view from Oslo was that now, more than ever, Australia had no choice but to take the survivors ashore.[20]

Maltau was with the SAS doctor on the deck. He recognised the man's voice and challenged him. Wasn't he Dr Hammond who they had thought was a civilian from Christmas Island? Hammond was working astonishingly swiftly. According to military records, the medical assessment was '50% complete' after only eight minutes. A further twenty minutes later, details of the 'medical state' of the 438 survivors had been collected 'in prep[aration] for PM announcement to parliament'. Hammond was not issuing a clean bill of health. He reported: 'General health of UBA [unauthorised boat arrivals] is reasonable, 4 pers[ons] required IV (2 urgent, including 1 woman 8 months pregnant), 2 others pregnant. 3–4 sprains and 1 poss[ible] light break to leg.'[21]

At 2 pm, Howard rose in parliament to denounce the *Tampa* for defying Australia. 'The ship is now in control of the SAS.' He moved at once to the health issue. 'I should inform the House that the preliminary assessment carried out by the Australian Defence Force doctor indicates that nobody—and I repeat: nobody—has presented as being in need of urgent medical assistance as would require their removal to the Australian mainland or to Christmas Island. I repeat that that is the result of the preliminary investigations and a further medical assessment continues.' He added that Australia's offer of medical help was 'not in any way conditional on the return of the vessel to international waters'. Not any more, because Rinnan had just faced down exactly that threat.[22]

The failure to deliver swift medical help to the *Tampa* was Howard's great tactical mistake. He had repeatedly assured the Wilhelmsen Line—and the country—that Australia stood ready to provide medical assistance, but he waited for a cumbersome military operation to deliver it. While giving those humanitarian assurances, Howard was simultaneously ridiculing claims of a health crisis on the *Tampa*. He and Philip Ruddock would continue to do so ruthlessly, directly accusing Arne Rinnan of misrepresenting the situation on his ship. Graeme Hammond had now confirmed there *were* sick people on the *Tampa*, but Howard sidestepped the fact with the clever formula that no one was so sick 'as would require their removal'. Ruddock and other ministers all used exactly those words over the next few days. This spin worked perfectly because no one—certainly not Howard—explained that Hammond's patients were not being dealt with according to the Royal Flying Doctor's civilian principle that 'the moment someone sneezes, they are evacuated'. The military was running this show under orders from the top. As events would show over the next few weeks, Canberra was extremely reluctant to allow medical evacuations. The pregnant woman Hammond identified as urgently requiring rehydration was one of at least three seriously ill people treated for the next two days or more on a cargo boat about half a dozen kilometres from a fully equipped hospital on Christmas Island.

I

The Prime Minister disappeared from Question Time. There was mayhem back in his office and among the bureaucrats grappling with the crisis. Each refusal by the Norwegian skipper to heed Australia's threats had come as a shock. High hopes that Rinnan would sail once the SAS boarded his ship, had also come to nothing. He was refusing to budge from Flying Fish Cove. Canberra's next threat to the shipping line would be if the *Tampa* did not sail, Australia would tow it out to sea. Alexander Downer would tell ABC-TV's *Lateline* that night, 'Obviously, there are an almost infinite number of methods that could be used to move a ship out of your waters. You could tow it out, for example, just to make the point'. The Foreign Minister described this as 'an entirely reasonable and entirely normal proposition. We've got to have the capacity to protect our territorial integrity as a country'.[23]

The Wilhelmsen Line and the Norwegian government were acutely aware HMAS *Arunta* was approaching Christmas Island. It had 'crash-sailed' from Fremantle the previous day—that is, come in, refuelled and sailed straight out again—and would be at the island in two days. A spokesman for the line in Oslo, Per Ronnevig, had warned that if the military took control of the *Tampa*, Australia would be accused of piracy. 'I mean I would not say anything if the ship was in the vicinity of a banana republic, but I mean this is supposed to be a civilised country. It is not behaving like it.' Peter Dexter in Sydney spent a good part of this extraordinary day hosing down Ronnevig's piracy talk. 'It's not coming into our vocabulary at this time.' Yet the issue was clearly on their minds. 'Taking command of the vessel', said Wilh Wilhelmsen, 'is I think what you call piracy'.[24]

Lawyers for the shipping line were working on a strategy to prevent the *Tampa* being forced out to sea. Even before the SAS boarded the ship, James Neill of Aus Ship P & I was putting together a legal team in Sydney led by a QC and supported by a senior maritime law expert from the local Bar. The aim was to be ready to go to court to seek an injunction to prevent the government from towing or forcing the ship out of Australian territorial waters. The basis for the injunction would be, essentially, that the *Tampa* was unseaworthy. The team was preparing not only to get an injunction— that was not so difficult—but to be ready to fight the case immediately. So the lawyers were at work compiling an immense, 250-page affidavit setting out why the *Tampa* could not legally sail. Calculating that it would take 45 minutes to force the boat out onto the high seas, the lawyers planned to be able to get the injunction they needed within twenty minutes or less. A judge was on stand by.[25]

The lawyers and the shipping line assumed their telephone calls were being intercepted and saw this as an effective way of letting Canberra know they were preparing to fight. No notice was given to the government through normal channels.[26] Their calculations were absolutely right. The electronic signals gathering Defence Signals Directorate (DSD) was unlawfully reporting to the government on conversations James Neill was having with his client. The inspector general of Intelligence and Security, Bill Blick, would later conclude this surveillance breached the privacy provisions of the *Intelligence Services Act* and also violated 'legal professional privilege'.[27]

The intelligence gathering involved more than snooping on the shipping line's lawyers. DSD's immensely powerful system at Geraldton on the Western Australian coast would have intercepted all communications with the ship. The government had an almost open slather on the use of this material. All foreigners talking to the ship could be reported on lawfully. DSD must junk domestic Australian material sucked into its system, but the law at this time allowed very wide exceptions to this rule. Any calls, faxes and emails Australians made discussing any indictable offence (for instance, people smuggling) or the activities of foreign powers (Norway) and of foreign corporations (such as the Wilhelmsen Line) in respect of Australian interests, could be intercepted, analysed and reported to the government.[28]

A couple of road blocks in Canberra's way may also have been dealt with lawfully by intelligence authorities. Blick personally approved DSD reporting on 'one Australian person' whose identity has never been revealed.[29] This target's connection to the *Tampa* appears to have been through a foreign corporation, so it may have been Peter Dexter. The Attorney General also granted a warrant allowing the domestic intelligence agency, ASIO, to assist 'with foreign intelligence collection activity that DSD was not empowered to conduct'.[30] DSD is expressly forbidden to intercept diplomatic communications in Australia. The Attorney General's warrant possibly allowed the Norwegian embassy's telephone traffic to be monitored.

Not long after Question Time, the Secretary of the Attorney General's Department, Robert Cornall, the First Assistant Secretary, Office of International Law, Bill Campbell, and the government's Chief General Counsel, Henry Burmester QC, were called to Howard's office. The Prime Minister's solution to the impasse at Christmas Island was to pass a quick law giving the government power to do essentially what it liked to the *Tampa* and, thereafter, to any boat bringing asylum seekers to Australia's shores. Howard outlined what he wanted. This was *his* law. The fundamental requirement was that Canberra would be left to operate with almost complete freedom from scrutiny by the courts. Campbell, Burmester and the First Parliamentary Counsel, Hilary Penfold, sat in the Prime Minister's office for the next few hours drafting the Border Protection Bill.

There was a strong element of bluff in Howard's strategy. He and Downer would hint that the *Arunta* was heading for Christmas Island to tow the *Tampa* out to sea. It was technically feasible. The navy had calculated the *Arunta* could tow the Norwegian ship but not very far, not very fast and only with the *Tampa*'s co-operation. If the ship resisted it would have to be seized and a naval 'steaming party' put at the controls. This was an extremely serious step to take and would cause a major diplomatic incident. The government never seriously considered doing this, not least because it was clear the navy might refuse.[31] The government's best hope for getting rid of the *Tampa* was that the threat of *Arunta*'s arrival plus the passing of the Border Protection Bill would persuade the Norwegian ship to leave of its own accord.

No such legislation had ever been put to the Australian parliament. Its full title was *A Bill for an Act to provide for the removal of ships from the territorial sea of Australia, and for related purposes*. It was to operate from 9 that morning, half an hour before Rinnan's MAYDAY. The Prime Minister would have the power to direct soldiers, police, customs officials and public servants to seize 'any vessel' and use force if necessary to take the ship and everyone on board 'outside the territorial sea of Australia'. This would happen out of sight of the courts. No matter what happened—deaths, disasters and injuries—no civil or criminal proceedings could be taken against the Commonwealth or the officers carrying out these operations. And no shipping line or asylum seeker could go to the courts 'to prevent a ship, or any persons on board a ship, being removed to a place outside the territorial sea of Australia'. This new regime was to operate 'in spite of any other law'.

Howard rang Kim Beazley's office at about 5.50 pm. It was the first inkling the leader of the Opposition had of the Bill. Howard said, 'I want to bring it in at about 6.30. I want to show it to you first'. Up until this point Beazley had approved every move Howard made in the *Tampa* crisis. Labor was not quizzing or criticising the government, but standing in the government's shadow while hoping this distraction would go away as soon as possible.[32] Beazley and his chief of staff, Michael Costello, sat down with Howard and his chief of staff, Arthur Sinodinos. Howard gave the Bill to Beazley. 'He literally tossed the Bill across the table to me and said you know, words to the effect, this is the Bill that ensures we're going to be able to protect our borders and drive ships away. It actually fell open as it hit the desk at the part which exempted or indemnified government servants against any form of civil or criminal liability.' Howard made no attempt to explain the legislation. He remarked, 'I don't really need it'. Beazley flicked through the Bill for only a few moments and said: 'There is no way we can support this, John.'[33]

SEVEN
Labor cornered

TO AUGUST 31

Until now, nothing much had gone wrong in Kim Beazley's career. The Labor leader was a man of ambitions rather than causes; he picked as few quarrels as he possibly could; he left the party bosses alone and the unions alone; he teamed up with winners. And he won every time: his seat, his place on the front bench and the deputy prime ministership in 1995. When Labor was routed the following year, Beazley was the most senior, most loved and most presentable man left standing. The leadership of the party came to him by unanimous vote. Even his loss in the next election was a kind of victory, for no one expected he could come so close, so quickly to beating John Howard. Until the arrival of the *Tampa*, the general assumption of his party was that sometime before Christmas, Kim Christian Beazley would be the next Prime Minister of Australia.

Beazley was not a brutal opponent. Over the previous six years, he had often had Howard on the ropes but never landed a knockout blow. He never set out to make Howard hated nor turn his opponent into a figure of fun. Why? 'Probably because I don't find him very funny.'[1] He never laid a line on the Prime Minister as cruel as Howard's charge that Beazley did not have the 'ticker' for the top job. Beazley's friends, enemies and the press talked ticker ever afterwards. It was so obviously the big question about

Kim. He was decent, intelligent, likeable—but did he have the ruthlessness the job required? Beazley's patron Bob Hawke said: 'You see some in politics, on both sides, who really hate their opponents. Kim hasn't got a killer hatred element to him.'²

Beazley and Howard thought very much alike on economic and social issues. Howard was a lifelong—and very effective—opponent of the union movement, but the two men shared many of the attitudes political commentators dismissed as 'old fashioned' until it became clear in the mid-1990s that the votes of those for whom such views had never gone out of date was the key to power in Australia. In 2001, Howard and Beazley were two conservative leaders chasing the same very conservative voters. Beazley presented himself as a bigger, more civilised version of the man whose job he was after. Labor was not campaigning for a new Australia, only a new leader.

Labor was banking on a 'small target' strategy to carry the party to victory. It would emphasise key differences on education, health and taxation but otherwise pick few quarrels with Howard's government. Though Labor essentially controlled the Senate, Beazley supported legislation deeply at odds with traditional Labor attitudes: to cut capital gains tax, channel a fortune to private health funds and increase public subsidies to rich private schools. Howard repaid this co-operation by posing a new question in 2001 almost as devastating as the 'ticker' question of 1998: what, if anything, does this man stand for? When Beazley invoked the spirit of Ben Chifley during the centenary of Federation celebrations in May, Howard responded savagely: 'I didn't agree with much of what Ben Chifley stood for, but at least Ben Chifley stood for something.'³

Labor always stood for border control. The party voiced the deep Australian fear that any trickle of boat people meant a flood was on the way. Gough Whitlam was prime minister when the first Vietnamese took to the boats in 1975. He declared he was 'not having hundreds of fucking Vietnamese Balts coming into the country'.⁴ Bob Hawke branded the next wave of boat people queue jumpers and threats to Australia's immigration policy. 'Let no one think we are going to stand idly by and allow others, by their autonomous action which reflects perhaps some unhappiness with the circumstances in which they find themselves in their own country . . . to determine our immigration policy.'⁵ It was Hawke's government—with the enthusiastic co-operation of the Liberal and National parties—that began the system of mandatory, indefinite incarceration of boat people without trial in the early 1990s. Labor was not deterred by Australia having signed—and often championed—a list of international conventions that ruled out just such a strategy.[6]

Beazley was no new broom on boat people. 'Our views on this were not light years away from the government at all, never had been.'[7] Beazley backed an idea John Howard took from Pauline Hanson's One Nation Party for punishing boat people. Refugees who came by boat would be kept on probation for a few years in case they could be sent away again once things settled down back home. When these temporary protection visas (TPVs) were introduced in 1999, Australia's unique notion of 'good' and 'bad' refugees—those picked by DIMA versus those who turn up under their own steam—was translated into law.[8] 'Good' refugees could bring their families to a permanent home in a new country where they were given social security, settlement support and language training. 'Bad' refugees would be incarcerated in desert camps, have reduced social security benefits on their release and have to wait many, lonely years before their families could join them. If TPV families wanted to stay together, they all had to make the same dangerous journey. When Beazley and Howard joined forces to create TPVs, the smugglers' boats began filling with women and children.

Beazley had baulked at only one of Howard's immigration proposals: to cut the courts out of the process entirely. Labor governments had been so frustrated by the courts that Hawke passed a law in 1992 severely limiting judicial review of immigration decisions.[9] This did not end the hostilities between politicians and judges. The courts kept insisting on due process and the government kept demanding total control. Labor tried to legislate around the judges. Beazley said, 'The last court decision determines the next piece of legislation'. But Howard's government proposed taking all review of immigration decisions on any ground whatever away from the judges. From May 1997, Labor had resisted heavy pressure to pass this legislation.[10] Four years later it was still before parliament and Labor still opposed the Bill, regarding this sort of treatment of the courts as an attack on the rule of law. Labor's opposition was not on behalf of asylum seekers, but decent government.

|

As late as the week before the *Tampa* steamed over the horizon, the polls were telling Kim Beazley that Howard 'was going to lose and lose heavily. And their polling must have been telling them the same. I didn't actually think immigration issues could flush that away. They had never been so potent. Plus I was also quite confident we had a reasonably impregnable position on the immigration-type issues where we've always been strong'. Beazley thought the way the detention centres were being run 'stank' and Labor's policy was to bring them back under government control, settle them down and hold a 'proper enquiry' into allegations of mismanagement and cruelty behind the wire. But the issue here was good administration. 'That was not a position against mandatory detention, which we supported.'

Polling in marginal seats convinced Labor that boat people, refugees and immigration were not big issues in 2001. The polls seemed to confirm the party's long-term strategy of concentrating on health, education and the GST. 'People's sense of insecurity about those sorts of things vastly outweighed any more esoteric views they might have on migrants', said Beazley. Certainly, there were no votes to be won softening Labor's stand on boat people. 'A sympathetic position for people who came to the country illegally is non existent. A more generous policy towards letting in people on humanitarian grounds—refugees, whatever—not quite as non existent but close to it. But as a salient influence on your vote: nothing.' Beazley could see there was some 'angst' about border control but people seemed more worried about drugs and quarantine than illegal immigration. Party strategists even saw the possibility of turning the immigration issue *against* the government. Since Howard came to office in 1996, 11 000 boat people had reached Australia's shores. Under Labor in the 1980s and 1990s, Australia received a mere 2000. 'They knew they had a vulnerability given the massive increase in boat people there had been under them compared to the previous situation', said Beazley. 'Obviously they had a vulnerability.'

Labor has no excuse for getting it so wrong. Other pollsters were on the scent. Hugh Mackay gave his clients—including newspapers—a chillingly accurate forecast in July: 'There is a widespread view that people who have arrived illegally . . . are likely to *behave* illegally once here . . . some of the most ugly and vicious outpourings of hatred occurred in discussion of boat people/illegal immigrants . . . so strong are the passions aroused by fear of illegal immigrants and of Australia being "swamped by Asians" that such matters have the potential to overwhelm factors like the GST in the coming federal election campaign.'¹¹ Nascent racism, ancient fears of invasion by immigration and talkback radio ranting against Asian crime were about to fuse into a new and extraordinarily potent political force. Labor missed what was coming. Looking back to these weeks and the election he was about to lose, Beazley could see that Howard was on the brink of doing something no federal leader had ever been able to do before: fight a law and order election and pitch it in terms of national survival. What was coming was 'a sea change in Australian politics', said Beazley. 'You can see its antecedents but you can't see its potency.'¹² Others did.

Labor was also underestimating John Howard. By August, he had spent a fortune on the old, on voters in marginal seats and on advertising his government's achievements. The economy had been faltering but was again performing strongly. The national secretary of the Labor Party, Geoff Walsh, said, 'The net effect was to shift the Coalition from a desperate position to one where it was back in the fight'.¹³ The man who had seemed finished earlier in the year was clawing his way back. Polls in the middle of August showed Howard was as much approved as disapproved by the electorate. But the government's primary vote was still drifting to One Nation. Across 'frontline marginal seats' the Coalition's primary vote had collapsed 7.5 per cent. Labor's most astute strategists failed to guess how Howard might win these votes back. 'I kept racking my brains as to how in the hell he can do this', said the former NSW Labor party boss John Della Bosca. 'Early that year I decided there was no way to re-embrace One Nation for Howard and therefore he was gone. And I was wrong because what he did was go *around* One Nation. Even knowing the problem, it never occurred to me that an issue would arise like the *Tampa* which would allow Howard to waltz around Hanson, claim the constituency for himself, indeed ignite the rest of relatively civilised Australia, to feel a sort of sense of solidarity about this preservation of the borders.'¹⁴

Even before the ship appeared, there were doubts in Beazley's own circle that the encouraging polls would be translated into a Labor victory. There was not much sense that Australia was ready for change. The voters didn't dislike Howard enough. Nor did they admire Beazley enough. Labor's strategy of finessing its way to victory had left this big, eloquent man without much presence in the political landscape. Beazley couldn't command national attention. The problems of the man and his party's tactics came together in the terrible mistake of thinking they were 'strong' on border control. Labor was only 'strong' here because it had been so determined to live in the government's shadow. 'Labor had no position of its own on boat people', said one of the party's most trusted strategists. 'And it was much too late to work up a position when the *Tampa* happened. The public knew Labor had no position. The party was cornered right at the end of the political cycle.'[15]

I

On the first day of the crisis, with Canberra in turmoil and the story breaking around the world, Beazley had had just 25 words to say to parliament about the *Tampa*. 'We support the government's actions in regard to the motor vessel *Tampa*. They seem to us to be appropriate and in conformity with international law.'[16] The Opposition asked no questions: nothing about the safety of the crew, the welfare of the survivors, the impact on sea rescue in the region, the damage to Australia's international reputation or the prospects—if any—of another country taking these asylum seekers if Australia refused to allow them to land. Labor neither interrogated nor debated this astonishing policy reverse. The Opposition signalled it was on for the ride. Howard repaid Beazley by attacking him once more for blocking the old Bill designed to bar the courts from deciding refugee matters. 'I express the hope that the Opposition will now withdraw its objections to legislation in the Senate so that we can send yet a further signal—a very clear signal—to those who would seek to trample on our sovereign rights.'[17] Beazley was being shown no quarter.

Labor showed no interest in challenging the government's legal assertions about sea rescue, asylum seekers and Indonesia's obligations. The Opposition made a few calls to maritime lawyers but did not retain experts to give systematic advice during the crisis. Beazley's own grasp of the legal issues was shaky. He shared John Howard's mistaken belief that Australia's 1990 rescue arrangements with Indonesia compelled Arne Rinnan to take the *Palapa* survivors to Merak. 'If [the rescue] had occurred within the Australian zone, the ship would be making landfall in Australia', said Beazley. 'It occurred within the Indonesian zone, therefore it makes landfall somewhere in Indonesia.' But he never read the terms of that 1990 agreement, nor did he seek legal advice on its meaning. He believed it was all part of the old—but defunct—arrangements for disembarking Vietnamese boat people rescued in the South China Sea. 'And it is a reasonable thing for Australia to demand that the operation of that law should be in its purest form.' The point of this mess of misconceptions and poor research was that Labor was just as anxious as the government not to find any legal or moral obligation that might stand in the way of the *Tampa* operation. They were in this together.[18]

Labor asked no questions at all about the *Tampa* on the second day of the crisis. None at all. But on the third day—Wednesday, August 29—Beazley's instincts were suddenly engaged when Howard called at 1.45 pm to tell him the *Tampa* had been boarded by a detachment of SAS. This was absolutely Beazley's cup of tea. His happiest years in politics had been spent as Minister for Defence and he loved to see the military in action. He was not the man to argue that the operation was both political and military overkill. 'You can have criticisms of how many of the SAS should have been put on board', said Beazley. 'And whether it should have been done with the level of drama it was done with, whether there should have been the deception involved in it, but you've had a captain signal in that he is under duress and he is being obliged to do certain things that he would not otherwise be obliged to do. It's not a completely unreasonable proposition in the circumstances that you put on board somebody who might be able to deal with them.'

After Howard's dramatic announcement to parliament of the SAS boarding, Beazley rose to bless the operation. 'I join the Prime Minister in the first instance in expressing gratitude to the members of the Australian armed services engaged in this very difficult situation both at sea at the moment and also on land.' Then he said the words that would be used to flay him all the way to the ballot box. 'In these circumstances, this country and this parliament do not need a carping Opposition; what they actually need is an Opposition that understands the difficult circumstances in which the government finds itself, and to the very best of my ability I will ensure that that situation prevails.'[19] Four hours later Beazley was in Howard's office reading the grim clauses of the Border Protection Bill. Howard had pressed him too far. The Bill could not be supported by Labor, said Beazley. 'But we would probably accommodate you rapidly in terms of its debate.'[20] The two leaders parted.

Howard went into a joint party meeting. Waves of 'hear hear' swept the room as he declared something must be done about the boats. Members had nothing in front of them. The Bill had not been run through a photocopier. No time, said the whips. They would see it when debate began in the House in about twenty minutes. Howard told them briefly what the legislation was about. There was no discussion. No dissent. No one asked questions. Several members had the impression Howard was assuring them Labor would support the legislation. The meeting broke up soon after 6.30 pm and the members trooped back into parliament.

I

Kim Beazley held court in his office. Not all the party leaders had been alerted to what was happening. He told those sitting stunned in the armchairs around him, that the Bill was not acceptable. Labor could not vote for a law to put all other laws aside, place lives at risk on the ocean and forbid any scrutiny by the courts. It was law for dictatorships not democracies. The room accepted Beazley's verdict. There was no debate. Someone suggested giving the Bill a cut off date, a sunset clause. Beazley rejected the idea. 'We haven't time to call a caucus', he said. 'I think we should accommodate them on voting on it immediately and we should vote it down immediately. We shouldn't allow pressure to build on us to pass this.'[21]

They knew what was at stake. Labor's election victory was very likely being plucked from them. If Howard was going to drive home his advantage in the *Tampa* crisis, he needed to force Labor into opposition. He had done it. 'He was looking for the wedge and he was going to get the wedge in some way', said Beazley. 'Whether this was going to provide the wedge he wasn't to know. But the search for the wedge was out there.' Somehow in the mood of the moment, their electoral sacrifice struck them as almost heroic. The Bill was impossible. The cost to Labor would be very high but they would block it in the Senate and go down with all guns blazing.

Swept up in the drama of the night, the leadership group failed to consider the benefits of delay. 'We all knew it was a huge shit sandwich', said one of those present. But did they have to eat it straight away? Only later was it clear that their only hope of making the public understand why this Bill had to be rejected, was to argue the case *before* the deed was done. But they were mesmerised by the pain they knew they were about to suffer. 'The view was that voting against it would devastate us', said Beazley. 'I advocated that view. I accepted that view. But the Bill had to be rejected. That would be the consequence whenever we dealt with the Bill, therefore best deal with it quickly and get on with the subsequent debate as best we could.'[22] Beazley headed for the House. Labor members only learnt what was happening—and how they were to vote—as they filed into parliament.

Howard rose at 6.47 pm. 'This Bill will confirm our ability to remove to the high seas those vessels and persons on board that have entered the territorial waters under Australian sovereignty contrary to our wishes. It is essential to the maintenance of Australian sovereignty, including our sovereign right to determine who will enter and reside in Australia.' He told parliament it was essential that the removal of boats from Australian waters 'not be able to be challenged in any court' because 'the protection of our sovereignty ... is a matter for the Australian government and this parliament'.[23] Howard was proposing that one of the three arms of government be lopped away.

Haste was crucial. 'This is an unusual Bill for unusual circumstances. I am seeking, unusually, the authority and support of the parliament to facilitate the passage of the Bill through all stages in both houses of parliament tonight.' He rammed the point home. 'I again say to the Opposition—to their representatives in this house and also in the other place—that it is in the national interest that this Bill go through tonight. It is in the national interest that, in legal terms, what we have done today is put beyond all shadow of doubt. It is in the national interest that the courts of Australia do not have the right to overturn something that rightly belongs to the determination of the Australian people, as expressed through their representatives in this parliament.'[24]

Beazley delivered a ragged speech that was no match for the rhetoric of the Prime Minister. The big themes of lawfulness and good government deserted him. Howard made it sound as though this law would stop an invasion. Beazley complained about wedge politics and called for calm. 'What we have is not a national catastrophe but a serious problem.' Yet his critique of the Bill was damning: 'No matter what the circumstances, it will be a reasonable and authoritative thing for an Australian officer to take a boat that is sinking, and in which there are life threatening situations involving the people on board, and order it out. That will be capable of being sustained by this Bill—drag the boat out, sink it, people die. It does not matter what you think ought to happen; that is what this Bill permits.'[25]

Peter Andren, the independent member for the conservative bush seat of Calare in NSW, joined Labor in opposing the Bill. 'Perhaps my electorate supports this legislation right up to the hilt but I do not.'[26] An even braver Liberal member, Judy Moylan, left the House rather than vote. The debate was over by 7.30 pm. The Bill was passed by the House 73 votes to 62. Beazley returned to his office utterly devastated. He told his colleagues he absolutely believed the election was lost.

Howard rang and there was a clumsy attempt to broker a compromise. He offered a sunset clause of six months. Beazley rejected it. Now Beazley repeated the offer he had made in the House: Labor would support a '*Tampa* specific' Bill that gave legal protection to all those involved in the operation that day and support the expulsion of the ship but on condition that Howard found a safe haven for the asylum seekers. 'We didn't isolate a place of safe haven', said Beazley. 'It could have been Australia. It could have been New Guinea. It could have been the Pacific. That was a matter for the government.' Howard seemed interested for a moment. 'But then he said "Safe haven? Orwww!". He laughed, "That's ridiculous" and just dismissed it.' Beazley offered to come with a team to Howard's office and talk through the night to find a solution. He wasn't interested.[27]

The Senate began to debate the Bill at 9.30 pm. That it would fail there was a foregone conclusion. The Greens railed against the Bill. So did the Democrats and independents. Labor senators, many of whom had profound misgivings about the Opposition's support for the government over the last couple of days, were now off the leash. They too attacked Howard, not just for an evil piece of legislation but for the whole policy of blocking the *Tampa*. Debate ground on for four and a half hours before the Bill was killed by 34 votes to 30.

That night, the Prime Minister made a rare tour of the press gallery. He strode into the *Australian*'s office 'bristling with nervous energy. "That boat will *never* land in our waters—*never*", he emphatically told a small group of reporters. The politician—whose career is a testament to his stubbornness—appeared to be operating on pure adrenalin at the end of one of the most dramatic days of his Prime Ministership. Howard's eyes bulged, his face reddened and he shifted restlessly as he spoke'.[28] The loss of the Bill was a blow to his efforts to force the *Tampa* to sail, but it came with a bright silver lining. Labor had been manoeuvred into opposition and Beazley's high-flown promises of co-operation could now be used to crush him.

Howard could tell Australia that the Labor Party, dithering and disloyal, had thwarted his efforts to guard the nation's sovereignty.

I

The phones began to ring in Beazley's office early in the morning. The calls were terrible. 'It was awful, just awful', said one of his staffers. The emotion was raw. So was the racism. People were sobbing and screaming down the line. How could Labor have done this? 'My staff were completely shell-shocked', said Beazley. 'I mean I can make a political argument but a girl on the switchboard finds it very hard to handle a sophisticated set of propositions about what you do when you suspend all laws.' The phones were feral from this point right to the end of the election campaign. Labor members would go home to their electorates at the end of this first week and be spat on in the streets. Beazley said, 'It was unprecedented in my experience. Never had it in my career'.

Most of the papers were on their way to bed even before the debate began. A couple of grabs from Beazley's speech were quoted everywhere next morning but he earned no praise for his stand. In the remorseless logic of the press, it was simply a waste of time to dwell on the Border Protection Bill now that it had been rejected. The episode was over. Beazley held a press conference that morning and a great river of words flowed from the Labor leader. He was at his most eloquent. 'The legislation was not in the national interest, the legislation was draconian, the legislation was not legislation about law but about suspending law.' The press was barely interested. The *Tampa* story had moved on at a headlong pace and the media was struggling to keep up.

Beazley was shocked to find he was given no credit for rejecting the Bill. The electorate was unused to the sight of Beazley taking a principled, unpopular stand on any issue. That had not been Labor's game plan under his leadership. He couldn't, with this one gesture, convince the public there was a great issue here. The public backed Howard. Gun control, tax reform and East Timor had given him the aura of a tough little man of principle. His extravagant claims that Australia's sovereignty was imperilled by a boatload of refugees were believed. 'There was a profound conviction that John Howard was taking a stand on principle', said Beazley, 'and that the Labor Party was playing politics.' Howard was once again taking a 'tough' stand in support of an immensely popular issue. That was his trademark. Public and private sources would, by this time, have been confirming that Howard was on a winner. The Liberal Party's pollster, Mark Textor, would have been taking soundings on the *Tampa* almost from the moment the ship appeared. Talkback radio had been red-hot for border protection all week. A readers' poll in Melbourne's *Herald Sun* on Tuesday, August 28, produced 13 572 votes for keeping the *Tampa* people out and only 615 votes to let them in.[29] John Howard had struck oil.

Advice was pouring in to Beazley's office from all corners of the party. 'The night before, people had said there was no choice', said one of Beazley's staffers. 'But faced with this terrible reaction they were now saying there *was* a choice and they should have voted for the Bill.' Particularly blunt advice is said to have come from the Sussex Street headquarters of the NSW Branch of the party: 'Just pass the fucking thing and repeal it when you're in power.' Beazley was not budging, at least not now. He told his staff he would reject the same Bill if it were served up again. 'I'm not changing my position.' But as the catastrophe unrolled, there was a consensus among party leaders that whatever happened in the weeks ahead, Labor must now stay in step with the government on boat people. No reservations. No dissent.

Howard was on Alan Jones early that morning. The talkback king of Sydney could take Howard to the breakfast tables of nearly one in five Sydney families. He was a key player in the Liberal campaign to hold onto the votes of those disgruntled, cautious people who might otherwise drift to One Nation. Ethnic crime was one of Jones' big subjects and he played an important role in establishing, in the popular imagination, a link between queue jumping boat people and Muslim criminals in Sydney's western suburbs. Jones was denouncing 'Muslim Lebanese rubbish' and 'mongrel minorities' the week before the arrival of the *Tampa*. Earlier that month he had conducted a shrill campaign against young men responsible for a series of horrific rapes in those suburbs, suggesting Sydney was all but defenceless in the face of these 'Muslim teenagers'.[30] Jones' support for the *Tampa* solution was absolute, except to urge John Howard to be even tougher.

Jones gave the Prime Minister a platform to deliver his message all over again: the neglected obligations of Indonesia, the defiance of sovereign authority, the fibs of Rinnan, the decency of Australia—'we are not closing our doors to genuine refugees'—and the unprincipled behaviour of his opponents. 'We've been done over by Labor and the Democrats.' As the day went on, Howard began a lethal personal attack on Beazley as the man who stood for nothing, the man who promised not to be a 'carping' opponent then voted down the Border Protection Bill, a man and a party 'trying to walk both sides of the street'.[31]

EIGHT
Pacific Solution

AUGUST 30 & 31

Crowds of proud and patient East Timorese, dressed in their best and carrying fresh identification cards, began gathering at polling booths before dawn. The world's newest state was electing a constituent assembly. East Timor had endured centuries of Portuguese neglect, exploitation by the Indonesian military and, in 1999, militia slaughter after these same people voted for independence. That brought United Nations forces to East Timor under Australian command. Thousands of Australian troopers were on alert this morning—August 30—in case violence broke out again after polling. The early morning crowds were peaceful and happy but no one knew how the day would end. In the middle of this fragile civic occasion, the United Nations administrator of East Timor, Sergio Vieira de Mello, took a call from Alexander Downer. He wanted to know if an empty refugee camp could be found to house the people from the *Tampa*. De Mello, indebted to Australia, was anxious to please but he had to pass the request to the secretary general of the United Nations Kofi Annan.

The *Tampa* showed no sign of budging. Wilh Wilhelmsen was threatening to take Australia to the International Court if it seized control of his ship: 'That would mean the capture of the vessel which we would consider illegal.' Rinnan was bluntly contradicting Howard's clumsy remarks that the SAS 'effectively control' the *Tampa*. The master said the soldiers 'don't interfere with the control of the ship. They only handle our passengers.'[1]

Life had changed for them. The asylum seekers now lived within a ring of armed men nicknamed by the shipping line 'the humanitarian assistance workers'. All contact with the crew was broken off and they felt this keenly. Boredom was rife. The food flown out from the island seemed not as good as the food that had been cooked on the ship. The deck was still filthy. One of the men wrote: 'There was a doctor but the number of sick people had increased. Because when they brought food for us, there were only fifty dishes. When we ate, the dishes were stacked and were left on the ground. There was no water to wash them. They allocated one container for men and one container for women to use as toilets. Sometimes we used buckets and sometimes plastic [bags]. There was a foul smell in these containers and urine was overflowing and made the place very dirty for us to sleep. For example, one night we all slept and when we woke up in the morning the place was covered by urine. We were all very dirty and if we talked to them about our situation they would be cross with us and shout at us with negative answers.'[2] Very disturbing for the asylum seekers was the way the SAS videoed everything. They suspected the worst. 'They were filming us to show we are wild people, we are inhuman, we are not worth accepting into civilised society.'[3]

In Sydney, the Wilhelmsen legal team was confident everything was now in place to win a court order preventing the *Tampa* being forced out to sea. Jane Halton's taskforce appears to have discussed these preparations. The taskforce minutes for August 30 read: 'AGs [Attorney General's] gave an update on the legal proceedings.' The shipping line had said nothing to the government and filed no documents in court. No other legal proceedings involving the *Tampa* were on foot. The information before the taskforce appears to have come from continuing DSD surveillance of the Wilhelmsen lawyers. One of the two unlawful intelligence reports of James Neill's discussions was dated this day. Quizzed directly on this point, Halton said those words in the minutes refer 'to the fact that there had been advice from the Attorney-General's Department that legal proceedings were likely'.[4] They don't read that way.

Fearing it could not move the ship, Canberra was now trying to move the people. Hence Downer's early call to Sergio de Mello. Halton's taskforce had been looking at several possible places to send them: East Timor,

Papua New Guinea and the bankrupt island republic of Nauru. Someone in the government christened this the Pacific Solution. The taskforce wanted to know how long it would take to get the asylum seekers to those locations and 'how long it will take to get Nauru ready?'. For the first time there is a mention in the minutes of the troopship HMAS *Manoora*.[5]

After making his call to de Mello, Alexander Downer summonsed the High Commissioner for New Zealand, Simon Murdoch, to his office. A request of this kind is a weighty matter in the diplomatic world and Murdoch suspected it was about the *Tampa*. He rang his prime minister, Helen Clark. How should he respond? She said, 'Hard call. I'm disposed to be helpful if we can be, so let's see what they're going to ask'.[6] Howard's Canberra had a long list of complaints against New Zealand and Helen Clark, not least that she ran a soft immigration policy and didn't pull her weight in defence. Australian ministers felt free to criticise their New Zealand counterparts in public, but Clark's ministers don't reply in kind. They prefer to find ways of demonstrating that their country is a more civilised place than Australia.

Murdoch arrived at Downer's office at 1.30 pm. Downer was desperate. According to impeccable sources he said, 'For God's sake, help us. What can you do? Can you take them please?' He wanted New Zealand to take all the people on the *Tampa*. He told the high commissioner he was 'looking for a means of solving the humanitarian question without compromising their [Australia's] national policy. One way would be to get them off the *Tampa* and process them'. Murdoch left saying New Zealand would do whatever it could.[7]

Sometime that afternoon, Downer learnt the East Timor option had been rejected by Kofi Annan. In the words of de Mello's political officer, Jonathan Prentice, it was 'a definite no'. There were many worries: would the survivors on the *Tampa* be willing to leave Australian waters and would force have to be used to get them to disembark at Dili? Could East Timor's resources cope? The view in Geneva and New York was that Australia was counting on these people becoming entirely the legal responsibility of the United Nations once they were landed in East Timor. 'It was a bad idea', said Assistant High Commissioner for Refugees Soren Jessen-Petersen who was handling the *Tampa* situation. 'There was also a risk—this was the feeling of the Secretary General—that the problem was being handed over not to an independent state but to the United Nations.'[8]

Rebuffed by the United Nations, Australia turned to Nauru. John Howard was in the habit of treating the island's government with the contempt it deserved. He had not bothered to attend the annual South Pacific Forum when it was held there earlier in August. An advance party from the Department of Foreign Affairs and Trade had come back in despair. This once rich island had no water, no electricity and no money. Australia had propped it up so the forum could actually go ahead and Howard sent Peter Reith in his place. Reith got on rather well with the island's prime minister, Rene Harris. It was Reith who first suggested this little island halfway to Hawaii as a staging post for the people from the *Tampa*. Reith and Downer made the call to Harris together. 'We rang him and said look, this is the issue, this is the situation, would you be able to give us a hand?'[9]

The government of Nauru would do just about anything to make money. By farcical coincidence, Australia was thinking of shifting the asylum seekers from one almost exhausted phosphate island to another. Mining had devastated Nauru. The mines went bust but the government kept spending so that by the late 1990s the place was bankrupt. Con men had filched the islanders' patrimony. Fortunes had been wasted on an airline, a property empire, even a London musical on the life of Leonardo da Vinci. Nauru took to selling passports to international criminals and established one of the world's shonkiest banking systems through which the Russian mafia washed tens of billions of dollars. It left Nauru as poor as ever. The bottom line for the island was this: it owed millions for the fuel that ran the desalination plant on which 12 000 people relied for water. If Rene Harris felt like drawing the line at Australia's proposition, he was in a very weak position to say no.

'Peter said: "How are you Rene? Great forum. Blah, blah" ', Harris told Craig Skehan of the *Sydney Morning Herald*. 'Then Peter said: "We have a bit of a problem. I'll put your friend on, because you know Alex better than me." Alex went off about the whole shebang, Australia's problems with sovereignty and back-door, front-door issues and that kind of stuff.' According to Harris, Downer offered flattery, money and the prospect of earning international respect by being part of a humanitarian solution to the crisis. All Nauru had to do was let Australia build a 'processing centre' somewhere on the island and Australia would do the rest. Harris told Downer, 'I'll meet with my cabinet and call you back tomorrow'.[10]

I

The Pacific Solution was not a new idea. The British blockading Palestine before the Second World War sent Jewish refugees to Mauritius and Cyprus. When thousands of people fled Haiti in the 1980s and 1990s, the United States scooped them out of the sea and took them to be processed at its military base at Guantanamo Bay in Cuba. There were famous confrontations on the beaches of Florida to stop asylum seekers setting foot on land because once they did they had the protection of United States law. The Guantanamo Bay solution was designed as much to keep Haitians out of the legal system as the territory of the United States.

That purpose was driving the Pacific Solution, too. Asylum seekers on Nauru would have no recourse to the safeguards and appeals process of the Australian courts. Nauru must also have promised to close its own courts to these people. The Pacific Solution could not work any other way. The islanders were allowing a camp to be built to detain hundreds of people for an indeterminate period without any authority under Nauruan law to hold them behind barbed wire. They could only be kept there if they were effectively placed beyond the reach of the courts of both countries.

Australia wanted the co-operation of the United Nations High Commission for Refugees. Nauru was not a signatory to the Refugee Convention and there were no officials on the island qualified to assess refugee claims. Australians could do the work, but part of the attraction of the whole scheme was to have the asylum seekers on the *Tampa* processed according to the more stringent rules of the UNHCR. The problem here was that Australia would now have to go cap-in-hand to the United Nations after earlier refusing to attend discussions at UNHCR headquarters in Geneva with representatives of Norway and Indonesia 'to address immediate humanitarian concerns'. Jessen-Petersen remarked: 'At that time the Australian authorities felt they did not need UNHCR.'[11]

The UNHCR was shocked by Australia's actions. Geneva had declared the Border Protection Bill incompatible with the Refugee Convention because 'it could have led to the rejection of asylum seekers at the frontier by the forcible removal of ships from Australia's territorial waters'. What worried the world body most was that Australia's new policy threatened to undermine the Refugee Convention in the region. 'That was our concern', said Jessen-Petersen. 'Other countries might say, "If Australia can do it, we can do it", and there goes the whole international protection principle down the drain.'[12]

The UNHCR was working to find homes for all the refugees on the *Tampa* in other countries.[13] But throughout this crisis, the bottom line for Geneva was that Australia must first allow these people ashore to be processed. Canberra refused. The Howard government treated the UNHCR solution as a kind of diplomatic trick. Ruddock explained: 'People were saying land the people at Christmas Island and let's sort it all out later. The focus of my attention was what would be the implications of that— and the implications were very clear. Once we had brought people ashore and they were in the migration zone, it didn't matter whether the UNHCR had given any assurances about what would happen and about how processing might be able to happen and [people] resettled elsewhere— they were in Australia. And then [Australia's legal] obligations kick in and . . . it was game, set, match.'[14]

But Australia wanted the United Nation's help on Nauru. So on the night of August 30, Howard rang Kofi Annan to brief him 'on discussions that have been underway with a number of countries' and to ask him to set up the meeting with Indonesia and Norway which only the day before Australia had refused to attend. Australia now wanted Annan to help persuade those two countries to 'take some responsibility for the problem' and he wanted the UNHCR to organise the screening of the asylum seekers, but not in Australia.[15] Howard came away from the conversation with nothing.

I

Helen Clark's domestic and external security committee worked into the early hours of the morning. 'We very quickly came to the conclusion that there were some problems with the 433 you just couldn't solve', said the committee's leader Dave Hill. 'The critical issue in all of this was the capacity of the Immigration service.'[16] The people from the *Tampa* would have to be processed at the Mangere centre, a tidy Second World War military camp down an unmarked road in a poor suburb of Auckland. Mangere had lately been given a fence and there were plans to put up a gate and hire some guards. It could handle only 150 refugees at a time and seventy places had already been reserved for refugees expected to arrive from Africa in the next few days. Dave Hill concluded New Zealand could only offer eighty places to the people on the *Tampa*. That decision was conveyed to Canberra later on the morning of Friday, August 31.[17]

Australian officials begged New Zealand to reconsider. Such requests have to be taken seriously by New Zealand. After all, Australia is her only great friend. Britain deserted her for Europe; the United States jilted her when she declared her ports nuclear free. Now Australia was asking, as a great favour, that New Zealand be what Canberra so frequently complained she was: a soft touch on immigration. New Zealand had never had boat people. From time to time there were rumours of boats but they never materialised. New Zealand was more relaxed and its government braver about these issues. But the decent gesture it was now being asked to make would help Australia escape its own obligations. New Zealand was about to let Australia off the hook by giving the Pacific Solution an air of respectability.

'Maybe that is the case', said Lianne Dalziel, the Minister for Immigration. 'But at the time the pressure was on to respond to what was becoming an increasing crisis where it was kind of stalemated between the captain of an international ship ... and a country that had been faced with thousands and thousands of asylum seekers making their way to its outer reaches and claiming refugee status. So it was a stalemate situation and I always felt that somebody had to help. We saw it as a humanitarian situation and we responded in that way.' This attitude to Australia's plea for help was being driven by Helen Clark. 'The Prime Minister indicated to me that she wanted my officials to come back with the best figure that they could ... The pressure was on all of us I guess to see what was the best response we could make.'[18]

While New Zealand was still reconsidering its offer, Nauru let Australia know it could put a camp on the island.[19] The price was extremely high: $16.5 million. The terms of the deal would be settled over the next ten days but the single biggest item was $10 million to pay the fuel bills that kept the island's generator and desalination plant running. No Australian aid officials were involved in the haggling. Australia's aid priorities in the South Pacific—good governance and economic reform—were not on the table. There would be some kit homes, police training, scholarships to Australian schools and measures to bring Nauruan aviation up to scratch, but the big money involved was a million dollars or so to wipe off unpaid hospital bills in Australia and those millions for the desalination plant. The nub of the bargain was simple: drinking water in return for asylum seekers.

At 2 pm Canberra time, Clark rang Howard from a hotel room in Hamilton. The upshot of their conversation was that New Zealand would empty Mangere and take 150 people from the *Tampa* for processing and settlement. These would be women, children and families. New Zealand only asked Australia to pay the cost of flying them to Auckland. 'Someone had to get them off the boat', said Clark. 'Unless someone agreed to accept them, sight unseen in effect, they weren't going to get off the boat.'[20]

In Geneva, Soren Jessen-Petersen was still gathering pledges from western countries willing to take refugees from the *Tampa*. 'We decided whether Australia needed us or not we would have to play a role.' The countries of resettlement included the United States and Sweden. 'We already had enough indication to know we could have solved the problem very quickly.'[21] At about 5 pm Canberra time, Jessen-Petersen called together representatives of Australia, Indonesia, Norway and New Zealand to propose a three-point solution to the *Tampa* crisis: temporary disembarkation on Christmas Island; immediate screening if necessary by UNHCR teams; transfer of refugees to third countries. Australia walked out claiming to be insulted by a press release announcing the proposal before it had been considered in Canberra. By this time John Howard had his Pacific Solution.

While those officials were gathered in Geneva, two teams of lawyers were heading for the Federal Court in Melbourne. The press had been reporting rumours of legal action all day. The government had been alerted to the progress of preparations by DSD intelligence reports and late on this Friday afternoon learnt officially that an application was about to be made to compel the government to bring the asylum seekers on the *Tampa* ashore. The Commonwealth hurriedly briefed its own team of barristers who were also converging on the court. Canberra's *Tampa* strategy might still unravel.

NINE
The rule of law

AUGUST 29 TO SEPTEMBER 3

John Manetta grew extremely irritated as he watched Alexander Downer on television talking about the 'illegals' on the *Tampa* who would never be allowed to enter Australia. It was the evening of Wednesday August 29, the day the SAS boarded the ship. Manetta, a Melbourne barrister, knew the law made sure that all those 'who tried to land in Australia without a visa were arrested, brought in, and put in immigration detention . . . Yet here was the Foreign Minister explaining how the government was going to do whatever it took to make sure that none of these people were brought into Australia . . . and that the government would see them pushed right back where they came from. Well the illegality of it was blatant'. As he turned in that night, he assumed Amnesty International or the Red Cross would already be on the case. 'I knew how the writ of *habeas corpus* worked, and I had no doubt [Downer]—or one or other of his Cabinet colleagues—would be getting one.'[1]

The fugitive Mexican banker Carlos Cabal, fighting extradition to his homeland, had engaged Manetta to release him from his Melbourne prison. For two years, Manetta explored every nuance of *habeus corpus* law on behalf of his Mexican client. Julian Burnside QC joined the team to fight the extradition proceedings. By the time the banker was duly returned in handcuffs to Mexico, the two barristers were friends and Manetta was an authority on what he called 'the hallowed procedure by which the courts of the common law world called to account those who held others captive in circumstances of dubious legality'.

When he woke next morning, Manetta was suddenly struck by doubt: what if no one was working on the *Tampa* case? He rang John Pace, an academic at the University of NSW and former lawyer for the United Nations. Had Pace heard of any cases on foot? He hadn't. Manetta decided he would do the job himself. Pace offered to try to find him a client on the ship. The word in Sydney was that one of the Afghans on board the *Tampa* had somehow managed to ring a relative in Sydney. From his chambers in Flinders Lane, Manetta enlisted Burnside. The team that failed to spring one fugitive banker would now try to release 433 people held by the Australian army on the deck of a cargo boat. Burnside's instructions to Manetta were to keep trying to get a line to the ship, start collecting the facts and find solicitors willing to brief them.

The big commercial firms Manetta approached that morning—firms he had worked with, whose partners he knew—either hesitated or knocked him back. Manetta was asking them to give their time without fee, to act *pro bono publico*. Not all the partners in these firms were convinced fighting for the asylum seekers on the *Tampa* was, in fact, in the community's interest. While they agonised, Manetta approached Melbourne's Public Interest Law Clearing House (PILCH), a small organisation staffed by a few bright young lawyers who find law firms willing to work *pro bono* on issues of public importance. PILCH is the conscience of the big end of the legal profession in Melbourne which largely funds its work. It accepted the *Tampa* case and Emma Hunt, Phil Lynch and Danielle Brennan were immediately at work. Eventually PILCH persuaded the big labour firm Holding Redlich to be the instructing solicitors.

Most of all they needed a client on the ship. Pace discovered there was no Afghan on the *Tampa* with a mobile. Hunt and Lynch began ringing the ship. At 12.30 pm Melbourne time the communications officer on the ship told the lawyers they could not speak to any of the asylum seekers and asked them to put their request in a fax to Rinnan. That was soon ready but the lines to the *Tampa* were so clogged it was not until 2.30 pm that the fax went through asking Rinnan to provide urgently 'the name of an asylum-seeker aboard your vessel. This person will need to give us the authority to lodge the writ of *habeus corpus* and the application for an interim injunction on their behalf. For this purpose, we attach a form for the nominated asylum seeker to fill out and return to us immediately'. Emma Hunt also offered help to Rinnan: 'If you require, the Public Interest Law Clearing House could also arrange urgent free legal assistance for you in this matter.'[2]

Pleas for asylum were being handed to the soldiers. 'We wrote a letter to the authorities. We explained our problems. We also asked what were the factors which would prevent us to Christmas Island. We also wrote letters to human right organisations. We also wrote letters to people and Australian government to help us to be allowed to Christmas Island. We in our letter, urged to the women and children of Australia to let us stay with them in peace. They took the letters. They told us that the letters had been faxed. They said they are waiting now for the response.'[3]

One of the letters reached Jane Halton's People Smuggling Taskforce. The minutes for August 30 read: 'AG's gave . . . advice on the status of the letter from those on board.' Under the rules of the Refugee Convention, that letter should have brought them ashore. They were in Australian territorial waters, they wanted asylum, they were not a threat 'to national security or public order', so they must have their asylum claims properly assessed. Australia could not simply expel them.[4] But Australia had shrunk its borders for refugee purposes. Pleas for asylum have to be made inside the 'migration zone' which does not include the territorial seas. Canberra had closed Flying Fish Cove and put a ring of SAS troops around the asylum seekers to keep them from reaching the zone, defined as Australia's dry land and harbours. As an added precaution, anyone with power to accept asylum pleas made *outside* the zone—DIMA officers and agents, police, soldiers flying the flag—were being kept a very long way from the ship. In the eyes of the refugee world, the asylum seekers had reached Australia, but according to Australian law they were still a kilometre or two from safe haven.

This was briskly confirmed by the legal advisers to Halton's taskforce, including, on this morning, the Commonwealth's General Counsel, Henry Burmester QC. They listed and dismissed each possible ground for taking the asylum seekers' letter seriously: 'A plea for help: they are getting it. Didn't go to a person under the Migration Act; no obligation to process in Australia provided they are not refouled.' Throughout this mess, Australia would claim to take very seriously the principle of *non-refoulement*: the obligation not to send asylum seekers back to countries where they might face persecution.[5]

Those letters to the soldiers were still a time bomb under the bureaucrats because they made it impossible for DIMA to pretend not to know if the survivors wanted to land in Australia. The pretence was always nonsense. Why else did they risk their lives on the *Palapa*? Why else beg Rinnan to take them to Christmas Island? Did Philip Ruddock ever doubt at any time that there were people on the *Tampa* who wanted to enter Australia? 'I would never have questioned it.'[6] But officers of his department did exactly that to avoid obligation under the Migration Act to bring these people ashore. DIMA officials were sitting on Halton's taskforce on August 30 when the asylum letter was considered. From that point on, any claim by the department not to know there were people on the *Tampa* wanting to land in Australia was simply a lie. But the pretence continued.

The soldiers returned the letters to the asylum seekers saying they had never been delivered. 'The soldiers came and said they did not have the authority to send letters or fax them.'[7]

|

PILCH kept ringing the ship. These calls were being monitored by Australia's Defence Signals Directorate and an unlawful report on the conversations was being prepared for the government.[8] One of the officers on the *Tampa* told the lawyers to ring a senior vice president of the line, Hans Christian Bangsmoen, at the Lysaker headquarters. Emma Hunt spoke briefly to Bangsmoen at 6.30 pm. He was about to go into a meeting to discuss the PILCH requests to Rinnan. He would ring her back. She never spoke to him again.

The Wilhelmsen Line was not going to help PILCH. As far as the line was concerned, Australia had a duty to disembark the people on the *Tampa*'s deck simply because they were survivors of a shipwreck. Wilh Wilhelmsen was aware Norway was also pressing Australia to recognise these people had rights as asylum seekers. He didn't want the shipping line drawn into that. 'We had to let government sort out this issue.' To help PILCH at this point 'would have seriously interfered in the political discussion that was going on and we didn't want to do that. We are not a political organisation'. The line didn't like Australia's tactics but had no quarrel with the government's political objectives and no wish to put at risk a century of fruitful business dealings with Australia.[9]

But the Wilhelmsen Line's lawyers recognised that if the ship were held up at Christmas Island indefinitely, then the Migration Act offered a way of breaking the impasse. The line would not intervene to help PILCH but as a last resort would position itself to take a very similar action on its own account to get the survivors ashore. Partly to prepare for this, James Neill now flew to Christmas Island leaving instructions that his office was only to talk to solicitors already representing clients. He'd done some rough figures and was worried that a firm collecting the business of 433 asylum seekers stood to make millions from legal aid. He said he wasn't going to encourage the ambulance chasers of the law.[10]

So after all the Wilhelmsen Line had done for the survivors, it would not take the one small step that would give them their best chance of disembarkation in Australia: putting an asylum seeker in contact with a lawyer. When Emma Hunt arrived at PILCH next morning, Friday August 31, she found a fax waiting on the machine that thanked her for 'offering your kind assistance in the awkward situation which MV *Tampa* finds itself. However, I have been in contact with our office in Oslo, and they have instructed me not to follow up on the matter. Again, thank you very much for your interest. Yours sincerely, Arne Rinnan'.

The Norwegian ambassador to Australia, Ove Thorsheim, had arrived on Christmas Island by private jet some hours before dawn that day. Later in the morning, he and James Neill presented themselves to the SAS commander Gus Gilmore and asked to be taken out to the *Tampa*. Neither sought Gilmore's permission, only his assistance. Thorsheim was relying on the Vienna Convention on Diplomatic Relations. Neill was asserting his right as Rinnan's solicitor. They waited for hours. Along the edge of Flying Fish Cove, islanders in crudely painted T-shirts were demonstrating against Canberra. The slogans read: 'SHAME AUSTRALIA SHAME' and 'CAPTAIN OF THE SHIP STAY IN AUSTRALIAN WATERS'.

No civilians had been allowed out to the *Tampa*. Even the Red Cross, which has a right to go almost anywhere in the world to assess and meet humanitarian needs, found its way blocked. The Red Cross had brought to the island a team including a doctor, a registered nurse and a 'tracing' officer who worked in the mainland detention centres and was fluent in both Afghan languages, Dari and Pashtu. What was planned as a routine Red Cross operation to lend a hand on the ship was being frustrated by Canberra. DIMA would not help nor would the SAS allow the team to go out with the ambassador. Who in Canberra was blocking the way was a mystery to the Red Cross for a few days. Eventually the final, formal refusal came from the Department of Prime Minister and Cabinet.[11]

Thorsheim and Neill were both togged up by the SAS in camouflage suits while they waited. Finally, Canberra said no to the lawyer and yes to the ambassador, who was put into a zodiac a little after 2 pm and whisked out to the ship. The ambassador understood that the decision to allow him on board was made by John Howard.[12]

Rinnan left the bridge to meet Thorsheim. It was the only time during these days that Rinnan came down to the deck and most of the survivors now caught their first real sight of the man who had rescued them. 'Rinnan was short and the ambassador was tall', recalled an Afghan teacher who was standing close to the mesh barrier that separated the survivors from the crew. 'We want to give you this letter', said Mohammed Wali, stepping up to the mesh. 'It is addressed to the people of Australia.' When Thorsheim went to take it, one of the SAS officers intervened. The ambassador was visibly furious. 'Why not?' he asked the soldier.[13] Wali was left with the letter in his hand. Rinnan, the soldier and the ambassador disappeared.

Oslo considered this incident—an Australian soldier blocking the Norwegian ambassador on a Norwegian ship—a grave breach of diplomatic convention and the lowest point in its dispute with Australia. 'If it had continued, it would have had very big dimensions', said Hans Longva at the Foreign Ministry. 'There was a very sensitive situation.'[14] He refused to elaborate. Australian officials, when they learnt of this incident, were amazed by and grateful for Norway's forbearance. From the bridge, Thorsheim rang the Foreign Ministry which alerted the Australian ambassador in Oslo, who in turn contacted Downer in Canberra. It took Australia less than twenty minutes to back down. The ambassador and Rinnan returned to the deck. Thorsheim said to Wali, 'Now I want to take your letter'. It read:

> To the Australian government, human rights organizations and Australian ladies and gentlemen,
>
> We hope you accept regards and warm feelings of the miserable and oppressed Afghan refugees turning around Christmas Island in the middle of sea, while having no shelter, cloths to change after ten days and even toilet and bathroom.
>
> Respected Australian government and gentlemen and ladies. You know well about the long time war and its tragic human consequences, and you know about the genocide and massacres going on in our country and thousands of innocent men, women and children were put in public graveyards, and we hope you understand that keeping in view all aforementioned reasons we have no way but to run out of our dear homeland and to seek a peaceful asylum. And until now so many miserable refugees have been seeking asylum in so many countries. In this regards before this Australia has taken some real appreciable initiatives and has given asylum to a high number of refugees from our miserable people. That is why we are wholeheartedly and sincerely thankful to you.
>
> We hope you do not forget that we are also from the same miserable and oppressed refugees and now turning around Christmas island inside Australian boundaries waiting a permit to enter your country. But your delay while we are in the worst condition has hurt our feelings. We do not know why we have not been regarded as refugee and deprived from rights of refugees according to international convention in (1951).
>
> We request from Australian authorities and people, at first not to deprive us from the rights that all refugees enjoy in your country. And in the case of rejection due to not having anywhere to live on the earth and every moment death is threatening us. We request you to feel mercy for the life of (438) men, women and children.
>
> Thank you.
> Yours sincerely,
> Afghan refugees
> Now off the coast of Christmas Island.[15]

Before leaving the ship, Thorsheim faxed the letter to the foreign ministry in Oslo which then distributed copies to the UNHCR in Geneva, to the Australian ambassador and to the Norwegian ambassador in Canberra to be forwarded to the Australian government. Back on shore, Thorsheim also presented a copy of the letter to the administrator of Christmas Island and faxed further copies directly to the Department of Foreign Affairs in Canberra and to Alexander Downer. Norway was acting discreetly but with great determination to compel Australia to face its obligations to the people on the *Tampa*.

Thorsheim addressed the press. He had received a letter but he said nothing of its contents. All was calm on the boat. Water was running low and was being rationed. Sanitation was unsatisfactory. The crew was extremely tired. Three of the survivors were still very ill and being treated by army medics. He reiterated Norway's position: Arne Rinnan had carried out a rescue and brought the survivors to port. 'We hope that all the rescued people can be put ashore and the ship can sail.'[16]

All afternoon, Rinnan had been pestered by another Melbourne lawyer, Eric Vadarlis. He was a wild card, a solicitor with no particular profile in Melbourne who knew nothing much about migration law but was determined to mount his own rescue effort. Vadarlis had rung around the Melbourne Bar to put together his own legal team. He netted Dr Gavan Griffith QC, a former Commonwealth solicitor general, and Jack Fajgenbaum QC, who in turn enlisted a fearless migration barrister Debbie Mortimer. Riordans were the instructing solicitors and advice was also given by Erskine Rodan a Melbourne firm of immigration lawyers. These lawyers were all working *pro bono*.

Vadarlis is a terrier. He managed to speak to Rinnan three times. 'He advised me that Australian military personnel were on the vessel and were monitoring all communications with the vessel.' Vadarlis asked to speak to the SAS commander who refused to give his name, refused to put him through to an asylum seeker, suggested he contact the shipping line's Sydney office 'and promptly hung up the phone'.[17]

Vadarlis' calls were, indeed, being monitored by DSD and an unlawful intelligence analysis of them was available to the government this same day. The press had been reporting since morning that a court challenge was in the air and it appears Canberra was taking urgent and unscrupulous steps to find out what was going on. The unlawful report of PILCH's calls to the ship on Thursday had taken the usual 24 hours to be analysed and fed to government. Vadarlis' calls on Friday were being reported almost immediately.[18] The great irony was that Canberra may have been caught off guard by intelligence reports of the difficulties PILCH and Vadarlis were both facing in finding a client on the ship. Those unlawful DSD reports seem to have lulled Canberra into a false sense of security.

The president of Liberty Victoria, Chris Maxwell QC, had joined the PILCH team that morning. Burnside now asked Maxwell if Liberty would be the client. This was a second or third best option. The lawyers could always mount a *habeas corpus* case—the ancient rule is that you can't be kept out of court because you can't reach your client—but they also wanted to force the machinery of the Migration Act into action. For that they really needed a client on the ship. Perhaps taking the case in the name of Amnesty International or the Human Rights and Equal Opportunities Commission (HREOC) would give them a chance to argue the Act. But both those organisations were reluctant to become involved for fear of what it might cost them if they lost. Liberty Victoria's business was to promote lawfulness, due process and civil liberties. That might just offer the leverage the lawyers needed. So Maxwell agreed the fight could be taken in Liberty's name.

In which court? Manetta had originally wanted to go straight to the High Court but that would be slow. Delay would be tough on the asylum seekers trapped on the deck of the ship and the cost of holding them there while the High Court found time to hear the case could be prohibitively high. The Federal Court, on the other hand, prided itself on being able to hear big cases immediately. So late in the afternoon, the PILCH team alerted the Commonwealth, put out a press release, gathered up the documents and set out for the Federal Court in William Street. Vadarlis and his team were on their way to the same destination.

'It was late winter, and twilight outside', said John Manetta. 'But when we arrived at the atrium of the Court, for a moment, it seemed like day again. It was flash bulbs, and television camera lights. I don't think I'd ever seen so many of them before.' The two teams met in the registry office. They agreed to fight the one case together and a few minutes later they found themselves before that night's duty judge, Tony North.

That North would be the judge coloured the whole proceedings. Three years earlier, he had halted an attempt by Patrick Stevedores to clear union labour from its wharves. The Howard government was deeply committed and privately implicated in the operation. The dispute and the court challenge rocked Australia. North was supported by both the Full Bench of the Federal Court and the High Court. The men went back to work. It was a high profile victory for Julian Burnside, counsel for the wharfies and a humiliating loss for Patrick and the government. Right-wing commentators and politicians once again abused the judiciary but the outcome was reassuring proof for others that the courts could still cut through political uproar to find a lawful resolution of great public disputes. Many of the same lawyers were now gathered in front of the same judge—and the underlying contest between the law and popular politics was absolutely unchanged.

Burnside and Gavan Griffith asked North to order Canberra to leave the *Tampa* in Australian waters. HMAS *Arunta*, dispatched by Howard early in the week, was due to arrive at Christmas Island at any moment. North adjourned to allow the Commonwealth's dazed barristers to try to get instructions. This was not easy. Ministers and officials in Canberra were putting the finishing touches to the Pacific Solution, due to be announced the following day. These court proceedings were, at the very least, going to ruin the timetable. The Commonwealth's barristers were instructed, eventually, to agree to nothing. North ordered the *Tampa* to be left where it was so they could 'consider the matter coolly, responsibly, tomorrow'.[19]

I

The Battle of the Pot of Jam is not the most glorious campaign in the annals of the SAS. A soldier put a big pot of jam in the middle of the *Tampa*'s deck as the asylum seekers were queuing for lunch. There was a mêlée. 'People rushed to grab their share. At that very moment they had their filming cameras and photo cameras ready so they could take photos and films of this scene.' The SAS videoed everything, but at the sight of the cameras at this moment there was an outpouring of rage. 'Why do you want to show us to the world as lawless people and for a mouthful of bread embarrass us?' One man was thrown to the ground, had his hands pinned behind his back and was then led away. A second man then erupted in anger. He too was taken behind the containers. The crowd assumed they were to be punished. This was not so, but people were yelling, gesticulating and calling for Rinnan. They had no idea how far the SAS would go. 'Their guns were ready and they had also a hose. If anyone moved they would use that.' The SAS commander Major Vance Khan appeared and restored order. He apologised and promised to destroy the film. The two young men were released.[20]

Khan had a second fraught confrontation with the asylum seekers at about 9.20 the morning after the court case began. They knew nothing of the case and were not going to be told now. Instead, Khan announced that they were to be shipped away. 'Mr Major Khan who was the high ranking official of Christmas arrived and read the Australian Prime Minister's statement. In that statement he had indicated that 150 of the migrants would go to New Zealand, as the New Zealand government was prepared to accept 150 persons and priority was given to women and children. The rest were going to Nauru to go through legal processes.' The asylum seekers made their distress very clear. They quizzed Khan but he refused to give them any further details. They told him 'the Australian Prime Minister's decision was unfair'.[21]

The announcement of the Pacific Solution at a press conference in Sydney an hour or so earlier was one of John Howard's most accomplished performances. Never was the spin more subtle. 'Naturally, the UNHCR and the International Office for Migration will both be involved and indeed their involvement is part of the process of resolving this very difficult situation.' Once they were well away from Australia, the asylum seekers from the *Tampa* would have their claims assessed 'under the normal processes applying to refugees around the world'. It was 'envisaged' Norway would take some and Australia would take its 'fair share' as well, 'consistent with our open policy concerning refugees'. Once more the Prime Minister advanced the statistical fib that Australia is 'the second most generous country in the world in taking refugees after Canada. Now that is a pretty good record and we aim to keep that record'.[22]

Howard was hardly questioned about the Pacific Solution. The journalists were far more excited by the hazy first details he gave of Operation Relex: 'Commencing immediately the Australian Defence Force will conduct enhanced surveillance, patrol and response operations in international waters between the Indonesian archipelago and Australia. This will involve five naval vessels and four P-3C Orion aircraft.' Howard called this an 'intensification' of present practice designed to deter people smuggling.

He had no answer for the most obvious question: how would the navy grapple with boats? 'All I can say to you . . . is that as always Australian defence personnel will act in accordance with the law and in a humane fashion.' He added: 'We don't in this nation sink boats.' As journalists continued to ask what the navy actually planned to do, Howard resorted to his stock reply during the *Tampa* crisis. 'I am not going to hypothesise about that. I mean the worst thing you can do, the most unhelpful from Australia's point of view is for me to start hypothesising about that. I mean there comes a point where there are some answers that shouldn't be given by me or Mr Ruddock because, to the hypothetical propositions, because it undermines the purpose of what we are trying to do.'

Howard was wrong to suggest he had Norway's support. Once Oslo heard about the Pacific Solution, the Australian ambassador was summoned to the Foreign Ministry to be told, 'Norway cannot support a plan which calls for the refugees to be transported to another country before being processed . . . Australia's unyielding stand on the issue may undermine the UN Refugee Convention'.[23] Australia was also handed a diplomatic note blasting its treatment of the people on *Tampa* and demanding Canberra respond to the plea for asylum that the Norwegian ambassador had carried off the ship. 'The Norwegian Government therefore urges the Australian Government to strictly observe its obligations under the United Nations Convention on the Law of the Sea, the Safety of Life at Sea Convention and the United Nations Convention relating to the Status of Refugees.'[24]

Howard's hints of UNHCR approval were also misleading. The UNHCR was unwavering in its insistence that the asylum seekers on the *Tampa* should be brought ashore and processed in Australia. But given Australia's intransigence, the UNHCR could not stand in the way of the 150 asylum seekers offered protection in New Zealand. Nor could the UNHCR refuse to carry out on Nauru its customary function of processing applications for asylum in countries that aren't able to do the job for themselves. Shortly before Howard's press conference, Jane Halton had offered the Canberra UNHCR team a briefing. It was only a briefing: no negotiations. The team brought a copy of the asylum letter which had arrived overnight from their Geneva headquarters. They told Halton this was a valid application for asylum and if it were ignored, Australia would be failing in its international obligations. Halton dismissed the argument and ended the briefing.

Howard also misrepresented the position of Kofi Annan. The Secretary General of the United Nations had arrived in Durban where Howard rang him twice to explain the details of the Pacific Solution. Howard came away from these calls declaring that Annan accepted his plan and even 'expressed satisfaction' with its details.[25] In fact, the Secretary General was unhappy with the solution and told a press conference in Durban he would still prefer refugees on the *Tampa* to be given protection in Australia. Howard's plan was 'a compromise solution. It is not an ideal situation, and I feel for the refugees who are on this ship in the heat, in containers'. For their sake, the United Nations was not going to stand in Howard's way. 'The men and women and children on that boat . . . are in need of refuge and support. And so we accept the compromise.' In Howard's brutal summary that became: Kofi Annan 'accepts' and even 'supports' the Pacific Solution.[26]

The ground shifted in Justice North's courtroom when the portly but nimble Solicitor General David Bennett QC, read out the Prime Minister's statement on the Pacific Solution. The court rose for over an hour while the Melbourne lawyers decided if they still wished to pursue their case. They did. Burnside attacked the new plan head on. 'The really essential point is, here are people who are being held, presumably not at their own wishes, and who the Commonwealth wishes to abduct from Australian territory and put them out in the middle of the Pacific. Ordinarily, civilised nations don't allow that to happen and courts intervene if it's threatened. That's what the process of *habeas corpus* is all about.'

Bennett, meanwhile, was mounting a last-ditch stand to keep the asylum seekers' letter secret. A member of the Vadarlis legal team had seen a line in an early edition of the *Age* about a letter handed to the ambassador on the ship. The lawyers called for its production in court. When Bennett began blustering about diplomatic immunity, there were loud mutterings of disbelief from the gallery. He protested to North: 'I wish the people in court wouldn't gasp with horror every time I say something.' The judge agreed but ordered the letter be produced. That would take another 24 hours.

Bennett played the deadpan comedian with some skill, compelling North to pay attention to the government's essentially farcical argument. The men and women on the deck of the *Tampa* were free, the Solicitor

General told North, free to go anywhere in the world but Australia. It was not the fear of SAS guns that kept them on the ship, but their fear of sharks. And perhaps they were perfectly happy to proceed to New Zealand and Nauru now that they knew about the Pacific Solution. Several times, North offered to release the ship and end the case if that was, in fact, the case. It would only take a telephone call to the SAS to find out what the asylum seekers wanted to do. Bennett's team never made that call nor did they allow their opponents to ring and confirm what they must all have known: these people still wanted to come to Australia.

Bennett's Alice in Wonderland postures hid an able strategic mind. The *pro bono* lawyers wanted to examine Rinnan, the commander of the SAS and senior public servants to gather the evidence needed to fight the case. Instead, Bennett proposed to admit just enough of the facts and allow the case to proceed at once. Bennett had apparently calculated that the government was going to lose this round before North. Admitting the facts was risky, but it would move the case swiftly to the inevitable appeal which the government stood a better chance of winning. The *pro bono* lawyers were uneasy but North was keen. The rest of Saturday was spent arguing the terms of the real contest that would begin next day which Bennett, for some reason, kept pointing out was Father's Day.

That night was the worst spent on the *Tampa*. The chicken and rice flown out from the island smelt odd but everyone ate. People were hungry. There was lots of food. At about 10 pm, a wave of food poisoning hit the asylum seekers. People were retching and shitting all through the night. When daylight came, there were long queues for the overflowing latrines. To the distress of these people, the SAS kept videotaping. 'This was another psychological blow to us and we felt very low. We did not want to be filmed.' Khan promised the film would never be shown. They did not believe him.[27]

The Prime Minister began the day by misrepresenting them on ABC-TV. 'I am encouraged by advice I received this morning that the reaction of the people on the *Tampa* when being informed of the arrangements that we had negotiated with Nauru and New Zealand was fairly positive.'[28] They were further misrepresented by Bill Farmer, secretary of the Department of Immigration and Multicultural Affairs, when he entered the witness box at 3 o'clock that afternoon.

Farmer admitted it was unprecedented for a boatload of asylum seekers to turn up at Christmas Island and not be brought ashore under the Migration Act. He conceded it was a 'reasonable working assumption' that 90 per cent of the Afghans on the *Tampa* would be granted refugee status if they could get ashore. He conceded that neither he nor anyone in his department had taken steps to inform these people about the court case. 'I don't think that's my responsibility. I'm not acting for them.' He conceded the government had, in fact, taken steps 'to ensure that the people on board the *Tampa* are not able to contact lawyers'. But he would not concede that they still wanted to land in Australia. A 'number' may have approached Australia with that intention, said Farmer, but since the announcement of the Pacific Solution he could no longer say what they wanted. For hours, Farmer kept denying the obvious as he was quizzed by Griffith and Burnside. The Afghans' asylum letter had at last been produced in court—and released to the press—but Farmer would not concede even this was evidence any of them wanted to enter Australia. 'I really have no basis for forming an opinion on the statements in the letter. And if I could just explain why: we receive numbers of claims or statements by people which, in accordance with law, are examined. Some of those statements are found to have a basis; some are not.'

Howard had, meanwhile, called a press conference to announce the next step in the Pacific Solution. An amphibious troopship, HMAS *Manoora*, had arrived at Christmas Island to take the asylum seekers away and the well-being of these people was now a matter of urgent concern for the Prime Minister. 'I believe that the humanitarian consideration and the best welfare of the people now on the vessel will be better met if they can be transferred as soon as possible to the *Manoora* where the conditions are obviously more comfortable than what they are on the *Tampa*.' Everything had to happen fast. Howard was anxious to keep the action rolling along. 'I am told by the chief of the Defence Force through the Defence Minister that as I speak the *Manoora* is ready to take people on board.' At 5.30 pm, David Bennett interrupted the court case to announce the *Manoora* 'is now available for immediate transhipment of the persons concerned'. Crunch time had arrived. North sent the parties into mediation.

Behind closed doors, the *pro bono* lawyers faced a very tough call. Howard was threatening to blame these legal grandees for putting the asylum seekers through hell on the deck of the *Tampa* as the case dragged on. They were already under attack. Liberty Victoria had had to close its office. PILCH was fielding abusive phone calls. Burnside was getting death threats. They had no way of knowing what their 'clients' would want: to tough it out on the *Tampa* or lose one of their few tactical advantages by shifting to the *Manoora*. Had they been able to make contact with the asylum seekers, the lawyers would have found these men and women were willing to stay put. That was the message they gave months later when asked in New Zealand. After all they had been through and having come so close, they would have sat on the deck of the *Tampa* for weeks if that's what it took to reach their destination.[29]

Now came the financial threats. Bennett produced an affidavit setting out 'the full cost to the Commonwealth' of the operation on Christmas Island while the court case continued. The *Manoora* was put down at half a million dollars a day and the *Arunta* at a million; three sorties a day by Hercules came with a price tag of half a million and the same again to keep two P-3C Orions in the air. Pay and food for 200 SAS and other troops came to another $90 000 a day. The total bill put before the lawyers was $2 974 230 for every day the court case continued. The figures were shamelessly—and fairly obviously—inflated.[30] Even so, what the lawyers saw was the risk of catastrophic financial repercussions if they lost the case.

They haggled for three hours. The result was an extraordinary deal. The government would not ask for an undertaking as to damages for this trial or the appeal to the Full Bench of the Federal Court. In return, the Melbourne lawyers agreed to the transfer of the asylum seekers to the *Manoora* where they would be held until that appeal was heard and decided. If the asylum seekers won they would be brought back to Australia. If they lost, they would be delivered into the Pacific Solution. The most daring aspect of the arrangement was a decision to argue the case as if the asylum seekers were still on the deck of the *Tampa*. Freezing the facts at this point had its tactical disadvantages. Any doubt that the asylum seekers were 'detained' on the cargo boat would be resolved by looking at the even closer confinement by the Commonwealth that awaited them on the troopship. But that was the best deal the lawyers could get. The arrangement did not cover any final appeal to the High Court. The prospect of paying damages of million dollars a day would hover in the air to discourage the Melbourne lawyers from taking the case all the way.

I

The *Tampa* was tense next morning as Khan announced the transfer to the *Manoora*. 'We will go to Christmas', asylum seekers shouted. They learnt for the first time about the court case—it was one of the conditions of the deal struck the night before—and some on the deck remember Khan being 'very optimistic that the court would make a decision in our favour'. The soldier had plans of the new ship to show them. '*Manoora* was described as a ship with laundry, toilet and bathroom facilities with enough food and fruit provided, things that we were deprived of while we were on board the *Tampa*.' Khan made no threats of force but said, 'It will be better if you co-operate with us'. They knew they had no choice.[31]

The transfer began that afternoon at about 1.30 Christmas Island time. A wind was blowing but the seas were calm. Each survivor was counted off the *Tampa* by the SAS and Christian Maltau. Many asked to embrace the Norwegian. He said: 'There will be no hugging and kissing.' They were taken across to the *Manoora* twenty at a time in barges. Some of the boys held out at the very end. 'They said if we don't get off the *Tampa* we wouldn't be forced; then 10 or 15 minutes later they came to say they had permission from the government that if we didn't get off we would be forced and that they could do that straight away without any problem.'[32] The boys joined the last barge which left at 5.15 pm. Everyone was waiting on the helideck of the *Manoora* with new numbers around their necks. They took a last look at the *Tampa* and all 433 of them were led below. They say they did not see daylight again for over a week.

When the asylum seekers were safely out of the way and there was no longer any risk of them making last minute—and effective—pleas for asylum to the police, a detachment of AFP officers went out to the *Tampa*. Their mission was to arrest and gather evidence against the Indonesian crew of the *Palapa*. The Wilhelmsen Line was only too happy to see this happen, for the greed and incompetence of those Indonesians had put at risk the lives of hundreds of people. But when the police asked for access to the *Tampa*'s crew, James Neill saw an opportunity to lay to rest Australia's threats to prosecute the line. He negotiated a handwritten deal with Steve

Jackson, General Manager, Western Operations, Australian Federal Police, 'by which it is undertaken, on behalf of the Australian Federal Police and the Commonwealth of Australia, that these authorities would refrain from prosecution or the taking of any criminal or civil action against the Owners, Operators, Agents, Lawyers, Master and Crew in relation to the *TAMPA* associated events that occurred during the period 26 August to 3 September (inclusive)'.[33]

Close behind the police were Neill and the Norwegian ambassador. A little later, the Indonesian four were taken off the boat and into custody. The police interviewed the *Tampa*'s crew for a couple of hours and left about 7.15 pm. The soldiers, meanwhile, were cleaning up after the asylum seekers. Maltau approached the army doctor, Graeme Hammond, and asked for a written report on the medical situation on board the ship to send to Norway. According to the first officer, Hammond promised to provide one but never did so. 'The SAS were great, friendly, polite', said Maltau. 'But the doctor was a complete arsehole.'[34]

When the clean-up was complete, the SAS presented Rinnan with a framed map of Christmas Island, the destination he was never allowed to reach. The inscription read:

> To the master and company of the MV *Tampa*.
> Thanks for the friendship and assistance.
> 29 Aug–3 Sept 2001
> Regards
> (The Third Herd)
> SASR.

Rinnan gave the soldiers in return a Wilhelmsen Line flag signed by himself and the crew. There were no protestations of affection, but that may just have been the Scandinavian way.

Vance Khan was the last of the SAS to leave at a little after 10 pm. All this time, a strong offshore wind had been blowing the *Tampa* away from the island. Rinnan now ordered the engines full ahead and took his ship right up to the shore. Along the water's edge crowds had gathered to cheer and wave farewell. Neill could see Macca's rough bar on the edge of Flying Fish Cove 'really going off'. Then the fireworks began: the islanders' tribute to Rinnan and his ship. The captain watched this amazing scene from a makeshift bar set up by the crew. 'Everyone was smiling that night. We brought out some beer and we were using the whistle and turning off and on the lights on deck. We were very pleased to leave Christmas Island.'[35]

TEN
The thick grey line

SEPTEMBER 3 TO 10

At midnight on September 3, as the *Tampa* headed towards the Sunda Strait, three warships, ten patrol boats, a supply ship, one transport vessel, Seahawk helicopters and P-3C Orion surveillance aircraft were ready to blockade the Indian Ocean. The military operation was backed by the intelligence agencies, Coastwatch, the AFP, diplomats and officers of DIMA working to 'disrupt' the smuggling rings on the ground and track their boats once they left Indonesia. The launch of Operation Relex was a triumph for Max Moore-Wilton's ambitious 'whole of government' approach to prevent asylum seekers reaching Australia. The military presence he advocated in mid-1999 was finally in place in September 2001.

The navy always doubted Operation Relex could live up to the high hopes of Canberra's bureaucrats. 'Those of us who've spent time up there on maritime exercises know that ships can hide', said Admiral Chris Barrie. 'And they are very bloody hard to find.' And bureaucrats did not grasp the impact safety of life at sea rules would have on the navy. Barrie told them 'there are serious limitations on what we can do here. The first premise is: "No one is to lose their life."'[1]

In the frantic week it took to plan Operation Relex, Barrie explicitly warned the Prime Minister and the Defence Minister, Peter Reith, of the dangers of these operations. Naval blockades of refugees have been mounted often enough in the past fifty years for the Royal Australian Navy (RAN) to know the work is messy and dangerous. When military force is used to stop asylum seekers reaching their promised land, there will be threats of self-mutilation, suicide and sabotage. They will try to sink their own boats. Barrie had researched the most famous border protection operation in modern history, the British blockade of Jews making for Palestine before and after World War II. The British carried out sabotage in the ports, surveillance of the sea lanes and interception of boats which led to violent confrontations with refugees. According to Barrie, when the Royal Navy intercepted the SS *President Warfield,* 'The Jews had three men killed, two by cosh, one shot by a ship's Bren-gunner when in the act of shaping up to cleave a sailor with an axe. Twenty-eight were admitted to hospital [and] 200 treated for injuries on board'.[2] Afghans, Iraqis or Jews, it would make no difference: these people, having risked so much and come so far, would be absolutely desperate.

Rear Admiral Geoff Smith had on his staff at Maritime headquarters in Sydney an American naval intelligence officer who pointed him to accounts of violent clashes between the US coast guard and asylum seekers fleeing Haiti. Smith had little doubt the Australian operation would see the navy involved in the same sort of controversial, difficult and dangerous work. Smith believed the ships' commanders and their crews would face ugly encounters rarely seen except in war. 'We made the assessment that increasing levels of aggression and increasing levels of behaviour specifically designed to intimidate our sailors and specifically designed to place pressure on our moral and cultural values would be a manner in which some of these people would behave. That is what we anticipated and that is what we found.'[3]

Both Barrie and Smith were acutely aware of the navy's obligation to rescue those in peril at sea. How these people find themselves in trouble does not matter. What they are up to on the ocean is irrelevant. Even the enemy in wartime must be rescued from drowning. 'Ensuring the safety and preservation of life at sea is a fundamental mariner's skill', said Smith.[4] These old rules were spelt out in a number of conventions in the twentieth century and are known to both military and civilian shipping by the acronym SOLAS: Safety of Life at Sea. They are not vague humanitarian objectives. SOLAS rules are part of the law of Australia, absorbed into both the Navigation Act and the RAN's Maritime Commanders' Orders. They must be obeyed.[5]

Until now, the navy had been a bit player in this drama on the Indian Ocean. Under Operation Cranberry, patrol boats would occasionally intercept asylum seeker boats and escort them to Christmas Island, Darwin or other ports where the passengers could be processed as refugees. This raised no SOLAS issues. Boat people were 'invariably co-operative and compliant' said Smith. Navy boarding parties were able to work in 'a relatively benign environment'. But the admiral could see that would change under Relex. 'What was a law enforcement activity had real potential to rapidly escalate into a violent situation or just as quickly deteriorate into a major safety or preservation of life situation or, worse, both.' His orders for Relex included a direction to all commanding officers to 'take every reasonable means to achieve the mission without needlessly risking the safety and well-being of their ships' companies, their vessel and the lives of the unauthorised arrivals on board SIEVs [suspect illegal entry vessels]'. Smith was supported in this by Barrie and by Rear Admiral Chris Ritchie who said, 'We are talking about people coming to Australia illegally. It is not World War III'.[6]

But would Relex work? Stripped of all military jargon, Relex was a *show of force* designed to frighten people smugglers and asylum seekers—while impressing the Australian electorate. It was a military version of the tactics DIMA had tried against the *Tampa*. The same threats levelled at Rinnan would now be delivered from fighting ships of the Australian navy on the high seas. The threats were drafted by DIMA: 'Notice to master and crew. The Australian government considers people trafficking to be a very serious issue. The government of Australia is determined to stop illegal migration to its territory. It is an offence under the Australian Migration Act to bring to Australia non-citizens who do not have authority to come to Australia.' Jail sentences of ten years and fines of up to $110 000 for each member of the crew were then outlined with the advice that 'You should now consider immediately returning to Indonesia with your passengers and not enter Australian territory'.

If the warnings were ignored, the navy had orders to board the vessels as soon as they entered Australia's 'contiguous zone' 24 nautical miles from shore. The wheelhouse would be seized and the boat returned to the high seas. The rules of engagement and the levels of force the navy could use were a closely guarded secret. The confrontation with each boat would be micro-managed by Canberra. Smith said, 'Actions taken following boarding in each case were specifically directed by government'.[7]

The government and the navy were still treading warily. There was little doubt the blockade would provoke harsh criticism from the UNHCR in Geneva and there was no knowing how the Indonesian air force and navy would react to a huge build up in Australian surveillance and naval patrols so close to their waters. Nor was it clear how the Australian public would respond if any of these operations went badly wrong. The night before Relex began, John Howard went on *60 Minutes* to reassure the nation. 'Of course, we are Australian. We don't behave barbarically. We don't shoot people, we don't sink ships but our generosity should not be abused.'[8]

|

Admiral Chris Barrie, like many military men who rise to the top, was a political operator with antennae finely tuned to the wishes of his masters. He was already into his second term as Commander of the Defence Forces (CDF) and was hoping for another reappointment to the top job. By the time of Relex, Barrie had been CDF as Australian troops took a leading role in the United Nation's operation on East Timor and he had survived turmoil in the Department of Defence after the axing of its first civilian secretary—and his friend—Paul Barratt, and then the departure of his minister. Howard had eased John Moore out of the job to make way for the more gung-ho Peter Reith largely, according to Liberal Party sources, to have Reith in that portfolio for the election.[9] Defence played well for the Howard government and Reith was the kind of man who would make the most of any electoral opportunities defence presented in the election of 2001. Very quickly, Barrie forged a working relationship with the new minister but his deference to Reith and Howard left some of his senior officers uneasy.

On paper there was a clear line of command in Operation Relex. Immediately below Barrie was Rear Admiral Chris Ritchie, Commander Australian Theatre (COMAST), and below him came Rear Admiral Geoff Smith, who first planned and then commanded the operation. Reporting to Smith was an army man, Brigadier Mike Silverstone, Commander of Joint Taskforce 639 based at Northern Command in Darwin. He directed the conduct of the operation, devised the tactics and decided the disposition of the navy's ships.

But in reality, Operation Relex was closely directed by Jane Halton's People Smuggling Taskforce. This micro-managing of Relex would cause enormous tensions between the military and the civilian bureaucracy as every confrontation with the boats was debated in Canberra by Halton's group of public servants who in turn answered to Max Moore-Wilton, Reith and John Howard. The view of the military was that she had inserted herself into the chain of command without any experience of operational reality. She denied being in the chain of command and claimed simply to be acting on the direction of her political masters. But her position was crucial. As Smith explained, 'Once these vessels were intercepted in the early stages of Operation Relex, every decision that was taken in terms of what to do with that particular vessel and the people in it was in fact directed from Canberra. It is my understanding that that came out of the interdepartmental committee process and therefore, from our perspective, it was a government direction'.[10]

Unique arrangements had been made to pass information swiftly from the blockade back to the government. Smith was told 'that this was to occur to maximise time available for consideration and policy decision-making at the national strategic level'. He was to get on the phone and tell his immediate superior Ritchie 'when significant SIEV events occurred' and Ritchie was to make sure the information passed 'by the quickest means available' to Defence headquarters and thus to government.[11] A great deal would never be written down. Raw information would flow through to Canberra unchecked and unanalysed. Howard, Reith and their staffs would be in a unique position to know what was going on in the Indian Ocean—and put it to use—almost as it was happening.

At the same time, the government was taking extraordinary steps to keep information about Operation Relex from the public. Even before detailed planning for the blockade began, Peter Reith had imposed far tighter control of information flowing from the military. The same day in early August that the National Security Committee of Cabinet began to look at a military option to deter people smuggling, Reith called Barrie and the secretary of the Defence Department, Allan Hawke, to a meeting in his office. Reith put before them a sweeping plan to give his office control over the release of all military information to the public. Existing arrangements for the military to brief the press were hardly open and candid, but Reith's new proposal amounted to a change of culture. The military would now have to clear all media releases with Reith's press secretary, Ross Hampton. The military PR machine defined the new policy as 'no surprises for the minister's office'.[12]

Barrie claimed there was little room to argue against Reith at the meeting. 'There was quite a long discussion between Alan and me and the Minister on this set of issues. And the Minister directed that this was the way it would all happen.'[13] They caved in. So tight were these new Defence Instructions (General), that the media was now barred from Defence seminars and conferences except by special clearance. Any approaches by the media had to be reported to senior officers. One provision even barred military officers from providing any information to the public 'which could place in doubt their political impartiality or acceptance of the obligation to implement the policy of the elected government'. The no surprises rule was set out in black and white: 'It is important that the private offices of our Ministers and Parliamentary Secretary are informed well in advance of any activities with the potential to arouse public or media interest.'[14]

Barrie and Hawke signed up to the code but their troops were not happy. The new arrangements were cumbersome and slow. The expensive Defence public relations machine and its 100 or more civilian employees were disempowered. Some military men candidly called this what it was: censorship.[15] But journalists in the Canberra press gallery were so used to the Howard government's obsession with controlling information, that the new instruction aroused little comment. It was ten days before the first journalist—Ian McPhedran, defence writer for News Limited—reported these extraordinary restrictions. He was joined by a handful of perceptive journalists but the government's tight hold over military information did not become a matter of general public concern. There were no editorials thundering against political censorship, no evidence of proprietors complaining to the government, no protests from the Canberra press gallery. This very significant failure by the press allowed Reith to impose even tighter rules for Relex three weeks later.

The military's hands were not entirely clean. Military PR proposed a media campaign with a strong political focus 'to ensure that we adequately and effectively communicate government messages'.[16] The plan—prepared by Brian Humphreys, director general of communication strategies for the

Defence Department, his civilian boss Jenny McKenry and the head of military public relations, Brigadier Gary Bornholt—set out strategies for delivering the government's message to local and international audiences. 'The Australian domestic audience will be targeted to emphasise the "get tough" message and to engender public support for this action.' The international press would be targeted with the same message that 'Australia is now determined to protect its borders'. But the Humphreys plan assumed the military would carry out its traditional role of briefing the press on the 'operational and technical detail' of Operation Relex plus 'distribution of large amounts of supportive materials such as video footage and still photographs of ships and aircraft involved in the action'.[17]

Reith did not want that. When Humphreys brought the plan to the minister's office on September 2, Ross Hampton rejected it. 'Mr Hampton then outlined his preferred way forward. We immediately set in train mechanisms to deliver that.'[18] Once again, the military gave up without much fight. 'The proposal we put involved putting military officers in that loop in terms of the provision of information', said Humphreys. 'The alternative offered was that the information would be released through the minister's office.'[19] There would be no military briefings of the press and journalists would not be allowed to quiz military officers about Relex. Even the commanders of Relex—Barrie, Ritchie, Smith and Silverstone—were gagged. Every press enquiry to the military about the operation was to be bounced back to the minister's office. Though this was only a policing operation, the level of censorship would be tougher than the media was used to in wartime.

Ross Hampton also gave a direct instruction to Humphreys that no 'personalising or humanising images' were to be taken of asylum seekers. The intent of the instruction went further. 'Basically, we were told: do not take any photographs of asylum seekers.' Again the military gave up without a struggle, indeed without discussion. Humphreys explained: 'I was aware of earlier concerns expressed by Immigration regarding the identification of asylum seekers.'[20]

For over a decade, DIMA had imposed a regime of censorship over the detention camps using the rationale that a photograph in the papers might help asylum seekers make a refugee claim or put their families at risk back home. As a result, Australians had only the haziest picture of what life was like behind the wire in Port Hedland and Woomera. When the same argument was advanced to cover Operation Relex, the military accepted it without question. DIMA's concerns were not entirely without foundation but the press has any number of methods of photographing events without identifying individual people. The government's aim here was to make sure Relex was conducted out of sight. Months later, when the government needed to defend its conduct of the operation, videotapes of asylum seekers—in close up, clearly identifying them—would be released. In the end, dozens of hours of these tapes would be made public.

Ross Hampton, once an unexceptional ABC reporter, was now among the most powerful people in Canberra. He was the single conduit of information between the defence establishment and the Australian public and he would become a critical player in the election campaign. Hampton was given a special hotline to the military's Public Affairs and Communications Office (PACC). 'We knew if that phone rang it was coming from the minister's office', said one official. 'We knew there was a priority on that and we could act accordingly.'[21] An unquestioning loyalist to Peter Reith and to the government, Hampton would swing from politeness to aggressive anger in his dealings with the media and the military. Ultimately, he would refuse to give any information to reporters that posed a problem for the government. As the operation became mired in controversy in the weeks ahead, Hampton would thwart attempts to scrutinise Relex.

These controls proved immediately useful. Just as the navy predicted, the operation would not go smoothly. Nor was it conspicuously successful. Neither the people smugglers nor their passengers were easily deterred by the 'thick grey line' Australia was throwing across the Indian Ocean.

I

With Relex in place, Peter Reith and Philip Ruddock flew to Jakarta on Wednesday September 5. Downer joined them from London. The 'three amigos', as the Opposition dubbed them, had a great deal of work to do trying to repair the damage done to relations with Indonesia since the appearance of the *Tampa*—and to prevent things getting even worse now Australia was establishing a new military presence off the Indonesian coast. They also had a number of favours to ask. They wanted cheap fuel for Australian ships engaged in Relex. They wanted Jakarta to take the two steps Australia had long advocated to help beat the people-smuggling trade: to make it a crime and to set up a detention camp on some remote island where all the asylum seekers passing through Indonesia could be held. Howard had pushed the plan for the camp—to be paid for entirely by Australia—when he was in Jakarta three weeks earlier. Now, despite the abuse Canberra had been heaping on the Indonesian government over the *Tampa*, the three Australian ministers were pushing the idea all over again.

President Megawati's government was in no mood to barter with Australia. The meetings were a debacle. Megawati said she was too busy even to meet the ministers. Ruddock lived up to his nickname, The Minister with No Ears, offending Indonesian officials by lecturing them. Jakarta was still upset over local covert disruption operations being directed by Australia and also by Australia's use of the dubious undercover operative, Kevin Enniss. A high priority of the ministers was to try to get the protocol for co-operation between the AFP and the INP back on track. They failed. It was set aside by the Indonesians in the days immediately after the ministers' visit, though the INP agreed to continue to work co-operatively with the Australians on a case by case basis.[22]

Downer spoke of the 'constructive spirit' of his talks with Foreign Minister Hassan Wirajuda but there was, in reality, little prospect that Indonesia would help hold back the asylum seekers still waiting in cheap hotels across the archipelago for boats to take them to Australia. Despite Canberra's coaxing and offers of aid, Jakarta was not going to be part of either Operation Relex or the Pacific Solution. In a contemptuous gesture, the Indonesians sent an air force plane to buzz the navy's operations at Ashmore Reef.

The amigos were still in Jakarta when Relex faced its first test: the interception by HMAS *Warramunga* of the *Aceng* heading for Ashmore Reef. The *Warramunga* picked up the boat on its radar on the morning of September 7 and sent a Coastwatch plane to confirm it was indeed a SIEV. While the frigate stayed out of sight over the horizon, an inflatable boat (RHIB) was despatched to deliver DIMA's warnings to the skipper who 'acknowledged his understanding of the warning by nodding his head up and down'. Pamphlets warning against illegal migration entry were also handed across to the curious asylum seekers. The RHIB withdrew, the *Aceng* changed course briefly but then set course once again for Ashmore. The RHIB returned to deliver the warnings again. The *Aceng* simply kept going. Later in the afternoon, the warnings were delivered a third time. 'The SUNCs [Suspected Unauthorised Non Citizens] seemed to be getting frustrated with the apparent lack of help from the BP [Boarding Party] and kept asking for "Australia" in broken and good English.'[23]

The Iraqis had sailed in this small boat from Lombok, believing they were 'seeking a better future for our suffering families and to save them from their threatened life and to reach a place where there is basic human respect without discrimination of religion, colour, race and opinion.' Nearly half the 228 on board were children. Then after a week at sea, 'Military men in a rubber boat belonging to the Australian forces stopped us'.[24]

Richard Menhinick, the commander of the *Warramunga*, ordered his men to board the *Aceng* when it entered the Australian contiguous zone at sunset. The frigate was now standing close by. The sailors took control of the wheelhouse without difficulty and steered the *Aceng* back towards the high seas. The asylum seekers were 'relaxed and happy'.[25] After an hour, the *Aceng* was again at the edge of the contiguous zone and the boarding party left. The boat turned immediately for Ashmore again. An hour later, a second boarding party found a very worried Indonesian skipper gesturing that he feared his throat would be cut. 'The master continued to plead with me to turn back to the south or he would be killed', reported the commander of the boarding party, Lindsey Sojan. As the boat was again steered north, the asylum seekers grew restless and began to 'ask why they were not going to Australia as they had paid to go there and it was their dream and they would all die if they returned to Iraq'.[26]

As soon as the Australian sailors withdrew, the *Aceng* again turned for Ashmore. By now, HMAS *Newcastle* had joined the *Warramunga*. A third boarding took place after midnight. Both navy ships were 'highly visible and imposing', but this display of naval might was no help to the sailors trying to regain control of the *Aceng*. Women in the wheelhouse 'began crying and screaming hysterically . . . upon noticing the hand of Chief Petty Officer King on the wheel, one of the female SUNCs screamed and pinched the BP's hand until he released the wheel'. The commander of this boarding party, Peter Armitage, found fifteen asylum seekers hidden in the wheelhouse, many of them hysterical, while 'a number of visibly angry SUNCs managed to remove the centre window of the wheelhouse and begin to move in'. As the situation deteriorated, Armitage judged it would take 'medium to high force with possible lethal force' to secure the *Aceng*.

Menhinick gave permission for the boarding party to withdraw. 'The extraction was conducted well, albeit hurriedly.'[27]

For the next hour the *Aceng* continued to putter towards the reef at five knots escorted by a fully lit destroyer and frigate. At 2.30 am, the *Warramunga* turned a blaze of light on the *Aceng* and warned the asylum seekers they were approaching a dangerous reef. The boat was still outside Australian territorial waters. 'Negotiations began and the SUNCs agreed to remain in the area until sunrise in exchange for food, water and blankets.' The asylum seekers were told 'processing' would begin at first light. They had been tricked into thinking refugee processing was about to begin. A boarding party from the *Warramunga* took control of the *Aceng* peacefully a little after dawn on September 8. The Iraqis sat there, 'high waves throwing our humble boat'.[28] A few hours later they were scooped up by the passing *Manoora*. They were content, believing Australia was about to process them as refugees. They had no idea what voyage the ship was on.

I

Relex was not a great success at its first trial. Later that day, a press release from Ross Hampton put the best possible face on the story: 'The Royal Australian Navy has intercepted, and prevented reaching Australia's migration zone, a people trafficking boat.' True, but the navy was supposed to persuade people smuggling boats to turn around and go away. Instead, the *Aceng* cocked a snoot at two warships and kept sailing for Ashmore until persuaded to stop a little outside territorial waters. The navy was left to face the unanswered question of Operation Relex: how far could they go to persuade boats to turn around?

Unanswered legal questions were also troubling the military. Canberra's motto throughout these weeks was: Action First, Legislation Later. Lawyers from half a dozen departments had been involved in planning Relex. They shared the navy's worries about the dangers of the blockade—sabotage, self-harm and deaths would come as no surprise to them either—and they were also deeply concerned about the basis in law for carrying out Relex. Air Vice Marshal Al Titheridge, head of strategic command, prepared a brief for Jane Halton's taskforce setting out the unresolved legal issues a few days before the appearance of the *Aceng*. The lawful duty of service personnel was still to bring asylum seekers *into* the migration zone, not repel them. 'If they see a vessel in Australian territorial waters that they have reason to believe is a SIEV, they are obliged to board, detain and take it into the migration zone.' If a distress relay went out alerting shipping to a sinking SIEV, the navy would be obliged to go to its rescue. 'If the UBA vessel sinks, either by accident or design, they should normally be taken to the nearest port.'[29] That meant Australia.

No legislation authorised Canberra to repel boat people. The Border Protection Bill would have plugged that gap. When it failed, the government's lawyers were left with only one possible argument to justify Australia's dramatic new strategy of refusing to allow asylum seekers to land: that Canberra had inherited from Britain an ancient prerogative right to repel people at its borders. Legislation honed for decades directed civilian and military authorities to do exactly the opposite, but Canberra was claiming to exercise an old right to shut the door in anyone's face. The government's own lawyers placed little faith in this argument. However, David Bennett pursued the line before Justice North: if those people had indeed been detained by the SAS on the deck of the *Tampa*—which he denied—then their detention was justified as an exercise of this ancient power. The lawyers put the same argument to the military to justify them taking part in Operation Relex. The admirals thought it dodgy but they went along with it even though North was putting the finishing touches to his judgement and no one knew which way he would decide the issue.

Later on the day the *Aceng* arrived, John Howard flew to Washington for a much delayed audience with President Bush. Australian prime ministers are not alone in performing this White House ritual, but it mattered particularly for Howard with an election looming before Christmas. Before he flew out, he held a brief press conference at Sydney Airport to discuss the *Aceng* and thank 'the men and women of the Royal Australian Navy for the work that they've undertaken on behalf of the national interest on this particular occasion. It remains the determination of the government to do everything we can, both legally and decently, to deter people coming illegally to this country'.[30] He had a 'farewell bombshell': the government proposed cutting Ashmore and Christmas Island entirely from the migration zone. Even reaching land there would not entitle a boat person to ask for asylum. 'That will act as an additional deterrent', explained Howard. 'And I would ask the Labor Party and the Democrats to consider supporting our legislation, with effect from 2 o'clock this afternoon, when it comes before the parliament. That will be a matter for them but I would ask them to consider supporting the legislation. It is hardly unreasonable or draconian or unfair.'[31]

What lay behind this was a plan to turn Christmas Island into a holding centre from where asylum seekers could be despatched to camps in the Pacific—without rights of protection or recourse to Australian law. The model was Guantanamo Bay, Cuba, with this difference: Guantanamo was never United States soil and Christmas Island was still Australian territory. A spokeswoman for UNHCR in Canberra said the excision plan 'perverts the principles' of the refugee convention. 'We don't consider the fact that the Australian Migration Act may or may not apply to Christmas Island or Ashmore Reef is relevant from an international law perspective.' She added, 'We are concerned about what sort of precedent this might set'.[32] Canberra was unmoved. Beazley announced Labor would support the legislation. Commentators spluttered. 'The government has gone completely bananas, they've gone bonkers', said Dr Jean-Pierre Fonteyne, director of the Graduate International Law program at the Australian National University. 'It is completely ludicrous. There is no way whatsoever that that can be in accordance with international legality.'[33]

He was not alone in predicting a wave of international protest. Australia's delinquent attitude to refugees had been a world story for two weeks. Except for a few Tory tabloids in London and some extreme Right politicians on the Continent, Australia had been offered almost no public support. A rich country with few asylum seekers landing on its shores was having a hard time winning the world's sympathy. The international response had fundamentally been disgust and surprise. But none of that was about to matter. Australia's behaviour was to become no more than a subplot in suddenly dramatic times.

ELEVEN
The shadow of the Twin Towers

SEPTEMBER 11 TO 19

On the morning of September 11, John Howard returned from his early morning walk in Washington to find the Australian press corps waiting on the steps of his hotel, the old Willard a few blocks from the White House. They had news from home that Tony North had ordered the government to bring the asylum seekers ashore.

They had been unlawfully detained, North told the crowd and television cameras jammed into his Melbourne court. The government 'directed where the MV *Tampa* was allowed to go and not to go. They procured the closing of the harbour so that the rescuees would be isolated. They did not allow communication with the rescuees. They did not consult with them about the arrangements being made for their physical relocation or future plans'. North saw the Pacific Solution not as a way out for the asylum seekers but proof of their complete detention. 'After the arrangements were made the fact was announced to them, apparently not in their native language, but no effort was made to determine whether the rescuees desired to accept the arrangements. [They] took to themselves the complete control over the bodies and destinies of the rescuees.'[1]

The journalists wanted to know Howard's response. He deflected their questions. There would be a press conference at 9.30 am. He then disappeared into the hotel. Journalists gathered in the press room on the hotel's fourth floor waiting for the conference to begin saw on CNN two planes slam into the World Trade Centre. Howard appeared a few minutes later in shock. 'Can I just say, before I start on the domestic things, how horrified I am at what I've just heard regarding what's happened in New York. I don't know any more than anybody else but it appears to be a most horrific, awful event that will obviously entail a very big loss of life.' But he pulled himself together to announce his government had already appealed North's decision. 'We believe very strongly that these are matters that should be resolved by governments.' He hammered Labor and Beazley and the Democrats for rejecting his Border Protection Bill. 'I think they failed the national interest in doing that, failed it very badly indeed.'

Mark Jessop of Channel 9 was stationed outside the press conference waiting to film the Prime Minister's departure. Suddenly, a secret service man rushed past him into an adjoining room. Jessop followed and saw out the window that the Pentagon was on fire. Flight 77 had crashed into the building while Howard was talking. Jessop went back into the press conference and whispered news of the fire to several journalists. Howard was winding up with a few more digs at the Federal Court and Beazley. 'Well look, I don't know what the Opposition's position is, I really don't. I mean, it changes every day. I mean, he must exhaust himself running from one side of the road to the other.'

A few moments later, Howard was at the lifts surrounded by secret service men—some talking to their wrists, some talking to the Australian Prime Minister. What they said was inaudible but the journalists heard Howard ask, 'Where am I going?' He disappeared on his way to the basement of the Australian Embassy.

On September 11, terrorism became the defining threat facing the western world. Australia would soon join her allies in a war to overturn the regime the Afghan boat people were fleeing. John Howard would be handed the huge electoral advantage of being Prime Minister in wartime. He and his ministers would speak of a world utterly changed by September 11 but Canberra's priorities were curiously unaffected by the events in New York and Washington.

Intelligence chiefs in Canberra immediately began switching their priorities to focus on the terrorist threat at home and abroad. But even after September 11, Australia's intelligence effort in Jakarta would remain strongly focused on people smuggling. This was despite consistent reports from the United States embassy in Jakarta that the terrorist group al-Qaeda was active in Indonesia. The then US ambassador, Bob Gelbard, told the Australian embassy of a plot to attack the United States mission in July that year. There had also been a terrorist attack on the home of the Philippines ambassador in Jakarta, on churches and on the Jakarta stock exchange.[2]

Australia's military chiefs were also told to keep their eye on the main game—people smuggling—even though Howard invoked the ANZUS treaty after September 11 and was one of the first allied leaders to pledge military support for the United States. With the War Against Terror looming, the military was less enthusiastic about its mission against people smugglers in the Indian Ocean. But Operation Relex remained a top priority with Howard. The military was told that Australia's commitments to the war in Afghanistan did not have to jeopardise the blockade of boat people. One of the most senior commanders of Relex said, 'The war on terrorism was there, but in our priority sense Relex was still on top'.[3]

I

Even while Tony North was working on his judgement, the Chief Justice of the Federal Court, Michael Black, was preparing behind the scenes for the inevitable appeal. Two of the most senior available judges were ready to join him on the case as soon as North's decision was known. One was Robert French, an intellectual heavyweight on the court; the other was crusty, irascible Bryan Beaumont, who left a native title case in Perth to fly over to Melbourne for the *Tampa* appeal as soon as North brought down his decision. The three men were at work on the documents next day and the appeal itself was heard one day later, on September 13. Black's court was a confused scene of barristers, books, trolleys and spectators but there were no television cameras as there had been in North's court. There was a peculiar tension in the air: great issues were at stake, so much of the legal territory being explored was abstract and unfamiliar, so much needed to be said—yet there was so little time. Just one day.

Did it have to be so swift? One of the key strategies of the government in the *Tampa* operation was to convince people everything must be done in a rush. It kept events moving, fed the sense of crisis and wrong-footed the government's opponents. North had refused to be hurried. The appeal might have turned out very differently if the court had again taken its time. But the pressure on the Federal Court was immense. Looming in the background were years of accusations by Howard and his ministers that the court was improperly standing in the government's way. This hostility had climaxed in the remarkable provisions of the Border Protection Bill. Howard was now sending the same, familiar message from Washington. 'This is a matter that relates to the integrity of Australia's borders and the integrity of our borders is surely a matter for the democratically elected government.'[4] The Federal Court's reply was: no, we do have a role here but we will be quick about it.

So the *Tampa* case came back to court in the atmosphere of heightened threat surrounding September 11. The morning of the appeal, talkback radio was alive with the idea that the terrorists of New York were linked to the Muslim asylum seekers forcing their way into Australia. Ever since the *Tampa* appeared, Howard and his ministers had been arguing that Australia was involved in a kind of war to protect its borders, with the right to take tough action that wars allow. September 11 seemed to make sense of that fierce rhetoric. The Solicitor General exploited the moment ruthlessly. 'Today, invasions don't have to be military', David Bennett told the judges. 'They can be of diseases, they can be of unwanted migrants.' The government must have power to protect Australia from the sort of people 'who did what happened in New York yesterday'.[5]

North had left the government in a stronger position than it first seemed. He had accepted the argument that only an asylum seeker from the *Tampa* could contest Canberra's failure to obey the Migration Act. There was no lawyer in his court with a client on the ship. Vadarlis and Liberty Victoria had no standing to complain because they were not asking to be brought ashore and put into migration detention. So, in the end, Canberra did not have to defend its strategy of ignoring the Migration Act. This was a considerable victory for the government's strategy of isolating the asylum seekers from DIMA officials, from police, from civilian doctors, from anyone at all who could accept an asylum plea—and especially from the *pro bono* lawyers looking for clients. That left only one question for the appeal judges to reconsider: were the asylum seekers unlawfully detained on the deck of the *Tampa*?

The Solicitor General, David Bennett, now returned to the only argument Canberra had up its sleeve: that it did not need legislation to do what was done to the asylum seekers on the *Tampa* because there was an ancient prerogative power allowing the government to repel people at the border even in peacetime. Bennett had to convince the three appeal judges first that this prerogative survived in modern Australia and, second, that it had not been superseded by the exhaustive provisions of the Migration Act.

The judges were difficult to read. Beaumont held fire for a few hours then peppered both sides with cantankerous, eccentric questions. At times he seemed unable to grasp the details of the trial before North. His sympathies appeared to be with the government. Black and French were calmer, more opaque and certainly listening to the argument pursued by Gavan Griffith and Julian Burnside. Their argument was this: the Migration Act is the only source of authority the government has to deal with asylum seekers because parliament designed it to take over entirely from the old prerogative. As the Migration Act says nothing about closing Australia to asylum seekers, putting them in military detention and sending them away to islands in the Pacific, the asylum seekers from the *Tampa* must be released and brought ashore. Burnside argued it would be bizarre to allow the Crown to decide, on a case by case basis, whether to operate under the Migration Act or exercise the prerogative. 'You would then have rights displaced at the whim of the executive, people being dealt with at the whim of the executive and either with or without statutory protection, depending on what view the executive took of the particular case.'

Bennett waited until late in the day to play the September 11 card. All sides agreed Canberra could act as it wished to repel enemy aliens in wartime. But what about friendly aliens like asylum seekers in peacetime? Bennett's argument was perfectly tuned to a world facing terrorist threat. He declared 'quaint, old-fashioned' the distinction between friendly and enemy aliens. 'All wars since 1945 virtually have been fought without declarations of war.' He asked the judges to suppose a vessel arrived in port with terrorists and weapons on board. 'There's no state of war. They're friendly aliens, as far as the cases define them. The people who did what happened in New York yesterday were friendly aliens as a matter of law.' Black interrupted him: 'One would expect that such persons could be stopped. But what's the power?' Bennett replied: 'That has to be under the prerogative.'

At about 6 o'clock the three judges left the bench for 20 minutes. When they returned, the Chief Justice announced they had given themselves three days to make up their minds. 'It will be our aim to deliver judgement at some time on Monday in Melbourne.'

I

More boats were heading for Australia. Despite all the resources of Operation Relex, the KM *Ratna Mujia* was only discovered after it ran aground on Ashmore Reef.[6] The navy sent HMAS *Gawler* to take a look at the boat now designated SIEV 2, and found 132 Afghans crammed into a small fishing boat 'in very poor condition with very few provisions (contaminated by vermin) remaining on board and only a small quantity of water'.[7] Though they were stuck fast on the reef, Canberra would claim the boat had come aground just short of the low water mark, so these asylum seekers never quite entered the migration zone.

They were transferred to the empty *Aceng* moored in the lagoon, while the navy worked to refloat the SIEV and repair its engines in the hope that it might take these people back to Indonesia. The weather was hot and still. The hulk of the *Aceng* was extremely crowded. Tensions rose next day and by mid afternoon, a group of four or five asylum seekers was threatening to jump overboard if they were forced to return to Indonesia. There were demands for interpreters and access to the media. Tempers cooled overnight but by the following afternoon the asylum seekers were 'refusing all assistance except medical with some threatening suicide and hunger strikes if taken anywhere other than Australia'.[8] Again, tempers cooled.

If this had been a United States operation in the Caribbean, authorities would have sorted roughly through the passengers by now to find who might have a claim to refugee status. Only those with no hope would be sent directly back to sea. But that sort of immigration triage was never part of Operation Relex. Admiral Smith explained: 'The status of these people was irrelevant as far as I was concerned. They were unauthorised arrivals and we were dealing with them in that context... My job was not to differentiate, my job was to intercept and to enforce the government policy.'[9]

While hunger strikes were threatening in the lagoon, HMAS *Warramunga* was a few miles away working to turn back another boat, the KM *Sumber Bahagia*. This big wooden coastal freighter flying the Indonesian flag now designated SIEV 3 had ignored three warnings the previous night and kept steaming for the reef. When it entered the contiguous zone, a boarding party of thirteen sailors from the *Warramunga* took control of the wheelhouse and headed it back out to sea. Most of the people on board were women and children: 28 women and 54 children on the upper deck and 47 men in the hold. They were all Iraqis and had been at sea for five days since leaving Lombok. The only navigation equipment on board was a very old magnetic compass. There was no radio. Food was low but there were thirty boxes of bottled water. Once the boat reached the edge of the high seas at about dawn, the sailors returned to their RHIB. The operation had gone without incident.

As soon as the sailors were out of sight, SIEV 3 headed south again. When the RHIB returned to issue fresh warnings, asylum seekers shouted that the boat was 'broken' and there was 'one sick pregnant lady' on board who needed attention. Even so, the skipper headed the SIEV vaguely in the direction of Indonesia with the *Warramunga* tailing him over the horizon. By mid afternoon, the *Warramunga*'s commander, Richard Menhinick, could see the boat was lost and its passengers at risk. So, at about 4 pm, he sent a chart over showing the boat's position and the course it should steer to Indonesia. The sailors on the RHIB reported the boat's skipper 'gestured with his hand his throat being cut indicating he was not safe. The PIIs [potential illegal immigrants] were becoming more and more agitated with women and children crying'. The sailors returned to the *Warramunga* at which point the SIEV—with the help of the chart—turned once again towards Ashmore. Menhinick noted: 'The master had totally ignored my advice, warnings of prosecution and the courses drawn on how to return to Indonesia.'[10]

By now it was nearly dark. Menhinick sent two boarding parties over to take control of the SIEV and as the first sailors climbed on board, 'one female PII was seen holding a child over the side and threatening to throw the child over the side'. It was an ugly but empty threat sailors were to be faced with many times over the coming weeks. They swiftly secured the deck and the engine room but the way to the wheelhouse was blocked by angry Iraqis. The sailors disabled the wheel and steered the boat from the deck. Once the course changed, the asylum seekers became very aggressive. Two of the three large kitchen knives found earlier in the day had disappeared from the galley. The boarding party commander reported: 'The situation continued to worsen with all the male PIIs starting to riot and threaten the BP as a mass. I assessed that the situation could not be controlled without the use of high force and possible lethal force.'[11] Permission was granted to withdraw. The *Warramunga* blasted its siren 'for a prolonged period' and bathed the SIEV in searchlights. The asylum seekers could be seen rioting among themselves.[12]

The night was dark and there was no moon. The SIEV was heading for dangerous reefs and Menhinick decided the safest course was to guide it into Ashmore Lagoon. Through his loudspeakers he ordered the SIEV to follow him but the boat refused to comply. Lieutenant Commander Simon Gregg took a RHIB alongside and negotiated for an hour and a half. The skipper was clearly not in control and there was no leader among the asylum seekers. The SIEV was a scene of shouting, confusion and anger. Menhinick reported, 'The final demand from them and the only consistent one in the end was for them to embark in *Warramunga*'. He agreed. By this time, the reef was only one nautical mile ahead and 'there were 54 children on board the SIEV with no lifejackets'.[13] The transfer began at about 11 pm and took nearly three hours. The Iraqis were searched—nothing was found—given numbers and photographed. The *Warramunga* headed to a spot just outside the lagoon with the empty Indonesian boat trailing behind.

By the morning of 13 September—the day of the appeal in the Federal Court—the navy had nearly a thousand asylum seekers on its hands. Those from the *Tampa* and *Aceng* were on board the *Manoora* heading for Nauru; those from SIEV 2 were waiting in Ashmore Lagoon; and the Iraqis from SIEV 3 were camped on the quarter deck of the *Warramunga*. Negotiations continued all day to persuade the Iraqis to return to their own boat. Finally, they agreed and in the early evening SIEV 3 steamed into the lagoon and anchored some distance from the Afghans. For the next ten days both groups of asylum seekers sat on the lagoon while their fate was decided.

The Afghans had settled down and apologised for their earlier outbursts. One confessed that 'tiredness often results in them saying things they don't mean'.[14] Their old boat—assessed by the navy as beyond repair—had been lashed to the *Aceng* to give them more room to move. Conditions were still terrible. 'We were eating expired date food', the people of the SIEV 2 wrote in a joint statement. 'We were having raw rice. Some of women and children and men got ill. Some people fainted. We were suffering from burning sun during the day and from freezing cold in the night time. We could not sleep because of the cold.'[15] For half an hour each day, the sailors allowed them to take a dip in the lagoon. A security team watched to see that no one swam ashore. Ashore was their goal: the migration zone of Australia.

I

Peter Reith was on Nauru horse-trading with Rene Harris when these new arrivals on SIEV 2 reached Ashmore. He persuaded the president to add them to the asylum seekers Nauru had already agreed to put in detention on the island. With the numbers blowing out, Reith put a new spin on the island's role in the Pacific Solution: 'People will come in and some people will go out and then other people will come in. So you'll have, you know, you'll have an in-and-out situation.' Harris was clearly happy enough but made noises about needing to consult his fellow parliamentarians about fresh arrivals.[16] The final deal with Nauru was done in three face-to-face meetings over 24 hours and signed at a steamy outdoor ceremony on September 10 before Reith jumped back into his RAAF jet and headed home to Australia.

A village by the sea built with Taiwanese money for an international weight-lifting championship was to be the main camp for the detainees. The championship had been another Nauruan flop and the abandoned village was left unsewered so there was work to be done. Some detainees would be put in tents on the neglected Topside sports oval in the bleak centre of the island. The infrastructure, the staff and the running costs were to be supplied and paid for by Australia. Facing the press back home, Reith tried to muffle the fact that the asylum seekers would actually be imprisoned on Nauru. When Harris made it clear they would be, Reith declared, 'I believe this is a humane response to a difficult issue'.[17]

Australia was already searching the Pacific for more islands on which to park boat people. New Zealand had signalled the limits of its generosity by declining to take any of the *Aceng* people. The remote, poor republic of Kiribati was offering one of its scattered atolls in return for an 'assistance' package. Kanton boasted two families, very little water, no electricity, a small wharf and an old airstrip left over from the Second World War. Canberra was interested. Canberra also made soundings in the tiny island states of Palau and Tuvalu. Fiji, still in a fragile condition after the coup of 2000, was also on Australia's list. Informal approaches were made to France for a site in French Polynesia and to the Kingdom of Tonga. But the most serious approaches were being made in great secrecy to Australia's principal client-state in the region, Papua New Guinea.

Now back in Australia, Reith was adding his weight to popular alarm that terrorists might be lurking among the asylum seekers. David Bennett was saying the same thing in the Federal Court, but Reith lent his authority as Minister for Defence to these claims in four separate radio interviews on the same day. Intelligence experts ridiculed the idea: why put terrorists on people smuggling boats knowing they will end up in immigration detention, perhaps for years, while their identities are scrutinised? But Peter Reith did not hesitate. His spin was extremely skilled. Might 'Bin Laden appointees' be hiding among the boat people, asked Derryn Hinch of 3AK. 'We shouldn't make assumptions about that', replied the minister. 'But there is a simpler, broader point to make and it was made by Jim Kelly the Assistant Secretary of State, the number two bloke to Colin Powell responsible for our region when he was in Jakarta only ten days ago and he said . . . you've got to be able to manage people coming into your country. You've got to be able to control that otherwise it can be a pipeline for terrorists to come in and use your country as a staging post for terrorist activities.'[18]

Jane Halton's committee was juggling all these issues: the Federal Court case, the new arrivals on Ashmore, intelligence on fresh boat departures, the logistics of establishing detention camps on Nauru, negotiations with PNG, hunger strikes among the Iraqis on the *Manoora* and the preparation of a bundle of immigration Bills to be put to parliament as soon as the Federal Court decided the Liberty Victoria/Vadarlis case. The men and women on the taskforce had never experienced a rolling crisis of such uninterrupted intensity, week after week. From time to time, Max Moore-Wilton would stroll into the meetings to demand answers 'otherwise you'll have egg on your faces'. Halton was ridiculed by one of the taskforce as 'the dachshund barking on her mobile'. Tempers were frayed.

The new legislation was designed to gut the remaining rights of asylum seekers who turn up in Australia uninvited. Once Christmas Island, Ashmore Reef and Cocos Island were excised entirely from the migration zone, boat people arriving at these remote points could be detained and removed by force to another country. This would be the legislative underpinning of Operation Relex. Asylum seekers on boats that made it all the way to the mainland might, in time, become Australians but not if they stopped along the way in any country—such as Indonesia—that could grant them 'effective protection'. Essentially, the thousands of would-be refugees waiting in cheap hotels in Jakarta for a smuggler's boat to Australia would now never have a permanent, secure home in Australia and the only family who could join them there would be the wives and children they brought with them on the boats.[19]

Seizing the moment, the government would try to break Labor's four-year opposition to the Bill designed to end the last court scrutiny of migration decisions.[20] Another new Bill would narrow the concept of persecution which stands at the heart of refugee law.[21] Petro Georgiou, the Liberal member for the prosperous Melbourne seat of Kooyong and a former director of the Australian Institute of Multicultural Affairs, attacked the Bill in the Liberal's party room for being 'the first time a Western nation had moved to tighten the definition of refugee status'. Georgiou declared the world would see Australia abandoning its standing as a humanitarian nation. 'Jews fleeing Nazi Germany would have been denied entry into Australia under the Howard Government's tighter rules on asylum seekers.' Small changes were made to the bill.[22] The courts had been too generous, said Ruddock, encouraging people 'who are not refugees to test their claims in Australia, adding to the perception that Australia is a soft touch'.[23]

The last crucial Bill in the government's bundle would declare lawful everything Canberra had done in relation to the *Tampa*, the *Aceng* and the two SIEVs still waiting in the Ashmore Lagoon. Though not as extreme as the failed Border Protection Bill, this was still a unique proposal to retrospectively exclude the scrutiny of the courts.[24] It was designed to stop the asylum seekers taking any action at law, prevent the Wilhelmsen Line from suing the Commonwealth and snuff out the case brought by Liberty Victoria and Eric Vadarlis. It was to be kept under wraps until the Federal Court decided the appeal. If the government won, it would make an appeal to the High Court all but impossible. If the government lost—and the law officers believed that that was the way things were shaping—then the legislation would reverse the court's decision at a stroke. Such action is not often contemplated by a democracy.

The court scattered the day after the hearing. Justice Beaumont flew back to Perth for the examination of a dying witness in the native title case and did not return. The Chief Justice Michael Black flew to Sydney for the funeral of a young and brilliant judge, John Lehane. Ansett Airlines was collapsing and Black's plane was delayed by industrial action on the tarmac at Mascot. He reached the church just in time and flew straight back to Melbourne to work through the weekend with Robert French. They were under extreme pressure to meet their own deadline, for the *Manoora* was expected to reach Nauru on Monday. The judges were receiving death threats. These were passed onto the police. Whenever they were out of the court building, Black and French kept their mobile phones with them. Their staff always knew where they were. At lunchtime on Saturday, the two judges walked up William Street and found—not entirely by accident— a pleasant place to eat near the Victoria Markets which turned out to be an Afghan restaurant.

These old friends found themselves on opposite sides of the case. They tussled with the issues all weekend. Black was for releasing the asylum seekers. He did not believe Canberra had any prerogative power to send them away. The power had died in Britain even before Europeans reached Australia. It was last used to close the ports to Jews fleeing France in the early 1770s. A century later, when there was a popular clamour—but no law—to forbid Chinese passengers on the SS *Afghan* from landing in Sydney, the great judge Sir William Windeyer had declared the government of NSW could only 'exclude foreigners from landing if they come infected with disease, or in such vast and overwhelming numbers as really to threaten danger to our liberties, though they should come in peaceful guise.' It was not enough to raise the spectre of 'half a million of Chinese' ready to flood the colony of NSW: the Chinese on the *Afghan* presented 'no impending danger to the country'.[25]

Black had no doubt the asylum seekers were indeed detained on the deck of the *Tampa*: 'The conclusion is inevitable that, viewed as a practical, realistic matter, the rescued people were unable to leave the ship that rescued them on the high seas.' Nor was the *Tampa* able to sail with them still on board: 'It is hard to see how in a practical sense Captain Rinnan was free to leave.'[26] Black could find no lawful basis for their detention and proposed to uphold North's decision ordering their release and directing the government to bring them ashore.

But French did believe the power to shut the border existed, not as an ancient surviving prerogative but as a sovereign power embedded in the Constitution, allowing Australia 'to determine who may come into its territory and who may not and who shall be admitted into the Australian community and who shall not'. That conclusion would not help the government unless French also believed there was room for the exercise of the power outside the confines of the Migration Act. Here French showed a capacity for judicial activism that would, in other circumstances, have infuriated Canberra. He declared the government's independent power to police Australia's borders must have survived unless prohibited by the 'clear words' of parliament. French conceded there was nothing in the Migration Act to authorise the government to do what it had done, but there was nothing forbidding it either. 'The steps taken in relation to the MV *Tampa* which had the purpose and effect of preventing the rescuees from entering the migration zone and arranging for their departure from Australian territorial waters were within the scope of executive power.'[27]

Beaumont supported the government for arcane reasons of his own. But he also backed French. Neither man thought the asylum seekers had been detained at all on the *Tampa* even by a ring of SAS soldiers. Beaumont was for allowing the government almost untrammelled power to protect the border. French was more circumspect. He compared the power he had identified in the Constitution to the defence power of the Commonwealth: 'it will vary according to circumstances'.[28] The particular circumstances of these days were not canvassed by either judge, but only the spectre of September 11 makes sense of the unprecedented notion that Canberra could ignore its own laws and repel the friendly aliens rescued by Arne Rinnan.

For some hours on Monday September 17, the judges still hoped they could finish writing their judgements in time to meet their own deadline. But at a certain point it became clear this was not going to happen and the lawyers were summoned at 4.15 pm to hear Black deliver the bare verdict of the court. The room was extremely crowded and the Chief Justice refused to appear until everyone was seated. Attendants rushed back and forth filling the aisles with chairs. Black then entered and announced the outcome without flourish. 'By a majority, comprising Justices Beaumont and French, the Court has determined that the appeals should be allowed and has set aside the decisions made by Justice North.' Black was heading for the door as Griffith rose to thank the court. The government lawyers shook hands and murmured congratulations to one another for this considerable win. Outside in William Street, Eric Vadarlis wept and declared there was now an 'open game on refugees. If they come near our shores, the government is going to push them out, tow them out, drag them out. I can't believe this is happening in this country'.[29]

As David Bennett left the court, he remarked that the Commonwealth would want its costs. Vadarlis and Liberty Victoria would face a bill of about $70 000. The *pro bono* lawyers were astonished. In cases like this—when great public issues are at stake, lawyers are working for no fee, novel questions of law have been explored and the judges are divided—a victorious Commonwealth usually bears its own costs. Justice French would praise these *pro bono* lawyers for acting 'according to the highest ideals of the law. They have sought to give voices to those who are perforce voiceless and, on their behalf, to hold the Executive accountable for the lawfulness of its actions. In so doing, even if ultimately unsuccessful in the litigation they have served the rule of law and so the whole community'.[30] That was very far from Canberra's view. The Attorney General, Daryl Williams, declared Vadarlis and Liberty Victoria would be made to pay because taking their case to court was 'from a government perspective, promoting unlawful activity'.[31]

I

That night Philip Ruddock and Jane Halton took the new border protection legislation to Beazley. The fight had gone out of Labor. The party had decided to pass *all* the immigration Bills, old and new, that would be presented to parliament next day. Beazley seemed hardly interested as Ruddock and Halton took him through the provisions of the retrospective validation of the Bill. 'I started a cursory reading of it and could see a very different kettle of fish', said Beazley. He was not perturbed that everything done to the people on the *Tampa*, the *Aceng*, and the two boats still moored in Ashmore Lagoon would be put beyond the reach of the courts. 'Nobody had been killed or beaten up or hurt in any way . . . beyond a bit of jostling there hadn't been anything of a particularly underworld character.'[32]

When Labor's capitulation was reported, the phones began ringing again in party offices across the country. Callers were shouting, sobbing and hysterical. 'How could Labor do this?', they yelled, slamming down the phone. Holocaust survivors rang to tell their life stories in terrible detail. Staffers were given fresh lines of spin each morning to help cope with the calls. They didn't do much good. Candour seemed to work best: 'I know. I think it's terrible, too. But, please, hang in there.' Of course there were others among the Labor faithful who were thrilled by this development. Staffers had no idea before they answered each call if they would be dealing with tears and pleading or triumphant congratulations. Labor veterans could not remember a time when the rank and file had been ambushed by such contradictory passions.

Liberty Victoria looked at the new border protection legislation and threw in the towel. Two judges including the Chief Justice of the Federal Court had taken Liberty's side but there was no point appealing to the High Court. 'The Federal Government—aided by the Labor opposition—is about to do what no other litigant in the same position could do—wave the legislative magic wand and validate conduct which, in the view of two judges of the Federal Court was unlawful', said Liberty Victoria, announcing its decision to quit. 'Due process of law should have been allowed to proceed to its conclusion, so that these issues could be ventilated in Australia's supreme court.'[33]

Eric Vadarlis and his team would bat on as much as anything to challenge the constitutionality of the new legislation which his lawyers, the former solicitor general Gavan Griffith and the eminent Jack Fajgenbaum saw as obnoxious to the rule of law. They were not able to hold the asylum seekers on the *Manoora* while they waited for the High Court to find time to hear their appeal. In the end they were beaten because the story had moved on: the people rescued by the *Tampa* would soon no longer be in Australian hands and no Australian court could order their release.[34]

The Melbourne lawyers were the government's last real opponents. They joined a distinguished list of those who had tried and failed to restrain Canberra: the United Nations, the government of Norway, the Wilhelmsen Line, legal commentators, human rights advocates and a few brave politicians—Greens and Democrats in the Senate, Peter Andren in the House of Representatives and one or two courageous but powerless members of the Liberal and Labor Party caucuses. The agility, resilience and daring the Coalition government had shown in out-manoeuvring these forces must be acknowledged. So must the fact that in the end the key to the government's success was the collaboration of the Opposition.

With the case won and the likelihood of an appeal crushed, the government's prospects now depended on the smooth execution of Operation Relex and the Pacific Solution. The next challenge would be the unloading of the *Manoora* for the troopship had reached Nauru.

TWELVE
The voyage of the Manoora

SEPTEMBER 3 TO OCTOBER 8

John Howard never promised to put the people taken from the *Tampa* into the soldiers' quarters on HMAS *Manoora*. The Prime Minister praised the facilities on board. 'Australian troops often spend weeks on that vessel', he told *60 Minutes*. 'Nobody can suggest that if these people are on it for a number of days that they're being treated in an inhumane, uncivilised fashion.' He told Kofi Annan, 'conditions on the *Manoora* are as comfortable as they can be, given that it is a large troopship'. He sent his solicitor general into Tony North's court to announce a 'large troopship with medical facilities on board' was waiting to take these people away. Howard's words played their part in convincing the *pro bono* lawyers it would be inhumane to keep the asylum seekers any longer on the deck of the Norwegian cargo boat. But no one noticed that John Howard wasn't promising these people would live where the troops lived on the ship. On the afternoon of September 3, the 433 asylum seekers took a last look at Christmas Island before being led below and locked into the *Manoora*'s garage, the 'tank deck' which usually held tanks and trucks. Admiral Smith explained, 'In that way we could keep them contained'.[1]

The *Manoora* was pressed into service on its way to Bangkok where its sailors were hoping to have a few days break after two tours of duty in the troubled Solomon Islands. The ship is a floating heliport, lightly armed and one of its functions is 'protection and evacuation of Australian nationals in the region in the event of serious civil disturbances.'[2] The *Manoora* was taking the asylum seekers only as far as Port Moresby so as to stay as close as possible to the Solomons where further violence and mayhem was expected. Also embarking on the ship at Christmas Island were the SAS troops under Major Khan and three or four members of the International Organisation for Migration (IOM) who would register the Afghans during the voyage. The New Zealand Immigration Service joined them at some later point to choose the families, single women and unaccompanied minors who would be flown to Auckland. The *Manoora* was in no rush to reach Port Moresby, for the asylum seekers would have to remain on board until the Australian courts had finished with them.

Transhipping the asylum seekers through PNG was part of a larger deal Canberra wanted to strike with Sir Mekere Morauta's government that would include a holding camp for asylum seekers in some remote corner of the country. Australia had its eye on the Lombrum naval base on Manus Island near the Equator. The Australian High Commissioner, Nick Warner, sold the idea to PNG as a solution to its own problems with foreign smugglers, illegal loggers, fish poachers and gun runners. Australia would use the camp for six months, after which PNG would have a secure, remote facility for detaining unwanted foreigners. Discussions with PNG were being held in the context of a $20 million promise Canberra had made to fund reform of the country's armed forces. The Howard government would later claim the two issues were quite separate but observers of the negotiations confirm the deals were being done together.[3]

Life on the tank deck was hard for the Afghans. There was no daylight, no relief from the stinking heat or the incessant noise from the engines, no privacy and nothing much to do but queue. 'We were always in a queue—food queue, toilet queue or bathroom queue.' They had been given clothes, a toothbrush, toothpaste, soap and a towel for every two people to share. They had access to three bathrooms from ten at night until six in the morning. Three minutes per shower. There seemed to them very little to eat. The sailors were brusque when children lost their numbers. 'They would say to them you are the last one to get your food because you lost your number. They were children. You can't police them all the time.' They begged to be allowed out on deck. After eight or ten days, the IOM officers persuaded the soldiers to allow the Afghans onto the helideck for a couple of hours twice a week. For those who had left their shoes on the *Palapa*—most of them—the deck was often too hot to walk on. Yet, for all these difficulties, they seemed to bear with the voyage patiently. They are patient people and they had some hope that the court case would soon deliver them to Australia. Assadullah Rezaee said, 'We were happy in some ways and thankful for that'.[4]

After four days at sea, the *Manoora* rendezvoused at sunrise with the *Warramunga* in international waters near Ashmore Reef and scooped up the 229 Iraqis from the *Aceng*. They had been tricked into thinking refugee processing would begin once they climbed aboard. Sub Lieutenant Lindsey Sojan of the *Warramunga* explained how the deception was done. 'They were informed they may go onto a large military vessel (*Manoora*) for further processing and a safe passage . . . the destination of their passage was not determined.' They climbed aboard the *Manoora* thinking they were on their way to Australia. 'When we saw the Australian flag on the *Manoora*, we were relieved. We thought that the flag will protect us from now on, particularly as we were told by some Australians that the ship will be heading for Darwin.'[5]

The Iraqis were held all day on the helideck while they were thoroughly searched and given numbers. The navy did not wish to mix the Iraqis with the Afghans, so the new arrivals were locked into the air-conditioned dormitories on the 'mess' deck which had been denied to the asylum seekers from the *Tampa*. The two groups were kept absolutely apart. Indeed, it was not until the last days of the voyage that they became aware of each other's presence on the ship. The now very crowded *Manoora*—with over 600 asylum seekers, a detachment of SAS and 180 sailors on board—sailed to the edge of Australian territorial waters near Darwin on September 9 and took on fresh supplies. Two RAN heavy landing craft, a civilian tender and the *Manoora*'s helicopters loaded 150 tonnes of fresh and frozen food, medical supplies, aviation spares, bedding, dry stores, waste bins, and all necessary safety equipment for everyone on board.[6] There seemed no limit to the budget for the Pacific Solution.

The Iraqis were difficult all the way. Within three days, they were on hunger strike. They refused to co-operate with IOM officials. They brawled amongst themselves. There was absolutely nothing for them to do either but queue, sleep, pray and fret. Later, they wrote an angry account of their weeks on the *Manoora* for Amnesty International. They complained about the food: 'Food supply was unimaginably low, very bad quality, some was outdated and it was distributed in an insulting manner sometimes.' About health: 'Generally the health situation deteriorated, specially for those with long term diseases . . . some dangerous diseases started to spread such as malaria, liver virus, skin diseases. There was one special day for treating skin diseases only. We were not subject to the sun for a long period which extended more than two days and on many occasions.' About children: 'On board the ship we had about ten babies under two years old of breast feeding age, and 35 children between 2–10 years and about forty children between 10–15 years. They were deprived of their minimum needs (except some of them received some toys not exceeding ten toys) this created problems and jealousy between the children. As the children required special attention, many problems resulted.' They complained there were not enough nappies; not enough milk; not enough baby food. The air-conditioning failed from time to time and they believed this was deliberate. Being videoed by the SAS was a new experience for these people and they assumed the soldiers were gathering evidence to use against them: 'Taking photos of negative situations only, for example when the toilet is not clean and when we are sleeping.'[7]

Eight days into the voyage, Khan came down to the tank deck to tell the Afghans they had won their court case but they would have to stay on the ship because the government was appealing the decision. He had other news: he and his men were leaving and new soldiers would be coming to take their place. The commander of the *Manoora*, Bob Morrison, had negotiated with Admiral Smith for an army unit to take over from the SAS. This was the first of the controversial Transit Security Element (TSE) units which were then deployed on most ships involved in Operation Relex. The look of the soldiers delivered a message. 'Helmets and the whole thing', explained one of the officers involved. 'It was our form of intimidation, I suppose.'[8]

The asylum seekers were *not* told the ship was now heading straight for Nauru. PNG had had second thoughts about the transhipping deal. Port Moresby had no big buses and there weren't enough trucks to take six hundred asylum seekers from the port to the airport. They would have had to walk. As usual, there was trouble in town and the possibility of an ugly mêlée. The press would be on hand in droves, the press the Australian government had so far successfully kept away from the operation. And there was trouble with the safety certification at the airport. It was unclear if pilots would be willing to land the large planes needed to fly the asylum seekers out. The National Security Committee of the PNG Cabinet canned the deal sometime around September 10, just as North was finishing work on his judgement. The Solicitor General then assured Jane Halton's taskforce there was nothing in the court orders to prevent the *Manoora* heading straight for Nauru.⁹ So the ship sailed on.

Australia had a fortnight to build camps for a thousand people in one of the poorest countries on earth, half way across the Pacific. Ten million dollars was thrown at the challenge. A couple of days after Rene Harris and Peter Reith signed the deal between the two countries on September 10, a huge airlift began to Nauru bringing everything needed from mattresses to plumbers, mosquito nets to stoves. The operation was directed by Jane Halton. She made it very clear that her instructions were coming from the top. 'Do you understand me—from the highest level of the Australian government, this has to be done.'¹⁰

The operation faced difficulties on all fronts: no tradesmen, no building supplies, very little fresh food, few local staff and not enough Nauruan police. A division of the European catering giant Compass was hired to cook in the camps. Chubb Protection Services from Australia was engaged to provide security inside the wire. The first of the Chubb staff began arriving on the island on September 13. The President announced that Australian police would also help train his men to maintain security outside the wire.¹¹ Police, Australian Protective Services (APS) personnel and soldiers were being flown in from Australia by Hercules.

In the midst of this, local landowners began asking an outrageous price for the use of the weight-lifting village, so it was decided that the camp on the Topside sports field in the desolate remains of phosphate mines would become the main holding centre. When Canberra heard of the trouble with the Iraqis on the *Manoora*, construction began on a second camp to isolate them at State House in a hollow near the coast. Both camps were built out of corrugated iron, plastic sheeting and green shade cloth.

Canberra remained undeterred by what looked like an absolute obstacle to the Pacific Solution. The people about to be imprisoned in these camps had committed no offence against the laws of Nauru. The Constitution of Nauru guarantees 'no person shall be deprived of his personal liberty except as authorised by law' and guaranteed all prisoners on the island the right to a lawyer of their own choice. Australia was faced with the same problem in PNG where the Constitution forbids imprisonment without trial.[12] Legality was a second or third order consideration still unresolved as the *Manoora* headed for the island. Indeed, hundreds of asylum seekers would already be sitting in the Topside camp when the minutes of Jane Halton's taskforce record: 'Attorney-General's looking at question of authority to detain on Nauru—need access to Nauru legislation.'[13]

The 'legal' scheme adopted in the end combined brute force with tricky interpretation. The asylum seekers would not be detainees at all. They would be visitors to Nauru on special visas which were issued on condition that each person remained within the confines of a camp. Asylum seekers who left the camps would land in the Nauruan lock up, but only on a breach of visa conditions. And their detention would be put beyond practical challenge by persuading Nauru to block entry to any lawyers wanting to come to the island to cause trouble. Among the many messages Australia was sending to the region in these dramatic weeks was a curious message about law and lawfulness.

I

Chilli appeared in the food on the last days of the voyage of the *Manoora*. 'Very hot pepper was added to the food', the Iraqis reported to Amnesty International. 'It was impossible for humans to tolerate it, never mind children. The type of pepper resulted in infections to the lips of some of us. Although we pleaded with the Australian and the doctor to stop this practice they even added more black pepper to our food.' The same complaints came from the Afghans on the tank deck. 'The last few days they used chilli in the food', said Wahidullah Akbari. 'It was so hot the children were unable to eat or touch, even the adults they couldn't eat.' Perhaps the cooks thought Afghans liked chilli? 'We were saying to them, we don't want chilli. There was no mistake.'[14]

On September 17, Major Dunn, the new commander of the soldiers on the *Manoora*, told the Afghans the bad news that the Federal Court appeal had gone against them. 'Therefore you must disembark in Nauru for legal processes.' Dunn added to their great surprise, 'You are now close to Nauru'.

They had imagined they were somewhere near Port Moresby. Dunn attempted to reassure them. 'The Australian government has decided that you should go to Nauru to be processed legally. From there some will go to New Zealand, and some of you will stay in the camp that is built in there.' They quizzed one of the IOM representatives about the camps. 'Mr Hosai said, "every room is for five people and they were equipped with fans and other facilities".' Eighty of the Afghans would go ashore first to help make the camp ready for everyone else. 'The Australian soldiers led by Mr Major Dunn had strict orders to ensure that the first group disembark and it was not to their benefit to stay on the ship. Therefore we had no other choice. The first group disembarked.'[15]

Large Nauruan women with garlands in their hair danced and sang on the wharf to greet the Afghans as they came ashore on September 19. The men had made a banner for the occasion which they held aloft in their boat: 'Thanks from honourable government of Naru for giving protection and shelters for Afghan refugees.' They looked gaunt after a month at sea on the *Palapa*, the *Tampa* and the *Manoora*. They carried their few belongings in green plastic garbage bags. The women gave each of the men a small posy of flowers as they stepped onto the wharf.

The press was also waiting. Until this moment, Australia had been able to make sure no one saw or spoke to these people who had been at the centre of a world story for weeks. Their first words were shouted complaints about life on the *Manoora*. The journalists followed the buses taking them to Topside and interviewed them through the wire. A teacher told Craig Skehan of the *Sydney Morning Herald*: 'We came from Afghanistan to Pakistan and then to Jakarta and we tried to get to Australia because we had heard that Australians are kind people. But I think the Australian government was kind of cruel to us. Your Prime Minister should know that things are very bad in Afghanistan and they are getting worse.' Since coming ashore they had heard about September 11. They expressed sympathy for those who had been killed. They laughed at the suggestion there would be terrorists in their number. 'We don't want to make any trouble. We are respectable people.'[16]

Topside was nothing like the camp they had been promised on the ship. 'We saw that tents with 50, 60 people capacity were erected for us and there were no fans or other living facilities. We asked for these facilities.' Along the front of the camp were impressive wire fences. Skehan reported:

'At the rear there are only strands of wire between steel posts. The real and formidable barrier is the surrounding coral pinnacles, jagged and fossilised, and beyond that the vast expanse of the Pacific Ocean.'[17] Into this hell, another 222 of the asylum seekers from the *Tampa* were unloaded peacefully over the next few days. The only Afghans left on the ship by that time were those families, women and boys waiting to be flown to New Zealand.

The boys and pregnant women came ashore on September 26 with another banner thanking the governments of Australia and New Zealand. A chartered Boeing 707 flew them to Auckland where they arrived in the early evening on a distant runway out of sight of the press. They were fed, photographed and given medical checks at the airport. Few were chronically ill but these people from the *Tampa* would need about four times more medical attention—both physical and psychological—than refugees who normally reach New Zealand. Many were traumatised and depressed. Many had acute minor illnesses like scabies. A very high number of women were pregnant. Though they had complained about the food on the *Manoora*, tests showed their diet had been good. The more devout were now giving thanks for their rescue by fasting. They had to be persuaded to eat.

Buses took them to Mangere camp. Boat people had never reached New Zealand's shores—not since the great canoes brought the Maori—but local opinion was sufficiently hostile to the Afghans to present a political challenge to Helen Clark's government. The polls were against her. Talkback radio had been hitting the *Tampa* issue hard in the previous weeks and demonstrations were expected, but the turnout of demonstrators at Mangere that night was meagre: a couple of people with placards and a campervan covered with angry slogans parked near the fish shop at the top of the drive. Security was now a little tighter: there was a guard, a boom gate and a wire fence.

The second airlift arrived at Mangere very late the following night. There were no protesters this time. Within weeks, opposition to New Zealand's role in the Pacific Solution died away. All but one of the 131 Afghan asylum seekers flown from Nauru were confirmed to be refugees and given permanent visas to begin a new life in this unexpected country. Of the couple of thousand people eventually caught up in the Pacific Solution, these were the luckiest: secure in New Zealand before history shifted under Afghanistan, deposing the Taliban government they had fled, leaving all but a handful of the Afghans on Nauru without a claim to refugee protection.

I

Once the Afghans were off the *Manoora*, Australia faced the challenge of clearing the Iraqis from the ship. Halton's taskforce had only turned its mind to this problem in the last days of the voyage: 'What if they won't get off?' Nauru had insisted no one be forced ashore from the *Manoora*. 'Jesus, they can't drag them off', said Rene Harris. 'There are women and kids on the ship. I believe they will not do it.' The only ones they were going to welcome ashore were those who were willing to leave the ship. The IOM was also refusing to accept asylum seekers forced off the *Manoora*. 'The Afghanis were very good and did as they were asked', said Admiral Smith. 'The Iraqi group ... proved very difficult ... they knew they were on Australia. A warship is Australia. They were reluctant to get off it because they knew that by getting off it they were not achieving their objective.'[18]

Soon after the *Manoora* reached the island, thirteen Iraqis were persuaded to disembark. That left nearly 90 men, about 55 women and 80 children refusing to budge. They were angry at being tricked onto the *Manoora* in the first place and then lied to about the ship's destination. Relations with IOM, already poisonous, grew worse after the Iraqis were filmed reading old newspapers in which they learnt for the first time about September 11. 'We were reading about this whilst some of them were taking videos of us to record our reaction. But the following day when we stood for one minute of silence to mourn the victims and condemn this cowardly act, they did not record this.' The Iraqis did not believe what the soldiers and sailors told them about Australia. They continued to believe Australia was a country that encouraged people to flee oppressive regimes and was, even now, preparing a welcome for them. At the end of their very long, expensive and dangerous road they were staying put.[19]

After five days of this stalemate, an Australian government spokesman suggested peaceable disembarkation was only Nauru's 'preference'. This was denied by Nauru: 'Our position is not negotiable.' The UNHCR continued to insist no one be forced off the boat. Peter Reith retorted, 'Well, they're not going to stay, I can tell you that'. His fellow minister,

Warren Entsch, proposed starving them off. 'If they want the food, it's on the beach. It's as simple as that.'[20]

Australia paid Nauru more money. For weeks, phosphate miners, teachers and other public servants had not been paid their wages. The millions Australia was already pouring into the bankrupt island were not reaching them. 'Can I go and eat with the refugees?' an islander wrote to an underground newsletter, *The Visionary*. On September 25, the island's Minister of Finance brought home $1.4 million in cash in his suitcase, an advance on the sale of one of the island's last investment properties, the Savoy Tavern in Melbourne. Reith was back on the phone to Harris. The following day the President stood weeping in the island's parliament: 'The Australian government is giving us cash today.'[21] One million was on its way to pay outstanding wages and salaries by the end of the week. Another $3 million was promised.

Howard signalled that Australia was not going to be deterred by the objections of Nauru, the IOM and UNHCR to forced removals. 'I should make it clear that the people on the *Manoora* will go to Nauru . . . We would like to do that in a calm manner, but in the end it has to be understood that we're not going to change our position.' Reith was all for using the military to frogmarch the Iraqis off the ship but Halton persuaded him to see what a team of hostage negotiators from the AFP could achieve. They reached the ship on Saturday, September 29 and were given two days to do their best. They achieved nothing. At 7.10 pm on Sunday September 30, Reith signed an order for the forced removal of the Iraqis. 'The prospect of voluntary disembarkation by these people remains unlikely. The government remains of the view that the remaining Unauthorised Boat Arrivals should be removed as soon as practicable, but commencing no later than tomorrow.'[22]

Reith rang Rene Harris early next morning. What passed between them is unclear. Reith claimed Harris was 'quite happy with the arrangements' but Harris disappeared from the scene soon after this conversation, citing urgent kidney problems.[23] Like very many Nauruans, the President was diabetic. Harris was flown by Hercules to a hospital in Melbourne but the officials left behind continued to insist there be no forced removals from the ship.

Meanwhile on the *Manoora*, their people were asked to select six negotiators. They chose five men and a woman. After some hours of negotiations they were asked to divide their people into groups of 25. According to the account they later gave to Amnesty International, the groups were taken up on deck and asked if they wanted to disembark. They said they did not. 'Australian officials became convinced that the position is the same for all.' According to their account, the six were then taken to an unfamiliar room on the ship where the captain, flanked by an Arabic interpreter, read a statement: 'You must understand exactly what I am saying. You must disembark this ship quickly.' Suddenly thirty soldiers arrived, two soldiers cornered each one of the six delegates, they held them and led them to a boat and transported them to the island.[24]

Australian soldiers in full combat dress brought the six ashore in a landing craft. Twelve APS officers on the wharf walked the Iraqis to the bus. The asylum seekers were shouting: 'We are not criminals. We are refugees.' One man was dragged. When the little bus reached the Topside camp, the six refused to get out. Angry IOM officials would not allow Australian soldiers into the camp to force them off the bus. The Iraqis sat in the bus all that afternoon in the blazing sun as the press interviewed them through the wire. 'We are the representatives of our group. Maybe they will cheat them, or bring them here by force. They tell us lies. How could you elect Mr John Howard when he does this illegally?'[25]

The Iraqis left on the ship had no idea what had happened to their six leaders. When the captain asked to see another six, they presented themselves and they were also removed from the ship. According to their report to Amnesty International, greater force was used to remove the second delegation. 'Thirty soldiers approximately came over, surrounded the poor six people from all directions. Three of them were held tightly to the table and the soldiers kicked them strongly and twisted their arms to their backs severely.' They were taken to the landing craft. They were calm for the 200-metre journey but began to struggle violently when they came within sight of the wharf and the press. They were forced, shouting, into another bus and taken to Topside.

That night on television, Peter Reith demonstrated his extraordinary ability to deny the obvious. Though he had signed an order—still secret—directing the ship to be cleared and though ABC audiences had, only moments before, watched footage of distraught Iraqis being brought ashore by the military, Reith insisted no force had been used. 'Look, obviously, from their point of view they want to say that this is a shocking business on behalf of Australia; that they've been forced against their will; that they've been badly treated. I appreciate that's what some of these people want to run as an argument. But the advice I have is that it went reasonably smoothly.' Surrounding the Iraqis on the landing craft with soldiers in helmets and full camouflage was not force? 'We took sensible precautions.' The man dragged to the bus? 'He was a bit difficult.' The UNHCR complaining it wasn't warned and the IOM now refusing to allow force to be used to empty the bus at Topside? 'Can we not exaggerate things.' The minister attacked the Iraqis as dissatisfied customers of criminal people smugglers. 'They're not coming to Australia. It's as simple as that.'[26]

Violence broke out on the *Manoora* that night. Admiral Smith described it as 'a riot of some significance' which developed 'within the mess deck where they were, and that was of sufficient concern to the ship that the ship's staff and the army people withdrew and sealed the hatch until they cooled down.' Lurid accounts of the riot would appear in the press during the election campaign: stories of women threatening to hang their children, a mother deliberately breaking her child's arm by throwing her to the floor, of bunks torn apart and used as weapons, of shit smeared on the walls and thrown at the soldiers. Smith said an investigation of these stories revealed no evidence of a child's arm being broken and only minor damage to bunks and bathrooms. 'That damage, as I said, was fairly minor in monetary terms, but there was some damage done.'[27]

The captain had appeared on the mess deck with about twenty soldiers to announce: 'Your families, relatives and friends are safe and they are on Nauru.' At this, there was an eruption of violence and the Australians withdrew and locked the doors. Somehow, the rest of the captain's proclamation was read to them through an opening in one of the doors. The gist of what he said was, 'They disembarked freely, do not be worried about them. They ask you to disembark quietly'. The Iraqis told Amnesty: 'The situation went from bad to worse as we knew that they were forced to disembark since it is not possible that a person will leave his wife behind or leave his children or his personal belongings or attempt to convince his family to disembark.'

Nauru managed to prevent further removals next day, October 2, but caved in the following day and fifty Iraqis were forced ashore in three groups. The soldiers say: 'We had cards which explained the acceptable level of force we could use and we followed them to the letter. We asked them three times: "Will you walk to the ship by yourself?" ' When they refused, they were escorted. The Iraqis say the soldiers used water hoses, batons and 'electric sticks' to force them into the boats. Vouching for the behaviour of the armed forces throughout Operation Relex, Air Marshal Angus Houston said, 'I have total confidence that our Navy and Army people who were out there throughout this very demanding operation used minimum force at all times'. He firmly denied military personnel ever carried or used electric prods.[28]

The press could see that some of those arriving at the wharf were 'visibly distressed'. As the third group neared the shore, a fight broke out on the boat. The Nauruans sent it back to the *Manoora* but a little later it reappeared manned by Australian soldiers in combat dress. The thirteen on board—including three children and a baby—sat on the boat for nearly three hours in fierce sun refusing to come ashore. Nauruan negotiators finally coaxed them into the buses.[29]

That left 166 Iraqis on the *Manoora* as night fell. Conditions in their quarters were terrible. They were refusing to use the lavatories for fear of being kidnapped. 'Women and children were afraid to go to the toilet, indeed, we put a screen in order to do our business in bottles ... can one imagine this!' Next morning soldiers cleared them all from the ship. 'The place was invaded by 20 armed soldiers carrying batons, electric sticks, water hoses and other strange weapons.' The Iraqis claim some of them were beaten. They say they were told to say nothing of this when they reached the landing stage. 'The reason, of course, is they wanted to convince the men from Nauru that we are disembarking freely.'[30]

The press watched the landings on the last day through very long lenses for they had been forced back about 80 metres from the landing stage. Six groups came ashore. There were shouts but too distant for the press to hear what was said. Three groups refused at first to leave the landing barge. One sat it out for an hour and a half. Iraqis were brought down from Topside to speak to them. An Australian doctor appeared to treat them. Nauruans coaxed them. They all, eventually, climbed out of the boat and into the buses. The *Manoora* was clear. A spokesman for Philip Ruddock said, 'We are happy the disembarkations were all voluntary'.[31]

The Iraqis were absolutely beaten, angry and embarrassed. Later, through Amnesty International, they extended an apology to Australia. 'Some of us, out of ignorance or being a child or as a result of the pressures experienced or because of lost dreams which were feasible but have disappeared or because of the loss of money or loss of time: all these resulted in uncivilised behaviour. We apologise for this. We are persecuted people. We ran away from fire with our families to a country which we respect. We respect its people and its will and we are sure [this country] will accept us and save us from the tragedy and suffering. We are sure that the ship of our dreams will land in the land of our dreams, Australia.'

For John Howard, the Nauru operation was almost a total success. He had kept his pledge that no one from the *Tampa* would set foot in Australia, and further demonstrated his government's resolve by expelling the Iraqis who came on the *Aceng*. HMAS *Tobruk* was collecting the latest arrivals at Ashmore and they, too, would be despatched to Nauru. Labor was offering no opposition to the Pacific Solution, nor was it objecting to the forced clearing of the *Manoora* or Canberra's carelessness with Nauru's sovereignty in the operation. Despite Australia's broken promises, the IOM and UNHCR continued to assist the Nauru operation. Nauru now almost disappeared from the news. Most of the journalists flew home. Events had moved on and they had to follow. It was the same to the very end: each new sensation in the story obliterated the last.

THIRTEEN
Launching the campaign

TO OCTOBER 8

The courtyard of the prime ministerial wing of Parliament House is a grey, cold space that would feel a little like Beijing even without the wisteria and stone lanterns. John Howard holds press conferences, flanked by flags and ministers, in a patch of sunlight at the doors to his office. Behind them, through those doors, hangs one of Sid Nolan's big Ned Kelly paintings. On the day the last Iraqi was cleared from the *Manoora*, Howard called the press to the courtyard to announce Australia's largest commitment of troops to a war since Vietnam. On one side of him were the hooded eyes of Alexander Downer and on the other, the high, bald dome of Peter Reith, still Minister for Defence for a last few weeks. Howard had farewelled Reith from parliament the week before, declaring 'of all the people with whom I have been associated in politics over the years, there is none I hold in higher regard than Peter Reith'.[1] He was a man on his way out but this absolutely suited his prime minister. Reith would not be accountable at the ballot box for anything he did in the weeks ahead. Nor would he ever have to face parliamentary scrutiny.

Reith was a skirmisher of daring, a head kicker with a celebrated knack of escaping tight corners. These brawling skills had made him a valued operator in the party and in government while they slowly eroded public trust and regard for the man. The brutal realist figured he would lose his seat at the coming election—he was probably wrong about that—but he knew that leadership of the party and the country were now beyond him so he had decided to retire from politics. The baton Reith always said was in his knapsack would stay right there. But he had lost none of his talent as a political fighter. He had wrecked the 1988 referendum campaign which had begun so hopefully as a bipartisan effort to make fundamental reforms to the Constitution; he was up to his neck in the waterfront battles of 1998; his radical republicanism helped defeat the referendum of 1999. Reith said of himself: 'I was born to plot.'[2] His last assignment was to see Operation Relex through to the election.

'Prime Minister, what are your plans this afternoon?' asked one of the journalists.

'To keep working and governing', Howard replied.

'What are the chances of a drive to Yarralumla?' None that afternoon, replied Howard. It was the following morning, Friday October 5, that he saw the Governor General to request a dissolution and then invited the press back to the courtyard to announce that the election would be held on November 10. Howard was already campaigning. 'The government I have led has endeavoured on all occasions to be a servant of the Australian people. And if re-elected I recommit myself to serve the Australian people and to lead a government that governs for the interests of the entire Australian community, for the great mainstream of the Australian public, and a government that will always put Australia's interests first.'

Howard declared leadership the great issue in the contest. 'This is not a time to change to either a prime minister or to a party that finds it difficult to articulate a clear view on the great issues that challenge the Australian nation.' His attack on his opponent was unerring. 'Mr Beazley's had five-and-a-half years to define himself to the Australian public. He's had five-and-a-half years to tell the Australian public what he stands for and what he believes in. He's led the Opposition now for the same time that I've been Prime Minister and I don't believe the Australian people have any clearer view now than they did in March of 1996 what he or the Australian Labor Party stands for. This was nowhere better illustrated than in his vacillating, chopping and changing over the issue of illegal immigration.'

John Howard was winning the leadership race. He had not been so popular, so trusted and respected since cracking down on gun ownership after the massacre at Port Arthur. 'Many of my stands have been unpopular', he said, announcing the election. 'But we haven't been reluctant to state a position.' Yet his genius lay in seizing policies such as gun control, East Timor and turning back boat people that were both tough and very popular. They earned him a reputation for strength of character and stubbornness under fire, which he used to fight for his tough but *unpopular* economic and industrial policies. Howard's approval rating soared ten points in the polls after *Tampa* and another ten points after September 11. In public perception of their handling of boat people, a chasm had opened between the leaders: only 32 per cent approved Beazley's approach while 74 per cent backed Howard. The man who had been trailing as 'preferred prime minister' back in May was now ahead of Beazley by 56 points to 34.[3]

One of the journalists asked, 'Can you believe the position you're in now compared to how things were eight weeks ago, compared how perhaps you felt eight weeks ago?' Howard was not going to gloat over the great political stroke of the *Tampa* or the supreme luck of finding himself prime minister as Australia prepared to join the War Against Terror. 'I simply ask the Australian people to look at our record, compare our capacity with that of the Labor Party at a difficult time for the Australian nation. I don't take anything for granted. I think we have a big fight ahead of us.'

I

The Liberal party campaign headquarters was a sprawling, open-plan office on Lonsdale Street, Melbourne. The campaign director was Lynton Crosby, federal director of the party since 1997. He had masterminded the 1998 campaign and was very close to Howard. His was usually the first call Howard took each morning. 'Every day virtually of our waking existence for the last six months we have worked together.'[4] The party pollster was the legendary Mark Textor. The three of them had settled on a slogan for the opening of the campaign: 'PUTTING AUSTRALIA'S INTERESTS FIRST— CERTAINTY LEADERSHIP STRENGTH.'

Textor looked like a reformed bikie with a bald head and goatee but was very good at his job, bringing sophisticated mathematics to bear on the gut instincts of Australians. He had honed his skills in the Northern Territory working for the Country Liberal Party (CLP) government of Shane

Stone. There, Textor introduced to Australia the US Republican Party's strategy of wedge politics: finding hot issues to fracture an opponent's traditional support. There is no more effective wedge than race. Andrew Coward, one of Stone's strategists, watched Textor polling on race issues. 'We studied it very carefully from year to year, including the attitudes of people who came [to live in the Territory] and found about 80 per cent of people who would describe themselves as Labor in another State would have an anti-black view, and many of them would vote for another party if, during an election campaign, they had the pants scared off them. Come election time, based on this research, the CLP sends a message to the electorate which essentially says, "You might not like us but if you elect the other mob, they'll give the rest of the place away to the blacks".'[5]

Exploring the nuances of race—and finding the language to telegraph race issues—had been a quiet development of the Liberals under John Howard, backed by Textor's polling and supported by Shane Stone who by the campaign of 2001 was no longer chief minister of the Territory but federal president of the Liberal Party. Distasteful as many found this—including many Liberal loyalists—the team of Howard, Textor and Stone gave the party a professional grasp of Australia's real attitudes to race. For a major party to be offering comfort, however covert, to white Australians who frankly disliked people of other colours, was attractive across the political spectrum. John Howard has always vehemently denied he deserves to be labelled a racist. 'I don't have a racist bone in my body and I do find that extraordinarily offensive and it is against everything that I've always sort of believed about the equality of men.' But he has demonstrated a willingness to *use* race at the polls. In his first term he targeted voters resentful of Aborigines. As his second term ended, he was pursuing voters who feared their country was being invaded by Muslim boat people.[6]

Under Howard, the most influential voters in Australia were those who most resented the economic revolution of the 1980s and 1990s and lived on the margins of the nation's new prosperity—in regional towns and on the edges of the booming cities. He was deaf to them on economic issues, but honoured their outlook everywhere else he could. The week before the election was called, the pollster Rod Cameron identified these voters as 'less well educated, insular, conservative and narrow minded, anti elites in a big way—whether the elites are big cities, big business, big media, big or organised anything—fiercely anti economic rationalism, they have a strong sense of discontent, of being ignored'. Even before the arrival of the *Tampa*, the analyst Hugh Mackay had identified the strong racial concerns of these people. 'Just below the surface, there is a high degree of anxiety about Asian immigration, about the idea that Australia's culture is being changed in unexpected ways, and that recent immigrants are associated with unacceptable increases in crime and violence.' He noted, 'Refugees previously referred to as "boat people" are now routinely described as "illegals"'.[7]

For Howard's opponents to accuse him of racism was extremely difficult. To condemn him was to accuse his supporters—some millions of Australians—of being racist, too. That was a brave call in the face of the ballot box. And Howard had prepared his defences well over many years. When Kim Beazley taunted him in 1996 for not condemning the emerging Pauline Hanson, Howard thundered: 'If someone disagrees with the prevailing orthodoxy of the day, that person should not be denigrated as a narrow minded bigot. That is basically what has been happening in this country over a very long period of time.'[8] Community debate on race had been muffled by coyness—he called it political correctness—but in the name of free speech Howard claimed an extraordinary privilege for himself, his government and his supporters: to be exempted from any allegation of racism.

He insisted on the right to pursue his policies—cut the budget of ATSIC, deny the existence of the stolen generations and close Australia to Muslim boat people—'without being accused of prejudice or bigotry, without being knocked off course by ... phoney charges of racism'. He wouldn't enter a debate on whether this was or wasn't racist. He simply *insisted* it wasn't. Critics were told that to accuse someone of racism was elitist and arrogant. This was a new political correctness. The xenophobia of Australians was to be shown democratic respect. To contest the prevailing fear of boat people was simply unpatriotic. Howard had found a perfect issue in border protection: tough but popular, crude racism combined with genuine concern for the security of the country, a concern intensified by the terrorist attacks on America. It was race wrapped in the flag.

I

Kim Beazley was at Rydges Hotel on Exhibition Street in Melbourne when he saw the jets slamming into the World Trade Centre. He turned from the television to his chief-of-staff, Michael Costello, and said, 'Well, there goes the election'. For the second time in a fortnight he declared the election lost—and it hadn't even been called. When Howard drove to Yarralumla three weeks later, the situation had changed very little. Beazley knew it was almost impossible for Labor to win. Howard knew that too. The challenge for the Labor leader was to keep his party from falling into a yawning pit. The party pollsters were saying—very quietly—that Labor could lose 45 seats in the House of Representatives. It faced the greatest wipe out in its history.[9] Beazley and the party would work themselves into a mood of faint optimism by the time the campaign ended, but when it began the challenge was to avoid absolute humiliation.

Labor's campaign headquarters was also in Melbourne, working class West Melbourne. The party's secretary, Geoff Walsh, was a veteran of many elections, having served Bob Hawke and Paul Keating. Walsh was running this campaign but one of the party's senior strategists was its Senate leader John Faulkner, a gloomy man of the Left with a large brain, an almost sentimental commitment to Labor history and a deep but hidden sense of humour. Saatchi and Saatchi was the party's advertising agency. Polling was in the hands of John Utting of Sydney. Labor's clunky slogan was: 'A FAIR SHARE FOR ALL AUSTRALIANS—JOBS. HEALTH. EDUCATION'.

Canada's Progressive Conservative Party was all but annihilated when it went to the polls in 1993 after introducing a GST. For the last year, Labor had been pinning its hopes on a massive backlash against Australia's GST. But Howard had done a lot of work to placate community anger. The new tax had not been imposed on food. The burden of paperwork on small business was lightened. Then the revival of the economy in the middle of 2001 had taken the edge off GST angst. With more money coming through the till, small business settled down a little over the new tax. Labor's pollsters still found an 8 per cent swing against the government because of the GST but Australia was getting used to it. The Liberals had seized the *Tampa* with relief; Labor was stuck with the GST. The shadow Justice Minister, Duncan Kerr, remarked ruefully, 'They had no plan A. We had no plan B'.[10]

That revival of the economy washed across the whole community, particularly encouraging young couples with mortgages to stick with the government. In Labor's old heartland seats in Sydney's western suburbs, families with big mortgages were riding a real estate boom. Howard's government had delivered them low interest rates and big capital gains.

A NSW Labor official told journalist Dennis Atkins, 'People in the so-called battler seats of western Sydney are sitting on asset values that are 30 to 40 per cent higher than in most of Melbourne and certainly in Brisbane and Adelaide. These people have substantial mortgages to back these house values and that makes them very cautious when it comes to interest rates'.[11] They were also the audience for Sydney's most accomplished radio broadcaster, Alan Jones. Throughout the campaign Howard would be a regular guest on Jones' breakfast show, speaking straight to what were once solid Labor households.

Labor did not have the cash to poll as often or as widely as the Liberals. The grim assessment of its position at this time was based on snapshot polling in individual seats where the issues of refugees, national security, border protection and leadership were all going against Labor. Queensland was looking particularly bad. The high-flying recruit Cheryl Kernot was travelling so poorly in the traditional Labor seat of Dickson that she was written off early as a lost cause and Labor withdrew much of its campaign support. Part of Kernot's problem was her 30-year-old opponent Peter Dutton, a former policeman who had sensed early on that immigration was the winning issue. Even before the *Tampa*, Dutton was distributing flyers throughout the electorate: 'The Howard Government is rock solid on protecting Australia's borders. Labor is soft on illegal immigrants.' He received very strong support. 'In all of the meetings I attended there was no criticism of the government's policy on border protection. It was a major issue.'[12]

Beazley's first policy launch—the day after Howard called the election—was an attempt to neutralise the immigration issue by pledging $100 million to 'border protection'. Labor was not challenging Relex or the Pacific Solution but proposing to set up a Coastguard to take over the blockade of the boats. Beazley was to be painted as unpatriotic for this proposal, but it was welcomed by the navy which was taking no pleasure in Relex. As Admiral Barrie said, 'A lot of our side just wanted this thing to go away'.[13]

I

Max Moore-Wilton had one last problem to clear up before campaigning could begin. Negotiations with Papua New Guinea to set up a detention centre either on the gold mining island of Misima or at the Lombrum naval base on Manus Island were dragging on. Soon the government would be in the 'caretaker' period of the campaign when the Opposition would have to be consulted before major policy initiatives were taken. Moore-Wilton consulted his department's first assistant secretary (Support Services for Government Operations), Barbara Belcher. She knew the Electoral Act backwards. He put a hypothetical question to her: would an agreement with an unnamed country to receive asylum seekers breach the caretaker rule? She asked: 'Could you see it as continuing new policy? Would there be money involved? etcetera. I was assuming that it was an urgent matter that could not be put off until after the caretaker period ended five weeks later.'[14] Her verdict was that if the deal was not done by the time the caretaker convention came into play at noon on Monday October 8, the Opposition would have to be consulted on its terms.

Australia had more important things to worry about that Monday morning. Overnight, the United States had launched its first air strikes against al-Qaeda and the Taliban. Australia would soon be moving ships, planes and troops to the War Against Terror. There was a great deal to organise. But at 9.30 that morning, Moore-Wilton called senior Australian and PNG officials to his Sydney office. There was no formal record of the meeting and no minute- or note-taker. The first two hours were spent settling the last details of Australia's $20 million contribution to the reform of PNG's armed forces. Michael Potts, head of the international division of the Prime Minister's Department said: 'After that agreement was reached, the secretary, Mr Moore-Wilton, then broached the issue of a probable PNG option for asylum seekers ... saying there was an avenue by which PNG might be able to assist Australia and then raised the problem that there were a number of asylum seekers and would there be a possibility of PNG being able to provide temporary accommodation for them?' Negotiations had, in fact, been continuing for weeks but now crunch time had come. According to Potts, PNG gave its agreement in principle to taking asylum seekers thirty minutes before the noon kick-in of the caretaker convention.[15]

Three days later, a memorandum of understanding was signed in Port Moresby by Australia's High Commissioner, Nick Warner, and the Secretary of PNG's Department of Foreign Affairs, Evoa Lalatute. PNG was given a million dollars in cash at this point. Australia would meet all the costs of establishing and maintaining the detention centre on Manus Island and pay all the costs of processing another 223 asylum seekers now waiting on Christmas Island.[16] It was assumed the UNHCR would do the processing and it came as a shock to the parties to be told by the UN body that as PNG was a signatory to the Refugee Convention it would have to do the processing itself. Australia would staff and meet the cost of the processing operation, too. Even before the first asylum seekers reached Manus, Australia would be pressuring PNG to expand the camp to take 1000 people, and not for six months but a year. And the prospects for Australia were good because PNG was always having a cash crisis.

That was still a few weeks away. On the morning of October 8, as Moore-Wilton clinched the first deal with PNG and the caretaker convention cut in, the 2001 election campaign was running at full throttle with Australia caught up in the latest public uproar of Operation Relex.

FOURTEEN
Orders from the top

OCTOBER 6 TO 9

Commander Norman Banks of the frigate HMAS *Adelaide* had been awake since 4.30 on the morning of October 6 waiting to intercept a boat bound from South Sumatra to Christmas Island. An RAAF P-3C Orion went out searching at dawn but it was early afternoon before the plane spotted the white-hulled fishing boat ploughing its way south with its Indonesian flag boldly displayed. The intelligence report on the *Olong*'s departure the night before was spot on. The 25-metre boat, overloaded with asylum seekers, was still over one hundred nautical miles from the Australian territory. She was given the 'identifier sign' SIEV 4.

Banks gave the order to shadow the boat. When it came into view, he saw a marginally seaworthy vessel with no lifeboats. It would have failed any mariner's safety inspection. As the RAAF Orion had already reported, some fifty people on the deck were wearing life jackets. According to Banks' superiors in Canberra, this was highly significant. Banks had an intelligence briefing warning that passengers on these rickety vessels might be wearing life jackets for an ulterior motive: they might be planning to sink their own boats in a desperate attempt to force the Australian navy to rescue them and bring them to Australian territory. This outcome, he was told, had to be avoided at all costs.

With the *Olong* still on the high seas, Banks sent out a small party to check it out. As he suspected, there were many more than fifty on board, perhaps over two hundred passengers: men, women and scores of children, including a little one holding an SOS sign.

Ibtihaj Al Zuhiry watched the navy come along side. She was crammed in among the asylum seekers with her three children, the youngest just five years old. An English literature graduate of the Mandaean faith, Ibtihaj had put her trust in God and the people smugglers when she stepped on board the boat. Waiting in Sydney was her husband, the children's father, Bashir. Although the Australian government had accepted her husband as a refugee—he had been jailed and tortured in Iraq—he was given only a temporary protection visa. This meant Ibtihaj and her children had no hope of seeing him for at least three years. So now, after nearly two years alone, Ibtihaj paid American dollars for a place on the boat. She had telephoned her husband just before they left Jakarta and was warned the navy might turn them back. But she had travelled all the way from Jordan and she was *not* going to give up. Now, she and her children were out on a leaky boat in the middle of the ocean face to face with Operation Relex.

The navy intelligence on SIEV 4 was swiftly passed to Canberra and to the head of the Prime Minister's People Smuggling Taskforce, Jane Halton. On this Saturday afternoon, the workaholic Halton swung into action. Her weekend with the family went on hold. She dialled Howard's two key advisers, Max Moore-Wilton and Miles Jordana. They agreed the Prime Minister would want to be right across this one.[1] This boat was the first to confront Operation Relex during the election campaign. SIEV 4 was sailing into Australian political history.

Every senior public servant on the taskforce was summoned to meet first thing next morning, Sunday October 7. Admiral Barrie's right-hand man, the head of Strategic Command at Defence headquarters in Canberra, Air Vice-Marshal Al Titheridge, was making excuses. Strategic Command was preoccupied with the war against terrorism. Admiral Barrie had just returned from Washington and the US-led bombing of Afghanistan was expected to begin any moment. And Titheridge had promised himself a few hours' break on Sunday at the races. It was Canberra Cup day. Halton and Titheridge compromised: he would brief her by phone in the morning and send his junior officer to the meeting. Defence also allowed Titheridge to brief Peter Reith directly in the morning—in time for the minister's appearance on *Meet the Press*.

On the *Adelaide*, Banks braced himself for a long night. His orders were clear. He must stop the SIEV reaching Christmas Island. He was to use 'every reasonable means' to achieve this without risking the safety of his crew, his ship or the boat people.[2] Banks did not take these orders lightly. An experienced, loyal officer with 25 years' service in the navy, he did not question the government's policy and considered himself 'unashamedly apolitical'. But he was not a fool and knew a little about the fraught politics of border protection. Two years earlier, he had sat on the first people smuggling taskforce with Jane Halton and Miles Jordana when Moore-Wilton first proposed using the navy to turn back refugee boats. The conflict between the civilian and military outlook had been obvious back then. How could naval officers square their duty to render assistance to those in distress at sea—even illegal immigrants—with orders to turn their overcrowded boats back to Indonesia? Banks was being told to do just that right at the beginning of an election campaign with the eyes of all the government on him.

I

In the early hours of Sunday morning, the *Adelaide* delivered repeated orders to the *Olong* to turn back to Indonesia. But the DIMA threats of fines and jail had made no impression on the crew of the little boat or its 223 asylum seekers who pushed on towards Christmas Island. Just before 4 am, as the boat neared the edge of the contiguous zone, Banks switched tactics. The inky sea in front of the little boat lit up like daylight and the *Adelaide* fired four warning shots. A message, in Bahasa and English, boomed out ordering the master of the boat to turn around. Panic erupted on the SIEV but it made no sign of altering course. The frigate fired another round over the SIEV's bow. Again there was no response. Banks manoeuvred the *Adelaide* aggressively towards the small boat and his heavy guns pounded 23 rounds into the water in a deafening blast of firepower. A boarding party left the frigate and sped towards the SIEV.[3]

The *Olong*'s passengers were now screaming and running from one side of the boat to the other. Ibtihaj thought she and her three children were about to die. Nine armed officers from the *Adelaide* boarded the boat and began separating the men from the women and children. In the pitch black there were scuffles, screaming and wailing. Navigation charts and equipment were wrecked by either the passengers or the crew as the naval party took the bridge and the engine room by force. Once in control, they turned the *Olong* around and steered her north, back towards Indonesia.[4] Panic and anger swept through the boat. The asylum seekers had been sailing for two days. Many were sick, exhausted and hysterical. One man grabbed a piece of wood and appeared to be holding it like a weapon. Some of the passengers were threatening to destroy the boat and commit suicide or throw their children overboard if they could not reach Australia. Banks' men radioed the *Adelaide* that they were losing control but Banks was resolute. Passengers jumping overboard must immediately be put back on board their boat. As dawn broke, he stood on the bridge of the *Adelaide* monitoring the unfolding chaos.

The *Olong*'s engine died just after sunrise and the small boat began rolling heavily in the swell. Banks spotted several heads bobbing in the water. As the *Adelaide*'s RHIBs sped to haul them in, more passengers started jumping overboard. Banks counted six, then twelve, then fourteen in the water. The sailors were reporting men and boys jumping in. The commander feared he was facing a mass exodus from the boat that would force him into a rescue. He had to maintain control. He ordered another boarding party onto the SIEV. All this was being videoed from the *Adelaide*.

Water was streaming over the decks of the *Olong* as it heaved from side to side. Suddenly, some of the officers spotted a small girl about five years old in a pink jumper being carried by her father up to the top of the wheelhouse. The child was one of the few on board without a life jacket. Her father now dressed her in one. He then took the child to the guard rail on the upper deck and held her over the side, gesturing to the sailors in the RHIB below to take her. Watching from the bridge Banks was stunned. He thought the father was about to drop the child. He ordered his men to intervene. The sailors below motioned the father to put down the child and two of the armed boarding party led them back to the wheelhouse.[5]

During this hectic effort to control the boarding operation, Banks was interrupted by a telephone call from Brigadier Mike Silverstone at Northern Command headquarters in Darwin. The brigadier was an army man but Banks answered directly to him in Operation Relex. The call was unusual and the timing was appalling. In any other circumstance, Silverstone would not interrupt a commander in the middle of an operational crisis but he needed an update for Canberra because of Reith's planned television appearance. Banks gave Silverstone some brief facts. He would later recall telling Silverstone some of the passengers were throwing themselves into the water and threatening to throw in their children.[6]

Silverstone hurriedly scribbled some notes in his diary: the boat's steering was disabled; it was dead in the water; the passengers were threatening a mass exodus; they were wearing life jackets, although some had discarded them. He wrote, 'Men thrown over side. 5, 6 or 7.' When Banks hung up Silverstone added the word 'child' to the note believing, he would say later, that Commander Banks told him a child about 5, 6 or 7 years old had been thrown over the side.[7]

For Banks and Silverstone, this brief conversation was a footnote to a difficult and dangerous naval action. They had no idea they were about to embroil the Australian Defence Force in its biggest political trauma since the Vietnam War. Silverstone picked up the phone and dialled the Strategic Command boss in Canberra, Al Titheridge.

I

Jane Halton opened that Sunday meeting of the People Smuggling Taskforce at 9 am. This would be a defining day in her professional career. She was a striking woman. In contrast to her flabby middle-aged male colleagues, she was taut and athletic, sported a trendy haircut and dressed with style. She swore by a rigorous exercise regime as she juggled the demands of a family and a relentless work pace. Though she had little public profile, she was known inside the bureaucracy as Max Moore-Wilton's right hand, and her power was enhanced by his patronage. By the time she arrived at the office, news of the SIEV's arrival had been leaked by the government and was running on the ABC news. It was obvious the fate of this boat and its passengers would be a big election story and a critical test for Howard. If the *Adelaide* could not stop the boat reaching Australia, all Howard's efforts since the *Tampa* would look like posturing. But if the boat would not make it back to Indonesia, the taskforce needed to come up with some politically acceptable options.

Present at the meeting that morning were the head of the Immigration Department, Bill Farmer, and his top bureaucrats from the *Tampa* operation, Philippa Godwin and Andrew Metcalfe. A senior Foreign Affairs officer, Peter Doyle, and Halton's number two, Katrina Edwards, also joined them. Titheridge's representative was a junior officer from Strategic Command, Group Captain Steve Walker. Just after 9.15 Titheridge rang Halton for the second time that morning and passed on the brief update from Silverstone. Halton believed she heard him say that the passengers were wearing life jackets, fourteen people had jumped overboard and, 'they were throwing their children'.[8] According to several witnesses, Halton relayed this claim to the meeting.

The image of children being thrown overboard grabbed the attention of the bureaucrats because it confirmed the warnings they had been given: determined boat people would go to any lengths to play on the Australian navy's obligations to rescue drowning people at sea. However, the news came as a surprise to Steve Walker. That morning before he left Strategic Command headquarters, he had read the reports on the operation and nowhere did they mention this startling claim. He thought Halton knew something he didn't and, somewhat embarrassed, said nothing.

About thirty minutes later, Bill Farmer's mobile went off. Philip Ruddock was about to walk into a press conference in Sydney and needed some media lines on the boat. As the others listened in around the table, Farmer passed on to Ruddock the slim details: the passengers were wearing life jackets, men had jumped overboard and some had thrown their children overboard. 'Is that okay?', Farmer asked his colleagues. Halton had her mobile glued to her ear but some of the others nodded their approval. This now fourth-hand version of Banks' words, gleaned during the confusion of an unfolding military operation, became formal advice to a government minister.

Philip Ruddock knew exactly how to spin that briefing. At the end of his statement about the latest changes to the Migration Act, he waited for questions about SIEV 4. Choosing his words carefully, Ruddock noted that this boat was exceptional: the passengers were wearing life jackets and they had thrown their children overboard. 'I regard these as some of the most disturbing practices I've come across in public life', he told the reporters. 'People would not come wearing life jackets unless they planned action of this sort.' Ruddock left the press conference, went to his car and made two calls, one to Howard and one to Reith, briefing them on his comments. The 'Children Overboard' story was off and running.

Howard needed no encouragement to kick the story along. This was the afternoon of Kim Beazley's suburban barbecue to launch Labor's much-touted $266 million 'family package' that would almost certainly dominate newspapers on Monday morning, the first official day of the election campaign. Howard was also campaigning in Sydney, in the marginal seat of Hughes. At a doorstop media conference, Howard picked up Ruddock's line: Australia was not going to be intimidated. 'I want to make that very clear, we are a humane nation but we're not a nation that's going to be intimidated by this kind of behaviour.'

I

The *Olong* was limping back towards Indonesia. Commander Banks knew the boat was only marginally seaworthy and then only with the help of the navy. With its navigation system destroyed and its steering sabotaged the *Olong* was now depending on a hand-held compass sent over from the *Adelaide* to find its way home. The passengers, too, were in bad shape. Women and small children had been at sea for two days in the northern heat, rolling around on an overcrowded boat. Banks' crew had used intravenous drips to re-hydrate some of them but many also had gastro, scabies and lice. Now the weather was turning bad and a swell was up. It was going to be a rough ride north. The 56 children on board were a worry, especially a 21-day old baby who was feeding poorly. Banks ordered his crew to keep shadowing the boat and keep it under observation.

Before long a white flag went up on the deck of the *Olong*. The passengers were raising and lowering their arms. This was an internationally recognised signal of distress at sea. The small boat was again dead in the water and heaving from side to side. Once the engine stopped, so had the main pumps. The boat was taking water and passengers were already bailing. As the *Adelaide* approached, the crew could hear passengers wailing. Banks sent a boarding party to investigate. They found the engine had been sabotaged, a charge later disputed by the passengers. The cause was irrelevant at this point. What mattered to Banks was that it would take a long time to repair. He could not abandon the passengers on the high seas but he also understood he could not rescue them. He needed to buy time. He called Brigadier Silverstone in Darwin asking for permission to tow the boat behind the *Adelaide*.

The reply, when it came, indicated the sensitivity of the operation. Silverstone told him that the decision would have to come from the Prime Minister. Like almost all key decisions in Relex, the military consulted

Halton's Taskforce which in turn took orders from Howard or Reith. A few minutes later, Silverstone was back on the phone. Banks could tow the boat but the Prime Minister would decide where it would go. The options were Christmas Island, back to Indonesia or way over to the territory of Cocos Island. Banks was shocked but Silverstone explained this was a big deal, 'the Prime Minister would make the decision where we would take this vessel'. The Cocos Islands were 530 nautical miles away and in Banks' opinion the idea was ludicrous. He was determined to resist the Cocos option at all costs.[9]

I

The navy had been astonished that afternoon when Howard's advisers requested a brief on the feasibility of towing a SIEV to Cocos. Rear Admiral Chris Ritchie ordered Maritime headquarters to produce a hurried report. The assessment was blunt: 'Previous experience with SIEVs and foreign fishing vessels, indicates that these vessels tend to disintegrate under sustained towing... any attempt to tow SIEV 04 to Cocos Island represents a high-risk activity, especially in terms of concerns for its structural intergrity and the consequential risks to the passengers and [*Adelaide*'s] boarding party.'[10] Admiral Barrie made it clear to Peter Reith that the navy had obligations under SOLAS regulations and would not risk the lives of the passengers regardless of the border protection policy.[11] Defence was drawing the line.

Meanwhile, Jane Halton was discussing the options for SIEV 4 with Max Moore-Wilton and Miles Jordana and drafting advice for the Prime Minister. One thing was clear: Howard's position was that no boat people were to be allowed onto mainland Australia and they would only be allowed to go to Christmas Island in the case of a SOLAS emergency. Halton reconvened the taskforce in the early evening to okay her advice to Howard. Halton's final position reflected the battle on the taskforce between the military and the civilians. Defence ruled out towing the SIEV 4 and its passengers to the Cocos Island or Ashmore Reef. But Halton warned that 'holding them on the high seas would be highly visible to the media', while taking them to Christmas Island 'could have disastrous consequences'. Not only would this send a 'strong signal to people smugglers' but once again, the media would be a problem. 'There is a very real prospect that the media would have access to the group.'[12]

Managing the media was now a critical factor. The revelations by the Prime Minister and Philip Ruddock about children having been thrown overboard were creating a media frenzy. Reith's press secretary, Ross Hampton, was busily briefing press gallery journalists filing for Monday morning's newspapers. All afternoon he had been hounding Strategic Command for more details on the children in the water. But Strategic Command could find nothing to back up the claims. When Group Captain Walker returned to Halton's meeting, he told the bureaucrats the same thing. Walker had searched the files at Strategic Command. He told them there were simply no written reports from the *Adelaide* to support the claim. A squabble broke out. Bill Farmer accused Walker of being the source of the claims. Walker heatedly denied this and pointed the finger at Halton. She said nothing.[13]

That night Halton faxed her report to the Prime Minister at the Lodge and to Peter Reith at home in Melbourne. She gave no hint that the 'children overboard' claim was under question. 'Unlike previous boatloads', she wrote, 'this group was wearing life jackets with the clear intention of frustrating official attempts to repel them'. When the *Adelaide* tried to turn the boat back, she continued, 'This [was] met with attempts to disable the vessel, passengers jumping into the sea and passengers throwing their children into the sea'.[14]

Soon after midnight, Melbourne's biggest selling newspaper, the *Herald Sun*, was on the streets. Under the banner headline, 'OVERBOARD: BOAT PEOPLE THROW CHILDREN INTO OCEAN', the paper quoted an 'angry' John Howard saying, 'I don't want people like that in Australia. Genuine refugees don't do that . . . They hang onto their children'. A 'Voteline' box on the front page asked the newspaper's readers to 'Have Your Say' with the question: 'Should boat people who throw children into the sea be accepted into Australia as refugees?'

Howard was set to appear on a number of breakfast radio programs first thing that Monday morning. But at 2.15 am, the United States began bombing Afghanistan. The newspapers scrambled to put out new editions headlining the air strikes. The war on terrorism had once again upstaged Howard's war on boat people. The Prime Minister was undeterred. In his interview that morning he pushed his message on boat people: they would not be allowed into Australia. He told Alan Jones on Sydney's 2UE, 'I don't want in this country people who are prepared, if those reports are true, to throw their own children overboard'.

When dawn broke off Christmas Island, the *Adelaide*'s commander was in a quandary. He had an urgent message from Defence headquarters ordering him to return to his fleet base as soon as possible and prepare to leave for the Middle East. The *Adelaide* was needed to relieve United States' warships enforcing sanctions against Iraq's Saddam Hussein. For Banks, it was an exquisite irony. Before he could join the operation against the Iraqi dictator he first needed to stop a boatload of Iraqis fleeing Saddam from setting foot on Australian soil.

The trouble was he had no idea what to do with the *Olong* and its passengers. Banks was aimlessly towing behind him a crippled boat filled with over two hundred men, women and children. Its hull was holed and there was a hole below the waterline. Its two main pumps had stopped when its engine died. A third small pump, attached to a petrol-driven generator had also died. The remaining portable pump had thirty minutes' fuel left. Banks sent a RHIB to Christmas Island for more fuel but it was a hopeless situation. If the seas rose and the passengers panicked he would be in real trouble. He fired off a message to his commanders: he could not tow this boat anywhere for any length of time.[15]

The *Olong*'s passengers bailed and pumped all day but the water level in the bilge kept rising. At around three that afternoon, the passengers began to panic when the level suddenly rose higher. The navy moved all the children to the upper deck. The Iraqis begged the sailors to allow the women and children off the boat. Banks refused. In desperation they wrote a letter to United Nations Secretary General Kofi Annan asking to be rescued, pressing the letter onto the sailors. But Banks had his orders. Until they were in danger of drowning, the SUNCs 'were not to be embarked on the *Adelaide*'. To do so, he understood, was 'mission failure'.[16] He distributed life jackets to passengers who didn't have them.

Around 4 pm, the boarding party warned Banks the forward part of the SIEV was taking water. They also had a woman on board vomiting blood and going into shock. But for almost another hour Banks held out, arguing with himself over when to rescue the increasingly terrified Iraqis. He kept resisting the rescue and ordered the passengers be fed on their own boat even with water coming in over the freeboard at the bow. As the water rose further, Banks was forced to stop the tow. Five minutes later, the boarding party radioed Banks again: the boat was sinking. Banks ordered a senior officer and engineer to go on board and confirm the report. He had to be sure. A few minutes later, Banks finally got the message. 'I think we're going to lose this one', his executive officer reported back. 'It is starting to go.'[17]

Three minutes later, the warning pipes sounded on the *Adelaide*. The *Olong* was going under. Several passengers grabbed the tiny three-week old baby and handed him over to a navy seaman in a RHIB. The infant was one of the first off the boat. Minutes later the bow of the *Olong* was under water. Banks ordered the towline cut and launched the life rafts as men, women and children began jumping for their lives into the sea.

From the second deck of the *Adelaide*, Able Seaman Laura Whittle saw a mother struggling in the choppy water with her young child. Without even waiting to put on her life jacket, Whittle dived twelve metres into the sea to haul the frightened pair to a life raft. Nearby, her mate, Leading Cook Jason Barker, was swimming out to a terrified father and child. Scores of passengers, supported by life jackets, bobbed in the water surrounded by debris as the *Adelaide*'s crew scrambled to get the 223 men, women and children clear of the sinking boat which threatened to drag them under.

It was a miraculous rescue. In just thirty minutes, the Australian sailors had everyone in life rafts. The ill-fated *Olong* had almost disappeared by the time Ibtihaj and her three children were finally brought on board HMAS *Adelaide*. They were alive. They were all alive. But their meagre possessions were gone. All that was left of their bags, money, papers and jewellery were flotsam and jetsam slopping around in the ocean.[18]

I

Max Moore-Wilton was not happy with the news. He called Admiral Barrie at home that night to question the call Banks had made for urgent assistance from Christmas Island when the SIEV 4 began to sink. Moore-Wilton told Barrie none of the survivors could go to Christmas Island. Everyone hauled from the sea must be kept on the *Adelaide* until the government decided what to do with them. They might be rescuees to the navy but they were still SUNCs to the government.

The Defence chief was furious. This was an operational emergency and the saving of lives at sea was paramount, he told Moore-Wilton heatedly. The first priority was to use every asset available, including boats or aircraft from Christmas Island, to make sure no lives were lost. The navy could not guarantee everyone rescued could or would be taken on board the *Adelaide*. 'If people had to be rescued and landed at Christmas Island, that would have to happen.' And he insisted this was properly Banks' decision. Barrie hung up and immediately called his minister. He told Reith the Defence Force would do what he, Barrie, told them, not Max Moore-Wilton. Reith agreed to talk to Howard.[19] The crisis blew over just a few hours later at around ten o'clock when Barrie got word that all the survivors had indeed been taken on board the *Adelaide* and were safe.

On the upper deck of the *Adelaide*, the exhausted asylum seekers, many dressed in navy surplus, huddled under a makeshift shelter. The crew had rigged up toilets and were handing out sleeping bags along with words of comfort. They found a navy towel to wrap up the three-week old baby, while his mother, dressed in a pair of navy combat overalls, fed him from a bottle. The children were hugged by the fretting sailors. In the few hours since the rescue, Banks had seen a surprising change in his ship's company. Many whom he thought were 'white Australia' types were some of the most compassionate and humane towards the survivors. As he told his sailors, 'These people are indeed human beings first, [and] whilst we could not understand their plight, we had to treat them as refugees'.[20]

But in the eyes of the politicians these survivors were the boat people who had thrown their children into the sea. As they settled down to sleep, Banks received an order from Darwin. He was not to bring the survivors to Christmas Island that night and must stay offshore until at least eight the next morning. It was an ominous sign. On the deck of the *Adelaide*, however, nothing could puncture the mood of pride and goodwill. Commander Banks and his crew faced a harrowing mission, one that put their orders to protect Australia's borders in conflict with their duty as mariners to save lives at sea. In the end, their commander followed his judgement and gave the orders to rescue just in time. Two hundred and twenty-three people were alive because of their efforts. They were heroes.

In the early hours of the morning, the *Adelaide*'s communications room sent out a series of photographs on its secret email system, recording an unforgettable day in the lives of the crew, 8 October, 2001. Two of the photos, captioned 'Courage' and 'Courage and Determination', pictured Able Seaman Laura Whittle and her mate, Leading Cook Jason 'Dogs' Barker, in their brave rescue of two stricken asylum seekers and their children, the open sea rising around them.

FIFTEEN
Truth overboard

OCTOBER 9 TO 12

A light rain fell on the deck of HMAS *Adelaide* in the early hours of Tuesday morning. Some of the exhausted Iraqis woke and moved their sleeping bags into the shelter of the awning on the forward deck. Commander Banks inspected his ship with a sense of relief. 'Quite a sight,' he recorded, 'a sea of bodies all at peace on a "foreign" warship forecastle'.[1]

Banks hoped to offload the survivors that morning at Flying Fish Cove before going back to scuttle the almost submerged wreck of SIEV 4, now a shipping hazard. But the Commander's plans, made in the peaceful dawn hours, were short lived. Canberra was still denying him permission to take the survivors to Christmas Island. Peter Reith was in the process of formally instructing Admiral Barrie that, despite their terrifying ordeal, the survivors were not to be landed at the island, 'except in extremis'.[2] Barrie's office was, in turn, preparing a directive to Northern Command: 'AD ARE NOT TO LAND PIIs ON CI—EVER'.[3] This was going to be another troubled day on board the ship.

Banks had been deeply affected by the events of the previous 48 hours and was extremely conscious of the survivors' welfare. Over two hundred people, many of them traumatised, were crowded on the deck of his ship sharing four toilets, with very little washing water, few clothes apart from navy gear and limited medical facilities. No doubt all this was on his mind when he decided to take a call from Channel 10's Elizabeth Bowdler, a resourceful television news reporter who had looked up the *Adelaide*'s satellite phone number on the Internet. Banks described the extraordinary rescue to her in some detail. He would not be drawn on the question of children thrown into the sea, but he was especially keen to talk about the children on the *Adelaide*, including the three-week old baby still wrapped in a navy towel. He said, 'It was quite a joy to hold the little kids' hands and watch them smile'. He told Bowdler there were pictures to go with her story because the *Adelaide* had emailed to Canberra two graphic photographs of Able Seaman Laura Whittle and Leading Seaman Barker rescuing children from the sea.[4]

The interview was in clear breach of Banks' orders under Operation Relex which barred all military officers from speaking to the media without clearance from the Minister for Defence. He had also, in another breach of the Relex media rules, 'humanised' boat people. So when Channel 10 called Defence public relations in Canberra asking for the photos, alarm bells sounded. Tim Bloomfield, media liaison officer at Defence, immediately notified Reith's press secretary, Ross Hampton. The minister's office then demanded an explanation from Rear Admiral Ritchie, commander of Australian Theatre Operations. The investigation of Banks' flouting of the media rules would consume the Defence hierarchy for hours. By lunch time, Reith's office was 'screaming' to see the photographs.[5]

Tim Bloomfield finally had them emailed to him from the navy at about three that afternoon. Attached to each was a colourful commentary by the amateur photographer who had taken the shots. One was tagged 'Whittle Courage' and a long caption read: 'Laura the hero. During the 08 Oct rescue of 223 SUNCs from a sinking Indonesian fishing vessel, Able Seaman Laura Whittle again typified this true quality through her immense courage in leaping 12 metres from the ship's 02 deck into the water to drag women and children to the safety of a life raft. Selflessly she entered the water without a life jacket and without regard for her own safety to help others in need.' The second photo was tagged 'Courage and Determination' and its caption read: 'Dogs and His Family. Jason "Dogs" Barker shows dogged determination as he helped rescue women and children by dragging them to safety during the rescue of 223 SUNCs from a sinking Indonesian fishing vessel. The big hearted Leading Seaman also demonstrated Navy's core value of COURAGE.'

Bloomfield did not think they were great shots. He told Ross Hampton they were just pictures of 'UBA's in the water' but Hampton wanted to see them. A flustered staffer in Bloomfield's office, under pressure to get the job done, copied the photographs on his computer desktop and sent them off to Reith's office stripped of their commentaries. The words did not seem important. 'The issue was to ensure that the photographs were provided to the Minister's Office as quickly as possible', the staffer would say later.[6] Hampton printed the photographs for Reith.

That afternoon, Bloomfield sat down and prepared an apologetic report for Hampton from Defence public relations. He agreed that Banks had spoken 'outside the guidelines' set down for Operation Relex and without permission from the minister's office. Bloomfield copied the email to every key figure in Defence public relations, reminding them of the media rules for Operation Relex: 'No imagery is to be released outside this system. All comment and Media Response/Inquiry is to be referred to MINDEF Media Adviser, Mr Ross Hampton . . .'[7] There was never any question in Bloomfield's mind that the two photos of Whittle and Barker were sent to Hampton for the investigation of Banks' unauthorised interview.

Silverstone put Banks' media transgression to one side for a time. He had far more pressing concerns. Reviewing reports from the *Adelaide*, Silverstone found nothing at all about children having been thrown overboard that Sunday. There was nothing to support his recollection of the conversation he had had with Banks during the boarding operation and nothing to back the message he then sent through to Halton's taskforce which had sparked the media frenzy of the last 48 hours. Silverstone was not the only one to notice this great gap in the paperwork. At Maritime headquarters in Sydney, the naval commander of Relex, Rear Admiral Geoff Smith, also realised there was nothing in the reports to confirm the children overboard claims. After two days of media coverage, Smith was 'acutely aware of the sensitivity of this particular subject'.[8] He picked up the phone and called Silverstone.

By now, Norman Banks had discovered his ship was at the centre of a major election story. Alerted by friends and colleagues, Banks went to the communications room and pulled down Monday's newspapers from the Internet. Reading the headlines and the lurid accounts of children being tossed into the sea, he was stunned by the serious 'misinformation' in the media coverage.[9] When Smith called and asked for an explanation, Banks must have realised what was at stake. The credibility of the Prime Minister, senior ministers and the senior command of the Defence Force was on the line right at the start of an election campaign. On the other hand, Banks had his own credibility—and that of his crew and commanders—to consider. He told Smith directly that he had been on the bridge for most of the operation and had seen no children thrown overboard. What he had seen was a child being *held* over the side. Banks offered one caveat. Some of the crew on the far side of the ship may have seen a child being thrown. Smith ordered Banks to interview them as quickly as possible and review the ship's videotape.[10]

Banks also had it out with Silverstone. He told his commander that a senior officer was at his side on October 7 and he could confirm his account of their telephone conversation. Silverstone, the tactical commander for Relex, was an experienced military officer. He did not shrink from his responsibility to correct the record if necessary. He instructed Banks to gather all the evidence on the boarding operation and determine whether or not children had been thrown overboard. This was, after all, just one detail in a difficult and confused military operation albeit a detail that was now causing a political sensation.

I

At Russell Hill, the headquarters of the Department of Defence in Canberra, Chris Barrie was trying to focus on the war. The bombing of Afghanistan had been underway for eighteen hours and Defence analysts were struggling to gauge the reaction from Australia's Muslim neighbours, Indonesia and Malaysia. The commander of Australia's defence forces could not remember experiencing pressure like this. The attacks on the World Trade Centre and the Pentagon were still consuming the military and intelligence chiefs. American intelligence had failed to foresee the attacks and thousands had died. Chris Barrie's greatest fear was a surprise terrorist attack in Australia, 'the risk of which I considered real and unprecedented'.[11]

The launch of America's Operation Enduring Freedom only added to the weight on Barrie. Howard had dramatically invoked the ANZUS Treaty in the days after the September 11 attacks, pledging all possible assistance to the United States but Barrie was still unclear just what that would be.

Also a problem, given the depth of America's pain and fury, were negotiations with Washington over the right of Australian commanders to maintain some control over Australian forces in this war. Barrie was adamant he did not want another Vietnam on his hands. He was insisting Australian forces be used 'in circumstances of which our community, our government and everyone would approve'.[12]

Howard and Reith would not concede that senior Defence leadership was under great strain in the aftermath of September 11 and in the execution of Operation Relex. Indeed, the Prime Minister was very effectively blurring the distinction between the war on terrorism and the war on boat people. Out in the marginal seats, Howard was campaigning hard on his ability to fight and win both battles. But inside the Defence Force, the pressure was being felt and the arguments between military officers and civilian public servants grew louder. What was to take priority here, Relex or Enduring Freedom? Howard said, however, 'The government was assured by its professional military advisers that the Defence Force could meet all the tasks asked of it'.[13]

At the afternoon meeting of Jane Halton's Taskforce on Tuesday, October 9—nearly 24 hours after Banks rescued the asylum seekers from the SIEV 4 and two days after the first children overboard reports—Defence asked once more that the survivors be taken immediately to Christmas Island so the *Adelaide* could prepare to leave for the Gulf. Howard and Reith were stalling. They had very publicly ruled out allowing 'these kinds of people' into Australia and were still trying to send them to the Cocos Islands. They were even suggesting airlifting them direct from the deck of the *Adelaide* until Banks informed them this was virtually impossible.[14] Urgent talks were underway with PNG to send the survivors to the new detention centre being set up on Manus Island but it was far from ready. Halton informed the meeting that the survivors would stay on the *Adelaide* for another night. Banks could not approach Christmas Island without Peter Reith's written permission.

Halton was acutely aware that serious doubts were being raised about passengers on SIEV 4 throwing their children into the sea. Her number two, Katrina Edwards, was concerned to find the daily Department of Foreign Affairs report had made no mention of the incident. She and Halton agreed the claims needed further checking. Journalists were already demanding evidence to back the first big story of the election campaign.

That morning's *Herald Sun* had reported Philip Ruddock fielding queries about the number and ages of the children involved. 'I imagine the sorts of children who would be thrown would be those who could be readily lifted and tossed without any objection from them', he replied without batting an eyelid.[15] The public servants were going to have to do a lot better than that. Halton knew she and the members of her taskforce were in the firing line. They had passed the original unconfirmed Defence reports on to Ruddock and Howard. She turned to Al Titheridge, the military man at the table, and warned him that Defence 'had better be certain about the veracity of the initial reports'. She strongly suggested they 'do some checking'.[16]

As night fell on the *Adelaide*, Norman Banks sent his own apology to his commander, Mike Silverstone, in Darwin. 'I am now fully aware of the political ramifications/sensitivities of this operation and will ensure that no further media questions are answered.' Back came an arch reproach from Northern Command, '[D]on't use the term "political" or "politics" to describe our current predicament as it is politically incorrect to do so. You should have said something like "awaiting policy guidance" and everyone still knows what you mean.'[17]

By next morning, Wednesday October 10, not only the media but the UNHCR, the Democrats, the Greens and—rather timidly—even Kim Beazley were casting doubt on the story. As the breakfast news bulletins went to air, Howard's press secretary, Tony O'Leary, called Ross Hampton with a question: were there any photographs of the children overboard incident that could be given out to the media?[18]

The hunt for evidence was on but it was clear to the Operation Relex hierarchy by a little after midday that the evidence they hoped to find was evaporating. Banks had found no eyewitness on HMAS *Adelaide* who saw a child being thrown overboard. The ship's official videotape operator, Able Seaman Wade Gerrits, had examined the hours of tape for the October 7 incident. It showed the five-year-old child being held over the side by her father and a 'youth' going overboard. Gerrits thought he saw a child in the water who had jumped voluntarily but there was no record of any child being recovered from the water that day.

Banks broke the news to both Silverstone and Smith. Silverstone instructed Banks to assemble all the evidence and send it through to him in Darwin. Smith urged Banks to put together a full chronology of the key events and send it as a personal message to him in Sydney. Banks promised both commanders he would keep making inquiries of sailors from the far side of the ship. Banks and Silverstone believed there was only a slim chance of any new evidence emerging. Smith was convinced by now that the incident simply had not happened.[19]

At midday Smith passed the difficult news up the line to Rear Admiral Ritchie who jotted some notes in his diary: the video only showed a man threatening to throw a child into the sea and one youth—maybe thirteen years old—being pushed over. But because there was talk of a child being seen in the water, Ritchie did not give up on the story entirely. Perhaps the crew on the far side of the *Adelaide* might have seen this child thrown in. He did note, however, that Al Titheridge's staff at Strategic Command had found no evidence to back the children overboard claims.[20]

Titheridge's office had put together a chronology of the October 7 incident from the *Adelaide*'s signals. None of the signals referred to any children being thrown overboard. A note on the chronology pointed out, 'There is no indication that children were thrown overboard'. But there was a qualification: 'It is possible that this did occur in conjunction with other SUNCs jumping overboard.' Soon after midday the chronology was sent across to the Department of Prime Minister and Cabinet where it landed on the desk of Katrina Edwards, Jane Halton's assistant on the People Smuggling Taskforce.

In Ballarat that day, the media pack trailing the Prime Minister was not very interested in the policies Howard had travelled to this marginal electorate to announce. He wanted to talk about giving money to private schools. The reporters were after the sort of story that could derail an election campaign. It was starting to look as if the sensational tale of children being flung from SIEV 4 was a government concoction. The first reporter to his feet put a devastating list of questions to Howard: 'Can you tell us how many children were thrown overboard, were they wearing life jackets, what evidence is there children were thrown overboard and can we have access to that evidence?' The Prime Minister sidestepped. His original claims were made, he said, 'on advice' from the Minister for Immigration. The journalists persisted, asking if there were photographs or videotape from the *Adelaide* showing children being thrown overboard. Under pressure Howard promised to 'make some inquiries and see what evidence can be made available'.[21]

But shortly after Howard made this undertaking, Admiral Ritchie rang Peter Reith's office to tell Mike Scrafton there were no reports, no testimony and no video to support the claims being made by the ministers. There were only two shreds of information: a youth *may* have been pushed overboard and there *may* have been children in the water. Statements from the crew on the far side of the *Adelaide might* substantiate these claims. Ritchie was waiting on those statements. Meanwhile, the senior commander responsible for the planning and conduct of all Australian military operations was telling the office of the Minister for Defence that there was no evidence any child was thrown into the sea from SIEV 4. Yet within three hours, Peter Reith would be offering 'proof' that was exactly what happened to every media outlet in the country.

Ross Hampton called Captain Belinda Byrne, a junior officer at Defence public relations, and asked her to get a breakdown of the ages of the fourteen people who had gone overboard on October 7. Byrne found Strategic Command had been searching for the same information with no success. Hampton did not take this news well. Captain Byrne said he became 'extremely agitated' and told her 'he had seen pictures that proved children had been thrown overboard'. She told the minister's press secretary she had not seen these but would keep looking.[22]

Reith phoned Admiral Barrie. The two men had been wrangling all day over the fate of the survivors of SIEV 4, who were still sitting on the deck of the *Adelaide* forbidden to land on Christmas Island. Now Reith was telling Barrie he had in front of him two photographs from the ship showing children in the water and he wanted to release them to the media. Barrie said he had not seen the photographs but he had no objection, provided the identities of the sailors were protected. Barrie said he would check with Titheridge over at Strategic Command.[23] Both Barrie and Titheridge were preoccupied with getting the survivors off the *Adelaide* and took little interest in Reith's request.

Just before three that afternoon, Hampton rang Tim Bloomfield from the minister's Melbourne office. Hampton said his computer was playing up and asked Bloomfield to email to Reith's Canberra office the two photographs 'Laura the hero' and 'Dogs and his family' which the minister had decided to release to the media. Bloomfield was surprised. Why would they want those photographs? Why was the minister still interested in Banks' Channel 10 interview? At this point, Bloomfield had no idea Reith would use the photographs as 'evidence' of children being thrown from SIEV 4. He asked Hampton if he wanted the pictures with or without the captions. By this, he meant the brief descriptions of the rescue that came with each. Hampton told him to send only the photographs. Later Hampton would insist he never asked Bloomfield to remove the rescue accounts, only the captions to protect the identities of the sailors.[24] In a move Bloomfield would soon regret, he removed all the text from the pictures and pressed the send button.

Ross Hampton told a sceptical press gallery that the minister would produce photographs and answer questions later that afternoon in Melbourne. To ensure maximum exposure for the evidence, Hampton told Defence public relations to email the photos to any media outlets asking for them. But the timing of the release was to be decided by Howard's office. Hampton would hold off until he got the nod from Howard's press secretary, Tony O'Leary.[25]

At Russell Hill, Brigadier Gary Bornholt, the senior military man on the Defence public relations team, suspected something was terribly wrong. Bornholt was an experienced military officer, intelligent, efficient and tough as nails. He commanded almost universal respect from his military colleagues and could walk into any office on Russell Hill and get answers. Belinda Byrne had already reported to him Hampton's agitated demands earlier in the afternoon. Now he was shocked to hear Hampton was about to release the photos. He feared the minister's press secretary was confusing the incident on October 7 with the mass rescue of October 8. He rang to set Hampton straight but found the press secretary 'irate' when he reached him on his mobile. Hampton claimed the photographs had come from Admiral Barrie's office with confirmation that they were from the children overboard incident.[26]

With only minutes to spare before Reith was due to go public with his evidence, Bornholt rang both Barrie's office and Strategic Command. He was told they had not supplied the photographs and they were not proof of the children overboard claims. Bornholt jotted a note in his diary and called Hampton again. But Hampton told him the minister was doing a doorstop media conference at 4.30 pm and the photographs would be released. Bornholt warned Hampton that 'there remained a question as to their veracity'.[27] A few minutes later, Bornholt finally got hold of the two pictures with their original long captions and it was absolutely clear these were photographs of the mass rescue on October 8. An officer at Strategic Command also confirmed that no children went into the water the day before. None.

Just as Bornholt received this report in Canberra, Peter Reith walked into the ABC-Radio studios in Melbourne. He planned to present his evidence to drive-time host Virginia Trioli before facing the press on the doorstep of his office. She asked for the photographs. Reith handed them over saying, 'Well it did happen. The fact is the children were thrown into the water. We got that report within hours of that happening. Given that there are people who weren't there of course, you know, claiming all sorts of, making all sorts of exaggerated claims . . . we have reproduced the photos on the basis that the identities were not shown publicly, as stated practice'.

Trioli was not convinced. 'Mr Reith, there's nothing in this photo that indicates these people either jumped or were thrown?'

Reith began ducking and weaving. 'No, well you are now questioning the veracity of what has been said. Those photos are produced as evidence of the fact that there were people in the water. You're questioning whether it even happened, that's the first point and I just want to answer that by saying these photos show absolutely without question whatsoever that there were children in the water.'

Trioli kept pushing and Reith went further out on a limb. 'Now we have a number of people, obvious RAN people who were there who reported the children were thrown into the water. Now, you may want to question the veracity of reports of the Royal Australian Navy. I don't and I didn't either but I have subsequently been told that they have also got film. That film is apparently on HMAS *Adelaide*. I have not seen it myself and apparently the quality of it is not very good, and it's infra-red or something but I am told that someone has looked at it and it is an absolute fact, children were thrown into the water. So do you still question it?'

Reith left for the full media briefing where he again faced sceptical questioning. Why were there no dates and times attached to photographs, asked one of the journalists. 'Couldn't these people be in the water after the boat actually sank?'

'Well,' Reith replied, 'I have this sequence of events from the navy personnel on board. They have film of the incident. They have photos of the incident, and for those who are questioning the report that I'm giving you, they are saying the ADF people are not telling the truth'.

While Reith was still giving this spin, Brigadier Bornholt tried to call Hampton again. Bornholt now had absolute confirmation that the photographs the minister had just released were from the rescue of the passengers on October 8, the day after the children overboard claims were made. But Hampton was not answering his mobile. Bornholt left an explicit message saying the photographs 'did not depict the events the minister was intending to portray'. Hampton did not return the call, saying later he never got the message.[28]

I

As Jane Halton walked into the five o'clock meeting of the taskforce, her mobile rang. Peter Reith was on the line. He had just finished his media doorstop and told Halton he had released the photographs to the press. He also told her there was video evidence of children being thrown overboard.

Halton was still on the line when Katrina Edwards hurried into the meeting. She had bad news. Strategic Command had sent through a document on the children overboard claims. It was the chronology of events from the *Adelaide* for October 7 and it undermined the original advice the taskforce had given on the children overboard claims. Edwards said she read out the critical endnote on the document to Halton: 'There is no indication that children were thrown overboard. It is possible that this did occur in conjunction with other SUNCs jumping overboard.' Edwards said she then gave the chronology to her boss. Halton would say she could not recall either reading the chronology or it being handed to her.[29]

Reith's news was a godsend for Halton. She began a series of frantic calls to nail down the new evidence offered by the minister. She finally spoke to Mike Scrafton in Reith's office. Just what Scrafton told her is unclear except that there *was* a videotape of the incident. If he passed on to her the briefing he had had from Rear Admiral Ritchie, Halton should have known the videotape provided no evidence to back up the original claims. But following her conversations with Reith and Scrafton, Halton was confident enough to table a report to the taskforce which still included the children overboard claims. No one in the room apparently objected.

The taskforce was about to wrap up the SIEV 4 case. Halton distributed a draft press release from the Prime Minister announcing that PNG had, that day, joined the Pacific Solution. 'Papua New Guinea has agreed to establish a processing centre to assist Australia in combating people smuggling and illegal migration in the Asia-Pacific region.' The first candidates for this new Nauru would be the survivors of SIEV 4. 'The unauthorised arrivals rescued by the HMAS *Adelaide* will be disembarked and held on Christmas Island temporarily, until they can be transferred to the new processing centre in Papua New Guinea.'[30] That night, under the cover of darkness, the *Adelaide* unloaded its sorry human cargo at Flying Fish Cove while the media was kept at bay. Many of the survivors shook hands with the crew, thanking them for their lives. They had no idea what lay ahead.

Commander Norman Banks settled down to compile a full account of October 7 for his commanders. He hoped to lay to rest the children overboard allegations. In front of him were sixteen statutory declarations from crew members who witnessed the incident. Not one had seen a child being thrown overboard. Many saw a father holding his child over the rail. Some believed he intended to jump with her, some thought he was about to throw her and some thought he wanted the sailors to save his child. As for the youth who was 'pushed' overboard, five sailors said they saw a teenager or a young man go overboard, one said he thought he saw a child. But all the witnesses said the youth or child jumped voluntarily and was wearing a life jacket.[31]

As Banks worked on his report, almost every other senior defence commander, it seemed, was watching ABC-TV's *7.30 Report* which flashed on the screen the two photographs Reith had released that afternoon as evidence of the government's children overboard claims. The commanders were stunned. Whatever had happened on October 7, these were pictures of the rescue on October 8. Rear Admiral Smith was the first on the phone to both Ritchie and the head of the navy, Admiral David Shackleton, to say this mistake had to be corrected. Those admirals, in turn, called the Chief of the Defence Force at home. Ritchie told Barrie bluntly, 'The Minister's words on the *7.30 Report* and photos shown of people in the water were not related to the "child throwing incident"'. Shackleton was equally direct. The photos 'are linked to the wrong event... They are people being recovered from the boat sinking'. Barrie had no option. He promised both men he would speak to Reith in the morning.[32]

On Christmas Island, some of the *Adelaide*'s sailors were also spreading the word to the stevedores and quarantine officers that no kids had been thrown overboard. The photos on the *7.30 Report* were just not right. The navy guys sought out the 'civvies' because they wanted them to know it didn't happen.

Brigadier Gary Bornholt at Defence public relations knew a scandal was in the making. The photographs were a gross misrepresentation. Worse still, sitting in the department's email system, available to scores of officers, were copies of the photos with their true date and the original captions detailing the rescue. He emailed the head of his section, Jenny McKenry, with a warning. 'It is only a matter of time before this possibly finds its way into the public arena.' He suggested they notify Mike Scrafton in Reith's office, in writing, first thing in the morning, 'so that the Minister is aware of the possibility of ensuing damage'.[33]

▌

The newspapers were still sceptical next morning, Thursday October 11. The *Herald Sun* ran the rather fuzzy shots of sailors and asylum seekers in the sea but wrote: 'The pictures provide graphic evidence children were in the water. But they do not shed light on whether adult people from Iraq pushed them unwillingly into the ocean.' The *Australian* led its report with Reith's refusal to release the *Adelaide*'s videotape, which he was now citing as conclusive proof of the original allegations. But on radio that morning, the Prime Minister was one of the few people who did not hesitate to back Peter Reith. 'You saw the photographs and I understand from Mr Reith that there is an infra red Naval video which is not of great quality but provides even starker evidence of what was alleged on Sunday.'[34]

At 9 o'clock that morning, Bornholt sat down with Jenny McKenry to demolish Reith's evidence. As they prepared a comprehensive critique of the photographs, two of Reith's senior advisers, Mike Scrafton, from the minister's office and Dr Allan Hawke, Secretary of the Department of Defence, called to discuss the pictures. McKenry told both men, in unqualified terms, that the use of the photographs as proof of children being thrown overboard was a complete misrepresentation. Bornholt also outlined his attempts to warn Ross Hampton the previous day.[35]

Reith's man Scrafton turned the attack back on McKenry, accusing her office of being at fault. The cause of the confusion, he said, was the failure of her officer Tim Bloomfield to send the captions and text with the photos when they went to Reith's office. McKenry promptly arranged to send Scrafton the photographs with their original attachments. They were also sent to Ross Hampton. 'We were left in no doubt that Mr Scrafton understood what we were saying about the photographs', McKenry said later.[36] She also warned Scrafton that the photographs with their original captions had been copied throughout the unrestricted Defence public relations computer system making a leak to the media more than possible. Reith's man told her to strip them out of the system. She agreed because, she told herself, 'I believed the minister's office should first have the opportunity to make the correction'. Reith never made that correction. He would tell his staff, 'How do I know these photos are [the right ones] attached to these emails?'[37]

The Prime Minister's department was also told by the Defence liaison officer, Commander Stefan King, that the photographs were not evidence of children being thrown overboard. He was stunned to discover the truth at that morning's daily briefing at Strategic Command. King worked in the department's International Division, which had given advice on both Operation Relex and the Pacific Solution. He was sure the department would want to be aware of the blunder and see it corrected. His immediate superior, the senior defence adviser Harinder Sidhu, 'instantly agreed that this information warranted being passed to our Assistant Secretary and that she should join me in briefing him'. They saw Dr Brendon Hammer, Assistant Secretary Defence, Intelligence and Security, at 3 o'clock that afternoon. King outlined the misrepresentation of the photographs. Hammer agreed the information was 'sensitive' but said very little and gave King no indication how he would act. King assumed he would take the matter higher. Hammer did not and justified his decision with the age-old public servant's excuse that this was 'something I did not have within my area of responsibility'.[38]

|

Etiquette matters a great deal in the armed forces. Good form is power. The only military officer with the right to advise the Minister for Defence is the most senior officer of all, the Chief of the Defence Force. Of all the military, only he can broach a subject with the minister. By this Thursday October 11, the chain of command was depending on Admiral Barrie to set the record straight with Reith. In the end, Barrie failed.

He had met the minister at 10 o'clock that morning. Reith was in a truculent mood and Barrie found their exchange 'testy'. When the admiral explicitly informed Reith the photographs were evidence not of children going overboard but of children being rescued from the sinking SIEV, Reith went on the attack. He castigated Barrie for not checking the photographs. In the face of Reith's aggression, Barrie backed off. Despite the concerns of his most senior commanders, he did not ask Reith to correct publicly the gross misrepresentation of the photos. 'We had an agreement; we would drop this matter,' explained Barrie, 'and it was not said but it was my understanding that he would deal with the consequences'. Nor would Barrie allow his own people to clarify the dates on the photos. 'I have fulfilled my duty. I have brought it to his attention', Barrie told himself. 'As far as I am concerned, because he is now managing public affairs aspects, that is where it lies.'[39]

Reith knew it might not lie there for long. He took the precaution of writing up Barrie's conversations in his diary for future reference. Barrie was snared. Later that day Chris Ritchie tried to convince his commander in a long telephone call that no child had been thrown overboard. Admiral Ritchie now had all the first-hand statements of the *Adelaide*'s crew. They killed the last faint hopes of finding something to support the politicians' claims. None of the crew had seen a child thrown overboard. No child was recovered from the water. The video showed nothing. 'From those three points I have drawn the conclusion that it probably did not happen.'[40]

Barrie was in an extremely tight corner. Accepting Ritchie's evidence would put him in direct conflict with his minister and his prime minister in the early days of an election campaign as Australian forces were preparing to take part in the War Against Terror. What's more, the military would end up wearing a great deal of the blame if the original advice to Ruddock and Reith now had to be corrected. This mess was proof that the military should never have agreed to the quick reporting arrangements demanded by the government during Operation Relex. If the news from SIEV 4 had been properly analysed before being fed to the ministers before their Sunday morning press conferences, there would have been no doubts then and no embarrassment now.

Barrie told Ritchie he would not change his original advice to Reith, saying there was not enough evidence 'to show that what had been originally reported to me was wrong'. Barrie would hold to this position right through the election and beyond. When Ritchie put the phone down he was convinced it was 'a dead issue'. He wrote up his own conclusions in his diary.[41]

Canberra officials—civilian and military—did not have to be geniuses to realise by this time that neither Reith nor Howard seemed keen to get to the bottom of the issue. Reith was refusing 'for operational security reasons' to release the videotape both he and the Prime Minister claimed was 'even starker evidence' than the photographs of boat people flinging their children into the sea. Howard's own language shifted slightly: he was more cautious about the claims. The story almost disappeared from the repertoire of the ministers, perhaps as a result of Barrie's agreement with Reith. Having made its indelible mark, the story died down. But its impact on the electorate was immense: here was damning proof of the base instincts of these 'illegals' from which the Howard government was saving Australia.

Journalists knew Reith too well to be satisfied by his assurances. He sourced the story to the navy but the media was now blocked from asking the navy any questions. Enquiries about photographs, videos and children overboard were flicked from the Prime Minister to Reith and on to the minister's press secretary, Ross Hampton—who would not answer them. Further precautions were already in place to guard against leaks from the front line of Operation Relex. Sailors had been banned from sending personal emails and digital photographs during the interception of SIEVs. A 'restricted priority' signal leaked to the *Australian* claimed the ban was 'necessary to ensure the integrity of current operations and essential to mission accomplishment'. Navy sources quoted by the paper described the bans as 'excessive'.[42]

That the lid would stay on the children overboard story forever was impossible to imagine. Apart from the hierarchy of senior officers who knew the truth by the end of the first week in October, the *Adelaide* had a company of 210 men and women who had known all along that the story was bogus. The *Adelaide* would now disappear from Relex but not yet from

Australia. The crew would be quizzed by their partners, families and friends. The truth would soon be known in the naval community. The only question for the government was whether the original story would hold until election day.

SIXTEEN
A military campaign

OCTOBER 14 TO 23

The first week of the election campaign climaxed with a television debate between the leaders on Sunday October 14. Beazley had spent the day rehearsing, with Labor's Senate leader John Faulkner playing the role of John Howard. By the time the Labor team arrived at the Channel 9 studio in Sydney, Beazley was confident he could answer the main charge he knew he would face: that Labor was weak on border protection, flip flopping, working both sides of the street. The Prime Minister was giving Labor no credit for supporting every move the government was making in its campaign against asylum seekers. The one brave act of rejecting that first Border Protection Bill was still being used mercilessly against the Opposition.

Howard won the toss. He was uncharacteristically nervous. His blunt, flat eloquence failed him at first. His thoughtful frown locked at times into a grimace of exasperation. Once or twice, he whined. The two leaders spent half their hour on border protection. Beazley scored unexpectedly well. 'Now the person who flipped flopped on this, Prime Minister—if you want to use those insulting terms, if you don't mind my saying—was you. You came back with a Bill that worked and a Bill that we could support.'

They were such different men. Howard looks Australians in the face and sees them not as they wish they were or hoped they might become—

but exactly as they are. His political assessment is ruthlessly unsentimental. He was the first prime minister since Robert Menzies to come to power without an agenda for the improvement of the nation. For half a century, every prime minister had offered some sort of program to enlarge the spirit of Australia and deal with its ghosts. With great differences of emphasis and enthusiasm, this was as true for Harold Holt as Paul Keating. But Howard came to office with a program for economic change and a pledge to make Australians feel 'relaxed and comfortable' about themselves. He was mocked for this and those words were cited as proof he was some political dwarf. Later it emerged he was making a potent pledge to Australians: to leave their consciences alone.

Beazley's main asset was that Australians *liked* him. He was affable, approachable, buoyant. He could give a fine stump speech, without notes, his black suit flapping in the wind, his words plain, his message clear: 'It's time this out-of-touch bunch were gone, time that ordinary Australians had a break, time they had a government on their side.' His politics were coloured by the great romance of Labor. Campaigning in the Hunter Valley one blustery day, he was piped onto the picnic ground by the United Mineworkers Federation Band. He beamed as he marched behind the kilts and drums into an old, white crowd of supporters and their grandchildren. He loved and was good at all this: the picnic, the band, three cheers and the warm-up speeches from union heavies who talked about 'workers' and 'comrades' without the chic irony of Labor in town. Beazley could also quote Lincoln to a crowd of artists in the back room of a city pub and flatter them with the idea that while he was a mere politician their task was to follow 'the deeper rhythms of society'. Often verbose and way off message, Beazley was one of those politicians who give the impression of being built on a more generous scale than their record might suggest; that inside him there was a big soul biding its time; that victory would see him grow.[1]

Yet he and Labor had no real quarrel with Howard over blockading boat people. Labor was not arguing that civilised nations don't shut their ports to refugees. Nor was Labor defending the latest arrivals as victims of some of the most brutally repressive regimes on earth, so brutal we were going to war to crush them. Nor was Labor trying to put into perspective the trivial numbers involved. Only about 15 000 boat people had arrived in fifteen years, during which time Australia accepted more than two million immigrants. Labor was silent on the racial fears underlying John Howard's campaign. No one in the Opposition was contesting—at least in public—Howard's brilliant manipulation of a complex issue into a simple question of national security. But how could these Muslim arrivals 'threaten' Australia's borders when they willingly presented themselves to be taken into migration detention? They were an expensive and difficult challenge, not a sovereign threat. All Labor was arguing throughout the election campaign was that it would do the same job Howard was doing, but do it better. Labor would set up a coast guard to relieve the navy in the Indian Ocean and Labor had the clout in Jakarta to do the tough deals needed to stop asylum seekers making the journey in the first place.

Even so, that impression of innate stature counted for Beazley in his television confrontation with Howard. He was quicker on his feet, quite crisp, the bigger man. While the cameras still rolled, Howard's hand-picked adjudicator, Ray Martin, offered the Channel 9 studio any night until polling day if the leaders wanted to debate again. Beazley was willing to go another round. Howard dismissed the idea. He said, 'I think we've done very well tonight'.

I

In the daily battle to win page one in the election campaign, Labor and Beazley enjoyed one of their few victories next morning. The almost unanimous verdict of the press was that Beazley had won the television contest. 'BEAZLEY TALKS HIS WAY INTO THE RACE', announced the *Australian*; 'COALITION FINDS IT HAS A FIGHT ON ITS HANDS', declared the *Financial Review*; 'BEAZLEY TAKES POINTS IN DEBATE', said the *Age*. The press verdict was confirmed by a boost in the opinion polls. Since the arrival of the *Tampa*, nothing had done so much to reinvigorate Labor as Beazley's one hour on television.

But in the battle for the front page, Howard had two great advantages. First, he was prime minister of a country preparing to go to war. It was page one across the nation on October 17 when President Bush rang Howard and Australia committed ships, aircraft and a detachment of SAS to Operation Enduring Freedom. The war helped the government in more subtle ways, too. At a time of dramatic military initiatives, it didn't seem so very odd for Australia to be mobilising its navy to repel a few hundred boat people at the height of an election campaign. And with all this talk of terrorism in the air, it seemed not so outrageous for Peter Reith to suggest terrorists might be lurking among the boat people.² While Labor plodded on with its agenda of health, education and the GST, the Howard machine brilliantly combined absolute opposites—the western world's stand against the Taliban and Australia's military blockade of refugees fleeing the same enemy—into a single potent campaign.

Howard's second advantage in the battle to dominate the media was the extraordinary political control of news from Operation Relex, control that tightened after the debacle of SIEV 4. Military commanders would later complain that Reith's office had, in effect, made them accessories in a political exercise. But no evidence has emerged that the military tried very hard—if at all—to remedy the situation during the campaign. Indeed, records for these weeks show the military falling in with the idea that Operation Relex had to provide good publicity for the government. 'Potential mission failure leading to negative PR' was an early issue of concern in the planning of the operation. Admiral Barrie's minutes to his minister warned, 'Australian Defence Force operations to deter unauthorised boat arrivals will attract significant media attention'. The Relex files contain extensive analyses of press conferences, international reporting and clear warnings of public relations pitfalls. The military advised that the unloading of the *Manoora*, for instance, would be 'subject to close scrutiny by IOM, the media and the government of Nauru'. At times, the military was clearly using the prospect of bad publicity to pressure the government. In a failed effort to allow a pregnant woman on SIEV 3 to be airlifted to hospital, an unnamed officer advised: 'Consequences of delivery complications could give rise to potential adverse public image issues.' Medical evacuations had to be approved personally by the Prime Minister. None was allowed to the mainland during Relex.³

From the government's point of view, the news blackout was working smoothly after the Banks hiccup. Journalists could not get onto the ships; public affairs officers on the ships could not speak to the press; the commanders could not be interviewed. Experienced defence correspondents found their contacts extremely reluctant to talk. All questions about Relex were being flick-passed to Peter Reith's office. Ministers spoke and statements were issued but there were no press briefings from the military on operational detail: no maps, no photographs, no Q & As. There was nothing journalists could use to tell the human story of the operation, not from the sailors' nor the asylum seekers' points of view. There was no access to asylum seekers held on Christmas Island. The only photographs from the blockade released in these weeks were the two Reith published to shore up claims of children being thrown from SIEV 4. The only video was later released for the same reason.

This political blackout came at some price for Canberra. What better way to 'send a message' to people smugglers and asylum seekers than to release dramatic video footage of the navy intercepting the SIEVs? What better way to tell the world Australia was no longer a 'soft touch' than to have journalists writing vivid accounts of these confrontations? The intense censorship surrounding the operation pointed, once again, to its principal purpose: to impress the Australian electorate. Not only was the propaganda impact on the outside world muffled by censorship but Australians saw neither the hard work and courage of the military, nor the suffering, despair and sometimes violence of the boat people. All the electorate had to know was that Canberra was winning a contest in the Indian Ocean with a tide of faceless and ruthless 'illegals'.

At this point in the campaign—six weeks after the appearance of the *Tampa*—little of what was happening behind the scenes had been reported. None of the asylum seekers had had a chance to give their accounts of confrontations with the navy. The first details of Canberra's treatment of the *Tampa* and the bizarre threats to fine and imprison Arne Rinnan were only about to appear in print. Norway and Australia had managed to keep a lid on their diplomatic brawls. The sordid negotiations with Nauru were vividly reported almost as they happened but far less had been written about the parallel negotiations with PNG. Hidden entirely from public view were the frantic efforts of Howard's ministry and bureaucracy to drive the crisis. Canberra was shut tight. Ministers' offices weren't leaking. Neither was the military. So tightly was information held that the existence of Jane Halton's People Smuggling Taskforce went almost unreported. The crucial role of Max Moore-Wilton was only hinted at. The name Operation Relex had appeared no more than half a dozen times in print. What was really going on was barely known.

|

Canberra's most remarkable secret was this: Relex was not working. After five weeks, the navy had not persuaded a single vessel to turn back to Indonesia. The latest boat to outface Australia's fighting ships was the *Hara-*

panindah, making for Ashmore with 238 Afghans on board. Its engine had failed two days out from Lombok. Food ran low. Water was rationed. Mechanics among the passengers eventually got the engine going again. In their eight days at sea, these people suffered all the usual afflictions: sea sickness, diarrhoea, scabies. A baby died in the heat. Another was born whom the mother would name Ashmorey. After all this, they were delighted to see the *Warramunga* on the morning of October 12 but then sailors came in a little boat and told them, 'Go back. The Australian Government will not accept illegal immigration'. They replied, 'We are not illegal immigration. We are asylum seekers'.[4] The Australians boarded them and took them back to the high seas. They left and after a few hours the boat turned for Ashmore once again. This time the master declared it was impossible for him to sail back to Indonesia, so the Australians escorted the boat into the lagoon.

On their first day at anchor, the new mother, Fatama, began to experience uterine bleeding. A navy doctor saw her twice that day. Her husband Saeed told Debbie Whitmont of ABC-TV's *Four Corners*: 'When he came back in the afternoon, he said he might take her away and asked if I had any objection. I said I had none. I would have been happy with anything that would get her treated.' The doctor returned again the next day, according to Saeed. 'He said he had asked for a security permit but hadn't got it yet but that he would try to get it soon to take her away.' On the third day, the doctor told Saeed he was still trying to get permission to evacuate Fatama. With him was a woman whom Saeed also took to be a doctor. He recalled her saying, 'She really needs something. Try to get her out of here'. The Prime Minister of Australia considered her case. 'I said that if that were necessary, if her health was seriously in danger or was threatened, she should be medically evacuated if necessary to the Australian mainland to ensure that she received proper medical advice.' Fatama was not evacuated. The official summary of the incident read: 'The mother's condition had improved, and following specialist advice, the medical officer declared that medivac wasn't necessary.' Saeed told *Four Corners* she bled for a month.[5]

The Afghans sat quietly for five days on their grossly over-crowded, filthy boat designated SIEV 5. The navy fed them. When they asked about their fate, they were told: 'The government did not decide on you. Maybe they will ask you to come to Australia.' Ruddock answered just as evasively when the press began asking the same question. 'There are no immediate plans to move them. We are looking at a variety of options.'[6]

Even before the fiasco of SIEV 4, it was clear Relex was doing nothing much to persuade the boats to go home and the government began to consider forcing the issue. The idea was initiated by Moore-Wilton, then driven by Reith, Ruddock and Howard. While the Iraqis rescued from SIEV 4 were still camped on the decks of the *Adelaide,* Indonesia was alerted that 'vessels coming into Australian waters would henceforth be returned to the place from which they'd come'. There was no diplomatic eruption and, three days later, a 'sub-group on towing vessels back' presented Jane Halton's taskforce with a draft paper on the 'active return' of boats.[7]

Halton was meeting resistance from bureaucrats on three fronts. Lawyers were worried about the legality of the operation; diplomats were nervous about Indonesia's response; and the navy was concerned about the safety of lives at sea. There was a great deal of discussion about SOLAS issues. Pushing boats out of Australian waters was dangerous enough, but the risks would rise dramatically if these rotten and overcrowded boats were seized and driven all the way back to Indonesian waters. The navy would have to expect more sabotage and more violence. The strain on sailors and army units would be extreme. So would the danger. The navy was very unhappy about the prospect. Halton persisted. Her response to the doubters in her ranks was to demand they come up with the best possible arguments—legal, diplomatic and military—to support the government's new policy. It was not a time for frank and fearless advice.

Next day, October 12, Halton's taskforce officially advised the Secretaries Committee on National Security (SCONS) that the new strategy was difficult and dangerous but 'subject to a range of caveats, obviously, about seaworthiness and a series of other issues [it was] possible to return vessels'. SCONS took 'a slightly different view in respect of a couple of elements of the advice' then passed it to the Prime Minister for decision. Howard approved the advice and issued new orders for Relex at once. The first boat to be forced back would be SIEV 5. Admiral Smith said, 'With SIEV 5, we received new instructions which were, where possible, to intercept, board and return the vessel to Indonesia'. Relex was now a fundamentally different, more aggressive operation.[8]

This was a big decision for Australia to take but it was made in a rush, without public debate of any kind, despite the reservations of senior bureaucrats and military officers and without consultation with Labor at a time when the 'caretaker' conventions of election campaigns clearly mandated that the Opposition had to be consulted. But Labor made no fuss and fell in with the new policy. Indonesia made no public fuss either. Senior Foreign Affairs officials in Jakarta told Australia's ambassador Ric Smith that Indonesia believed the new Australian strategy was in breach of international law. Indonesia was ignored but chose to have no brawl with Australia. A leaked memo from Smith claimed that Canberra's wish to involve the Indonesians in the fate of the boats was being 'frustrated by the crude and unsatisfactory device of simply not communicating with us'.[9] But Australia could not be more pleased. In the end, the legal basis for the revamped Operation Relex was the doctrine of acquiescence: Australia could drive boats back to Indonesia because Indonesia allowed it to be done.

I

The Afghans on SIEV 5 had no idea what was happening when Lieutenant Commander Simon Gregg of the *Warramunga* boarded the boat with a party of sailors backed by TSE troops in the early afternoon of October 17. The asylum seekers claim they were told 'Australia has accepted you' and that they were being taken to a camp on the mainland. Gregg said he merely told them 'the Australian Government was considering their situation' and they could no longer stay at Ashmore. Either way, the Afghans remained 'calm and quiet' throughout the afternoon. The 'family elements' were transferred to the *Warramunga* and SIEV 5 was then towed towards the open sea while sailors finished repairing the sabotaged engines. The ignition key and fuel pump had been thrown overboard, the cooling pump was wrecked. After two hours, the engines came to life, the tow rope was dropped and the boat set out for Indonesia at top speed—3.5 knots—with Gregg at the wheel.[10]

According to the asylum seekers, the 160 single men left on SIEV 5 had been forced into the hold by Australian soldiers. It was extremely crowded. 'Most of the people were standing. And there were also the smoke of the engine.'[11] Meals and water were brought over from the *Warramunga*. Men who fainted in the hold were taken up on deck, revived with a splash of salt water and put back in the hold. The journey took 30 hours.

Peter Reith expected to be briefed throughout the operation and ordered 'a regular stream of sitreps [situation reports]—preferably in writing—two or four hourly'. His direction was scrawled on a kind of contract he and Barrie now signed before each SIEV was forced back to Indonesia. It seems a deal had been struck to try to end the tension between civilians and the military over SOLAS issues. The minister acknowledged the navy's responsibility to 'render all possible assistance to save life at sea' but coupled this with a bizarre direction to the navy to persuade Indonesia to take responsibility should disaster strike the tow backs. 'In the event of the UBA [unlawful boat arrival] vessel sinking in the Indonesian Search and Rescue zone, Indonesian authorities will be asked to provide assistance.'[12] The notion that BASARNAS would leap into action while an Australian naval vessel was already at the scene was simply delusional.

Before dawn on October 19, SIEV 5 reached the edge of Indonesian territorial waters off Roti Island and Gregg handed command back to the Indonesian crew thirteen nautical miles from land. When the men in the hold were told they had been returned to Indonesia they 'became hostile stating, quote kill us we no go unquote, and trying to break down the wooden bulkhead between the hold and the engine room'. The bulkhead collapsed and the TSE had to clear the engine room and then douse a fire lit by the angry men. A man in the hold began to mutilate his chest and arms with a razor blade. He could not be reached by soldiers in the crush but 'the wounds were assessed as not life threatening'. Meanwhile, amid scenes of grief and violence, the families were being returned from the *Warramunga* in what was officially described as a 'forced removal'.[13]

A Tajik from Afghanistan named Aziza told an investigator from the New York based organisation Human Rights Watch, 'We tried to put our babies at the soldiers' feet and begged them to have mercy on the children: "Where are the rights of the children?", I asked in Persian, and a man translated that question for me.' The soldiers were unmoved and proceeded to clear the ship. 'They had iron military badges on their shoulders, and one man touched it with his stick to show the electric sparks. Then they beat the sides and ribs of my husband with the electric sticks until he was unconscious. He was hit at least four times.' Aziza claimed two Australian soldiers then used their electric batons to force her into the RHIB. 'I fell on top of my baby. The baby was not injured, but I was badly bruised on my arms and legs. Where they had hit me, there were bruises that felt hot.

The pain from those strokes got worse a little later, and I continued to feel pain in those spots for nearly a month afterwards.'[14]

Australian military authorities insist no more than 'minimum force' was ever used against asylum seekers during Operation Relex. The use of electric batons has been specifically denied by Air Marshal Angus Houston speaking for the armed services. Human Rights Watch claims the use of these batons on SIEV 5 was corroborated in a number of interviews. Afghans from the same boat also told *Four Corners* that soldiers used electric batons to clear them from the *Warramunga*. 'It was like a black stick . . . When they pulled it out, they first hit the shoulders. They had badges on their shoulders. When it hit, it gave off electricity.' These reports closely resemble those made by the Iraqis forcibly cleared from the *Manoora* a fortnight earlier. The Iraqis—who had no subsequent contact with the Afghans of SIEV 5—spoke of their quarters on the ship being 'invaded by twenty armed soldiers carrying . . . electric sticks'. Air Marshal Houston's explanation is that TSE units carried metal detectors to help in the search for weapons. 'I understand the metal detectors have little lights on them, and when they detect metal the lights flash.' He stressed these were not 'cattle prod type' implements. 'Our people are not issued with those, nor do they carry them.'[15] Beyond dispute is that whatever these implements were, they frightened the asylum seekers.

The sun came up while this desperate operation continued. The Australians had provisioned the SIEV with food and water, new fire extinguishers and charts. 'The Indonesian master was informed that he had enough fuel for a one way trip to the nearest port [Kupang] and that he had enough four stroke fuel to operate his bilge pump for five minutes every twelve hours.' Threats of mass suicide were ignored. 'The aggressive PIIs stated that most PIIs will kill themselves if returned to Indonesia and wish to wait in international waters for the United Nations.' Although Gregg believed the engines had been disabled by the asylum seekers again, he took his men off at 7.30 am and withdrew over the horizon. Once it was clear that SIEV 5 was heading back into Indonesian waters, '*Warramunga* was ordered by Commander Joint Taskforce to depart the scene at speed and return to patrol of Ashmore Island'.[16]

That afternoon, before John Howard flew to the Shanghai summit of APEC, he called a press conference in Brisbane to announce that a vessel bringing illegal immigrants to Australia had, for the first time, been escorted back to Indonesian waters. 'It was all carried out in accordance with very careful legal advice we'd been given. There was no violence. We gave humanitarian assistance; we gave medical assistance; we particularly looked after the person who'd had the child.' Henceforth, he announced, all such vessels would be 'returned to the place from which they'd come'. He painted a picture of harmonious relations with Indonesia. 'We continue to work cooperatively with the Indonesian government to tackle the shared problem of people smuggling.'[17]

Australians took in their stride the news that their country had joined the shabby ranks of 'push off' nations. Perhaps if the public had known then what this meant for the asylum seekers on the *Warramunga* and SIEV 5, the response might have been different. The UNHCR made a fuss: 'The Australian government may have placed itself in breach of its legal obligations under the 1951 Refugee Convention.' But such polite dissent from the international body did not dent the general mood of support at home for this vigorous and effective action to protect the borders. Australia remained in the eyes of Australians, a decent country.

Shanghai gave the Prime Minister a chance to walk on the world stage for a few days in the middle of the election campaign. Any Australian leader would seize the opportunity and Howard ignored demands by Labor and Beazley that he stay home and stick to the hustings. In Shanghai, Howard wanted to meet Megawati Sukarnoputri who had refused to take his telephone calls since the *Tampa*. She cut him again in Shanghai. Howard wanted to hold talks with President Bush but would be given an affectionate photo opportunity instead. One leader ready and waiting to meet Howard was Sir Mekere Morauta. PNG was in financial trouble again and Australia had a favour to ask.

Frantic efforts by Canberra to find other places in the Pacific to process asylum seekers were getting nowhere. Nauru was full. After the *Tobruk* landed the people from SIEVs 2 and 3 on the island, the government's chief secretary, Jesaulenko Dowiyogo, said firmly: 'At this stage we have as many as we can take.' The Iraqis from SIEV 4, being flown up to Manus as world leaders gathered in Shanghai, would fill the PNG camp. Kiribati, Fiji, Tuvalu and Tonga were proving either unsuitable or unwilling to join the Pacific Solution. Australia's best hope was to persuade PNG to vastly expand the Manus camp: a group of old Nissen huts plus some converted shipping containers sitting on a malarial patch of ground between the jungle and the sea. Jane Halton's taskforce had already been looking at the possibility of both enlarging the camp and extending its life from six months to a year. The main logistical challenges were sewerage and staff accommodation, but if Australia was given the go ahead it would not take long to quadruple the facilities—'Minimum of 4 weeks to expand to 1000'.[18]

Morauta met Howard and Max Moore-Wilton 'in the margins' at Shanghai on October 21. The deal they struck was that Canberra would urgently examine the early payment of $34 million in aid to assist PNG 'face difficulties in maintaining health, education and infrastructure spending' in return for permission to enlarge the Manus camp. Howard and Max Moore-Wilton played down this quid pro quo but Morauta reported Howard speaking at the meeting of 'the need to increase the capacity of the facilities to accommodate additional asylum seekers'. Sir Mekere added: 'Is it not fair when Papua New Guinea receives 500 million kina from Australia [each year], to give a hand?'[19] The details were left to be settled by officials.

This proved messy. The Manus deal exacerbated old tensions between Morauta and his foreign minister, John Pundari, who dug in his heels when he received Australia's official request. 'My secretary immediately came up to me and said, "We're not going to do it, this wasn't the right way". He said the Australians were interfering with our internal affairs again.' The Foreign Minister's view was that Australia had the resources to deal with its own refugee problems. He knocked back the request. 'We said we will not accept further asylum seekers to be processed in PNG and if we have to take any more we will have to give it time and have it properly considered not like the previous one that was dumped down on us.' Pundari then briefed the press. Within 24 hours, both he and the secretary of his department, Evoa Lalatute, had been dismissed. 'I had no choice but to sack them', said Morauta. 'The worst crime here is leaking confidential letters before the foreign government has seen it.'[20] The Manus deal went ahead.

I

Operation Relex was hard work. Even before the SIEV 5 operation began, Admiral Barrie had been begging Reith to give his sailors a break. 'I am very firmly of the view that *Warramunga* should be released from the Relex commitment for a period of personnel respite of around seven days in port.'²¹ That was not to be. Once the *Warramunga* had delivered the Afghans back to Indonesia, it was sent across to Christmas Island where the *Mulya Jaya*—SIEV 6—had been moored for three days off Smith Point with 200 Afghans and 27 others on board. Though Canberra had decided the boat would be forced back to Indonesia, Jane Halton's taskforce minutes noted: 'Ministers will maintain public line that the government is still considering handling of SIEV 6 and will advise on decision in near future.'²²

Women and children were taken on board the *Warramunga* to relieve the overcrowding while the engineers began to repair the extensively sabotaged engines. Violence broke out as soon as it was clear the boat was being prepared for a return journey. A fire was started and doused. The *Warramunga*'s commander, Richard Menhinick, reported: 'A number of PIIs started ripping the bilge area apart, tearing up deck boards five metres in length, attempting to kick out the hull planks and starting a second fire.' He took the *Warramunga* to action stations in readiness for a SOLAS situation. 'Riot, fire and destruction only ceased when PIIs were shown evidence that they were being video taped and told that their actions would not assist their case with the Government of Australia.'²³

Forcing SIEV 6 back to Indonesia was a terrible prospect but next day—October 23—everything appalling about Operation Relex was put in the shade. The day began very early with a call to Jane Halton at 2 am. Halton was asleep and the mobile rang out before she could answer. When she hit call back she reached Shane Castles, the federal police officer on her taskforce. He had news about the next boat they were expecting at Christmas Island, the boat that would become known as SIEV X. 'He told me the barest bones—that he understood there was a report but that a cable would be coming later in the day that a vessel had sunk. That was it.'²⁴

SEVENTEEN
The boat that sank

OCTOBER 17 TO 28

Just before midnight on October 17, in the grounds of a cheap Indonesian hotel, a young Iraqi woman stood with her three daughters for their last hours together on dry land. Only 26 years old and a devout Muslim, Sundous Ibramam covered her head and kept watch over her girls. Emaan, her eldest, was eight, Zahra was six, and Fatima, just five years old. Her husband was not there to protect them and she had no idea where she was. But her sister was beside her for support and the people smugglers were saying they would soon be on the boat to Australia.

They had been travelling for days: first by bus, snaking along the roads from Jakarta to the west of Java, then by ferry to the city of Bandarlampung in South Sumatra and, finally, on another bus to this discreet hotel down on the coast. But tonight it was almost impossible to maintain discretion. Chaos engulfed the hotel. Hundreds of desperate asylum seekers were lining up for the voyage to Christmas Island. They had paid thousands of American dollars for their passage. For some it was their life savings. The smugglers were saying there was only one boat available, not two as they had promised. Sundous ignored the angry talk around her and followed orders.

Women and children were separated from the men and under cover of darkness were taken on yet another bus to the fishing village of Canti, just a short distance away.[1] Near the beach, a fence barred their way but security guards opened the gates and armed men in uniform, who looked like police, stood talking in Indonesian to the head of the syndicate, Abu Quassey, dressed in a safari vest with bulging pockets. He was clearly in charge, demanding the passengers' silence and issuing instructions over his mobile phone to the men back at the hotel still loading buses. Many of the Iraqis on the beach knew Abu Quassey as the Egyptian people smuggler who had recently branched out to run his own syndicate. He had taken their money but his operation had been plagued by bad luck and police harassment since August when this trip was first attempted. Now he was determined to get these passengers away on his boat anchored in the bay.

Sundous was going to join her husband, Ahmaed Al-Zalimi, whom she had not seen for almost two years.[2] He did not want her to come to Australia this way. Indeed, he had pleaded with her over the phone from his little flat in Sydney not to take the boat. He knew the Australian navy was turning back boats and he knew from experience the voyage was perilous. But Sundous felt she had few options. They had been unwanted aliens in Iran: the girls could not go to school, they could not legally rent a house and she was virtually a widow. Sundous put her eldest girl on the telephone to speak to Ahmaed. The child told him: 'I want to be with you again father. I want to see you.'[3]

Sundous' husband had supported the uprising against Saddam Hussein at the end of the first Gulf War and when it failed, he fled first to Iran and then by boat to Australia where he was accepted as a refugee. But by that time Australia was only granting boat people temporary protection visas (TPVs) which did not allow them to bring their immediate family to Australia for at least the first three years. Rather than working as a deterrent to boat people, the new visas were turning wives and children into new, very vulnerable customers for the people smuggling trade.[4]

On the shoreline that night were many Iraqis who had waited in Indonesia to be processed as refugees. Only a few had qualified, some had been rejected and others felt it was pointless to join the endless queue for resettlement. A number of the women and children, like Sundous and her daughters, had set out on this journey because they believed it was the only way to re-unite their families. So now, with nearly three hundred other women and children, Sundous and her daughters were being herded onto Abu Quassey's boat anchored off a beach on the Bay of Lampung.

Behind Sundous was another TPV wife, Amal Hassan Basri, travelling with her son Rami Abbas. Amal had her wits about her. A worldly middle-aged woman who once worked as a bank clerk in Baghdad, she had negotiated personally with Abu Quassey. She had trusted the people smuggler but now Amal was nervous and when she took her first step onto his boat she had a strange feeling. The boat was just 18-metres long, too light, she thought, and not very stable. 'I am normally a strong woman,' she recalled, 'but when I was on the boat I felt dizzy and felt like vomiting'.[5] She was sent below deck, but the smell of fresh paint made her ill. When she forced her way up higher she found the boat was already overcrowded, even though the men had still not boarded. When they arrived, many had to sit with the luggage on top of the cabin. The night was punctuated by raised voices. Some of the passengers left the boat, angrily demanding their money back. Amal had been told there would be life jackets on board but she soon discovered there were not enough to go around. There was only one for about every four passengers. She did not get one.

Before first light, in the early hours of Thursday, October 18, Abu Quassey's desperately over-crowded boat carrying some four hundred men, women and children was ready to depart. But it was so weighed down, so low in the water, the captain could not shift the anchor. As Amal looked out, she believed she saw Abu Quassey and his two men in their runabout alongside the boat screaming at the passengers to help the captain. 'Come on,' he cried, 'in two days time you will be in Australia'. But Amal had a bad feeling. 'The boat was very sad,' she thought, 'it didn't want to move'.[6] Finally, the anchor was hauled in and the boat slipped out into the Bay of Lampung and headed for the Sunda Strait, en route to the Indian Ocean.

Earlier that night, an Australian police officer in West Java rang Coastwatch in Canberra to say the Abu Quassey boat was on the move. Canberra was given the wrong point of departure—an unidentified port on the Java side of the strait—but the general thrust was correct: the boat was at last on its way.[7] Coastwatch had the information at about 10 pm and passed it on that night to both Operation Relex headquarters at Northern Command in Darwin and to the intelligence hub for the military, the Australian Theatre

Joint Intelligence Centre (ATJIC) in Sydney. But for the next 48 hours this 'human intelligence' on Abu Quassey's boat was given little credibility by the military who considered it unreliable.[8]

The Australian authorities had had their eyes on Abu Quassey for some time and already knew a great deal about him. Since July, federal police in Jakarta had been sending intelligence on his operation to the DIMA/AFP strike force on people smuggling. Abu Quassey's name already appeared on some forty DIMA intelligence notes. According to one Canberra source, the Abu Quassey boat was also a target of ASIS, Australia's foreign intelligence service, which had been 'tasked' to disrupt people smuggling operations in Indonesia. The information on Abu Quassey apparently included a DIMA intelligence report about midday on the day the boat left that referred to a smuggler's boat being loaded with passengers. The report added that, 'the departure of the boat has yet to be confirmed'.[9] Ten hours later, the fresh AFP intelligence came from Jakarta that Abu Quassey's boat was, according to this informant, actually on its way. As well as being fed into the military intelligence system that night, it was passed next morning, October 18, to the special DIMA/AFP strike force and to Jane Halton's taskforce.

Though mistrusted by the military, this new intelligence was of vital importance when Halton's bureaucrats met that morning because the taskforce believed that up to 1200 boat people were trying to leave Indonesia over the next few days. The Prime Minister's border protection policy was under assault from a virtual flotilla of boats right in the middle of the election campaign. DIMA briefed the taskforce on five boats believed to be on their way. Three were sailing down the corridor from West Timor to Ashmore Reef. The other two were sailing through the Sunda Strait 'with total 600 PUAs [Potential Unauthorised Arrivals] expected Christmas, with one possible arriving today . . . Some risk of vessels in poor conditions and rescue at sea. No confirmed sightings by Coastwatch but multi-source information with high confidence'.[10] One of those boats was SIEV 6. The other was Abu Quassey's boat, which the press would call SIEV X.

The military placed its greatest trust in aerial surveillance and in signals intelligence from DSD, which can monitor mobile phones and radio traffic on asylum boats. Police reports on boat departures had been wrong in the past and were generally viewed as suspect. As one senior Relex commander would later say, 'It was all human intelligence, it was conversations between two people. That's what was behind all that intelligence. And we had a track record of that being unreliable'.[11] The military's scepticism was not unjustified. Often syndicates would give information on competitors that was either wrong or flawed. Hours after Abu Quassey's boat sailed from Canti beach, DIMA's intelligence director was also reporting the boat had departed hundreds of kilometres away in Java two nights earlier. But whatever confusion there was about the time and place of the departure of SIEV X, civilian intelligence in Australia on the morning of October 18 believed it was possible that the boat was on its way. Military intelligence did not.

This suspicion of civilian intelligence highlighted a fundamental problem with Operation Relex. In the space of just six weeks, John Howard had taken a difficult civil problem—the boat arrivals—and tried to find a military solution to it. But the government had ended up with an uncomfortable combination of military and civilian agencies running the border protection operation. Communication between these two very different arms of government was often fraught. The intelligence chain became so extended that at times the military simply could not assess the original police or DIMA input.

All civilian and military intelligence on the boats was analysed by ATJIC and fed to Relex headquarters in Darwin where it was used to brief the P-3C Orion crews conducting the aerial surveillance of the Indian Ocean. The military now had direct responsibility for aerial surveillance of the route to Christmas Island. This area, some 34 600 square miles, was dubbed 'Charlie' and divided into four blocks. Charlie stretched up almost to where the Sunda Strait meets the Indian Ocean, as close as politically possible to the border of Indonesian territorial waters leaving a buffer of about 12 nautical miles. The Orions were equipped with high-tech surveillance gear including a maritime search radar and infra-red capability for night vision or poor weather conditions. Their crews reported directly to Operation Relex.[12] Coastwatch chief, Rear Admiral Mark Bonser, said the operation in the northern waters was 'probably the most comprehensive surveillance that I have seen in some thirty years of service'.[13]

But critically the purpose of Operation Relex was not search and rescue. It was a military operation to stop the boats and turn them back before they reached Australia. This border protection mindset had, since the arrival of the *Tampa*, blunted basic humanitarian concerns in both the military and the bureaucracy about the fate of the boat people. The failure of a boat to arrive did not trigger an alarm that a human tragedy might be unfolding. It was just one less boat to worry about.

I

Abu Quassey's vessel had been sailing for only a few hours when more arguments broke out on board. A group of Iraqis of the Mandaean religious sect confronted the captain about the terrible conditions on board. They had paid good money to the people smugglers but they had been put on a dangerous vessel. It was badly over-crowded, travelling slowly and the engine was already having problems. The captain sympathised but told them many on board had paid with their life savings and they were determined to keep going.[14] By now the boat was heading towards a group of uninhabited volcanic outcrops called the Krakatau Islands, a landmark in the middle of the Sunda Strait. At about 9 am, the Mandaeans hailed a fishing boat and about 24 of them hurriedly left SIEV X. Six of their party decided to stay on.

Tough as Amal was, her courage began to fail her as she watched all this. She thought she and her son Rami should abandon the boat too. Rami tried to contact Abu Quassey but discovered the boat's radio was dead. A fellow passenger tried to console Amal. 'Why go back to Indonesia? You will have no money and no support.' She saw a mother with her children, crying. The mother told her, 'either it's Australia or the whale's mouth'.[15]

All day the boat chugged south. That night the weather changed for the worse and by the morning of October 19, the sea was terrible. The boat was tossed in all directions and the rain poured down. Nearly everyone on board was seasick and many were vomiting. Waves were crashing over the deck and the rain blew in on the women and children through the open windows. They had, it seemed, hit the high seas.[16] Around midday, the boat's engine fell silent. With the engine gone, the pumps were useless. Almost immediately the boat began filling with water and men began bailing frantically.

They had by now been travelling some thirty hours. A rumour spread that they were just six hours from Christmas Island. Asylum seekers were always told the journey to Christmas Island took 36 hours but that was only a useful estimate when everything went well. This boat was grossly overloaded, travelling in heavy weather with a dodgy engine. The rough seas suggested they had hit the Indian Ocean at the end of the Sunda Strait but where, exactly, they were was impossible to know.

Sundous, sitting with her three little girls, saw some birds flying in the distance and prayed the boat was not too far from land. Some men came into the women's section and told them not to worry, the problems would be fixed. 'They kept calming the women down because they didn't want them to panic and start running around the boat causing more danger', she remembered.[17] Some of the men worked with the captain on the engine but as the hours ticked by it refused to kick in and the boat kept heaving heavily in the water. There was no functioning radio on board to call for help and no other boats in sight. The passengers were told to throw their luggage over the side in the desperate hope it might float towards a passing ship that would follow the trail and rescue them. Sundous was in trouble but her sister found her a life jacket. Now at least they had one each.

By about three in the afternoon, the sea was relentless. Sundous remembers 'the waves were hitting the boat and lots of water was coming through the windows'. As the water flooded the decks, the passengers panicked and started running to the dry end of the boat. Some of the men began tearing planks from the side to allow the waves to wash right across the deck and not be trapped on board. It was a last hopeless attempt to keep the vessel afloat. As the boat heaved again, the passengers fell on top of one another. Just minutes later it rolled and began to break up.[18]

I

SIEV X went down with frightening speed. The hull split and the women and children crammed below deck were sucked under. Few had life jackets but even they stood little chance. Those who jumped into the sea were surrounded by fuel flooding from the boat which choked them if they opened their mouths. Sundous found herself in the sea with her three little girls. But in the chaos, her beautiful daughters, Emaan, Zahra and Fatima disappeared under the water.

Another young mother, Roukayya Satta, tried desperately to hold onto her daughters, Kawthar who was five and Alya who was just two. As the boat went down, frantic passengers began stepping on the five-year-old who drowned when she could no longer hold onto her mother. Left with little Alya, Roukayya began searching for her husband. Thrashing passengers kept pushing her under and the third time she went down, she lost

Alya. It was only then she spotted her husband among the debris. He grabbed a plank and together they held onto it for their lives. Then bodies of their dead daughters floated by and their father despaired. 'I have lost my family, I have brought you to this, I do not deserve to live', he told Roukayya. 'I do not want to see you die in front of me.' She remembers her husband's overwhelming grief just before he, too, disappeared in the sea. 'He was crying, his grip became loose because of his exhaustion, a wave then came and washed him away from the timber.'[19]

Everywhere children were drowning: a three-week-old baby sucked into the sea with his mother; a ten-month-old girl who fell from her father's arms; a child whose crying mother tried to save her by placing the Koran on her head and reading a prayer; a foetus with its umbilical cord attached to its dead mother. Those still alive saw bodies all around them; they littered the water. Wherever you looked, said one survivor, 'you see dead children like birds floating on the water'.[20]

Twelve-year-old Zainaab fought for her life. She had been lifted from below deck by her mother, who screamed at her to get out. Now her parents had disappeared, having drowned along with her two brothers, the youngest who was just six years old. 'He was only a little boy and he drowned', said Zainaab. 'He swallowed a lot of sea water and it suffocated him. He could not breathe.'[21]

Amal Hassan Basri was saved by her son. She heard him in the water calling out to her, 'Mama come to me, come over here'. She had swallowed a lot of seawater and was trying to make peace with her God, praying for forgiveness before she died. But she instinctively clung to a dead woman floating by in a life jacket. Her son Rami wrestled the jacket from the corpse and put it on his mother. Along with Amal and her son, there were about 120 others left alive as the sun went down.

The only RAAF plane sent to look for Abu Quassey's boat did not leave Christmas Island until two hours after SIEV X capsized. One of the two boats Canberra thought to be heading south had been found that morning. SIEV 6 was spotted north of Christmas Island and stopped by the *Arunta* in a textbook exercise in surveillance and interception. Now the Relex commanders wanted the area closest to Christmas Island 'sanitised' to make sure the second boat did not slip through during the night. If the RAAF waited for the next regular surveillance flight at dawn, it could be too late. So at 5 pm, this special flight left Christmas Island looking for SIEV X. The Orion's crew had been tasked by the *Arunta* to concentrate on searching the southern sectors of Charlie where the route to Christmas Island narrowed and the frigate had a better chance of intercepting the asylum boat.[22]

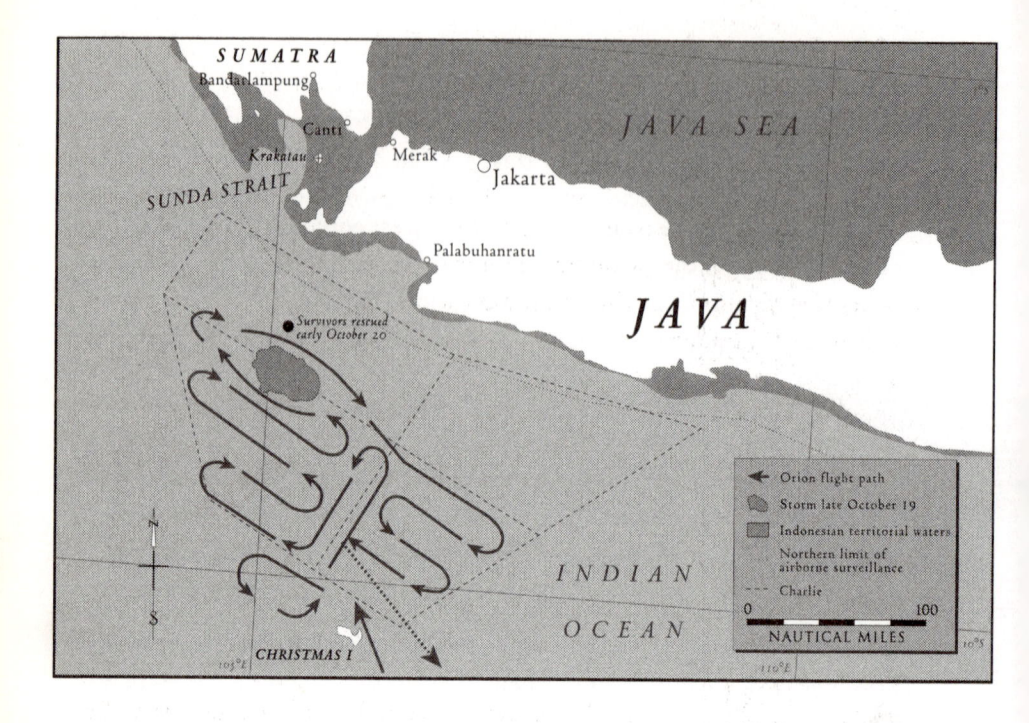

No one knows precisely where SIEV X went down but the few survivors eventually rescued were taken from the sea in the middle of the north-west block of Charlie at 07° 40 00 south/105° 09 00 east.[23] Wind and current would play their part in bringing survivors to that spot, but the position of the rescue suggests very strongly that Abu Quassey's vessel was inside the Australian surveillance zone when it sank. But what chance did the Orion have—hours later with night falling—of finding survivors in the water? According to a naval source, the Orion's radar could not detect people in the sea but might be able to pick up wreckage if it were not too widely dispersed. The infra-red equipment on the plane would be useful after dark searching for people in the water but the Orion would have to be very close by and infra-red results are severely degraded in bad weather. It was not impossible for the Orion to find survivors, but it was always a long shot.

As the plane followed its looping pattern in Charlie, the crew detected eight radar contacts and confirmed six were legitimate fishing vessels. The seventh contact was outside the 34 600 square mile zone and the crew ignored it. That left one contact in the north-west corner of Charlie up near the Sunda Strait. As the plane flew into that block, it ran into trouble. The weather was terrible. The Orion hit high winds, heavy rain and an impenetrable area of thunderstorms about 30 miles long and 10 miles deep.[24] The battle with the weather left the plane low on fuel. The Orion swung around the storm up into the north-west block, which it had been tasked to search. But that area of Charlie was not the military priority and the plane headed south again. Operation Relex was most interested in sweeping the seas close to Christmas Island. So the Orion looped through the south-east block of Charlie before heading home to base. In their mission report the crew noted, 'The need to conduct weather avoidance manoeuvres led to the aircraft reaching its limit of endurance before completing patrol of its designated area'.[25]

That was it for the night. As far as Operation Relex was concerned, the failure to find Abu Quassey's boat was a *good* sign. If this had been a search and rescue operation, the failure to locate the boat should have sparked an intensified search either for the boat or survivors. Perhaps another plane would have been sent into that far corner of Charlie. But on the night of October 19, there was no military reason to send another flight up there. 'The tactical priority was to ensure there was nothing in the southern part of the area', explained Air Commodore Phillip Byrne of the Maritime Patrol Group. 'That is the reality of tasking priorities. It was just the luck of the game.'[26] The Orion was back at base and the *Arunta* was over a hundred nautical miles away from the survivors of SIEV X praying for deliverance in the Indian Ocean.

A number of those who struggled to hold off death that night believe that someone did spot them—perhaps a merchant vessel or a fishing boat—and then deliberately sailed by. As the black night engulfed them, they clung to debris and floating corpses. The survivors were cut by nails sticking out of the wreckage and sickened by fuel, seawater and their own vomit. At least the pool of diesel kept the sharks away. As night wore on, many would give up, lose their grip and be washed away. Those who held on prayed. Throughout the night Amal could hear their voices crying out 'Help, Help' and 'Allah is Great'.[27]

Sundous was carried away from the other survivors. She was alone in the dark with the rain pelting down, exhausted, ill and certainly traumatised. Sometime late that night, she saw two bright lights suddenly appear on the water. She was certain they were lights and she was caught in an arc that beamed down on her. 'The light was only coming from one direction', she recalled. She thought they were lights from two boats. 'The lights were quite high, a squarish type of light shining down, not from high up but angled, about 100 metres away.'[28] Amal also saw the lights in the distance and so did others. When they came on, she could hear other survivors screaming 'help, help' and blowing the whistles on their life jackets. She thought she heard a ship's horn in the distance. But no one answered their cries. Shortly before dawn, Sundous realised the lights had disappeared but by then she could well have been hallucinating. She thought a dolphin was pushing her through the sea.

I

At roughly that hour in Canberra, AFP intelligence officer Kylie Pratt had a call from the Australian police in Jakarta confirming Abu Quassey's boat had left Indonesia. Pratt was given the wrong port and the wrong day of departure but Pratt's colleague described the boat, 'allegedly as small and with 400 passengers on board, with some passengers not embarking because the vessel was overcrowded'.[29] It was about 9 am in Canberra on Saturday October 20. Pratt immediately called the Coastwatch officer. She said she 'didn't want to cause a panic' but she was now more certain than ever that the Abu Quassey boat had left and its passengers could be at risk.[30]

Coastwatch noted Pratt's concern in its report: 'The vessel may be subject to increased risk due to the numbers reportedly on board.'[31] Within twenty minutes, the agency passed the information to the Australian Theatre Joint Intelligence Centre and to Operation Relex in Darwin.[32] The Joint Intelligence Centre believed the AFP information confirmed the departure of the Abu Quassey boat and within fifteen minutes issued a report warning of the imminent arrival of the SIEV, possibly that afternoon, in the waters off Christmas Island.[33]

But somehow Pratt's assessment that the boat was at risk was dropped from the intelligence report by the time it reached military headquarters at Northern Command in Darwin. Rather than sounding a warning that the passengers and the boat could be in peril, Northern Command thought the new information on the boat's overcrowding just meant it would take a slower course to Christmas Island. Its report blandly stated: 'Due to its overcrowding and need to maintain stability it may be limited to a slow passage and therefore a later time of arrival could be expected.'[34]

By now, a P-3C Orion had taken off on a morning surveillance mission over the north-west corner of Charlie zone. But in yet another intelligence breakdown, the Orion's crew was not told of the new report confirming the departure of SIEV X or Pratt's assessment that the boat was at risk. Military intelligence apparently felt there was no need to get this new report to the crew while it was airborne because 'there was nothing of any criticality' in it. The crew was not told there could be a SOLAS emergency north of Christmas Island or that 400 men, women and children could be at risk. Nothing was done to launch a search and rescue operation for SIEV X that day. Indeed, in a further intelligence breakdown, the new report was not even passed to the DIMA intelligence officers despite the fact that Kylie Pratt was on the joint DIMA/AFP strike force. Nor was it passed to Jane Halton's People Smuggling Taskforce.

The Orion crew flew its regular mission over the area and saw nothing, no bodies in the sea, no survivors, no luggage, no flotsam or jetsam.[35] But without being 'tasked' to look for the wreckage, it was unlikely it would have been spotted by radar. And unless the crew flew over the survivors, there would have been little chance of seeing them.

Some hours after the sun came up, Sundous saw a miraculous sight: a fishing boat was coming towards her, hauling survivors out of the sea. She was among the first rescued. The fishermen dragged her on board the *Indah Jayah Makmur*, sick and distraught but alive. The men could not speak her language but they treated her cuts and sores and gave her some fresh water and food.

For the next two or three hours the fishermen rescued survivors, including Amal and her son. How did you find us, the survivors asked? We saw the luggage and followed it, they replied.[36] Their boat was new and seaworthy, with a radio on board. The captain contacted the owners and conferred. Another fishing boat appeared to help with the rescue but that crew found mostly corpses in the sea. In all, 46 pitiful people were hauled from the water alive. Only four children had survived. Only 33 men and nine women were left alive. The total death toll was believed to be 353.[37] At any time on any ocean, this would count as a maritime catastrophe.

The survivors told the captain they wanted to go back to Jakarta. He explained he could not take them all that way for he was heading to his fishing ground, but would hand them over later to another fishing boat, the *Arta Kencana 38*, sailing back to the capital. So they set out on a two-day voyage. No news of their tragedy broke and Australian intelligence, both military and civilian, apparently heard nothing of the disaster, still noting in their reports that the Abu Quassey boat was on its way to Christmas Island. Australia launched no search and rescue operation for SIEV X despite its failure to arrive over the next two days and despite the intelligence report of October 20 that the boat was grossly overloaded. The navy was ready to fulfil its SOLAS obligations but under Operation Relex and in the political climate of these weeks, the failure of a boatload of asylum seekers to appear over the horizon was a relief, not a presage of a terrible maritime disaster.

On Monday October 22, the AFP in Jakarta told Coastwatch the boat was now 'overdue' but asked Coastwatch not to release this 'sensitive' intelligence to Australian search and rescue authorities for several hours until 'some suitable words' to convey this information could be found.[38] The AFP's source was not revealed. Coastwatch did pass the report to Jane Halton's taskforce which now, briefly, referred to the boat as SIEV 8: 'Not spotted yet, missing, grossly overloaded, no jetsam spotted, no reports from relatives.' It was 2 pm that Monday afternoon before the AFP finally authorised Coastwatch to tell RCC Australia that Abu Quassey's boat was overloaded and overdue.

Australia's rescue agency found itself back in the same quandary it was in weeks earlier when it discovered the overloaded *Palapa* was in trouble out on the Indian Ocean. Through Canberra's political eyes, rescuing these people and bringing them ashore meant trouble. The idea was to try to send them back from where they came. Rescue was not exactly mission failure, but it certainly wasn't operation success. In late August, RCC

Australia had done all it could to find someone else to rescue the *Palapa* before eventually calling on the *Tampa*'s help. Now it appeared to act under the same impulse—attempting to pass the problem of SIEV X to the Indonesians and the military. CEO Clive Davidson said, 'It was wanted to be sure the problem was passed over to the military and Operation Relex'.[39]

After about an hour, RCC Australia belatedly issued an overdue notice and then told the notoriously inadequate Indonesian search and rescue agency, BASARNAS, that the boat was overdue and that 'concerns have been expressed for its safety'. The Indonesians didn't reply and the Australian authorities took no further action, not even issuing an alert to shipping in the area, later saying there was insufficient information on the vessel's location to do this. According to Davidson, 'The nature of the information from Coastwatch was hardly alarmist and hardly raised a high degree of concern'.[40] RCC Australia also took comfort in the belief that Operation Relex was conducting comprehensive aerial surveillance in the area. That was that.

About the time the Australians were trying to flick the problem to BASARNAS, the exhausted survivors of SIEV X arrived at the Jakarta docks on board the Indonesian fishing boats. It was lunchtime in Jakarta, and police and immigration officials were waiting for them. But the survivors refused to disembark until an aid worker from the independent agency IOM was called. He arrived a few hours later. He knew many of them personally and indeed many of the dead. They hugged him and cried as they were helped into ambulances. Sundous, exhausted and in shock, was taken to hospital along with the other survivors. Her wounds were treated but the despair over the drowning of her three daughters was almost unbearable.

That night reporters in Jakarta were alerted to the tragedy. So was Jane Halton by that 2 am phone call, followed an hour later by a very detailed message from the defence attaché at the Australian embassy in Jakarta setting out the fate of SIEV X. The head count was a little out: '41 adults and 3 children survived, 352 drowned. Survivors taken to Jakarta—being cared for by IOM at Bogor outside Jakarta. Vessel likely to have been in international waters south of Java.'[41]

When some of the SIEV X survivors were sufficiently recovered, two officials from the Australian embassy and their Indonesian colleagues paid them a visit. They were investigating Abu Quassey and his accomplices.

The survivors nominated two of their group to meet the officials in the presence of a representative from the IOM. Ali Hamid and Karim Jaber Houssein were happy to pass on all they knew. An Indonesian led the questioning. At one point in the long interview he asked them to look at some 20 photographs of boats. 'Which is your boat?' the officer asked. Ali Hamid was amazed. According to him, there among the photographs was a grainy, black and white picture of Abu Quassey's boat before its departure. It looked like a satellite image or a surveillance picture. Ali's amazement turned to anger. 'You knew about our boat', he said. 'Why didn't you try to find us?'[42]

EIGHTEEN
The worst of times

OCTOBER 23 TO NOVEMBER 4

Kim Beazley was on the campaign trail in Brisbane on October 23 when the first details of the tragedy of SIEV X were broadcast on the ABC. After listening to the early news, the Labor leader went for a walk along the river with his press adviser, Greg Turnbull. They returned to face journalists on the steps of the Marriott Hotel. Beazley made a perfunctory statement of sympathy. 'It's a major human tragedy if that has occurred. And that is a very sad thing indeed.' Then he tried very ineptly to turn the catastrophe against Howard. 'What it points to is the failure of policy. We have not got the agreement we need with Indonesia in order to be able to ensure that those who put themselves in such danger are not encouraged to do so.'[1] Beazley's lack of empathy in the face of so many deaths stunned his colleagues. So did his clumsy footwork.

Howard launched a savage counter-attack later that morning on Perth's Radio 6PR. He told listeners Beazley's remarks were 'A desperate slur. A desperate slur'. He expressed the most heartfelt sympathy for those who had died and lost family in the wreck of SIEV X. Then he blamed Indonesia. 'This vessel sunk in Indonesian waters. Now I am saddened by the loss of life, it is a huge human tragedy and it is a desperately despicable thing for the Leader of the Opposition to try and score a political point against me in relation to the sinking of a vessel in Indonesian waters. We had nothing to do with it, it sank, I repeat, sunk in Indonesian waters, not in Australian waters. It sunk in Indonesian waters and apparently that is our fault.' Howard was still repeating this mantra a fortnight later at the National Press Club just before polling day. 'I was very touched by that tragedy in Indonesian waters . . . I'm human like everybody else.'[2]

No evidence has ever emerged to support the Prime Minister's emphatic claim. While Howard and Beazley were still sparring on the morning the news broke, two intelligence reports on the sinking were being prepared for distribution that day in Canberra. The one for Jane Halton's taskforce said SIEV X was 'likely to have been in international waters' when it sank. The other, for the Department of Immigration, said the tragedy occurred 'approximately 60 nautical miles south of the Sunda Strait'. The *Australian*'s correspondent in Indonesia, Don Greenlees, learnt that day that the boat had gone down 'about 80 kilometres from land'. The harbourmaster at Sunda Kelapar Port, North Jakarta, reported the survivors were picked up at a point 51 nautical miles south of Java. Essentially, it was impossible for SIEV X to have sunk in Indonesian waters.[3]

Howard's claim immediately blunted the political impact of the tragedy but left both military and civilian authorities in a bind. They could not publicly—or perhaps even privately—contradict the Prime Minister. The day after news of the sinking broke and Don Greenlees' report appeared for everyone to read in the *Australian*, Jane Halton provided a 'state of play brief' for Howard which fudged the issue. 'Boat capsized and sank quickly south of the western end of Java', she reported, but she placed these words beneath a subheading that read, 'Indonesian Waters'. She later explained this may have referred to the Indonesian search and rescue zone. 'Our experience of the description of Indonesian waters right throughout this period was, to say the very least, confused.'[4]

Beazley was crushed by Howard's ferocious attacks. His bungled attempt to turn the SIEV X strategy against Howard 'bit' and Labor fell back a crucial few points in the polls. Beazley's electioneering had seen Labor's fortunes slowly but steadily improve. Now the line on the graphs stopped rising. Hard heads among Labor Party strategists reckoned this was their leader's one big mistake in the whole campaign. Labor could not count on any change of heart in the electorate following the sinking of

SIEV X and these hundred of deaths. A Newspoll taken at this time showed that support for turning all boats away kept on rising. The *Australian* reported 'the biggest rise among women, the young and those over 50'.[5] Beazley tried to rescue himself by emphasising—absolutely accurately—that the primary responsibility for these 353 deaths lay with the people smugglers. That did him no good. Nor was it much use him sticking to his original accusation of 'failures of policy'. That was perfectly accurate, too, but the policy that loaded SIEV X with women and children—the 1999 creation of temporary protection visas—had been enthusiastically backed by Beazley and the Labor Party.

News of the tragedy quickly reached frantic relatives waiting in Sydney. When Sundous' husband, Ahmaed Al-Zalimi, heard his three girls had drowned, he collapsed in despair. He wrapped a white sheet around his head for hours on end, refusing to talk or move from his little flat until a social worker from Sydney's Muslim Association, Kaysar Trad, feared the man would lose his sanity and arranged for his friends to take him to hospital. Other refugees on TPVs who had lost wives and children on the boat were also deeply traumatised. 'They hadn't seen me for two years so they decided to come and join me', said one. 'If I could have brought my family here this would not have happened . . . We call it the Howard *Titanic*.'[6]

If these men flew to comfort their distraught wives in Jakarta, their TPVs would automatically be revoked and they would not be allowed re-entry to Australia. Al-Zalimi was refused a waiver to allow him to fly to Sundous. Howard explained to Tony Jones on ABC-TV's *Lateline*, 'If the policy is altered in one case, questions are going to be raised as to why it should not be altered in other cases'.

'You're a father yourself', said Jones. 'Do you not think that Australian voters would have forgiven you for allowing that man to go back to his wife and then come back to Australia?'

'Well, Tony, it's you who are choosing to put it in crude political terms like that, not me.'

'Let's talk about the politics of it. Were you advised that the images of him going back to Indonesia would have somehow mitigated against the tenor of your campaign?'

'I never take advice on the political impact of something like that', the Prime Minister replied.

'It's not too late before the election to change your mind on this issue', said Jones. 'Is there a chance now of you saying to him, "You can go back to your wife"?'

'Tony, the decision is in the hands of the Immigration Minister. Under law, it's not in my hands. I just want to, for the record, reject your suggestion that I would seek day-to-day political advice as to the political impact of a decision like that. I do find that question being close to offensive.'[7]

Heart-wrenching photographs of the Al-Zalimi children were splashed across the papers. This time, Peter Reith's office could not control the press coverage. The media carried desperately sad interviews with Sundous and other survivors in Jakarta and the 'humanising' photographs of three little girls dressed in their finest clothes playing for the camera a few days before their deaths. At Sydney's Randwick Racecourse that night, October 25, Labor held a huge fundraiser. Beazley came to press the flesh but the guest of honour was one of his patrons, the wily and ancient ex-premier of NSW, Neville Wran. It was late when Wran rose to speak. 'When I saw those three little girls, something told me Mr Ruddock was wrong. We're not dealing with a problem here, we're dealing with people.' Wran very deliberately spoke to the issue Beazley and his frontbench had been so anxious to avoid for weeks: the role of race in this campaign. 'The race card has been introduced into this election. It's a card, and an introduction, which we and our children will live to regret. We live in a country in which, despite the smoldering resentment and objections to newcomers, we have handled it all thus far. We have been able to run our country in a sensitive, compassionate and dignified way.' Wran's message to the faithful was that all this was being put at risk.[8]

Howard's response next day was sharp. 'If the Labor Party's policy on illegal immigration is, as Mr Beazley claims, the same as ours, then Mr Wran's criticism last night was a criticism of Mr Beazley as well.' Howard was dead right. Labor was trapped. Trailing around St Mary's Villa Nursing Home in the Sydney suburb of Concord, Beazley clung grimly to the official Labor line that race was not an issue at the 2001 poll. He would keep saying so right up to polling day, he told the press, 'because I'll tell you what I think this election is about, a fair society. And I'm going to keep plugging away at that until hell freezes over'.[9]

At this low point in the campaign, Beazley was encouraged to call on Howard to allow Al-Zalimi to fly to Jakarta. He refused. He wanted the issue to die. He did not want another front page lost to those drowned children. 'I was not going to go down the road of giving the government another day's worth of debate on the subject.' He told some of his colleagues he had another idea up his sleeve: a visa for Sundous to come to Australia. But no journalist asked Beazley about this and the Labor leader did not volunteer the idea. Asked why he never did that, he said, 'You can pass all the moral judgements you like on me. I couldn't care less. I'm trying to win an election campaign and get these evil bastards out of office.'[10] None of Beazley's frontbench was willing to challenge their leader even in the face of such profound human suffering. Too deeply ingrained in their political thinking by this time were the electoral consequences of appearing soft on asylum seekers. Labor's shadow Minister for Justice, Duncan Kerr, said, 'By then, we were just sick with cynicism'.[11]

I

The *Mirnawaty* was intercepted by HMAS *Bunbury* steaming towards Ashmore with about 200 Iraqis on board. They were combative from the start and began yelling in English and Arabic as the boarding party approached. One man stripped off his shirt and plunged into the sea. Another raised a small child above his head and gestured as if to throw her overboard. 'This child, a small girl, was obviously frightened', reported Petty Officer Christopher Smart. The sailors boarded and took the boat into the lagoon. That afternoon, eight 'restless and irate' men demanded to know where they were to be taken and declared they would not allow their boat to be forced back to Indonesia. Calm was restored with the soothing lie that their fate would not be decided for a week. In fact, the decision had already been taken to return SIEV 7 to Indonesia once the *Arunta* was brought over from Christmas Island.[12]

The calm on the boat lasted less than 48 hours. At about 10 am on October 24, fifteen asylum seekers leapt overboard. People on board began screaming and throwing life jackets at the men in the water. Two sailors from HMAS *Bendigo* witnessed what happened next. A woman dangled a small child in a red jumpsuit over the side. 'Other women were gesticulating towards the child shouting "Oh, no, look at the poor child, it's going to die" or words to that effect. They were obviously attempting to unsettle us. The child, about three years old, was also screaming.' This time the child *was* dropped overboard. 'Soon after the child hit the water, one of the male SUNCs swam to it and held it above the water on his chest.' He swam back to the SIEV and a number of other asylum seekers helped both the child and her rescuer aboard.[13] No video or photographs were taken of this appalling incident. Nor was it mentioned by the government during the election campaign. According to Human Rights Watch, several of the asylum seekers spoke of people being beaten with 'iron sticks' after the Australians fished them out of the water.[14]

Two SIEVs—6 and 7—were now waiting to be taken back to Indonesia but the operation was suddenly in limbo. The engines of SIEV 6, moored off Christmas Island, were running again after the navy had spent a week working furiously on the problem. The seas were rough—the minutes of Jane Halton's taskforce on Tuesday October 23 recorded, 'Weather has closed in, choppy with high seas forecast for two days'—but SIEV 6 still didn't budge once the weather improved. Petty sabotage continued all week: sugar in the fuel pump, water in the fuel, damage to the exhaust system. The *Arunta* was expected at Ashmore on the Thursday to take SIEV 7 back to Indonesia, but it did not arrive until the Sunday. Life on the overcrowded boat in the lagoon was, meanwhile, extremely uncomfortable for the Iraqis. 'We begged in English "Please just take us into the shade, or let us get on land so that we can lie down and sleep" but this was refused. We had no bath for seventeen days, and so we all had skin diseases.' They reported suffering, in particular, from sunburn, ulcers and viral conjunctivitis.[15]

So heavily censored are the minutes of the taskforce at this time that it is impossible to gauge why the 'active return' of both boats was on hold. These were the days when news of the sinking of SIEV X was reverberating around Australia. That coming Sunday, October 28, the Prime Minister was to officially launch his party's election campaign. A source on the *Arunta* told *Four Corners* of an announcement over the ship's loudspeaker, 'maybe tongue-in-cheek, that the delay was to make sure that the operation wouldn't interfere with the Liberal Party launch'.[16]

I

Security was tight around the City Recital Hall, tucked away in a lane behind Sydney's Martin Place. Police staked out all entrances to the hall. Only invited guests and accredited press were being allowed through. A noisy group of men from the Lebanese Muslim Association was demonstrating in the lane against Howard's refusal to allow Al-Zalimi to join his wife in Jakarta. A large photograph of Sundous and her three dead children was being held up for the television cameras. The Liberal Party guests walked past, unperturbed by the raw emotion of the protesters or the pranks of a smooth bunch of satirists from ABC-TV's *Election Chaser*, who also had their cameras set up in the lane. Chas Licciardello was selling souvenirs under a banner that read LIBERAL VICTORY STORE, but there were no customers for 'Tampa in the bottle' or 'GI John', a doll in battle fatigues that came with a clip on 'George Bush attachment'. *Election Chaser* had also set up an old-fashioned kissing booth offering the party faithful a chance to kiss Sir Robert Menzies' arse. No one was laughing. Howard's hard man, Senator Bill Heffernan, hovered in the lane keeping an eye out for trouble.

The City Recital Hall was perfectly chosen. No sound could enter from the street. There were no windows for yobbos to bash as they did in Parramatta at the last Liberal campaign launch. And a good recital hall makes applause sound great for both the assembled faithful and the television audience. For Philip Ruddock, the protector of Australia's borders, there was a tumult of whistling, stamping and clapping. The needle went right off the dial, not once but twice. The first time he stood and awkwardly took a bow. The second time he kept modestly in his seat, inclined his head and mouthed 'thank you very much' to a beaming John Howard, who had just congratulated Ruddock on the 'fantastic job' he had done for Australia.

Howard spoke for over an hour, on song all the way. He is very good at reading applause. He knows when to smile, when to gesture in triumph and when, as now, to stay resolutely grim as he drew together September 11 and boat people. National security was the connection. 'National security is . . . about a proper response to terrorism. It's also about having a far-sighted, strong, well thought out defence policy. It is also about having an uncompromising view about the fundamental right of this country to protect its borders. It's about this nation saying to the world we are a generous, open-hearted people taking more refugees on a per capita basis than any nation except Canada, we have a proud record of welcoming people from 140 different nations. But we will decide who comes to this country and the circumstances in which they come.'

Great breakers of applause broke over his head. This was the campaign's slogan, the television message for the last weeks, the full page ads being prepared for the newspapers, the posters being printed for distribution from one end of Australia to the other: 'WE WILL DECIDE WHO COMES TO THIS COUNTRY AND THE CIRCUMSTANCES IN WHICH THEY COME.' The old premiers of NSW brought out for the occasion, the shattered ranks of the Liberal Left which once rolled Howard for suggesting a faint shadow of the *Tampa* policy, most of the Cabinet, a squad of sitting members and senators, Liberal contenders for hopeless seats that had suddenly become winnable, and the Howard family superbly turned out in the front row clapped and clapped and clapped. They knew this was the winning ticket and John Howard had found it for them. In the centre of Sydney on a quiet Sunday morning, ringed by police, inside an elegant recital hall, a crowd of prosperous, white Australians was baying for border protection. When Howard finished, there was a standing ovation. He took what bushmen call a dingo's breakfast—a sip of water and a quick look around—then plunged into the applauding ranks of his supporters.

I

SIEV 6 was on the move a few hours later. 'That boat is a death trap. It will sink', warned Gordon Thompson, secretary of the Union of Christmas Island Workers. 'It's criminal. It's against the law to send an unseaworthy boat to sea.' Thompson had bluntly asked Customs: 'Had the ship been cleared for sea?' His unanswered question was listed by Halton's taskforce among the problems of the SIEV 6 operation.[17]

The old, timber boat sailed for only three and a half hours with Lieutenant Commander Simon Gregg at the wheel before the bilge pump failed. So did two portable backup pumps sent over from the *Warramunga*, destroyed by oily debris in the bilge. The problem wasn't sabotage: SIEV 6 was simply too old and rotten for the journey back to Indonesia. Water was entering 'through the seams of the hull boards' and Gregg realised the SIEV 'would eventually sink and that, as water level increased, the danger in foundering was very high'. Menhinick on the *Warramunga* ordered the asylum seekers be evacuated to his ship. It would soon be dark and there were 164 people to transfer. A helicopter hovered overhead throughout the operation, which finished at about 6 pm. 'All PIIs were transferred safely and without incident and were happy we had saved their luggage', said Menhinick. 'All PIIs were fed and given blankets to keep warm.'[18] He had handled the situation sensitively but it was a debacle for the government.

The second attempt at an 'active return' had come to grief inside Australian territorial waters.

Halton's taskforce met that afternoon to assess the mess and prepare a brief for Howard. It appears the navy had established a ground rule by this time that only the Prime Minister could order asylum seekers to be kept longer than a single night on a naval vessel. There was no talk of dragging these people off to Cocos Island. Instead, the sports hall on Christmas Island was readied to take them. They spent that night on the ship and next day, before the *Warramunga* took them to the island, Menhinick turned his guns on the hulk of the SIEV, firing a 'minimi machine gun, then 12.77 heavy machine gun and finally by 127 mm main gun' to sink the boat at 3.30 in the afternoon. The asylum seekers were then unloaded at Flying Fish Cove.[19] All of them eventually ended up on Nauru but some were to remain incarcerated on Christmas Island until February 2002.

SIEV 7 made it back to Indonesia. A few hours after the recital hall launch on October 28, it headed out of Ashmore Lagoon at about 5 knots with an Australian 'steaming party' at the wheel. Women, children and some of the men had been transferred to the *Arunta*, while a TSE detachment guarded about 160 men confined below decks on the SIEV. None of the asylum seekers had been told what was happening. During the night, the SIEV slowly changed course and next morning the asylum seekers were informed for the first time that they were being returned to Indonesia, now only three hours sailing away. There was mayhem. Men shouted, women screamed, children cried. 'You can kill me now, kill me now. Saddam will kill me', yelled one asylum seeker. An Australian soldier begged the men to be calm. 'I'm concerned about your safety and I'm concerned about my people's safety.' All this was videoed. Men started jumping overboard. A man held a child above his head shouting, 'What law allows Australia to deport this child and these people in a broken wooden boat?'.[20]

Leading Seaman William Taylor grabbed a fire extinguisher and forced his way to the bow where men were dousing themselves with diesel and threatening to set the boat alight. 'I shot the extinguisher at these people yelling at them to calm down.' They used the anchor to pierce a fuel drum and diesel drenched the sailors. 'More PIIs were lighting rags and threatening to ignite the drum and burn the boat.' Taylor feared for his life. 'I told them that we had helped them, that this was a government decision and not ours. I continued that we were here to help them, that we had given them food and water, and that they weren't going to solve anything by killing themselves and burning everybody else.' Railings were being torn out; the stays of the mast were cut; a fire started in the hold. When a group of men broke through a bulkhead into the engine room, they were repulsed by soldiers using capsicum spray.[21] It was a shocking mêlée that lasted for one and a half hours.

A number of men told *Four Corners* they were beaten with batons and sprayed in the eyes. Some claimed they were blinded for days by the spray, perhaps because their eyes were already inflamed by conjunctivitis. Human Rights Watch was told once again that electric batons were used against the asylum seekers. A man called Faizan said, 'I was a relatively healthy man, but I blacked out after being struck only once or twice. It felt like having your finger in a socket. It made my body jump'. Faizan also reported two soldiers crying. 'I asked them why they were crying, and they said, "We are also human, but we can't do anything because these are orders from our superiors. If it were possible I would take you back to my own home".'[22]

Meanwhile, the families were being brought over from the *Arunta*. Human Rights Watch again alleges 'disproportionate force' was used in the operation but the rioting on the SIEV subsided as the women and children climbed on board. When at last the transfer was complete, the Indonesian crew was taken to the wheelhouse and ordered to take over. One of the Australian sailors reported: 'Master appears very distressed and reluctant to take control of vessel after talking to aggressive SUNCs, but heads into wheelhouse and takes control of the helm.' The Australians then departed in their RHIBs. Speaking for the armed forces, Air Marshal Angus Houston insists no more than 'minimal force' was ever used in Operation Relex and that electric prods were never carried by defence personnel.[23]

The asylum seekers were hysterical. 'They took their boats and they left us there to face our destiny', said Mohammad Ali. 'Of 230 people, children and women, sick people—so many sick. People passed out, you know. I cannot describe that moment because they were very horrible. I cannot describe it at all. All the people were down, crying, you know, shouting, hitting themselves, slapping, you know. It was a very horrible situation.'[24]

The nearest land was Roti Island. Many hours later the boat ran aground about 300 metres from shore. It was night. The Indonesian crew abandoned ship. The asylum seekers left the ship, too. The water was just shallow enough for the adults to walk ashore carrying their children. Ali said, 'Most of the people had children and they cannot swim'. Next day, at least three men were missing. One had been sprayed in the hold. Months later, the survivors of SIEV 7 still trapped on Roti Island, claimed Hussein Yahia, Thamer Hussein and Haithem Dawood had completely disappeared.[25]

The Australian public, ten days out from the election, saw none of this. Ruddock told the press the bare bones of the story. The Prime Minister boasted, 'The good news in the last few weeks is that we have successfully returned, without injury, two groups of asylum seekers to Indonesian waters'. Yet the boats were still coming, observed Phil Clarke to the Prime Minister on Radio 2GB. Howard agreed. 'But if we throw up our hands and say we're going to stop doing this we'll be saying to the world anybody can come and I promise you that would be a recipe for the shores of this country to be . . . thick with asylum seeker boats, thick with asylum seeker boats.'[26]

I

SIEV 8 was a boat from another time. The people on board were Vietnamese who had left Saigon in mid-September and reached the island of Madura in early October where they loitered for a while before the Indonesian police reprovisioned the boat and forced it back out to sea. With the help of a compass and atlas, they set out for the Australian mainland. The patrol boat HMAS *Wollongong* found them off the north-west coast of Western Australia a little after midnight on October 28, stopped in the water, showing no navigation lights and flying a white flag painted with the letters SOS. A boarding party met no resistance. For a day and a half the commander of the *Wollongong*, Wesley Heron, waited for orders. Eventually he was instructed to ask the master of the vessel to steam under escort to Ashmore. Heron reported: 'Master and UA's responded negatively with an emphatic no that they would not proceed to AI and wanted only to go to Australia.'[27]

The sailors worked all afternoon to convince the 31 Vietnamese that Ashmore was an Australian island. The asylum seekers refused to eat 'stating that they were too sad and wished to die if they could not go to Australia'. They took down the boat's awning and sat in the sun. When this passive protest failed, they began 'ripping clothes, shouting at the steaming party and gesticulating in an aggressive manner'. The sailors kept repeating the familiar lie from these operations—that Australia had yet to decide whether to accept them—so they should co-operate and 'voluntarily go to Ashmore Island, behave and await the government of Australia's decision'. Calm was restored by evening and next day SIEV 8, with 'still some mixed feelings', followed the *Wollongong* to Ashmore, dropping anchor on the evening of November 2.[28]

The *Sinar Bontano III* slipped into Australian waters and was intercepted near Ashmore early on the morning of October 31. She was a big, old ferry flying the Indonesian flag and displaying two signs. One read, 'SORRY YOU ARE THE LAST HOPE', and the other, 'WE ARE IRAQI PEOPLE'. Among the 152 asylum seekers were also a few Afghans, Iranians, Sri Lankans and Bangladeshis. A TSE party from the *Arunta* came on board and herded them all into the hold while work began to repair the sabotaged engine. SIEV 9 was to be 'removed from AI and relocated towards the Indonesian coast'. After some time in those stifling conditions, a group of men began tearing up planks and trying to smash through the hull. The TSE then moved everyone to the upper deck where the disturbances continued. 'Many female PIIs were crying and many of the male PIIs were yelling at the TSE or at each other.' Several of the sailors saw a solidly built man threaten to throw a two-year-old child overboard. 'The TSE de-escalated the situation and the male calmed down and sat down. He was not restrained.'[29]

Trouble broke out again at sunset at the first attempt to restart the engine. 'All PIIs were standing up, chanting in an aggressive tone, "UN, UN, UN".' They threatened to jump overboard en masse if the boat got underway. The engine spluttered into life but died. The same 'large Middle-Eastern looking male' was again seen trying to throw a child overboard. This time a woman was struggling with him. 'The mother was holding onto the lower legs of the child, whilst the male had his right arm wrapped around the child's torso.' The TSE calmed him down then led him in handcuffs to the forecastle where he was held for some hours. In the mêlée, one of the asylum seekers was observed violently restraining his nine-year-old daughter. 'This incident occurred because the young female was trying to join in the riot and the father did not want any of his family members involved.' This was first reported as an attempted strangulation.[30]

The navy worked for three days to get the boat going again. There was more violence at the next attempt to start the engine. This time punches were thrown at the Australian soldiers. A few asylum seekers leapt into the sea. Lieutenant Andrew Hawke saw a woman run 'to the vessel's side with her child. I instructed BP personnel to stop her from throwing her child over the side and remove her from the area'. Once again, the asylum seekers settled down but remained truculent, occasionally violent, terribly sea sick and frequently on hunger strike as the days passed and the soldiers worked on the engines. Six of the TSE soldiers later wrote that 'during the riots, self harm and threats to children became commonplace and were not seen to be out of the ordinary, almost a "modus operandi". During "quiet" times the PIIs in general did not treat their children very well and used them as bargaining tools. During the many hunger strikes, the majority of the children were not allowed to eat'. The Relex high command was sceptical of some of these allegations.[31]

As the days passed, the boat wallowed and drifted. At one point, the current carried SIEV 9 into Indonesia's contiguous zone and a futile call was made to BASARNAS to render assistance. Then the current carried the boat back out again. The asylum seekers were begging to be towed to Ashmore. The navy refused but on Saturday November 3, 'to allay seasickness a steadying towline was connected to the vessel' and tensions eased on the SIEV. The navy kept on working on the engine. Canberra had still not given up hope of getting the boat back to Indonesia. New parts were dropped from a P3-C Orion but even they failed to do the trick and permission was finally given for the *Arunta* to tow SIEV 9 to Ashmore. 'The news was well received by the PIIs and their demeanour was happy and excited.'[32] The boat dropped anchor on the morning of November 4 not far from the Vietnamese waiting on SIEV 8. Both boats would sit on the lagoon until the early hours of polling day.

NINETEEN
The navy leaks

NOVEMBER 4 TO 8

The small NSW town of Bungendore is a tourist stop on the road between Canberra and the coast. On the Sunday before the election, a middle-aged man left a family barbecue on the Bungendore oval and ambled across the grass to the war memorial. The lanky Patrick Walters was a familiar figure in Canberra's corridors of power for he had worked on Kim Beazley's staff during the years Beazley was a minister in the Hawke government. Walters had returned to journalism, joining the *Australian* to establish its Jakarta bureau before moving back to Canberra. He never thought the children overboard story rang true but he was stuck in a desk job in Sydney editing the paper's election coverage and had been unable to pursue his doubts. He pressed the Canberra reporters to keep putting questions to Reith and Howard and to push the ministers to release the *Adelaide*'s videotape.

Local volunteers were refurbishing the little war memorial. One stood next to Walters and he offered a few polite words about the defence forces. 'My son's with the navy', the woman said. 'He's on the *Adelaide*.' The reporter's ears pricked up. 'That ship's been in the news a lot', he said hopefully. 'Yes', she answered. 'All this talk about the children, it's a load of rubbish, my son's very upset about it.' Walters was in a quandary. The woman had no idea who he was and he felt it wrong now to reveal his interest and press her for information. When he flew back to Sydney that night he went to see his editor, Michael Stutchbury, and said, 'We have got to nail this story'.[1]

The *Australian* had been the steadiest critic of the government's handling of the *Tampa*, Operation Relex and the Pacific Solution. While individual journalists across the media were producing tough stories throughout these weeks, most of the commercial proprietors supported Canberra's line. They had good commercial reasons for wanting to see Howard re-elected. The Minister for Communications, Senator Richard Alston, announced out of the blue in the middle of the *Tampa* crisis that a Coalition government would dismantle the cross-media ownership rules. Labor was committed to keeping this ban on proprietors owning newspapers as well as a television station in the one city. Media organisations also knew their readers, listeners and viewers overwhelmingly supported Howard's campaign against the boats. In the newsrooms of the nation, these were exceptionally tense weeks.

The *Australian*'s Perth bureau chief, Natalie O'Brien, had been ringing Christmas Island to question nervous locals who had spoken to the *Adelaide*'s crew. Walters' news from Bungendore confirmed what she was hearing. On Wednesday November 7, the paper reported on page one that 'Christmas Islanders allege that naval officers told them claims that asylum-seekers had thrown their children overboard during a confrontation last month with HMAS *Adelaide* were untrue'. It was a brave call, for the paper was relying on anonymous sources. The report noted that Peter Reith was still refusing to release the videotape, and criticised his press secretary for continuing to insist 'the Minister has no reason not to believe the reports he's received from senior officers in the navy'.

Unfortunately for the minister, the Defence Force Chief Admiral Barrie was in Hawaii that morning and not due back in the country until election day. Sitting in his chair was Air Marshal Angus Houston. A career military officer with 32 years in the service, Houston was not known for political guile and believed the military should give 'frank and fearless' advice to its political masters. The rest was up to government. This rule had served Houston well as he rose through the ranks to become Chief of the Air Force. As a member of Barrie's inner circle, he had sat through weekly briefings on Operation Relex and was well aware of the controversy within Defence over the children overboard claims. He knew the photographs released by Reith were a misrepresentation and 'that there was no documentary evidence to support the statement that children had been thrown overboard'.[2]

Houston decided to face his minister that day. First, he needed to assess the latest state of knowledge within Defence. He wanted to see the video for himself but it was in Sydney so he called Al Titheridge, head of Strategic Command, and the two old air force colleagues talked. Titheridge gave him the same briefing on the video that Reith's office had received three weeks earlier: there was no evidence there for the claims. The video showed men, and possibly a youth, jumping into the water voluntarily. At most, the video showed a child being held over the side of the boat by her father. Titheridge warned Houston, 'Minister Reith is chasing you' because the media was demanding a response to the *Australian*'s story.[3]

Houston also conferred with Brigadier Gary Bornholt, the chief public affairs officer for the military. Bornholt gave Houston a chronology of events for October 7 prepared by Norman Banks, commander of the *Adelaide*, and distributed to his superior officers on October 10. It was a military signal in a form totally familiar to Houston. 'What I read here gave me a very good picture, straight from the tactical level, as to what was happening out there', Houston explained later. 'If a child had been in the water, it would have been reported in the text of the message.'[4] Bornholt also filled Houston in on the thwarted efforts to have the minister's office correct the claims that photographs released by Reith were of children thrown overboard.

About noon, with Bornholt at his side, Houston put a call through to Reith on a speaker phone. The acting Chief of the Defence Force was going to have a witness for everything he said to the minister. Houston got quickly to the point. 'I felt that it was a very confused situation', he later recalled telling Reith, 'but from this evidence that I had seen, it appeared to me that there had been a boarding operation on the 7th, people had jumped into the water, there had been an incident with a child being held over the side, but fundamentally there was nothing to suggest that women and children had been thrown into the water'. Houston moved methodically to the photographs. He told Reith they were taken when the asylum seekers were forced to abandon their boat and were not evidence of children being thrown overboard the day before as the minister had claimed.

He told Reith he had not seen the videotape himself but was assured it did not prove children were thrown overboard. When Houston finished there was silence at the other end of the line for some time. Houston thought Reith was stunned. Finally the minister said, 'Well, I think we'll have to look at releasing the video'.[5]

This was not the first time senior military officers had told Peter Reith directly that there was no evidence on the video for the sensational claims that launched the election campaign. Only a week previously, the minister sat with Brigadier Mike Silverstone at Northern Command headquarters in Darwin and discussed the video. Reith later claimed he could not remember this conversation but Silverstone had reported it immediately to his boss, Rear Admiral Ritchie. Silverstone recalled telling the minister, 'the video does not show things clearly and does not show children overboard. We also have concerns that no children were thrown overboard and we have made an investigation of that'. Silverstone paused, expecting to hear a 'yes'. Instead, Reith turned to his adviser, Peter Hendy, and remarked, 'Well we had better not see the video then'.[6]

For weeks, Reith had been saying the video could not be released 'for operational security reasons' but while talking to Houston after the *Australian*'s story appeared on November 7, he came up with the tactically daring idea of showing it to the public. The government had only to hold the line for another three days until the election. Shifting the public's attention onto the video—even though he had again been told it contained no evidence of the claims—would buy precious time. Another minister would have called his prime minister to alert him to Houston's news. Another minister would also have issued a public retraction. Reith said he didn't because he did not consider the air marshal had given him 'a proper, detailed and conclusive report'. He planned to wait and discuss the matter with Barrie after the admiral's return—on polling day.[7]

▌

One of the fixed rituals of Australian federal elections is the prime minister's lunch at the National Press Club in the last days of the campaign. This confrontation with the massed ranks of the press is televised live. It is their best chance to land a last blow and a magnificent opportunity for the prime minister to speak to the nation. The lunch can make and break reputations on both sides of the divide. John Howard was preparing for this event when the *Australian*'s report appeared. It was clear to everyone at that point that the governments claims of children being thrown overboard would again face thorough scrutiny.

Howard faced a test of his integrity. The Coalition was well ahead in the critical marginal seats the government needed to hold power. By an overwhelming majority, the public endorsed the Prime Minister's leadership and his treatment of asylum seekers. If no child had been thrown from SIEV 4, Howard could admit this and trust to his genius for putting a good spin on bad news to get the government through the next few days. He could blame the military for the original mistake, point out that a child had been thrown into Ashmore Lagoon from SIEV 7 and that only in the last few days soldiers had saved children from being thrown from SIEV 9 as they tried to start its engines. John Howard chose, instead, to stick to his guns though he knew the evidence for the original story was evaporating.

He asked his senior adviser, Miles Jordana, to put together a brief for his Press Club interrogation. Jordana was not to carry out the sort of exercise Angus Houston was conducting at much the same time that day. Howard did not want a briefing from the military on the whole record—a phone call would have done it—but wanted Jordana to gather what evidence there was to support the old claims. Howard called this, 'a request to be refreshed, if I can put it that way, on the advice, particularly written advice I'd received about a month earlier regarding the children overboard incident . . . I'd asked Miles to go through the material I'd already seen, or the office had received. He wasn't making a fresh request for new information'.[8]

Jordana directed one of Jane Halton's staff, Jenny Bryant, to track down reports that might contain references to children overboard. That search led to the office of Harinder Sidhu, a senior defence adviser in the Prime Minister's department. Three weeks earlier, Sidhu had heard from the department's Defence liaison officer that the photographs were not of children overboard. She and the officer had gone to report that to her superior, but nothing had come of it. Now as she helped Bryant fruitlessly search for documents, Sidhu said, 'Haven't you heard there are rumours circulating in Defence that the photographs are not actually as they have been presented?' Soon afterwards, Bryant rang Jane Halton at home and told her this. Halton claimed to be 'shocked' and immediately called Jordana. But his response, said Halton was sanguine. She recalled him saying, 'This was not an issue. It had been dealt with. They were discussing it with Minister Reith's office'.[9]

By this time, Howard was cloistered with senior staff at the Lodge. With him were his senior private secretary, Tony Nutt, his press secretary, Tony O'Leary, and Jordana. The Prime Minister spoke on the telephone to Reith about the evidence for the children overboard claims but both men insist they did not specifically discuss Houston's briefing. 'I not only spoke to him about the issue of whether he got contrary advice from Defence but I also spoke to him about the video', said Howard. The Defence minister knew the truth but Howard would remain adamant that no one at the Lodge that night—or at any 'relevant time'—ever told him the military had contradicted the original story. 'In my conversation with Mr Reith he said that there was debate about the photographs and we agreed that that was the reason why we should release the video.'[10]

Howard also spoke to Reith's senior advisor, Mike Scrafton. 'The reason I spoke to Scrafton was that Scrafton had looked at the video... He was in Sydney and the video was apparently in Sydney so he had a look at the video.' Scrafton at the very least warned the Prime Minister the video was 'inconclusive'.[11]

That night, Howard knew the key evidence—the photographs and the video from HMAS *Adelaide*—was useless. Moreover, he must have suspected by now that Reith's use of the photographs had misrepresented them to the public. But Howard would not concede this. Nor was he provoked to clear up this immensely complicated puzzle by ringing *anyone* in the military. He did not ask his staff to do so, nor did he put in a call himself. That would not have been 'normal channels', he later explained. 'In the context of what was happening then, it was a perfectly legitimate thing for me to ask the Defence Minister, which I did.' And that was enough. It appears Howard was relying on Peter Reith to shield him from the Defence Department's verdict on this mess, and his own staff appear to have understood that they were not to make life more complicated for him by making fresh enquiries. Howard said, 'There was nobody in my office who had been provided with any advice that contradicted the original assertion'.[12]

Apart from his own phenomenal ability to talk his way through a crisis, the Prime Minister did have one feather to fly with. Earlier that day, Jordana had telephoned Kim Jones, head of ONA, to ask him to find any intelligence analysis containing a reference to children thrown overboard from SIEV 4. At seven that night, Jones faxed Jordana a flimsy ONA report on tactics used by asylum seekers worldwide. Only one and a half pages long and nearly a month old, the document contained just two sentences about the SIEV 4 incident: 'Asylum seekers wearing life-jackets jumped into the sea and children were thrown in with them. Such tactics have previously been used elsewhere, for example, by people smugglers and Iraqi asylum seekers on boats intercepted by the Italian navy.'[13]

Jones' fax came with several warnings. He warned Jordana that these sentences were written *after* ministers had been talking about the SIEV 4 incident for two days, so 'the ONA report could not have been a source of the information used in their statements'. He also warned the Prime Minister's adviser that ONA wasn't even clear where its information had come from: perhaps there was military input, but it was also drawn from the politicians' own words. Jones believed Jordana 'was aware that we were uncertain about the origin of the reference to the "children overboard" and that it may have been based on ministers' statements'. Helpfully attached to the ONA document were early media reports from AAP and the *Age* quoting Howard, Ruddock and Reith making the original claims. This highly secret ONA report was largely drawn from these press statements and contained no primary source confirmation of the incident. Howard's own unsubstantiated claims had been sent back to him in a classified document.[14]

I

Ships and men were leaving to fight the War Against Terror and the last days of the election campaign were punctuated by ceremonial farewells. November 8 had been designated a national day of prayer. Kim Beazley would speak in St Paul's Cathedral in Melbourne. John Howard read the first lesson in the chapel of the Royal Military College Duntroon, where top brass—including Angus Houston—had gathered with senior bureaucrats and political leaders to pray for Australian men and women leaving for the war. 'There is a time for everything, and a season for every activity under heaven', read the Prime Minister. 'A time to search and a time to give up, a time to keep and a time to throw away, a time to tear and a time to mend, a time to be silent and a time to speak, a time to love and a time to hate, a time for war and a time for peace.'[15]

He had already had a busy morning. On ABC-Radio's *AM* he confirmed he would be releasing the video while, at the same time, disowning it as evidence of children overboard claims. Reith and Ruddock 'got that information from navy sources and I've checked that with both of them as recently as last night', he told Catherine McGrath. 'And on top of that I was provided with written advice from intelligence sources on the 10th of October to the effect that people on the vessel had jumped into the water and that children had been thrown into the water.' He invited Beazley to come to his office and read the document. 'He'll know that I can't make it public.'

The navy had begun to leak. Sources were talking to journalists again. Howard was facing well informed questions. 'Now can I ask you this?', said McGrath. 'The initial information you say came from the navy, was there subsequent advice to the minister from [the] navy that in fact children had not been thrown overboard?' The Prime Minister appeared not to hesitate. 'My understanding is that there has been absolutely no alteration to the initial advice that was given. And I checked that as recently as last night.'

All that morning, Jenny McKenry, head of Defence public relations, had been pressed by Howard's and Reith's staff to have copies of the videotape ready for release at noon. The reporters were still analysing its contents when Howard arrived at the Press Club with a phalanx of advisers who took their places in the audience with, among other senior bureaucrats, Jane Halton. What followed was one of Howard's great performances. In his address he had nothing to say about children being overboard but the questions soon came thick and fast. Fran Kelly of ABC-TV's *7.30 Report* told Howard her Defence sources said that the two photographs had been misrepresented by the government. 'Will you ask the Minister of Defence to release those photos with captions as originally provided by the navy?'

Howard ducked and wove. His ministers had acted on Defence advice for their original claims, he said. In turn, he had relied on his ministers. Then he produced the ONA report and read the critical two sentences about the children being thrown into the sea and how these tactics had been used by people smugglers in the Mediteranean. He wrapped up his answer. 'If the Defence Minister and Immigration Minister get verbal advice from Defence sources and the Prime Minister gets that kind of written advice I don't think it's sort of exaggerating or gilding the lily to go out and say what I said.'

The impact was immediate. No one could remember a prime minister reading ONA advice at a press conference before. The journalists were stopped in their tracks and switched their questioning to Howard's border protection policy. But then he was brought back to the point. 'Given that there is some uncertainty about this video about the children being pushed overboard, do you regret saying they're not the sort of people we'd like to have in Australia?' 'Well in my mind there is no uncertainty because I don't disbelieve the advice I was given by Defence.' When a reporter tried to return to the issue of Reith misleading the public over the videotape, Howard said vaguely, 'Well I'll have a look at Mr Reith's comments'. But he added, 'I think Mr Reith has been an extremely good member of the Government and I have a very warm regard for what Mr Reith has done'.[16]

I

HMAS *Adelaide* and *Kanimbla* were leaving for the Gulf that day from the Stirling naval base in Perth. Vice Admiral David Shackleton, Chief of the Navy, had flown over for the event. He had been out of the country for some weeks. Over the Nullabor, his travelling companion, Rear Admiral Geoff Smith, brought him up to date on the kids overboard business. He told Shackleton 'there was no evidence to support the allegation that a child had been thrown overboard, and that the photographs that had been used were a misrepresentation of that alleged incident'. Smith was satisfied Shackleton understood what he was saying.[17]

The *Adelaide's* commander, Norman Banks, had spent his last night at home before a long tour of duty poring over the video and documents, certain both Shackleton and the minister would want to be briefed when they came to farewell his ship next day. In the morning he joined Shackleton, Smith and Reith for national prayers in St Mary's Catholic Cathedral. To Banks' chagrin, the Minister for Defence decided afterwards to skip the *Adelaide* altogether and just go on board the *Kanimbla* berthed nearby. It was an astute—though hardly brave—move on Peter Reith's part. When the Chief of the Navy turned up at the *Adelaide*, Banks took him to his cabin for coffee. It was the first time the two men had spoken face to face about this wrenching controversy. Banks continued to insist he had never claimed children were thrown overboard and he played Shackleton the videotape. At the end of their discussion, the admiral told Banks not to worry. 'There's an election going on. It's a hot item. It will pass with time.'[18]

Reporters, starved of contact with the military throughout Operation Relex, were gathered on the wharf waiting for Shackleton. As the *Adelaide* pulled out, Banks caught sight of the navy chief surrounded by the media in an impromptu press conference. The admiral was bombarded with questions. He tried to steer a course between his minister's public statements and what he had learned from Smith and Banks. He fudged as best he could but when asked directly if the video showed children being thrown into the sea, he replied, 'it doesn't appear they were thrown in'. A reporter asked: 'Did the navy's advice at all say that children had been thrown into the water?' The admiral replied, 'Our advice was that there were people being threatened to be thrown in the water and I don't know what happened to the message after that'.[19]

Shackleton's media adviser, John Clarke, wound up the press conference as soon as possible but the admiral knew he had a problem. Clarke called Jenny McKenry in Canberra to say the admiral 'feared' his comments had contradicted the government. McKenry ordered her staff to monitor the AAP wire. Sure enough, at 4.40 pm a story appeared on the screen headed, 'NAVY DENIES OVERBOARD ADVICE TO REITH'. Commander Banks, out on the Indian Ocean, saw the story on the 6 o'clock television news and was 'delighted that someone had had the courage to speak out at last and set the public record right'.[20]

I

Kim Beazley had been battling all day to get anyone to listen to Labor's message about tax, health and education. At the Royal Melbourne Institute of Technology, the medical students were attentive enough as the Opposition Leader ploughed on with his prepared spiel but the journalists were paying no attention. Through double doors they could see a teaching ward full of dummies in beds, staring back at them with plastic eyes and open mouths. Somehow, it seemed right.

The Beazley camp was furious that public attention was back on refugees and border protection. Labor was living on the hope that the gap was closing and that if only they could keep to their set text there was a chance of snatching a last-minute victory. Any press coverage of asylum seekers—even coverage sharply critical of the government—was 'off message' for Labor and a plus for Howard. The *Australian*'s report from Christmas Island the day before had been a body blow. Beazley's chief of staff, Mike Costello, was also beside himself about the *Sydney Morning Herald*'s front page that morning: a gallery of religious leaders, former politicians, diplomats, academics and public servants attacking both Beazley and Howard for their 'xenophobic and inhumane' policies on refugees. The headline read: 'HOWARD, BEAZLEY LASHED OVER RACE'.

'I don't remember a time when there has been an election with such a clear moral issue but treated by the major parties with such clear amoral electioneering', said the Reverend Tim Costello, president of the Baptist Union and brother of the Federal Treasurer. Former Liberal leaders Malcolm Fraser and John Hewson were there on page one, so were former Liberal ministers Fred Chaney and Ian Macphee. The chancellor of the University of NSW, Dr John Yu, condemned the 'heartless and xenophobic extremes' used to exclude asylum seekers fleeing Afghanistan and Iraq. Yu had arrived as an 'undocumented' refugee in 1937, a baby fleeing the Japanese Rape of Nanking, who was carried ashore in Sydney by his father's friend Sir Earle Page, founder of the Country Party. 'I tell this story to ask what will "queue jumpers" or "illegal" really mean when today's history is written.'[21]

Beazley battled through his morning press conference fielding questions about the children overboard claims. The Opposition Leader tried to dismiss the issue with a mild rebuke for Peter Reith: he 'should have been more careful in the language that he used in relation to the video'. Then, shortly after noon, he headed to St Paul's Cathedral to pray for the armed forces and offer his thoughts to the departing troops. 'My friends,' he said, 'consider yourselves fortunate when all kinds of trials come your way for you know that when your faith succeeds in facing such trials the result is the ability to endure'.

When Admiral Shackleton's remarks hit the wires later that afternoon, Beazley's advisers argued over how he should respond to them. He had to say *something* but they were afraid any attack on the children overboard claims could backfire. Beazley settled on a strategy of criticising Reith, 'more in sorrow than anger'. He told the press corps: 'We can protect our borders without lying about the circumstances. Border protection is vital to this nation but you don't have to lie about it.' And he tentatively pointed the finger at the Prime Minister. 'There is no question Reith lied, the question is what was Mr Howard advised.'²² Beazley's team worried he might have gone a bit far with that last remark, especially when the news broke an hour later that Shackleton had put out a 'clarification' of his comments.

I

The admiral had spent a hell of an afternoon. Reith's chief-of-staff, Peter Hendy, had had what Shackleton described as a forceful conversation with him. 'He recalled the minister being advised by navy people of this incident, and he advised that I should issue a clarifying statement to remove the apparent contradiction.' Hendy was correct. The original error—to which the government was now clinging for grim life—had come from the military. Shackleton's words on the wharf had glossed over the fact. But Hendy did not leave it at that. According to the admiral, Reith's staffer claimed the original story had never been corrected: that 'at no time had the minister been told otherwise'. Shackleton was unaware at this stage that Angus Houston had thoroughly corrected the story to Reith only the day before. The admiral set to work on a statement.²³

Max Moore-Wilton was furiously shoring up the government's position. In a round of rapid telephone calls he talked to Jane Halton and to Bill Farmer. They were the two crucial public servants, for the story had come into the People Smuggling Taskforce meeting via Halton and out to Ruddock via Farmer. Halton went back to search the records for the fateful meeting on October 7 and rang Moore-Wilton to confirm there were handwritten notes showing the briefing had originally come from Defence. Moore-Wilton also rang the secretary of that department, Dr Allan Hawke, who assured him a 'clarifying statement by Admiral Shackleton was imminent'. Hawke had already spoken to Jenny McKenry to point out Shackleton's slip. He told her the original source of the story was the military and 'that needed to be clarified'.²⁴ But Hawke must have realised this flurry of clarification was beside the point. He knew the military's latest state of knowledge on this issue. But it would not be Shackleton's role to reveal the truth. Instead, he and the military were preparing a statement that would put the best possible spin on the situation for the government. It would need to be very carefully drafted.

McKenry's phone was running hot. Reith's staff wanted the 'clarifying statement' sent to Howard's office as soon as possible. When she finally reached Admiral Shackleton, she talked him through the problem. 'Somehow we had to find a form of words', she told him. They decided to keep it short. The first attempt didn't work and wasn't entirely accurate so McKenry rang Shackleton again and walked him through a new statement.[25] Before it went out, it was given to Hawke and General Peter Cosgrove, who had taken over from Houston as acting Chief of the Defence Force. Cosgrove and Hawke read the statement and let it go. It was faxed to all the key players: Max Moore-Wilton, Jane Halton, Bill Farmer and, of course, Reith and Howard. AAP put it out a little before 7 pm. It was just three brief sentences. The first called the original wire report 'inaccurate' and the rest read: 'My comments in no way contradict the Minister. I confirm the Minister was advised that Defence believed children had been thrown overboard.'[26]

Late in the afternoon, Howard faced two tough interrogators: Jenny Brockie of SBS's *Insight* and Tony Jones of the ABC's *Lateline*. He recorded interviews with both to be televised that night. Just as Howard sat down in front of the cameras in Canberra, Shackleton's original statement landed on Brockie's desk. She abandoned her prepared questions. Howard was extremely edgy. 'Nothing can alter the fact that I have in my possession an ONA report that states baldly, as I said at the National Press Club today, that children were thrown in the water.' If that were not so, the navy should have told Peter Reith. 'Mr Reith is not a person who makes things up. He was allowed to go on saying that without any contraction being delivered to him . . . if in fact that advice is wrong, it would have been a good idea if we had been told that a month ago by the navy.'[27] He tore the microphone off and crossed the Parliament House corridor to be given an equally ferocious grilling by Tony Jones.

When Shackleton's 'clarification' was released just over an hour later, Howard's press secretary, Tony O'Leary, insisted both programs record a further interview. After some energetic toing-and-froing, the Prime Minister got his way. Jones went straight for the jugular. 'Who was it that convinced Admiral Shackleton to make this new statement?' Howard appeared deeply affronted. 'I think that's a bit offensive for him. I certainly didn't speak to him and I didn't ask the Defence Minister to speak to him and I'm not aware that anybody has spoken to him.'

Howard was furiously angry. Jones pointed out that Shackleton had not withdrawn his original remarks but simply confirmed Reith's *belief* that children were thrown overboard. Howard dismissed that as 'splitting hairs'. Jones again probed Reith's use of the photographs. 'Would you agree with this', asked Jones, 'if those pictures were taken after the boat was sunk and then represented to the public as pictures of children who'd been thrown overboard by asylum seekers, would that be a scandal?'

Howard replied, 'I'm not going to answer your hypothetical questions'.[28]

He left Parliament House over two hours late for his plane. More reporters were waiting for him on board. They were all flying to Sydney for the last day of the campaign.

TWENTY
The burning issue

NOVEMBER 8 AND 9

Lieutenant Commander Wesley Heron was a long way from a cathedral on the national day of prayer for the armed forces. November 8 found him in command of the patrol boat HMAS *Wollongong* in the seas north of Ashmore Reef on the front line of Operation Relex. After 21 years in the navy, serving on submarines and frigates, Heron had taken part in over 150 boarding operations but a call on his satellite phone at 3.45 that afternoon directed him to one he would never forget. The Customs vessel *Arnhem Bay* had intercepted an old Indonesian coastal trader, the *Sumber Lestari*, slowly making its way towards Ashmore Reef with at least sixty people in life jackets crowded on its deck. SIEV 10 had appeared on the radar just in time for the climax of the election campaign.

Heron headed for the scene and instructed the master of the *Arnhem Bay*, Bradley Mulcahy, to deliver the standard Department of Immigration warning to the Indonesian boat to turn back. It was ignored, as Heron expected. He had orders from Operation Relex headquarters by this time to board SIEV 10 as soon as it crossed into Australia's contiguous zone and then take it under escort to Ashmore Reef. Heron's mission was just a holding operation. SIEV 10 would be kept at the reef pending its 'active return' to Indonesia.

The warning pipes sounded on the *Wollongong*, ordering the crew to boarding stations. Less than half an hour later, Heron could see SIEV 10 in a stand off with the *Arnhem Bay*. He directed the Customs vessel to one side of the Indonesian boat as he manoeuvred the *Wollongong* to the other. Standing by with loaded weapons was a six-man boarding party led by his deputy, Lieutenant Commander James McLaughlin. Also in the party were two marine technicians, Matthew Philp and Gregory Hogarth, the *Wollongong*'s security officer, Malcolm Yeardley, and two seamen, Darren Walker and Jason Hillier. The six climbed into a RHIB and set off for the Indonesian boat with instructions to wait for further orders before boarding. But as they approached the Indonesian boat it was clear something was terribly wrong.[1]

The SIEV was dead in the water and rolling heavily. From deep within the boat came the sound of hammering. Planks were falling into the sea. Fuel was pouring over the side and a large rainbow slick had formed round the SIEV. People on the deck were yelling and gesticulating. 'It was made clear they did not want us to board them', Matthew Philp reported. 'They had the vessel's sideboards all blocked and people guarding them.' Watching from the *Wollongong* about 150 metres away, Commander Heron feared the SIEV was being sabotaged and a disaster was imminent. He called Relex headquarters again, asking for permission to board immediately. Five minutes later, the signal came through and the boarding party moved alongside. It was extremely difficult for them to clamber up the high hull onto the deck. Heron could see 'light smoke emanating from the forward end of the SIEV'.

When the sailors climbed on board, the SIEV's engine was almost certainly already on fire. The security officer, Yeardley, tried to push the passengers away from the railing but they were in uproar. The navy technician, Matthew Philp, grabbed the senior officer and pulled him forward so he could see the scene. Smoke was pouring out of the large entrance that led down to a hold and the passengers were hysterically pointing towards it. McLaughlin ordered the technician to investigate but before Philp could take more than a few steps down the ladder, a man staggered up from the void and fell on him. An explosion burst from the engine room and thick, black smoke poured out. The engine room was ablaze. Philp was overcome and forced back onto the deck. The boarding party had been on the SIEV a little over a minute.

The billowing black smoke set off mass panic on the deck. Scores of frightened men, women and children began running to the starboard side of the boat which started to tilt badly. Water was swirling around the legs of the sailors. McLaughlin thought the boat would capsize and ordered his men to move everybody to the port side. It was then one of the young seamen, Darren Walker, spotted two large barrels of water on the deck near the hold. With a knife from his senior officer, Walker began stabbing at the barrels, accidentally cutting his own hand through his glove. But once the water was released, the smoke thickened almost immediately. McLaughlin realised 'the greater danger to all on board was now the smoke and fire'.

The boarding party was choking and so were the passengers. Flames engulfed the hold and the heat could be felt through the deck. The sailors began shouting at the asylum seekers to jump overboard. Most of the terrified men, women and children obeyed. Those who didn't were pushed overboard. They grabbed at the navy crew, refusing to let go. Matthew Philp tried to push his way to the front of the SIEV but was surrounded by frightened asylum seekers and cut off from the rest of the boarding party. Every few seconds, McLaughlin radioed Heron on the *Wollongong* with reports on the fire as he kept pushing the passengers to jump. Over fifty people remained on the burning boat when McLaughlin decided he had to get his own men off. He called out to his security officer, Yeardley, who shouted the code word into the radio, 'RECOIL'. The sailors inflated their life jackets and jumped into the sea.

Philp was almost overcome by smoke when he heard the order and jumped. As he hit the water, two of the asylum seekers tried desperately to cling to him as his mates hauled him into the RHIB. Frantic survivors grabbed a rope on the RHIB, refusing to let go. The sailors tried to push them off but one would not let go until he was hauled on board.

From the bridge of the *Wollongong*, Heron watched unfolding exactly the kind of SOLAS nightmare that the navy had been warning the bureaucrats about since Operation Relex was in its planning stages. His crew had never practised a mass sea rescue and now, in front of him, SIEV 10 was on fire; well over a hundred people who could not swim were in the sea; most had cheap life jackets but others had no more than inner tubes and children's pool toys to keep them afloat. Baggage was scattered everywhere. Survivors clustered in groups clung to anything that floated. A two-week-old infant and a twelve-month-old baby wrapped in several life jackets were among those bobbing up and down on the sea. Heron had already called in a tender from the *Arnhem Bay* to assist in the rescue. He also called Coastwatch for spotter aircraft and posted lookouts on the bridge of the *Wollongong* to watch for survivors being carried away by the current. Three RHIBs were picking people out of the water.

I

A young Afghan farmer, Sayyed Shahi Husseini, stood with his wife Fatima in their red life jackets on the deck of the burning boat. She was four months pregnant. Sayyed grabbed her hand when the shouts of fire first went up but she was terrified of the water and would not jump. The waves were frightening and the wind was whipping up the sea. Neither Fatima nor her husband could swim. One of the boarding party saw them and shouted at them to abandon the boat. Fatima held her husband's hand and jumped. But as she hit the water, the waves carried her away from Sayyed almost immediately.[2]

Musa Husseini jumped from the deck clutching his six-year-old daughter Samira. As he hit the sea, the waves broke over his head and he gulped down salty water. Struggling to hold his child, he looked around for the rest of his family: his mother, his wife and their four other children. It was then he saw his wife with her head down and feet in the air, her trousers filled with water. The cheap life jackets made it almost impossible to stay upright in the water, forcing the survivors to float either face down or face up. With Samira in one hand and a piece of wood in the other, Musa struggled to reach his wife but the waves kept dragging him away. With immense relief, he saw his brave eight-year-old son right her in the water. She was alive.[3]

When Musa was hauled onto the deck of the *Wollongong*, he looked down and saw his mother still in the sea. He recognised the scarf on her head. She was being held by a teenage boy who was struggling to keep her head out of the water. The boy, Ali Reza, had found the woman face down in the water, not moving her arms. 'When I reached her I took hold of the back of her neck and pulled her face out of the water', he said. 'I noticed that she was not breathing, so I pushed her chest and tummy in. Some foam and some water came out of her mouth. She started to breathe but could not speak.'

Reza tried to reach the *Wollongong* before realising it was easier to swim for the smaller Customs boat. The waves kept pushing him under and he saw RHIBs passing him by. Two Afghans tried to help but they were already holding another woman. Reza believes it took him more than half an hour to reach the *Arnhem Bay*. He thought Musa's mother was still alive when he grabbed one of the rescue ropes and they were hauled aboard by the boat's master, Bradley Mulcahy. The sailors began trying to revive the woman with CPR. She was foaming at the mouth and her pulse was gone.[4]

Wes Heron got a message from the *Arnhem Bay* that an old woman had been dragged from the water unconscious. He sent the *Wollongong*'s medical officer, Craig Duff, to assist. Duff was not a doctor but a young naval police coxswain. By the time he reached the Customs boat the woman was beyond help. The sailors had pumped two litres of water out of her lungs but she was still not breathing. Duff thought she was perhaps in her seventies but it was hard to tell. Nurjan Husseini was, in fact, just 55. Duff 'advised the crew member to cease giving CPR'. She was beyond help and the crew needed to spend their efforts saving others among the '90+ PIIs embarked' rather than concentrate 'on one deceased person'. He radioed Heron who concurred in the decision.[5] Nurjan's struggle to reach Australia was over.

Duff returned to the *Wollongong* where he found two men working in the wardroom to revive another unconscious woman, Fatima, the 20-year-old wife of the farmer, Sayyed. She had only a weak pulse when she was lifted from the water but no pulse by the time she was left in the care of the chief engineer, Dale Zanker, and Linden Mooney, the ship's cook, who doubled as the medical emergency officer. They had lain the woman on her side to try to unblock her airways. Water and bile flowed from her mouth, and her nose and eyes were foaming. The cook administered oxygen while Zanker pumped the woman's heart. Despite all their efforts, no pulse flickered to life. When the oxygen bottle was nearly empty, Mooney screamed for more and another bottle was brought.[6]

Duff asked the men how long they had been working to revive the woman but they had no idea. They told him there were still no signs of life and Duff left to consult his commanding officer. Heron agreed CPR should cease. Duff returned to the wardroom and told the men to stop. 'Two of the four available oxygen bottles had been used', he said. 'Members of the *Wollongong* Boarding Party were in need of oxygen after inhaling diesel smoke during the fire on board the SIEV. Logistically, I felt it prudent to preserve my resources and treat those that could be saved.' With some care, Duff and Mooney put Fatima's body into a human remains pouch. Duff said, 'I crossed her hands on her belly and closed her eyes and wiped her face as there was still quite a bit of fluid and bile on it'. The body was taken to be stored in the officers' showers.[7]

Mooney then followed Duff to the quarterdeck to treat the living. Two babies were seriously ill, suffering from hypothermia. One was on oxygen. Duff and Mooney put the infants under warm water in an effort to raise their body temperature. Then they wrapped them in blankets and put them in the arms of their parents. The older child responded well but the young infant did not. At times, Duff thought the baby might be drifting into unconsciousness. He kept vigil all night with the parents monitoring the child.[8]

The *Wollongong*'s crew had found some survivors who spoke English and learnt, through them, that nearly everyone on SIEV 10 was an Afghan. There were a few Iraqis and Iranians. They had conflicting stories about how the fire broke out. While Yeardley was still on the burning boat, he was approached by an English-speaking Afghan pleading for help: 'Baby sick from water, smoke.' Yeardley snapped, 'Well, I didn't set boat on fire to make baby sick, you did'. The Afghan denied the charge. 'Iraq set boat on fire, not Afghani.' On board the *Wollongong*, Craig Duff was told by a survivor that Iranians had started the fire.[9] Later, the survivors would deny making these statements.

The Indonesian crew blamed the passengers too. There had been a confrontation below decks between the crew and some asylum seekers— and among the asylum seekers themselves—just after the *Arnhem Bay* confronted SIEV 10. Equipment was interfered with and gear thrown over the side. The Indonesians thought it possible the fire started at that point. But there were asylum seekers who held the Indonesian captain responsible. At the sight of the *Arnhem Bay*, he had gunned the boat's engine in an effort to outrun the Customs vessel and reach Australian waters. Asylum seekers believed the overheating of the engine might have sparked the fire. There was consensus among them on only one point: there was no pre-arranged plan among the asylum seekers to set fire to SIEV 10 if they were intercepted. Ali Reza later said, 'I don't think people would be so mad to do that while they have got so many barrels of petrol and people on deck'.[10]

On the bridge of the *Wollongong*, Wes Heron had more immediate problems than sorting out blame for the fire. The search for survivors had continued for over an hour and a half and he was satisfied he had found everyone. He had 62 on board his own ship and another hundred on the *Arnhem Bay*. Some were injured and some badly traumatised. There were several seriously ill children and two dead women. The *Wollongong* and the *Arnhem Bay* set out at slow speed for Ashmore, 22 nautical miles away. Three hours later, a little after 11 pm, they dropped anchor not far from SIEVs 8 and 9, still waiting in the lagoon.

A report on the fate of SIEV 10 was sent at about this time by Operation Relex to Canberra. It was in Peter Reith's hands by the early hours of November 9. In sparse military language, it reported the interception, the fire and the deaths of the two women. The conclusion was that the vessel had been deliberately destroyed and the fire deliberately lit but the report carried an important caveat: 'This is an interim report subject to correction following more detailed investigation.' The AFP would come to a far less clear-cut conclusion later: 'It is unknown if the fire was deliberately lit or the result of the engine having been tampered with . . . There is no evidence of a common plan amongst the passengers or the crew to destroy or damage the boat if stopped by Australian authorities.'[11]

But that open finding was months away. The fire, the drownings, the thirty children at risk in the catastrophe were about to be fed into the election campaign to divert attention from the government's severe embarrassment over the children overboard claims.

❙

The front pages were not kind to the Prime Minister that morning. 'NAVY SCUTTLES PM'S STORY' was the headline in the *Australian*; 'HOWARD IN HOT WATER OVER CHILDREN OVERBOARD CLAIM', said the *Sydney Morning Herald* while the *Courier-Mail*'s verdict across page one was, 'PHOTO SINKS HOWARD'S CLAIM'. Navy 'sources' were quoted extensively confirming that the story was bogus. The *Australian* carried a detailed if slightly garbled account of what had really happened to SIEV 4. That Ruddock, Reith and Howard had deceived the electorate was the common suspicion of the media but the editorials of nearly every major paper in the country that morning endorsed Howard's re-election. 'Australians don't want the bloke next door', concluded the *Daily Telegraph*. 'They want energy and calculated daring.'[12]

No day is like the last day of an election campaign. Both parties knew there were many voters who still had to make up their minds. Howard was superbly prepared for the task of persuading them. A press release with the grim news about SIEV 10 had gone out early. Never before in Operation Relex had so much information on a boat been released to the public. Once more, the story had rolled forward. Journalists would ask savage questions that day about the children overboard claims but they had to follow where the new story led. Howard was making hay. On breakfast television and morning radio, he hinted that he was now quite keen to find the truth about those claims and would be looking into the matter over the next few days. Meanwhile, it was up to the navy. 'If there had been something wrong with the original advice, something fundamentally wrong, then I would have assumed that the navy would have got in touch with the minister and said "look, what you said then is wrong because the facts are as follows". Now that did not occur, so I am told. I have not been given different advice. If I were given different advice I'd make it public.'[13]

'Now we've got a boat on fire', said John Laws. 'Yes we have', Howard replied sombrely. 'It sunk and apparently, and sadly, there appears to have been two of the people on it drowned. What I've done is, particularly in light of what has occurred, I've told Mr Reith to release the navy report, unvarnished and in full and people can then make their own judgements. And if there's any correction subsequently to be made well that's fair enough and the navy will make that correction but I do not want people, particularly the day before an election, saying well Howard and Reith are making this up.' He read slabs of the report about the fire, the panic on board—'that's understandable'—and the rescue, particularly of the thirty children.

'The report goes on to say, they had prepared their vessel to obstruct Royal Australian Navy boarding parties and had set about deliberately destroying their vessel in order to avoid their return to Indonesia. The fire was deliberately lit and the exploding drum is indicative of an attempt to prevent the boarding party from extinguishing the fire. That this was a deliberate action by the people is reinforced by the fact that they all wore life jackets. While not confirmed the two deceased woman appear to have drowned. This is an interim report subject to correction following more detailed investigation. Now, that I'm reading from a navy report. I'm not making any of that up. That is not based on hearsay.'

Howard deplored the deaths; he praised the navy for doing 'a fantastic job in a very difficult situation', and he attacked the violent 'pattern of conduct' that 'illegal immigrants' were using to thwart Australia's efforts to send them back to Indonesia. He swept aside the fact that his government had put the navy in that situation in the first place; that he and his ministers were shamelessly attacking the navy that morning for its supposed failure to correct the record on the children overboard claims; and that the refugee claims of the human cargo on SIEV 10 could not be dismissed until those people were duly processed. 'I can't guarantee to the Australian people there won't be more of them', Howard told John Laws' audience from coast to coast. 'But I can guarantee to them that if I'm re-elected tomorrow I will continue to stop these vessels coming to Australia.'

The polls gave Labor a sliver of hope. That week's *Bulletin* Morgan poll had tipped a big win for the Opposition. It was a bizarre prediction. On those figures Labor might rout the government by a majority of thirty or forty seats. None of the other polls, nor Labor's own polling, was suggesting a result anything like that. But this rogue poll and the knowledge that as many as 15 per cent of the voters had yet to make up their minds gave Labor a little desperate hope in the last days of the campaign. What it needed was a few days without boat people in the news. What it got was the hullabaloo over children overboard and then the catastrophe of SIEV 10.

On the last morning of the election campaign, Beazley was bombarded by questions about all this, questions that were 'off message' for Labor. Beazley was convinced that every word he spoke about the asylum seekers only helped John Howard's re-election prospects. He was right—because he had spent the whole campaign locked in step with Howard's border protection policies. On *AM* that morning, the ABC's Catherine McGrath confronted Beazley over his failure to challenge the government about children overboard claims until Admiral Shackleton's statement. 'Can I ask you this,' said McGrath, 'if you lose the election anyway, will you regret the reluctance you have had to take a stand on the asylum seekers?'

Beazley immediately became defensive. He retreated to his position of criticising Howard 'more in sorrow than anger', while desperately appearing to stand tough on border protection. 'There are many unanswered questions and John Howard and Mr Reith and Mr Ruddock have to answer them all by the end of today . . . ', Beazley replied.

'You didn't push them on this?' McGrath interjected.

'Will you let me finish', said Beazley. 'The point is you do not need to make a disreputable case for a reputable proposition.'

Beazley and his staff were angry that the press was once again dominated by stories from Operation Relex. They deeply resented church attacks on the party's refugee policy and what they saw as the 'left-wing' moralists in the party criticising the leader. Beazley's rhetoric had often been as strident as Howard's against queue jumpers and those 'criminals [who] take advantage of our generosity'.[14] He had tried to neutralise Howard on border protection while talking about 'the real issues'. When one interviewer remarked that the campaign 'ends where it began on the boat people issue', Beazley upbraided her, insisting the election debate was focused on jobs, health and education.

On this final day of the campaign, Beazley flew to Adelaide still trying to talk about unemployment figures and the GST. It was as if he were fighting another campaign in another election. He toured a fish factory. He told the travelling media corps at his last press conference: 'Throughout this campaign, what I have attempted to do is . . . to bring the issues of the campaign back to the kitchen table.' In a complete misreading of his opponent and the election campaign he had just fought, Beazley summed up John Howard as 'a bloke whose heart wasn't really in it'.[15]

Labor had done badly during the campaign in the daily battle to dominate page one. As Geoff Walsh, Labor's secretary, ruefully noted, of the thirty front page stories in Sydney's *Daily Telegraph* in those weeks, only two had headlined Labor's agenda; three covered the Melbourne Cup but over twenty were devoted to asylum seekers, the war against terrorism, anthrax and jihads. But Beazley's dogged, good-humoured campaigning had managed to save Labor from the abyss that lay at the Opposition's feet when the election was called. That night, the Labor leader ate a last supper at one of Adelaide's fine restaurants with his wife Susie Annus and his staff. For a few hours their mood was buoyant until details of the latest Newspoll reached the party. Nothing in these figures collected over the past couple of days supported the Morgan prediction. The Coalition looked poised for victory with a two-party preferred vote of 53 per cent.[16]

In the newsroom of Sydney's *Daily Telegraph*, another page one was being prepared. Nothing about jobs, tax, health or education. The layout of the page left no doubt that Howard's message had triumphed. Above a photograph of one of the refugee boats anchored on Ashmore Lagoon and a story of SIEV 10 being 'deliberately set alight' was a long running headline: 'AS 12 MILLION AUSTRALIANS GO TO THE POLLS TODAY THEY ARE AGAIN CONFRONTED BY THE ELECTION CAMPAIGN'S BURNING ISSUE.'

Petty Officer Malcolm Yeardley had spent the day tagging the survivors on the *Wollongong*. For an interpreter he had an Afghan with a PhD in engineering. They interrupted their morning work to deal with the 'delicate matter' of taking Sayyed to see his wife's body.

Unable to find his wife and not knowing she was dead, Shahi had been brought over from the *Arnhem Bay* to look for her on the *Wollongong*. When he could not find her, he sat crying on the deck. Sailors tried to calm him, telling him his wife was not well. But Shahi was distraught and insisted on seeing her. An hour later, he was taken to the officers' showers and Fatima's body bag was unzipped. Shahi was given ten minutes to sit with her and mourn.[17]

Nurjan Husseini's body had been brought over from the *Arnhem Bay* and also placed in the showers. Yeardley was called away from his work later in the day to help the medical officer decide 'whether or not it was humane to let the family have a look, to ID the corpse'.[18] That night one of Nurjan's grandsons was allowed to sit next to her body bag and pray. Next morning, the bodies of Fatima and Nurjan were transferred from the *Wollongong* to the freezer room on HMAS *Tobruk* for the final leg of their journey to Christmas Island.

TWENTY ONE
Victory party

NOVEMBER 10

Every polling day, party workers appear in the early morning dark outside schools, town halls and kindergartens to skirmish for positions. The Liberals used to be rather casual about this but in the 1990s they learnt to match the professionals of the Labor Party, arriving before dawn to set up a card table and fix the party's poster to the fence as close as possible to the polling booth. The Liberal poster in 2001 showed a resolute John Howard with his fists clenched, flanked by flags. The message was: 'WE DECIDE WHO COMES TO THIS COUNTRY AND THE CIRCUMSTANCES IN WHICH THEY COME.' Pamphlets with that slogan and that shot of Howard had been dropped into letterboxes across the nation. Huge advertisements showing the same determined Howard defending his country against invading boat people appeared that morning in all the major newspapers of Australia. The ads reminded voters, 'A vote for your local Liberal team member protects our borders and supports the Prime Minister's team'.

Whatever the Liberals would later say about this campaign, there was no doubt the party saw border protection as its most potent vote-winner. In the previous few days, in the most closely contested seats, the party had pulled advertising on every subject but this. A fortune was spent hammering the message home. The party's federal director, Lynton Crosby, would cite the co-ordination of the message—in advertisements, posters and in the press—as evidence of the campaign discipline he believed brought the party victory. 'John Howard's press club performance and continuing discipline coupled with the strict discipline that our campaign displayed with polling booth dressing and messages helped lock away our vote.'[1]

Howard's discipline in those last days was formidable. With his credibility in doubt over the children overboard claims, he found himself dealing with a press corps sniffing blood, furious old public service mandarins, carping bishops, public enemies in the Liberal camp and disgruntled naval officers who had, at last, found their tongues. Retired Vice Admiral Sir Richard Peek, a former navy chief who had sprung to Shackleton's defence, attacked the use of the navy to turn back boat people and attacked 'the current rules where the services are completely muzzled and treated rather in the way the German population was treated by Dr Goebbels in World War II—not allowed to say anything in public'.[2]

Dr Duncan Wallace was not, at first, muzzled. A Naval Reserve officer and a psychiatrist from Sydney's St Vincent's Hospital, Wallace was back in Sydney after some weeks' service on the *Arunta*. Wallace had watched SIEV 7 forced back to Indonesia and had seen the violence that erupted on SIEV 9 as the navy tried, unsuccessfully, to force that boat back. These operations, wrote Wallace in letters to the press, 'merely serve to harass, frighten and demoralise people who are already weak, vulnerable and desperate. Not only are these actions physically dangerous to members of the ADF, but it is my expert opinion, as a senior consultant psychiatrist to the Royal Australian Navy, that they are highly likely to be harmful to the psychological health and moral development of all members involved. Nearly everyone I spoke to that was involved in these operations knew that what they were doing was wrong . . . the hard-hearted who speak loudly about the need for stern deterrent actions to solve this problem have not seen the faces of the boat people in their miserable conditions, imploring us for help'.[3]

Howard denied the work was taking its toll on the sailors and continued to thank them effusively for their efforts. 'I don't pretend it's easy. I wish we didn't have to do it, but I say to the critics of our policy, and this includes all of them, are they seriously imagining that if we abandon the policy we're now following, the result would be other than a signal around the world that this country once again . . . was going to become open and easy to access by illegal immigrants.'⁴

Wallace was then silenced by the navy but eloquent voices from the front line were now telling their stories. On polling day, the *Australian* reported the response of a senior officer on the *Tobruk* ferrying boat people to Nauru. 'In the middle of the night I looked down from the bridge', said the officer. 'There's two hatches open and it's hot. Through one, I could see a hundred people lying there on stretchers. I thought, "It's like a slave ship". I thought, "Jesus, I thought we were Australians. I thought we were a good bloody country." Onboard, they don't like to use the word prisoners, but they are. At Ashmore Reef it hit me—shit we're going like South Africa. If Australia continues down this political path, it will be like apartheid here. And people will think that's what we do here. But it's not what we should do here.' The unnamed officer reported divisions in the navy between those who supported Operation Relex and those who thought the government was turning the service into 'legally sanctioned people-traffickers'. Having decided these people were refugees, the officer concluded he could take no further part in the operation. 'They're fleeing the governments the Americans are trying to destroy, for Christ's sake. They're fleeing persecution.'⁵

As attention focused more closely on the role of race in the campaign, Howard insisted the boats would still be stopped even if the people they brought were 'white or Japanese, or North America or whatever—it is a question of protecting our borders'. He assured Australians he was not appealing to racism—for they were not racist. 'I don't find any racism in the Australian public. I find constant references to racism in articles and news commentary and in the utterances of my critics on the policy. I don't find, as I move around the community, people expressing racist sentiments about the illegal immigrants at all.' Of course there were always a few bigots about, he conceded one morning on Adelaide radio. But to suggest his fellow countrymen and women were racially prejudiced was 'self-flagellation of the Australian spirit'.⁶

Howard belittled his critics as bearers of personal grudges against him or their own country. Attacks from the old guard of the Liberal Party he dismissed as 'completely unsurprising'. He was, by this time, being assailed by the former prime minister Malcolm Fraser, a handful of Liberal ex-ministers and his own predecessor as leader of the Opposition, John

Hewson, who called the Pacific Solution 'ludicrous' and accused Howard of tapping into 'latent racial prejudice' both in this campaign and in the past. 'Ironically, Howard despite being carefully crafted has never had a genuine passion for policy. He has, however, successfully manipulated prejudice to his personal, political advantage.' But Howard shrugged these Liberal critics off. 'Many of them have been critics of mine for a long time. Many of them, on a lot of issues.'[7]

The Olympian figure of Laurie Oakes, Channel 9 correspondent and *Bulletin* columnist, brought some clarity to the race issue just before polling day. 'The key feature of this election campaign has been a clever use of what professionals call "dog whistle politics". A dog whistle is pitched so high that dogs hear it but humans do not. Dog whistle politics involves pitching a message to a particular group of voters that other voters do not hear. John Howard wanted One Nation voters back. He also saw a chance to attract some traditional "blue-collar" Labor voters with similar concerns. The *Tampa* episode provided him with the dog whistle he needed.' Oakes noted that Howard had experimented back in 1988 by calling for a slowing-down of Asian immigration. The idea was popular with the public but embarrassing for the party. Howard was dumped as Leader of the Opposition. 'He has learned from his mistakes—including the mistake of actually mentioning race.' Oakes was suggesting that in the years since that debacle, Howard had learned to whistle instead. Oakes concluded: 'Howard, clumsy 13 years ago, has been surefooted this time.'[8]

Challenged at the National Press Club about dog whistling, Howard denied Oakes' allegations. 'I don't believe at all what he says is accurate and I reject it completely', he said. 'It's politically offensive.' He had looked into his own soul and was content with what he found. 'I examine criticisms of my behaviour that have moral strictures contained in it like other strictures but I am satisfied within myself that what we are doing is in the national interest.'

John Howard had by this time crossed a crucial line. He gave an interview to the *Courier-Mail*'s political editor Dennis Atkins in which he crudely linked boat people with terrorists. Hitherto, Howard's linking of the two had been subtle, hard to hear, perhaps, unless you had acute hearing. He now threw restraint aside and made the same crude claims his Defence minister had been making for weeks. Atkins' report began: 'Australia had no way to be certain terrorists, or people with terrorist links, were not among the asylum seekers trying to enter the country by boat from Indonesia, Prime Minister John Howard said.' On Howard's plane late on the night of November 6, Atkins had his laptop open to show his press colleagues how the *Courier-Mail* would be splashing his scoop next morning. Howard appeared in the aisle and Atkins showed him, too. 'Good', said the Prime Minister. 'Excellent'.[9]

Howard's line was not based on the professional advice available to him from his own intelligence service, ASIO. Dennis Richardson, director-general of ASIO, rated the possibility of terrorists arriving disguised as asylum seekers as extremely remote. 'Why would people use the asylum seeker stream when they know they will be subject to mandatory detention?' he asked. 'They do not know how long they will be detained and they don't know if they will be allowed entry and they may be thrown out. I can't exclude it but I've not seen evidence of it. I believe a foreign government wishing to put someone into Australia has resources at its disposal beyond the need to slip people in as refugees or asylum seekers.' But Richardson would not be making that public statement for another six months.[10]

Terrorism had re-entered the campaign because the Taliban's ambassador to Pakistan, Mullah Abdul Salam Zaeef, had just declared a hazy jihad against Australia for joining the War Against Terror. The mullah's threats were disowned by Australia's Muslim leaders and Howard was at pains to calm the electorate. Extremists linking Australia and the United States in that way was not a surprise to Howard. 'We knew once the terrorist attack occurred that all countries which could be readily identified with the United States . . . ought to be on a heightened state of alert.' But he believed all security precautions that needed to be taken by Australia, had been taken. 'We have to get on with our lives, we have to continue to enjoy ourselves and continue to run our businesses and go on our holidays and travel around this wonderful country.'[11]

Australia's intelligence focus in Indonesia remained fixed on people smugglers—despite Australia's role in the Afghanistan war and despite fanatics in the archipelago dreaming of a vast Islamic state. The indolent government of President Megawati Sukarnoputri would continue to allow Jemaah Islamiah (JI) to flourish, particularly in the aftermath of crackdowns in Malaysia and the Philippines. JI was already linked to al-Qaeda. But at this time, Alexander Downer saw 'no specific threat to Australia or Australian interests' from the growth of al-Qaeda's influence in the region.

The AFP's chief of intelligence, Jeff Pentrose, was later to speak of a prevailing attitude in Australia of 'it can't happen to us'.[12] What mattered most urgently to Canberra for many months to come was beating the boats. Those hundreds of deaths on SIEV X had stirred Sukarnoputri's government to convene—at Australia's urging—a regional meeting of countries affected by people smuggling. That had been a useful success in the election campaign for the Howard government. But in retrospect, it would come to seem there were far more urgent issues for those countries to be gathering to discuss in early 2002 in Bali.

I

The Prime Minister emerged from Kirribilli House at 6.47 am walking briskly and smiling the smile that showed John Howard was, for all his talk about tight contests and cautious hopes, a relaxed and confident man. He visited his children working the Liberal pitch at Putney Public School. 'Fancy seeing you', said his daughter Melanie. 'You look familiar', said his son Richard. Around them were glowering WE DECIDE posters. Howard bought a raffle ticket and drove across his electorate to Eastwood Public School where he faced a last press conference in the playground. What did he think of the *New York Times* suggesting he wanted to keep Australia white? 'Well that's ridiculous, absolutely ridiculous. Look around you. You think I'm in favour of that sort of policy? I mean that is absurd, written only by somebody who doesn't understand this country. And that sort of remark is I think offensive to Australia.' He took the cameras inside for the ritual shot of him casting his ballot then bought a sausage on white bread from a fund-raising barbecue in the playground. He posed for photographs. 'Here I am in completely suspended animation, not knowing what the future holds and isn't that good. I mean, it's a tremendous exercise in democracy.'[13]

Kim Beazley arrived at Rockingham High School in his electorate of Brand, red-eyed and weary. The day was hot. Around him spread Perth's southern suburbs: dusty streets ringed by industrial parks with many English and South Africans living behind neat front gardens. Beazley seemed to be searching already for something to celebrate in the face of the loss bearing down on him. 'The polls this morning say this is a tight one. It's a miracle we're in this situation. When we began this election campaign all the polls told us that the Labor Party was facing annihilation.' He took his wife Susie inside and they voted for the cameras in one of the classrooms. There was not much more Beazley could do. He said, 'What keeps me alive is the smell of those suburbs in Western Australia near to the beach. It smells like relaxation and it smells like home and there is no better way to conclude an election campaign.'[14]

The leaders were joined at the ballot box that day by twelve million Australians. A great deal was happening in the polling booths. Labor's 'kitchen table' policies were, in fact, attracting large numbers of voters. In less dramatic times, when health, jobs and tax mattered more to the electorate, that shift might have secured Labor victory. But the trouble on November 10 was that Labor deserters were outnumbering recruits. The maths was turning in Howard's favour with about 15 per cent moving to Labor but about twenty per cent travelling in the opposite direction.[15]

Labor was always going to lose support to the government while the economy was buoyant and interest rates low. Young women, in particular, were voting in droves on November 10 to defend their mortgages.[16] Howard was always going to win votes by being prime minister in the aftermath of September 11, leading the nation into the War Against Terror. But the issue that was doing the sums for the government was immigration—not on its own, but border protection fused with national defence calling for resolute leadership. The appeal of the Prime Minister as a leader could not be disentangled from the issue on which he had shown such forceful direction since the *Tampa*. 'The issue of illegal entrants was . . . as much about leadership as the issue itself', Liberal strategists would later admit. '*Tampa* provided further evidence of this leadership strength. It reinforced an existing perception rather than creating a new one.' But the reinforcement was spectacular. Admiration for Howard's leadership had not stopped rising since the Norwegian ship was halted two and a half months ago at Flying Fish Cove.[17]

And Howard was demolishing One Nation. Across Australia its vote was halving. Liberals who had deserted their party in 1998 to vote for Pauline Hanson were coming home and bringing their friends with them. Along city fringes and in country towns—particularly in NSW and Queensland—seats that Labor might have won by shifting only a few hundred or a few thousand votes were holding firm for the government. Five marginal seats held by Labor were falling to the government. By carefully finessing his response to Hanson for years, then seizing her policy on boat people, John Howard had made One Nation irrelevant.[18]

■

At some point on election day, HMAS *Tobruk* set out from Ashmore for Christmas Island. The handful of Vietnamese from SIEV 8 travelled in the isolated comfort of the soldiers' quarters. They would be flown from Christmas to the Cocos Islands and then, many weeks later, home to Vietnam. Down on the *Tobruk*'s hot and noisy tank deck travelled three hundred Iraqis and Afghans from SIEVs 9 and 10. They were not aware of this yet, but these four days at sea were only the first leg of a long voyage that would take them to Nauru. Not all of them, of course, for in the freezer were the bodies of Nurjan Husseini and Fatima Hussaini who were to be allowed a patch of Australian ground in the Muslim graveyard on Christmas Island.

■

The polls closed at 6 pm. Howard had already returned to Kirribilli House, his official residence on the harbour. At some point early in the evening he sat down at the Australian Electoral Commission office computer in his study. 'It was not until the figures had been coming in for about an hour that I was completely satisfied that we were going to make it.' Labor's own number crunchers were on television a little before 8 pm admitting defeat. Beazley knew it was all over before the polls had closed in Western Australia. He rang Howard then drove to the Star Ballroom in Rockingham. 'I have to concede defeat', he told the unhappy Labor crowd. 'We have lost this election. There is no doubt about that.' He announced he was resigning. 'So I bow out of Labor Party history now.'[19]

Hotel champagne was flowing at the Wentworth in Sydney where guests were watching the early count on television screens. The celebrations had not yet taken off. The ballroom was still filling with Liberal Party workers in yellow t-shirts, North Shore matrons in pearls, university students on the piss, monarchists, relaxed businessmen, lawyers, candidates and their supporters and the beefy figure of Max Moore-Wilton. Was he not politicising his office by drinking at the Liberal victory party? Australia's Westminster system was 'evolving', he explained to the journalist. 'What we do on the weekend is our own business.'[20]

Suddenly, into the ballroom burst a man wearing a sandwich board, waving his arms and shouting, 'What a victory! We've won it! We've won this one! Congratulations guys'. He was one of the satirists from the ABC's

Election Chaser, the same people who set up that arse-kissing stall in Angel Place a fortnight earlier. On his sandwich board were silhouettes of the *Tampa*, turbaned heads and the words RACE CARD. 'We played well! We came through! John told me to come down and warm up the crowd like I've been doing the whole campaign.' No one pounced. No one laughed. People seemed to be struggling even to get the point. Moore-Wilton had no trouble. 'Go home', he snarled. 'Go home.' Someone threw a glass of beer. Then the plain clothes police arrived to hustle the RACE CARD out, still shouting for the cameras. 'I've been with him the whole campaign and now you're kicking me out. No respect. I tell you what, they just *use* you.'[21]

Loudmouths in the ballroom greeted the sight of Beazley conceding defeat on television with an outburst of booing. Chanting began: 'We want John.' The stage was empty, waiting. Pauline Hanson's face came on the screens. She had failed even to win a place for herself in the Senate. Now she stood in the hinterland of the Gold Coast and blamed John Howard for stealing her party's thunder. 'I believe that we saw the Coalition pick up the policies and issues of One Nation.' She declared she was unfazed by defeat. 'It's how I feel about myself. That's the most important thing. And you know what the next important thing is? My children, how they see me. And when my kids tell me, "Mum, we are so proud of you", I feel pretty good.'[22]

A few minutes later, the Howard family appeared in the Wentworth's ballroom and made their way to the stage through a tumult of applause. Howard stood flanked by his jubilant wife, their admiring children standing a pace behind. He had to beg the cheering crowd to let him speak. Oddly for him, he had notes. 'I cannot express to you the sense of honour and privilege I feel in once again being elected as Prime Minister of the greatest country in the world.' That brought another storm of applause and shouts of 'Johnnie, Johnnie, Johnnie'.[23] He was courteous to Beazley, thanked his party, his colleagues, his staff and his family. Once again, he called for unity as he had when claiming victory twice before on this stage. 'We have had a difficult and on occasions, as always happens in an election campaign, a bruising political exchange. That is part of a democracy. It is not something that we should ever shrink from, it is not something that we should ever recoil from. It is part of the democratic system that people will passionately argue their points of view but once that battle is over, we all have a duty, each to the other to come together as part of the great Australian nation.'

After 1998, a campaign bruising for Aborigines, Howard had caught the imagination of Australia by committing himself in his victory speech 'to the cause of true reconciliation with the Aboriginal people'. He had not delivered on his promise but the gesture, at least, had counted for something. In 2001 Howard made no gesture of reconciliation to those who had been battered by this campaign—Australia's 300 000 Muslims, tens of thousands of refugees already settled in Australia, the United Nations, Norway and Indonesia. Instead, he was laying the groundwork for the elaborate denials to come. 'To grasp the scale of what our party has achieved, we will remember the depths of political despair that many of us felt earlier this year and the long battle back begun months ago. And those who will seek to record wrongly that we only began to recover late in August'—he meant with the *Tampa*—'forget the great turning point of the Aston by-election, and the way in which our party and our National Party colleagues in Coalition responded to the concerns of the Australian people in many areas.'

Ballot boxes were still being emptied and the votes counted as Howard spoke that night. Yet even when all the counting was done and the analysts had crunched the numbers and all the exit polls had been published—even then, Howard and his ministers would deny the role in all this of border protection, the Pacific Solution, Operation Relex and the destruction of One Nation. They would say it was just a political myth put about by Labor, the Greens and those disgruntled elites only too happy to beat up on Australia.[24]

Standing on the stage with his family, John Howard rededicated himself to the service of his nation. 'Finally, can I say again tonight to all my fellow Australians I feel an enormous sense of honour and privilege at what has been given to me tonight. I won't let you down. It is a great trust. It is a solemn trust and I will discharge it to the very best of my ability.' The Howards had already plunged into the crowd when someone in the ballroom broke into the national anthem. Janette Howard led her family straight back to the microphones and they sang through, lustily to the end, word perfect. Then they made their way through the throng to a door that led to a private room. Max Moore-Wilton slipped in behind them to this more intimate celebration of their victory.[25]

Aftermath

By the time it was all over, Australia had shut its doors to about 2390 boat people. Not many: a couple of full houses at the City Recital Hall where John Howard launched his campaign with a pledge to defend his country's borders 'within the framework of the decency for which Australians have always been renowned'.[1]

Two more boats were forced back to Indonesia. SIEV 11 was a shark boat with 22 people on board. SIEV 12 was a grim operation involving 162 Iraqis, Iranians and Afghans. Men again jumped overboard, a child was held over the side, attempts were made to set the boat alight, an old woman doused herself with petrol. The navy left them off Roti Island a few days before Christmas. No more boats came after that.[2]

Australia had forced four boats and 670 people back to Indonesia. The fall of the Taliban, Australia's mysterious 'disruption' programs in Indonesia and the tragedy of SIEV X all helped stem the flow of asylum seekers. But the people smugglers were put out of business when they could no longer deliver their customers to Australia. Operation Relex worked.

The cost was about $500 million. The exact sum is impossible to calculate because the hundreds of millions of dollars spent by the military on

Operation Relex are hidden, somewhere, in the accounts of the Department of Defence. The Treasurer, Peter Costello, has admitted an extra $232 million was budgeted for the first year of the Pacific Solution: $196.5 million for DIMA's 'capital and operating costs'; $17 million 'in relation to costs involving Nauru'; and $18.5 million 'in relation to Manus Island'. Another $195 million has been allocated for a new 'reception and processing centre' being carved out of Christmas Island. When it comes to defending the borders from boat people, money is no object.[3]

Two women drowned. Three men went missing. A couple of thousand men, women and children suffered in detention in squalid boats on Ashmore Lagoon, in the Sports Hall on Christmas Island, in the holds of SIEVs forced back to Indonesia, and on long, frustrating voyages to Nauru locked in navy transports. Then they faced months and sometimes years behind barbed wire in tropical camps.

Australian sailors and soldiers were ordered to do some of the worst work of their lives out on the Indian Ocean. The military was drawn deep into the Coalition's election strategy, compromising the political neutrality of the armed forces. Some of the most senior military men in the land were outwitted, out-gunned and outmanoeuvred in a military campaign designed to re-elect the Prime Minister.

Australia did not kill those who drowned on SIEV X but their deaths can't be left out of the reckoning entirely. Canberra's response to that missing boat is a measure of what has happened here since the *Tampa*. When those in peril on the sea are asylum seekers, Australia hesitated to rescue. Not refused, hesitated. Only a miracle saved the *Palapa* from being another SIEV X right at the beginning of this story. In better times, the sight of that overcrowded boat in distress—or the failure of an equally overcrowded boat to arrive at Christmas Island—would have set off an immediate search and rescue operation. Not in late 2001. Canberra kept hoping somebody else would take these people off their hands.

Abu Quassey, the man responsible for the 352 deaths on SIEV X, served six months in a Jakarta prison for visa offences and was released on New Year's Day, 2003.

As the *Tampa* sat off Christmas Island, John Howard said, 'We are not closing our doors to genuine refugees'. When the last assessments were complete some fifteen months later, 879 of those barred from Australia were found to be refugees. This number included nearly all the Iraqis: 550

of the 655 processed by both Australia and the UNHCR.⁴ Most of the Afghans would also have qualified except for the defeat of the Taliban. The harsh—but necessary—rule of the refugee world is that once the source of persecution is removed, those seeking refuge abroad must return home. The danger is passed and so is the right of protection.

John Howard said of the people rescued by the *Tampa* and sent for processing to Nauru, 'We have always stood ready to take our fair share'. In the end, New Zealand took 186. Australia took one.⁵

The Pacific Solution turned out to be the New Zealand Solution. Australia has taken 318 refugees—mostly Iraqis—from the camps on Manus and Nauru. They have been given only temporary protection visas. New Zealand has taken 478 from those camps and given them permanent visas that allow immediate family reunion and there is no prospect of them being thrown out of New Zealand if the political tide turns in Iraq or Afghanistan. They have started new lives in a new home.⁶

Howard's high hopes of an international effort to clear the Pacific camps have been dashed. The rest of the world regards the refugees trapped in the Pacific Solution as Australia's responsibility. No other country except New Zealand has taken anyone from Manus. Sweden has taken fifteen, Denmark six and Canada eight refugees from Nauru. That's all. Hundreds of Afghans have returned home from the camps with financial assistance from Australia, but hundreds remain behind the wire. The camps are still operating nearly a year after they were first supposed to be cleared. Among the 530 still detained on Manus and Nauru in February 2003 were sixty refugees still looking for a home.⁷

After being chastised by the Geneva headquarters, Australia cut its annual core funding to UNHCR by half.

Pauline Hanson's One Nation Party completely disintegrated. Sir Mekere Morauta's government lost the PNG election. Rene Harris was left struggling to hold onto the presidency of Nauru once Australia's money began running out. In Oslo, the government of Jens Stoltenberg lost office to a right-wing coalition promising to cut the influx of foreigners to Norway.

Europe moved to tighten border controls under the pressure of vast numbers—about 400 000 asylum seekers in 2001—and with anti-immigrant parties transforming the political landscape. Philip Ruddock likes to suggest Europe is following Australia's lead, but the Europeans considered and rejected the three policies that set Australia's response to asylum seekers absolutely apart: naval blockade, offshore processing and mandatory detention.⁸

Ruddock was offered Cabinet promotion after the victory of 2001 but chose to stay where he was. His portfolio grew to include Aboriginal and Torres Strait Island affairs. Ruddock thus became responsible for all the most sensitive racial issues in national life as DIMA expanded to become DIMIA, the Department of Immigration, Multicultural and Indigenous Affairs.

Three months after Peter Reith left office, he became a consultant to the Defence contractor Tenix. Managing director Paul Salteri said Peter Reith would give 'valuable advice and guidance to Tenix in its relations with Government'.⁹

Jane Halton was awarded the Public Service Medal on Max Moore-Wilton's nomination. He described her as 'one of the most valuable and talented officers in the Australian Public Service'.¹⁰ John Howard appointed her Secretary of the Department of Health.

Wilh Wilhelmsen wrote to John Howard congratulating him on his re-election and suggesting a case of good Australian red was due for his contribution to the victory. He had no reply and no wine.

Howard, Moore-Wilton, Reith, Barrie, Halton, Scrafton, Hendy and Hampton remained absolutely adamant that the military had never corrected its original advice about children being thrown into the sea. Moore-Wilton ordered one of his senior bureaucrats—herself a bit player in the drama—to conduct an enquiry into this mess. Admiral Barrie directed one of his generals to conduct a parallel military investigation. Both concluded children were *not* thrown overboard but both concluded there was no evidence this news ever reached Peter Reith.¹¹

The shortcomings of these enquiries—conducted in private—were startling. Air Marshal Houston was not interviewed. Nor was Allan Hawke. Gary Bornholt gave evidence to the military enquiry of Houston's speaker phone confrontation with Reith on November 7, but this information was ignored. Neither the military nor the civilian investigators could clarify what passed between Admiral Barrie and the Minister for Defence on October 11. Neither drew adverse conclusions from this. Both enquiries stopped at that point in the story. No member of the Prime Minister's staff was interviewed. Nothing was said about attempts to tell Reith and Howard the truth in the week before the election. Both investigations brought down the curtain weeks earlier at October 11.

When Bornholt and Houston read those reports, they came forward and gave evidence to a Senate Estimates Committee. Houston blew Admiral Barrie, Peter Reith and both reports out of the water. Houston said, 'I stand completely behind my testimony. My job is to provide frank and fearless advice to government'.[12] Against all the evidence, Barrie continued for another week to insist that children *may* have been thrown from that boat. At a humiliating press conference on 27 February 2002, he finally conceded that was not the case. 'Do you feel like a dill, Admiral?' called Channel 9's Laurie Oakes. After a few more questions, Barrie fled.

Brigadier Bornholt left to command Australian soldiers fighting in Afghanistan. Chris Barrie retired, having failed to secure a third term as Commander of the Defence Force. Admirals Shackleton and Smith also retired. Dr Allan Hawke was not reappointed at the end of his three-year term as secretary of the Department of Defence.

Kim Beazley now sat on the backbench. When all the counting was done, the true depths of Labor's defeat were revealed: the party had won only 38.45 per cent of the primary vote—the lowest since Labor's collapse in the Depression in 1931.

On his last night as Leader of the Opposition, Beazley had pledged there would be an investigation into the children overboard affair: a judicial enquiry if Labor won, a Senate enquiry if the party lost. The Senate Select Committee on a Certain Maritime Incident came, in the end, to examine the whole of Operation Relex and the Pacific Solution. The questioning of civilian and military officials was driven by Labor's John Faulkner in a ruthless forensic exercise extending over many months. He and his colleagues on the committee laid bare much of this story.

Reith, Hampton, Scrafton and Jordana declined to appear.

John Howard survived all the revelations. He never retreated, never admitted error and just kept talking. As much as his election victory, the stonewalling of the revelations from the Senate gave Howard the appearance of being an unassailable political force. The Australian people continued to trust him as a leader and trust his strategy for border protection.

The protests, debate and public soul-searching that followed the *Tampa* did nothing to soften Australia's underlying hostility to boat people.

A Newspoll conducted a few days after the appearance of the *Tampa* found only nine per cent of Australians believed all boats carrying asylum seekers should be allowed to enter. A year later that figure was ten per cent. Australians were saying the same thing when the first boats appeared in 1976. Nothing had changed.

Max Moore-Wilton retired a year after the elections to become executive chairman and CEO of Sydney Airport, recently sold by the government to private investors. Howard called the press together to say how sorry he was this 'fantastic Departmental Secretary' was going after six and a half years of loyal service. Howard praised especially Moore-Wilton's determination to make the public service 'responsive to the wishes and the goals of the elected government'.[13] Moore-Wilton left Canberra unmourned.

Captain Arne Rinnan did a last lap of the world in the *Tampa* before his own retirement. He was now an Officer of the Royal Norwegian Order of Merit and Lloyds of London had declared him Shipmaster of the Year. Among those showering prizes on him were the Norwegian Ministry for Trade and the Norwegian Shipowners' Association, which both awarded him a plaque for heroic sea rescue; and the Anders Wilhelmsen Foundation, which gave him its Sailor's Prize. In the United States, Rinnan was given the Safety at Sea International Amver Award by the Coast Guard; the Lifesaving Award by the Seamen's Church; the International Rescue at Sea Award by the Association for Rescue at Sea; and the Friends of Seafarers Award by the Seafarers and International House. Spain nominated him for the Juan Maria Brande's Prize and awarded him the Premio de Derechos Humanos. Rinnan was declared 'Name of the Year' for 2001 by the media of several European countries. In Germany he was pipped at the post by Mayor Giuliani of New York. The United Nations High Commission for Refugees awarded Rinnan, his crew and the Wilhelmsen Line the US $100 000 Nansen Refugee Award for 'personal courage and a unique degree of commitment to refugee protection'.

Nearly a hundred Afghans gathered in a marquee on the Auckland waterfront to greet the man they called 'the wonderful angel who saved us from the open seas and gave us new life'. They brought him flowers, cards, letters, photographs and gifts. On the *Tampa* he had only ever been a distant figure to them, a shock of silver hair and a pair of binoculars. None had shaken his hand before this. Now they danced for him. A few days later, Rinnan brought his ship to Sydney. He joked; he was charming and discreet.

But he told the press that after his experience at Australia's hands he feared other ships might now be less willing to save lives. 'It is a terrible thing to be out there in a broken down boat. I'm afraid now there might be fewer rescues.' He denied being a hero. He called himself a simple seaman only doing what he had to do. 'It's an unwritten law of the sea to rescue people in distress. I would do it again and I hope all my seafaring colleagues would do the same.'[14]

Notes

The abbreviations used in the notes are listed below.

AFP	Australian Federal Police
Amnesty Statement	Compiled by the Iraqis from the *Aceng* for Amnesty International describing their ordeal on that SIEV, the *Manoora* and in detention on Nauru, Nov. 2001. Translated by Mike Nasir 28 March 2002, supplied to the authors by John Pace, who also authorised its publication on behalf of the Iraqis.
AMSA FOI	Documents provided under Freedom of Information legislation by the Australian Maritime Safety Authority to John Fairfax relating to the voyage of the *Palapa*, the rescue by the *Tampa* and the entry of the *Tampa* into Australian territorial waters.
CEDA	Committee for Economic Development of Australia
CMI	Senate Select Committee on a Certain Maritime Incident
DM	David Marr
Group One Statement	Compiled by Afghans from the *Tampa* for Amnesty International describing the voyage of the *Palapa*, their time on the *Tampa* and the voyage of the *Manoora*. Translated from Dari by Sharif Amin. Later retranslated for ABC *Four Corners* by Azadeh Fadaghi. Supplied to the authors by John Pace.

H of R	House of Representatives
MW	Marian Wilkinson
PST	People Smuggling Taskforce chaired by Jane Halton
RELEX FO	Documents provided under Freedom of Information legislation by the Department of Defence to John Fairfax. Essentially, what was requested was the complete Relex file held at Australian Defence Headquarters Strategic Command: 'All documents in ADHSC file SC DC 0957/01 and DHQ/28064.' After waiting for over a year, some documents were provided in full and some in heavily censored form.
RRA & T	Rural and Regional Affairs and Transport legislation
SS	Sue Spencer
Supplementary FOI	Further documents provided under Freedom of Information legislation to John Fairfax by AMSA, covering the interception of the *Tampa* and dealings between AMSA and the Royal Flying Doctor Service.

CHAPTER 1   FULL UP

1. *New Zealand Herald*, Section B, 22 Dec. 2001, p. 143.
2. All quotes from Sarwari are to DM.
3. All quotes from Merzaee are to DM.
4. All quotes from Hossaini are to DM.
5. Real name suppressed. All quotes from transcript of *R. v. Disun & ors*, No. 02/143, West Australian District Court, pp. 476 and 494.
6. All quotes from Rezaee are to DM.
7. *R. v. Disun* transcript: 'The smugglers', p. 472; 'It looked', pp. 468–9; 'I was told', p. 475.
8. *R. v. Disun* transcript: 'I saw', p. 499; 'You going', p. 473.
9. *New Zealand Herald*, 22 Dec. 2001.
10. All quotes from Akbari are to DM.
11. Pakistanis posing as Afghans, interpreters to DM; 'the right to', Article 14.
12. Engineering interpretation by asylum seekers and Andrew Marr.
13. *R. v. Disun*, transcript, p. 495.
14. *R. v. Disun*, transcript: 'Everybody was', p. 494; 'We all', p. 482.
15. *R. v. Disun*, transcript, p. 567.
16. Admiral Mark Bonser, director general of Coastwatch, letter to Jane Halton, 19 Oct. 2001.
17. To DM and MW.
18. 'Timeline for *Tampa* Incident', produced to CMI.
19. First summary supplied to the authors under FOI; second report in 'Timeline for *Tampa* Incident', supplied to CMI.
20. 'Timeline for *Tampa* Incident'.
21. 'best placed', Davidson to CMI, p. 1376. Arrangement of the Co-ordination of Search and Rescue Services between the Government of Australia and the

Government of the Republic of Indonesia, 1990. See especially, Clause (3)(a)(2) on prompt rescue.
22 CMI, p. 1387.
23 CMI, p. 1370.
24 'When we', Hansard, Senate Estimates, 19 Feb. 2002, p. 258.
25 *New Zealand Herald*, 22 Dec. 2001.
26 *R. v. Disun* transcript, p. 500.
27 *R. v. Disun* transcript, p. 500.
28 *R. v. Disun* transcript, p. 569.
29 'Timeline for *Tampa* Incident'.
30 'Timeline for *Tampa* Incident'.
31 AMSA FOI, doc. 10.

CHAPTER 2   SEA RESCUE

1 AMSA FOI, doc 11.
2 Wilh Wilhelmsen, *Speed and Service*, by Dag Bakka, Maritime Heritage Press, Sydney, 1995, p. 6.
3 *Speed and Service*, p. 129.
4 AMSA FOI, doc. 14.
5 All quotes from Wilh Wilhelmsen, to DM unless otherwise stated.
6 *Speed and Service*, p. 7.
7 To DM.
8 Peter Dexter to CEDA, 30 Oct. 2001.
9 The 1979 'Disembarkation Resettlement Offers' (DISERO) was followed in 1985 by 'Rescue at Sea Resettlement Offers' (RASRO). See Ryszard Piotrowicz, 'The Case of MV *Tampa*: state and refugee rights collide at sea', *Australian Law Journal*, vol. 76, pp. 16, 17, Jan 2001. Jean Pierre Fonteyne, in *Canberra Times*, 30 Aug. 2001, p. 11, states the number of rescues doubled in the first year of DISERO's operation to 14 560.
10 Article 98 of the UN Convention on the Law of the Sea incorporated into Australian domestic law as section 317A of the Navigation Act, 1912.
11 Norway's diplomatic note to Australia, 29 Jan. 2002.
12 From the Wilhelmsen Line's 'Sequence of events of the MS *Tampa*'s rescue of survivors of vessel adrift at sea'.
13 *WWWorld*, corporate magazine of Wilh Wilhelmsen ASA, No. 4/2001. p. 4.
14 Singapore press conference given by Rinnan and Maltau, 6 Sept. 2001.
15 'No sextant', to Singapore press conference; 'You can', *R. v. Disun* transcript p. 436.
16 Rinnan told *Norway Today*, 20 Nov. 2001: 'Several of the refugees were obviously in a bad state and collapsed when they came on deck to us. 10 to 12 of them were unconscious, several had dysentry and a pregnant woman suffered abdominal pains.' As told DM: 'There were 20 people unconscious, 6 pregnant women and several children with diarrhoea.'

17 'We said', Merzaee to DM; Maltau's account to DM; that the delegation was invited to the bridge, Rinnan at Singapore press conference; 'The tour operators', Wilh Wilhelmsen to DM.
18 First impulse, Maltau *R. v. Disun* transcript p. 437. The position of the *Palapa* 85 nm from Christmas at the time of the rescue—09 22 south 104 36 east—is taken from Wilhelmsen records. That the order to deal with the Indonesians came from RCC Australia: Rinnan at Singapore press conference. RCC Australia's exchanges with BASARNAS are at AMSA FOI, docs 12 and 14; 'We got one', Rinnan at Singapore press conference.
19 'For all intents', CMI p. 1381; request by DIMA: Davidson to Estimates, RRA&T, *Hansard*, p. 251 and 'Timeline for the *Tampa* Incident', 260542 UTC; Davidson's response: CMI 1378.
20 Excerpts from the *Tampa* log supplied to the authors by the Wilhelmsen Line; 'were very much distressed', NZ television's *Holmes Show*, 15 Oct. 2001.
21 'They were behaving', Lloyd's List, 28 Aug. 2001; 'We were all threatened', *Australian* 28 Aug. 2001, p. 1; 'dire consequences', James Neill to Neville Nixon, fax 27 Aug. 2001; 'Not blackmailed', Rinnan to Singapore press conference; Norwegians refusal to contemplate violence on the ship, Wilhelmsen to DM.
22 Rinnan at Singapore press conference. He actually said 'Tamil' instead of 'Taliban' but the meaning was clear.
23 '*Tampa* had been given', 'Timeline for the *Tampa* Incident', 261043 UTC; 'The captain wants', 'MV *Tampa*—Summary of Key Events Involving AMSA', evidence to CMI, 14 Aug. 2002; 'Custom and practice', RRA&T *Hansard*, 19 Feb. 2002, p. 264; 'It is difficult', 'MV *Tampa*: Some Law of the Sea Aspects', delivered at the Conference of the Maritime Law Association of Australia and New Zealand 3–4 Oct. 2002.
24 'It is entirely', WWL chronology; 'It was unclear', CMI p. 1382; 'if vessel goes', 'Timeline for the *Tampa* Incident', 261110 UTC; 'definitely', AMSA FOI, doc. 20.
25 Australia's 5 Oct. 2001 reply to Norway's first Diplomatic Note, 1 Sep. 2001.
26 This was said to Nixon either at the 7.10 or the 7.40 pm conversations with Rinnan, but makes much more sense at this point as it allowed Nixon's superiors to realise Rinnan could be given the orders which were relayed half an hour later. For the quote, see the commentary at the end of the 'MV *Tampa*—Summary of Key Events involving AMSA' in an email dated 14 Sept. 2001 from Davidson to Rachel Stephen-Smith of the Department of PM & C, supplied to the Senate CMI inquiry, 14 Aug. 2002.
27 Neill to DM.
28 Neill to DM.
29 *WWWorld*, p. 10.
30 Rinnan to MW.
31 'Amazed', Lloyd's List [Sept. 7]; 'surprised and disappointed', Century Newspapers, 7 Sept. 2001; 'Vessel is not', AMSA FOI, doc. 24; 'I was a little', to MW.
32 To DM.
33 Ruddock to DM and MW.
34 Sources to DM and MW.

35 Singapore press conference; the Wilhelmsen 'Sequence of Events' says Maltau called the bridge at 8.10 pm.
36 'You could see', Rinnan to MW; 'I'm not a big gambler', Singapore press conference; time he turned back to Christmas Island from the Wilhelmsen 'Sequence of Events'.
37 Who gave this order, Max Moore-Wilton to DM; 'Nixon's mood', Rinnan to MW; 'He told me', Rinnan to MW; fax to AMSA, FOI material, p. 29.
38 To DM.
39 To DM.
40 On obligations: Michael White in *Bimco Review 2002*, BIMCO, London, 2002, pp. 116–123 plus Norway's Diplomatic Note, 1 Sept. 2001.
41 To DM.
42 Wilhelmsen to DM; Neill to DM.
43 'because of', *WWWorld*, No.4/2001, p. 9; 'There was no', Dexter to DM.
44 Neill to DM.
45 Singapore press conference.

CHAPTER 3   AUSTRALIA V. THE BOAT PEOPLE

1 *Australian*, 2 Feb. 2002, p. 20.
2 'The courts have', press club 18 March 1998.
3 'Maybe you can', to Richard Guilliatt, *Sydney Morning Herald*, 27 April 2002, Good Weekend, p. 24.
4 The account of this conversation comes from senior AFP sources who were privy to Dixon's briefing of his commissioner.
5 Ruddock refused to dicuss with DM and MW what was said at this or subsequent meetings of the embassy's People Smuggling Group. He said, 'I have no formal recollection of any of those discussions which I am prepared to dicuss'. Ruddock maintained that position when given further details of what he was alleged to have said about both sabotage and pirates at those meetings. Ruddock wrote on 4 Nov. 2002: 'Briefings that I receive as minister are confidential and involve quite frequently matters that should not be revealed by me for a whole range of reasons including public safety, international relations and national security.' He provided an *Economist* article, 'Regional efforts to combat piracy are taking shape', 19 July 2001.
6 This account comes from one of the members of the People Smuggling Group at the Australian embassy in Jakarta.
7 *The Boat People: An Age Investigation*, Penguin, Ringwood, 1979, p. 179.
8 *Angels and Arrogant Gods: Migration Officers and Migrants Reminisce*, Harry Martin, Australian Government Printing Service, 1989, p. 95.
9 *Angels and Arrogant Gods*, ABC Radio Social History Unit, part six, broadcast but not published.
10 *Angels and Arrogant Gods*, AGPS, p. 107.
11 Katharine Betts, 'Boat people and public opinion in Australia', *People and Place*, vol. 9, no. 4, 2001, p. 40.
12 *Daily Telegraph*, 4 Dec. 1979, p. 4.

13 Article 31 of the Refugee Convention forbidding punishment of bona fide asylum seekers; Article 9(1) of the International Convention on Civil and Political Rights forbidding arbitrary detention; Article 37 of the Convention of the Rights of the Child.
14 Betts, 'Boat people and public opinion', p. 41, quoting a Saulwick Poll taken on a slightly different basis to the previous Morgan Gallop Poll.
15 *Future Seekers: Refugees and the Law in Australia*, Mary Crock and Ben Saul, The Federation Press, Sydney, 2002, p. 22.
16 Elizabeth Wynhausen, *Australian*, 13 April 1999, p. 4.
17 *Sydney Morning Herald*, 1 Nov. 1997, Spectrum, p. 1.
18 Migration Legislation Amendment Act (No. 1).
19 Moore-Wilton and other sources from those meetings to DM.
20 To MW and DM.
21 'Background Paper on Unauthorised Arrivals Strategy', DIMA website, downloaded 26 Feb. 2002.
22 'to target', Keelty to CMI, 11 July 2002, p. 1924; 'To prevent', Keelty to CMI, p. 1977.
23 To MW.
24 AFP media release, 24 Aug. 2002.
25 AFP Commissioner, Mick Keelty in written response to questions from the authors.
26 Enniss boasted, *Sunday*, 1 Sept. 2002; denial, AFP media release 26 Sept. 2002; 'It normally happens', to MW.
27 Denial of involvement in sabotage, media release 26 Sept. 2002; 'If we became', evidence to CMI, 11 July 2002, pp. 1980–1.
28 Interview notes supplied by Chris Tumelap.
29 Press release, 22 Dec. 2000.
30 Based on Ruddock's Background Paper on Unauthorised Arrivals Strategy.
31 Peter Mares, *Borderline*, University of NSW Press, Sydney, 2001, p. 143.
32 Those Who Come Across the Seas, HREOC, pp. 100–1.
33 See Keelty's evidence to Legal Constitutional Committee of Senate Estimates, 19 Feb. 2002, p. 193.
34 *Daily Telegraph*, 15 Feb. 2000.
35 To Alan Jones on Radio 2UE, 30 Aug. 2001.

CHAPTER 4   CANBERRA SCRAMBLES

1 Rajab Ali Merzaee to DM.
2 The first message reached Rinnan at 5.45 am island time according to Rinnan's log as read by Bangsmoen to MW. The time of the second call is not recorded in the log. That it happened is recorded in a letter of confirmation from Godwin to Rinnan on 27 Aug. The *Australian* suggests a time of 9.15 am AEST.
3 Evidence of Bill Farmer, secretary of DIMA, to Justice North, 2 Sept. 2001.
4 Howard and Ruddock's press conference, 27 Aug. 2001.
5 The time is taken from Rinnan's log as read by Bangsmoen to MW; Spencer told *R. v. Disun* he was given orders at 8.30 am island time to fly over the

Tampa; this account of the message to Rinnan is based on Howard's statement to his press conference about half an hour later; 'Captain Rinnan received', *WWWorld*, p. 11; Rinnan's reply to Coastwatch, AMSA, FOI doc. 32; 'The crew were', to DM.
6. *WWWorld*, p. 11.
7. Fax of confirmation from Neill to Godwin, 27 Aug. 2001.
8. 'MV *Tampa*: the Australian Response', a paper delivered at Headington Hill Hall, Oxford, 24 May 2002. There is an all but endless list of authorities on the point that the obligation to rescue is clear but the obligation to land the survivors is unclear. See, for instance, Prof. Don Rothwell in 'The Law of the Sea and the MV *Tampa* Incident: Reconciling Maritime Principles with Coastal State Sovereignty': 'While international law creates clear obligations upon coastal states to coordinate Maritime Search and Rescue operations and for ships to go to the aid of persons and other ships in distress, it remains unclear as to who has responsibility for the rescued persons after the actual rescue has taken place.' And Jean-Pierre Fonteyne at p. 17 of *Refugees and the Myth of the Borderless World:* 'From a law of the sea perspective ... the obligations of the captain of the *Tampa* ... were beyond any doubt. Which particular nation then inherited eventual responsibility of the rescued asylum seekers are unfortunately far from clear.'
9. Sources to DM.
10. Present at the first meeting were—from PM & C: Halton, Katrina Edwards, Michael Potts; from Transport: Lynnelle Briggs; from Defence: Tony Marshall and Al Titheridge; from AMSA: Clive Davidson; from DIMA: Andrew Metcalfe, Philippa Godwin; from Foreign Affairs: Gillian Bird and Geoff Raby; from AFP: Andy Hughes; from AGS: Bill Campbell.
11. Minutes, PST 27 Aug. 2001.
12. Migration Act, 1958 s. 189.
13. Seven Network, *Sunday Sunrise* 8.55 am, 2 Sept. 2001.
14. Sources to MW.
15. Seven Network, *Sunday Sunrise* 8.55 am, 2 Sept. 2001.
16. All quotes from Longva are to MW.
17. To MW.
18. *WWWorld*, pp. 10–11.
19. 'The Australian', AMSA FOI, doc. 37; 'would provoke', Davidson to PM & C, Aug. 27, AMSA supplementary FOI; 'We now have', AMSA FOI, doc. 39.
20. AMSA FOI, docs 41 and 42.
21. AMSA, FOI doc. 43.
22. Fax 27 Aug. 2001, supplementary AMSA FOI.
23. *WWWorld*, p. 11.
24. AMSA FOI, docs 46–7.

CHAPTER 5   PAN PAN

1. To SS.

2   Dietz's assessment, RFDS to SS, PST minutes early meeting Aug. 28 and AMSA notes of conversation with Dietz, 7.03 pm Aug. 27; Those 7.03 pm notes also the source for Maltau 'not panicking' and 'this sounds'.
3   To SS.
4   To Mike Munro, *A Current Affair*, 28 Aug. 2001.
5   To Neil Mitchell, Radio 3AW, 28 Aug. 2001.
6   'MV *Tampa*: Some Law of the Sea Aspects', delivered at the Conference of the Maritime Law Association of Australia and New Zealand 3–4 Oct. 2002.
7   To DM and MW.
8   'warning order', issued 2812192 UTC, released to CMI, 20 Sept. 2002.
9   To DM and MW.
10 *WWWorld*, p. 11.
11 'The process was', *WWWorld*, p. 8; 'I have been', to DM.
12 PST minutes for early morning meeting, 28 Aug. 2001; AMSA notes of conversation with Schuller at 3.46 pm, 28 Aug. 2001 and Schuller to SS.
13 'Timeline for *Tampa* Incident', entries at 280757 UTC and 280815 UTC.
14 The four conditions: Neill to Philippa Godwin, 27 Aug. 2001; attempts to help followed by dire warnings, Neil to DM. He had also spoken of people dying in an early fax to Godwin on 27 Aug. 2001.
15 'Owners deliberately', *Gard News* 165, Feb./April 2002, p. 9; 'surprised and disappointed', e.g. Rinnan at Singapore Press Conference, 16 Sept. 2001.
16 *Australian*, 29 Aug. pp. 1–2.
17 'A doctor from', to Mike Munro, *A Current Affair*, 28 Aug. 2001; doctors never saying illnesses feigned, '*Tampa* Crisis: doctors contradict PM', Kirsten Lawson, *Canberra Times*, 13 July 2002. Howard continued to maintain the shipping line was misrepresenting the position even after the SAS doctor had boarded the ship and reported cases of serious illness. For instance, Howard told Tracy Grimshaw of Channel 9's *Today*, 30 Aug. 2001, 'Those claims, certainly in relation to health, have been proved to be wrong ... there were no cases on board the vessel requiring medical evacuation. So that was a straight misrepresentation of the position.'
18 'We are thinking', to MW; 'In the Norwegian', Norway's diplomatic note, 1 Sept 2001.
19 'MV *Tampa*: Some Law of the Sea Aspects', delivered at the Conference of the Maritime Law Association of Australia and New Zealand 3–4 Oct. 2002.
20 Relex FOI, 281020 UTC.
21 AMSA supplementary FOI, 26 Aug. 2002 doc. 4 and Maltau to DM.
22 Schuller to SS.
23 Schuller to SS.
24 AMSA supplementary FOI, 26 Aug. 2002, doc. 7 and 'MV *Tampa*—Summary of Key Events involving AMSA', email documents submitted to CMI, 14 Aug. 2002; AMSA's précis of the fax is in 'Timeline for *Tampa* Incident' at 281315 UTC.
25 Rinnan demands a response, 'Timeline for *Tampa* Incident' at 281440 UTC; told Christmas Island doctor would contact, 'Timeline ... ' at 281446 UTC; Maltau's conversation with Hammond, Maltau to DM; 'authorities were investigating', WWL 'Sequence of Events'; 'If you have no', Rinnan to MW; permission to lower in 'Timeline' at 281540 UTC; 'not safe to launch', WWL 'Sequence of Events'.

26 'Timeline for *Tampa* incident' at 281646 UTC.
27 All quotes from Jagland are to MW.
28 Spokesman for Downer to MW.

CHAPTER 6 BOARDING PARTY

1 Relex FOI, doc. 1. According to the Wilhelmsen chronology, the MAYDAY was issued at 2309 UTC, 6.09 am at Christmas Island and 9.09 am in Canberra.
2 'You have', provided to CMI, 18 Sept. 2001; 'We're sorry', BASARNAS chronology and BASARNAS officials to MW.
3 Cast list from Malcolm Farr and Rachel Morris in *Daily Telegraph*, 30 Aug. 2001, p. 3; 'in shock', Hans Wilhelm Longva to MW.
4 To MW.
5 To MW.
6 Longva to MW.
7 'the company', Støre to MW; 'The shipping line', Howard to DM and MW; 'to request', Dexter to DM; 'It is my', Rinnan to RCC Australia 290048 UTC, Relex FOI, doc. 6; Howard's thanks, Malcolm Farr, *Daily Telegraph*, 30 Aug. 2001, p. 3.
8 Støre to MW.
9 Wali's threats, Rinnan telefax to RCC Australia, tabled House of Representatives 29 Aug. 2002; Wilhelmsen's concerns, to DM.
10 Instructions to survivors, WWL 'Sequence of Events'; 'the pulse rate' and 'We were looking', *WWWorld*, pp. 12 & 24.
11 'What *Tampa* was', 'Timeline for *Tampa* incident'; 'the *Tampa* entered', Rinnan telefax to RCC Australia, tabled House of Representatives 29 Aug. 2002.
12 *Australian*, 1 Sept. 2001, p. 1.
13 *Australian*, 30 Aug. 2001, p. 3.
14 ABC-Radio, *AM*, 29 Aug. 2001.
15 'I think', *Age*, 30 Aug. 2001, p. 3; 'We call', *Age*, 29 Aug. 2001, p. 2.
16 Bill Farmer, secretary of DIMA, to Justice North, 2 Sept. 2001.
17 Rinnan's protest, Rinnan to MW; assurances not taking over the ship, *WWWorld* p. 12; 'They said', Rinnan to DM; 'I told him', Rinnan to MW.
18 General verdict that *Tampa* was unseaworthy and could not sail from Christmas: 'surely obvious', Ernst Willheim, 'MV *Tampa*: The Australian Response' delivered at Headington Hill Hall, Oxford, 24 May 2002; 'It would seem a clear breach of international and maritime obligations to deliberately send a vessel out of our territorial waters in obvious breach of its safety obligations'. Dr Michael White QC in 'MV *Tampa* and Christmas Island Incident, August 2001' in *Bimco Review* 2002, pp. 116–23; 'The *Tampa* was accordingly ... unseaworthy (as eventually formally declared by the Norwegian Maritime Safety Board)'. Jean-Pierre Fonteyne in *Refugees and the Myth of the Borderless World*, p. 18. Fonteyne takes a further, controversial step of arguing that the unseaworthiness compelled Australia to allow the survivors to land. The Norwegian Foreign Ministry issued this press release: 'The freighter *Tampa* is not seaworthy for further voyage with more than 400 persons on

board. It is not a passenger vessel, it is not equipped to carry passengers, and it is not allowed to do that according to national and international regulations... Australia is now requesting the vessel to breach rules which Australia has accepted as an international commitment.' Zanker's verdict: 'MV *Tampa*: Some Law of the Sea Aspects' delivered at the Conference of the Maritime Law Association of Australia and New Zealand 3–4 October, 2002. Insurance questions: Wilhelmsen, Dexter and Bangsmoen to DM.
19   'Record of Events—*Tampa* boarding', ADFCC Ops Log Log Entry, HQ Australian Theatre.
20   'Whilst it appeared', Wilhelmsen to DM; 'bad but acceptable', Singapore press conference; 'The ship is', ABC-TV *7.30 Report*, 29 Aug. 2001.
21   'Record of Events—*Tampa* boarding', ADFCC Ops Log Log Entry, HQ Australian Theatre.
22   'The ship', House of Representatives, *Hansard*, 29 Aug. 2001, p. 30516; 'I should inform' and 'not in any', p. 30517.
23   *Lateline*, 29 Aug. 2001.
24   'I mean', *Age*, 30 Aug. 2001, p. 2; 'It's not', *Herald Sun*, 30 Aug. 2001, p. 8: 'Taking command', Wilhelmsen to DM.
25   Neill to DM.
26   Neill to DM.
27   Blick, *MV Tampa, August–September 2001—Collection and Reporting of Intelligence Relating to Australians*, 'Summary and introduction', pars 8 & 16.
28   *Rules on Sigint and Australian Person*, secret then and now. Amended October 2001.
29   Blick, *MV Tampa*, 'Summary and introduction', par. 10.
30   Blick, *MV Tampa*, par. 12.
31   Government sources to DM.
32   *Sydney Morning Herald*, 29 Aug. 2001, p. 13.
33   Beazley to MW and DM.

CHAPTER 7 LABOR CORNERED

1   To DM and MW.
2   ABC-TV *Australian Story*, 29 Oct. 2001.
3   John Button, *Beyond Belief*, Quarterly Essay, Black Inc., Melbourne 2002, p. 10.
4   Peter Mares, *Borderline*, UNSW Press, Randwick, 2001, p. 67.
5   Michelle Grattan in *The Politics of Immigration*, James Jupp and Marie Kabala (eds), Australian Government Publishing Service, Canberra, 1994, pp. 135–6.
6   See Mares, *Borderline*, p. 79, and for a full discussion of these issues, Ernst Willheim, 'MV *Tampa*: The Australian response', a paper delivered at Headington Hill Hall, Oxford, 24 May 2002.
7   Unless otherwise stated, all Beazley quotes are to MW and DM.
8   'Good' and 'bad' refugees, Mares, *Borderline*, p. 24.
9   Migration Reform Act 1992.

10 These provisions were first contained in the Migration Legislation Amendment Bill (No. 4) 1997 and then formed a separate Migration Legislation Amendment Bill (No. 5) 1998.
11 'Mind and Mood—Illegal immigrants', *The Mackay Report*, July 2001.
12 To MW and DM.
13 National Press Club address, 3 Dec. 2001.
14 To DM.
15 To DM and MW.
16 *Hansard*, H of R, 27 Aug. 2001, p. 30235.
17 *Hansard*, H of R, 27 Aug. 2001, p. 30236.
18 'If [the rescue]', *Daily Telegraph*, 29 Aug. p. 1; failure to read the agreement, Beazley to DM; failure to seek advice, sources to DM; 'And it is a', Beazley press conference, 30 Aug. 2001.
19 *Hansard*, H of R, 29 Aug. 2001, pp. 30518–9.
20 To MW and DM.
21 Beazley to MW and DM plus other sources.
22 To MW and DM.
23 'This Bill will', *Hansard*, H of R, 29 Aug. 2001, p. 30570; 'not be able', p. 30569.
24 *Hansard*, H of R, p. 30570.
25 *Hansard*, H of R, p. 30571
26 *Hansard*, H of R, p. 30574.
27 To MW and DM; for the offer of the sunset clause, see Howard to Alan Jones, Radio 2UE, 30 Aug. 2001.
28 *Australian*, 1 Sept. 2001, p. 1.
29 *Herald Sun*, 29 Aug. 2001, p. 1.
30 Quoted by Gerard Henderson, *Sydney Morning Herald*, 11 Sept. 2001, p. 10. Jones was one of many commentators at this time suggesting a link between race, religion and crime, a propensity in 'politically correct' commentators to silence discussion on these crimes, plus a failure of police to investigate and prosecute 'ethnic' crime.
31 'we are not', Radio 2UE, 30 Aug. 2001; 'trying to walk', *Daily Telegraph*, 31 Aug. 2001, p. 4.

CHAPTER 8 PACIFIC SOLUTION

1 'That would mean', *Australian*, 31 Aug. 2001, p. 2; 'effectively control', e.g. Howard to Alan Jones, Radio 2UE, 30 Aug. 2001; 'don't interfere with', *Daily Telegraph*, 31 Aug. 2001, p. 4;
2 Statement dated 19 Dec. 2001, translated by Azadeh Fadaghi.
3 The scholar to DM.
4 Date of reports on Neill, to DM; 'to the fact', Halton supplementary answers to CMI, provided 15 Aug. 2002.
5 PST minutes, 30 Aug. 2001.
6 Clark to Ruth Laugesen, *Sunday Star Times*, New Zealand, 9 Sept. 2001. We are especially indebted to Laugesen for much of our account of the negotiations with NZ.

7   *Sunday Star Times*, 9 Sept. 2001.
8   Prentice and Jessen-Petersen to MW.
9   Reith interview with John Laws on Radio 2UE, 11 Sept. 2001.
10 *Sydney Morning Herald*, 22 Oct. 2001, p. 15.
11 Jessen-Petersen to MW.
12 UNHCR press release; Jessen-Petersen to MW.
13 Press release, 29 Aug. 2001, 'UNHCR VOICES CONCERN OVER SHIP SAGA'.
14 To DM and MW.
15 This account is drawn from *Daily Telegraph*, 31 Aug. 2001, p. 1 and *Age*, 31 Aug. 2001, p. 1
16 *Sunday Star Times*, 9 Sept. 2001.
17 Cabinet minute, 'Irregular Migrants on MV *Tampa*: NZ's Response', executive summary, par. 3.
18 To DM.
19 That Nauru said yes before NZ made its final offer is clear from par. 5 of the Cabinet minute, 'Irregular Migrants on MV *Tampa*'.
20 *Sunday Star Times*, 9 Sept. 2001.
21 To MW.

CHAPTER 9   THE RULE OF LAW

1   All Manetta quotes unless otherwise stated are from an unpublished speech, 'How the *Tampa* case started', delivered to the Law Society of South Australia's Conference on Human Rights and the Criminal Law, 5 May 2002.
2   PILCH files.
3   Group One Statement.
4   1951 Refugee Convention, especially articles 32 and 33.
5   Whether the Pacific Solution amounted to a breach of this principle is debated at great length by academic commentators. For example, Ernst Willheim argues it did not in his paper 'MV *Tampa*: The Australian Response', while James C. Hathaway of the University of Michigan argues it did in 'Refugee Law is Not Immigration Law' in *World Refugee Survey, 2002*.
6   To DM and MW.
7   Group One Statement.
8   'MV *Tampa*, Aug–Sept 2001—Collection and Reporting of Intelligence Relating to Australians' by Bill Blick, Inspector-General of Intelligence and Security. That PILCH was a target of DSD reporting, see *Australian Financial Review*, 17 May 2002, p. 56.
9   'We had to', Wilhelmsen to DM; no quarrel and no wish to put business at risk, Neill to DM.
10 Neill to DM.
11 Red Cross to DM.
12 Sources to DM.
13 The teacher to DM.
14 To MW.
15 Spelling corrected.

16 *Australian*, 1 Sept. 2001, p. 8; *Sydney Morning Herald*, 1 Sept. 2001, p. 1.
17 Vadarlis' affidavit, 31 Aug. 2001, pars 9 & 13.
18 Date of DSD reports on PILCH and Vadarlis, sources to DM.
19 *Victorian Council for Civil Liberties & Ors v. Ruddock & Ors*, transcript, Friday 31 Aug. 2001.
20 There are many accounts of this incident. 'People rushed to' and 'Why do you', Group One Statement; 'Their guns were', Wahidullah Akbari to DM.
21 Group One Statement.
22 See p. 44, note 31.
23 *Norway Post*, 2 Sept. 2001.
24 Diplomatic Note, 1 Sept. 2001.
25 Howard press conference, 3 Sept. 2001.
26 Howard to Alan Jones, Radio 2UE, 3 Sept. 2001.
27 Group One Statement.
28 To Barrie Cassidy, ABC-TV *Insiders*, 2 Sept. 2001.
29 To Mortimer.
30 Affidavit of Commodore Warwick Gately, 2 Sept. 2001; the lawyers did not see a minute by Admiral Chris Barrie also released in the Relex FOI that read: 'These [figures] do not reflect the net additional costs to Defence, which will be lower because other budgeted activities have been cancelled.'
31 Group One Statement.
32 Unaccompanied minors to DM.
33 Account of the contents of the deal given by Christen Guddal of Gard P & I to MW.
34 To DM.
35 To DM.

CHAPTER 10   THE THICK GREY LINE

1 To DM and MW.
2 Evidence to CMI, 12 April 2002, p. 799.
3 Evidence to CMI, 5 April 2002, p. 493.
4 Evidence to CMI, 4 April 2002, p. 448.
5 First set out in Article 11 of the *International Convention for the Unification of Certain Rules with Respect to Assistance and Salvage at Sea* (Brussels, 1910) and most recently in Article 98 of the 1982 *United Nations Convention on the Law of the Sea* (UNCLOS); s. 317A of the Navigation Act 1912.
6 Smith, evidence to CMI, 4 April 2002, p. 448; Ritchie, evidence to CMI, 4 April 2002, p. 405.
7 Evidence to CMI, 4 April 2002, p. 448.
8 *60 Minutes*, 2 Sept. 2001.
9 Sources to SS and MW.
10 Evidence to CMI, 4 April 2002, pp. 459–60.
11 Evidence to CMI, 4 April 2002, p. 447.
12 Jenny McKenry, evidence to CMI, 17 April 2002, p. 1115.

13 To DM and MW.
14 Defence Instructions (General), lodged as an exhibit to CMI.
15 Tim Bloomfield, evidence to CMI, p. 1175.
16 Brian Humphreys, evidence to CMI, p. 1143.
17 'Operation Relex—Outline of Proposed Strategic Communication Approach', 31 Aug. 2001.
18 Evidence to CMI, 17 April 2002, p. 1148.
19 Evidence to CMI, 17 April 2002, p. 1150.
20 'personalising or humanising', evidence to CMI, 17 April 2002, p. 1151–52; 'I was aware', p. 1154.
21 Bloomfield, evidence to CMI, 17 April 2002, p. 1177.
22 Keelty to the Senate Legal and Constitutional Committee (Estimates), 28 May 2002.
23 Statement of Lindsey Sojan to CMI.
24 Statement to Amnesty International, Nov. 2001, translated by Mike Nasir in March 2002.
25 Statement of Peter Armitage to CMI.
26 Sojan statement.
27 'medium to high' from Menhinick's statement to CMI; all other quotes from Armitage's statement.
28 'Negotiations began', Sojan statement to CMI; 'high waves', Amnesty statement of Iraqis.
29 'Brief for HSC. Operation Relex/Gaberdine Issues for the SCG, 4 Sept 01'.
30 Press conference, 8 Sept. 2001.
31 'Farewell bombshell', *Sunday Age*, 9 Sept. 2001, p. 1; PM quotes from his press conference, 8 Sept. 2001.
32 *Sunday Age*, 9 Sept. 2001, p. 1.
33 *Sunday Age*, 9 Sept. 2001, p. 6.

CHAPTER 11 THE SHADOW OF THE TWIN TOWERS

1 *Victorian Council for Civil Liberties Incorporated v Minister for Immigration & Multicultural Affairs* [2001] FCA 1297, pars 81 and 82.
2 Bob Gelbard, interview with MW for *Sydney Morning Herald*.
3 To DM and MW.
4 Willard Hotel press conference, 11 Sept. 2001.
5 Transcript, *Minister for Immigration and Multicultural Affairs and Ors v. Eric Vadarlis and Ors*, No. V 1007 of 2001.
6 Probably on 9 Sept. 2001 according to statements to CMI by sailors, but Admiral Smith's 'Events Summary' for SIEV 2 says 10 Sept.
7 'Events Summary'.
8 'Events Summary'.
9 Evidence to CMI, 5 April 2002, p. 492.
10 From the statements of Lt Com. Simon Gregg and Com. Richard Menhinick to CMI.
11 Gregg statement.

12 Menhinick statement, p. 6.
13 Menhinick statement, p. 7.
14 Statement of Lt Com. David Moncrieff to CMI.
15 Supplied to DM and MW by Julian Burnside QC.
16 'People will come', to 2UE, quoted in the *Australian*, 12 Sept. 2001, p. 2; Harris on consultations, *Sydney Morning Herald*, 9 Sept. 2001, p. 6.
17 *Australian*, 11 Sept. 2001, p. 5.
18 Reith to Hinch, 3AK, 13 Sept. 2001.
19 Migration Amendment (Excision from Migration Zone) Bill 2001 and Migration Amendment (Excision from Migration Zone) (Consequential Provisions) Bill 2001.
20 Migration Legislation Amendment (Judicial Review) Bill 1998.
21 *Migration Legislation Amendment Act (No. 6) 2001*.
22 *Age*, 29 Aug. 2001 and Georgiou, Hansard, H of R, 20 Sept. 2001, pp. 31 and 164.
23 Hansard, H of R, 28 Aug. 2001, p. 30420.
24 Border Protection (Validation and Enforcement Powers) Bill 2001.
25 *Ex parte Lo Pak* (1888) 9 NSWR 221 at 243 cited by Black in par. 188 of his judgement.
26 'The conclusion', and 'It is hard', Black pars 80 and 83.
27 'to determine', French pars 192 and 193; 'clear words' and 'The steps taken' par. 204.
28 French, par. 197.
29 Black: summary of judgement pars 5 & 6; Vadarlis, *Australian*, 18 Sept. 2001, p. 11.
30 French, par. 216.
31 To Jon Faine, ABC-Radio, Melbourne, 23 Oct. 2001.
32 To DM and MW.
33 Liberty Victoria press release, 19 Sept. 2001.
34 *Vadarlis v Ruddock*, application for special leave, 27 Nov 2001.

CHAPTER 12   THE VOYAGE OF THE *MANOORA*

1 'Australian troops' to 60 *Minutes*, 2 Sept. 2001; 'conditions on the *Manoora*', to Alan Jones, 3 Sept. 2001; 'a large troopship', Bennett to the Court, 2 Sept. 2001; 'In that way', evidence to CMI, 5 April 2002, p. 465.
2 RAN website.
3 Sources to DM.
4 'We were always', Group One Statement; 'They would say', Wahidullah Akbari to DM; 'We were happy' to DM.
5 'They were informed', statement of Lindsey Sojan to CMI; 'When we saw', Amnesty Statement. One group of Iraqis on the *Manoora* expressly dissociated itself from these complaints: 'We do not wish to complain in any way against the honourable government of Australia despite our continuous suffering up until now. This is because it became clear to us whilst in this camp that the Australian Government works hard to extend the best of its possible assistance to us.'

6   *Navy News*, 17 Sept. 2001 and Smith's evidence to CMI, 4 April 2002, p. 463.
7   Hunger strike details from minutes of the PST for 11 Sept. 2001; Iraqi complaints are from the Amnesty Statement.
8   To DM and MW.
9   PST minutes, 11 Sept. 2001.
10 'Do you understand', a participant in the meetings to SS; ten million dollars spent on Nauru infrastructure, CMI, p. 327.
11 *Sydney Morning Herald*, 13 Sept. 2001, p. 22.
12 The Constitution of Nauru, Articles 5 (1) and (2) and Constitution of the Independent State of Papua New Guinea, Article 32 (2)
13 PST minutes for 24 Sept. 2001.
14 'Very hot', Amnesty Statement; 'The last few' to DM.
15 Group One Statement.
16 *Sydney Morning Herald*, 20 Sept. 2001, p. 11.
17 'We saw that', Group One Statement; 'At the rear', *Sydney Morning Herald*, 22 Sept. 2001, p. 31.
18 'What if', PST minutes for 17 Sept. 2001; 'Jesus, they can't', *Sydney Morning Herald*, 25 Sept. 2001, p. 9; 'The Afghanis', evidence to CMI, 4 April 2002, p. 465.
19 Amnesty Statement backed by the IOM's negotiator Chris Lom, *Herald Sun*, 29 Sept. 2001, p. 15.
20 'preference' and 'our position', *Sydney Morning Herald*, 26 Sept. 2001, p. 8; 'Well, they're not', *Sydney Morning Herald*, 24 Sept. 2001, p. 2; 'If they want', *Sydney Morning Herald*, 25 Sept. 2001, p. 9.
21 'Can I go', *Sydney Morning Herald*, 22 Sept. 2001, p. 31; 'The Australian government', *Sydney Morning Herald*, 27 Sept. 2001, p. 1.
22 'I should make', press conference, 29 Sept. 2001; 'The prospect', approval to begin removal of the UBAs from HMAS *Manoora* by Reith, 30 Sept. 2001.
23 ABC-TV, *7.30 Report*, 1 Oct. 2001.
24 The captain may have read the long message 'To the People on Board the HMAS *Manoora*' for the use of AFP, ADF and IOM negotiators approved by several departments including Prime Minister and Cabinet and Attorney General's which ends with the words: 'It is in your interests to leave the vessel immediately and co-operate with the UNHCR who will be determining your status under the refugee conventions. The quicker this happens the sooner your status can be determined and resettlement action started.'
25 'We are not', *Australian*, 2 Oct. 2001, p. 1; 'We are the', *Australian*, 2 Oct. 2001, p. 2.
26 ABC-TV, *7.30 Report*, 1 Oct. 2001.
27 Smith's evidence to CMI, 4 April 2002, pp. 463–4; lurid accounts, *Daily Telegraph*, 13 Oct. 2001, p.1.
28 'We had cards', *Daily Telegraph*, 13 Oct. 2001, p. 34; Iraqis on use of force, Amnesty Statement; 'I have total', Houston's evidence to CMI, 17 April 2002, p. 1081; for discussion of further complaints of electric prods made to *Four Corners* and Human Rights Watch, see pp. 219–20.
29 Scene at the wharf, Craig Skehan, *Sydney Morning Herald*, 4 Oct. 2001, p. 3.
30 Amnesty Statement.
31 *Sydney Morning Herald*, 5 Oct. 2001, p. 3.

CHAPTER 13 LAUNCHING THE CAMPAIGN

1   Hansard, H of R, 27 Sept. 2001, p. 31 677.
2   Pamela Williams, *The Victory*, Allen & Unwin, Sydney, 1997, p. 166.
3   Approval ratings and preferred PM: AC Nielsen 'Federal Voting Intention'; preferred handling of boat people: Newspoll 19–20 Sept. 2001. Figures and analysis from Murray Goot's 'Turning Points: For Whom the Polls Told', Nov. 2002.
4   Howard at victory celebrations, 10 Nov. 2001.
5   Coward to Mike Seccombe in *Sydney Morning Herald*, 8 April 2000, p. 42. Mark Textor's role in identifying and using race in election campaigns is the subject of extensive commentary over many years. Bob Hogg, a former national secretary of the Labor Party, told the *Australian Financial Review Magazine* (Oct. 2002, p. 24), 'He was their first advocate of wedge politics'. Hogg said he and Textor had had 'a long discussion about it in 1998. Don't forget, he practised and refined the art in the Northern Territory. All those very nasty campaigns that always occur in the last week of the election with black bashing and so on—he designed all that stuff; wrote the words and designed the ads'. Political analyst Malcolm McGregor writing in the *Australian Financial Review* (15 Jan. 1997, p. 12) detailed Textor's use of the 'wedge' in the wider Australian electorate, focusing especially on race: 'The Liberals' in-house market research expert in the lead-up to the last election, Mark Textor, has worked on a number of [US] campaigns through the Wirthlin firm, during which time he became a zealous convert to the technique known as 'wedge-issue' politics. There is nothing sinister or improper in any of this. Indeed, I believe Textor is one of the sharpest political minds I have encountered, and certainly the best political operator in contemporary Australian politics. But no understanding of the evolution of racial polarisation as a mainstream political issue is possible without understanding the dynamics of wedge politics.' Having detailed the US history of this technique, McGregor concluded: 'Seen in this light, Howard's handling of Pauline Hanson may be understood for the calculated poll-driven opportunism it was. Howard and the Liberals are the net beneficiary of any deterioration in racial civility in our public culture. Such conditions are the necessary if not sufficient conditions upon which Howard's appeal to alienated Labor voters depends.' Malcolm Farr analysed Textor's role in researching the 'We will decide' slogan at p. 136 of *Howard's Race: Winning the Unwinable Election* (ed. David Solomon, HarperCollins, Sydney, 2000). 'It wasn't serendipity or instinct which incited John Howard to use the words. They were the product of a long-running program of listening to voters through focus groups—small gatherings of people selected because their views reflected those of the mainstream electorate. "We will decide" summed up what many voters in regional Australia, on the fringes of big cities, and in Labor as well as Liberal seats, were thinking. It was the message refined from the focus group analysis of Mark Textor, long a Liberal pollster who spent a lot of time in the party's HQ in Melbourne.'
6   'I don't have', to Ray Martin, 15 Aug. 1998. Doyenne of the press gallery, Michelle Grattan, wrote in the *Sydney Morning Herald*, 19 Nov. 2001, p. 18: 'Ever since 1988, when he advocated a slowing of Australia's Asian immigration

rate, Howard has been dogged by allegations he holds racist attitudes. We can argue endlessly about this. Of course he strongly denies it. But what we've seen in this campaign is something worse than a personal racist view. Howard is willing to manipulate, shamelessly, these attitudes in sections of the community and the even wider fears people feel in times of international uncertainty.' Very extensive commentary on Howard's electoral use of race going back fifteen years is usefully analysed by Andrew Markus in *Race: John Howard and the Remaking of Australia*, Allen & Unwin, 2001.
7   Cameron's 'Federal Political Overview', updated 25 Sept. 2001, section 4; *The Mackay Report*, 'Mind and Mood', July 2001, pp. 30 and 31.
8   Hansard, H of R, 8 Oct. 1996.
9   Party sources to DM and MW.
10 To MW and DM.
11 David Solomon (ed.), *Howard's Race*, p. 151.
12 To SS.
13 To DM and MW.
14 *Hansard*, Budget Senate Estimates—Finance and Public Administration Legislation Committee, 28 May 2002, p. 142.
15 Hansard, Budget Senate Estimates, p. 140.
16 The survivors of SIEV 4, see Chapter 14.

CHAPTER 14   ORDERS FROM THE TOP

1   Halton to CMI, 16 April 2001, p. 900.
2   Commander Banks, statement to CMI.
3   This account is taken from the *Adelaide*'s chronology of events given to the Powell Inquiry and Banks' statement to the CMI.
4   This account is taken from an interview with Ibtihaj Al Zuhiry's husband, Bashir; the account of the boarding from the *Adelaide*'s situation reports given to the CMI, and the account of the boarding from other passengers on the SIEV presented in the Manus Island Asylum Seekers submission to the CMI.
5   This account is taken from the statutory declarations from sailors on board the *Adelaide*, the log of the videotape operator on the *Adelaide* who recorded the event and Banks' statement to the Powell Inquiry which were lodged as exhibits with the CMI.
6   Banks' statement to the Powell Inquiry.
7   Brigadier Silverstone's statement to the Powell Inquiry, lodged as an exhibit to the CMI. Banks' account is taken from his statements to the Powell and Bryant inquiries also lodged as exhibits with the CMI.
8   The participants differed in their recollections to the Bryant Inquiry over who first made the claim, some alleging it came from Captain Walker. He denied this in his statement. Both Halton and Titheridge agree he, Titheridge, passed her the information and Halton agrees she could have been the first one to pass the claim to the meeting.
9   Banks' testimony to the CMI, p. 298.

10 Report on the Cocos Tow Option released to the *Sydney Morning Herald* under FOI.
11 Admiral Barrie's statement to the Powell Inquiry.
12 Report of the PST, 7 Oct. 2001.
13 Group Captain Steve Walker's statement to the Powell Inquiry and Flight Lt Briggs faxes to Ross Hampton, lodged as exhibits to the CMI.
14 Report of the PST, 7 Oct. 2001.
15 Cable from Banks sent from HMAS *Adelaide*, given to the Powell Inquiry and lodged as an exhibit with the CMI.
16 Banks' statement to the Powell Inquiry, enclosure 2, amendments, lodged as an exhibit to the CMI. See also his statement to the CMI at pp. 185–7.
17 See Banks' evidence to the CMI at p. 294.
18 This account of the rescue is drawn from the *Adelaide*'s signal log, lodged as an exhibit with the CMI, Banks' testimony to the CMI and the Manus Island Asylum Seekers submission to the CMI.
19 Barrie's testimony to the CMI pp. 741–2 also pp. 786–7. See also Barrie's statement to the Powell Inquiry, lodged as an exhibit with the CMI.
20 Banks' testimony to the CMI, p. 166.

CHAPTER 15   TRUTH OVERBOARD

1 ADF Operation Relex Log Entry, 090055Z, attachment to Powell Report, lodged as exhibit to CMI.
2 Ritchie's statement to the Powell Inquiry, lodged as an exhibit to CMI.
3 Strategic Command file obtained by *Sydney Morning Herald* under FOI.
4 Bryant Report p. 15 and Customs deputy chief John Drury's statement to Bryant Inquiry, lodged as an exhibit to CMI. Also, Bowdler to DM.
5 Andrew Stackpool's statement to the Bryant Inquiry.
6 Stackpool to Bryant Inquiry, p. 16.
7 Tim Bloomfield's statement to the Powell Inquiry, lodged as an exhibit with CMI.
8 Smith's evidence to CMI, p. 592.
9 Banks' statement to the Powell Inquiry.
10 Smith's evidence to CMI, p. 584, and the Bryant Report, p. 28.
11 Barrie's evidence to CMI, p. 740.
12 Barrie's evidence to CMI, p. 802.
13 To DM and MW.
14 Documents in Maritime Headquarters file, 9 Oct 2001, released to *Sydney Morning Herald* under FOI.
15 *Herald Sun*, 9 Oct 2001.
16 Bryant Report, p. 31.
17 Documents from Northern Command released to *Sydney Morning Herald* under FOI.
18 Bryant Report, p. 20.

19 Silverstone's role and conclusions at this stage, Bryant Report, p. 28 and Silverstone's statement to Bryant Inquiry, lodged as an exhibit with CMI; Smith's conclusion, evidence to CMI, p. 585.
20 Ritchie's evidence to CMI, p. 369.
21 Ballarat doorstop interview, 10 Oct. 2001.
22 Captain Belinda Byrne's statement to the Powell Inquiry, lodged as an exhibit with CMI.
23 Barrie's evidence to CMI, p. 742.
24 Bloomfield's and Hampton's statements to the Bryant Inquiry, lodged as exhibits to CMI, and the Bryant Report p. 17.
25 Hampton's statement to the Bryant Inquiry.
26 Bornholt's statement to the Bryant Inquiry, lodged as an exhibit to CMI.
27 Bornholt's statement to the Powell Inquiry, lodged as an exhibit to CMI.
28 Bryant Report, p. 37.
29 Edward's evidence to CMI, p. 1705.
30 Press release, 10 Oct. 2001.
31 The statutory declarations of the crew members were attachments to the Powell Report and lodged as exhibits to CMI.
32 Shackleton's evidence to CMI, p. 93. See also statements by Shackleton and Ritchie to the Bryant Inquiry.
33 Jenny McKenry's statement to the Powell Inquiry, lodged as an exhibit to CMI.
34 Summary of media reports, Bryant Report.
35 McKenry's evidence to the CMI, p. 1101.
36 McKenry's evidence to the CMI, p. 1101.
37 Account from one of the key people present at the meeting, to MW.
38 King's evidence to CMI, pp. 1491, 1494 and 1501; Hammer's response, evidence to CMI, pp. 1805–6.
39 Barrie's evidence to CMI, p. 742 and 785.
40 Ritchie's evidence to CMI, p. 372.
41 Barrie's evidence to CMI, p. 742; Ritchie's evidence to CMI, p. 373.
42 *Australian*, 31 Oct. 2001, p. 1. The report calculated the policy to have come into effect about mid-September.

CHAPTER 16 A MILITARY CAMPAIGN

1 Quoted and reworked from DM's profile of Beazley, *Sydney Morning Herald*, 3 Nov. 2001, p. 29.
2 see p. 151.
3 'Potential mission', minute by Colonel MSJ Hindmarsh, 29 Aug. 2001; 'subject to', Lieutenant General DM Mueller, 'UBA Removal Strategy—HMAS *Manoora*', 28 Sept. 2001; 'Consequences of delivery', NCC AST Operation Relex Daily Sitrep, 15 Sept. 2001, identity of author and recipient censored.
4 'To Deter and Deny' by Debbie Whitmont, ABC-TV's *Four Corners*, broadcast 15 April 2002.

5   Howard to press conference, 19 Oct. 2001; official summary, 'SIEV 05 Event Summary' by Admiral Smith presented to CMI.
6   'The government did', *Four Corners*; 'There are no', *Sydney Morning Herald*, 14 Oct. 2001, p. 5.
7   Instigators of new policy, government sources to DM and MW; 'vessels coming', Howard press conference, 19 Oct. 2001; Indonesia was alerted in a third party note delivered 8 Oct. 2001; draft paper, minutes PST, 11 Oct. 2001.
8   Halton evidence to CMI, 16 April 2002: 'subject to', p. 917; 'a slightly different', p. 919; 'with SIEV 5', Smith's evidence to CMI, 5 April 2002, p. 508.
9   Opposition backing for returns, *Age*, 27 Oct. 2001, p.1; Indonesian advice to Smith, Jakarta officials to MW; 'frustrated by the crude', *Sydney Morning Herald*, 19 Oct. 2001, p. 1.
10 'Australia has accepted', *Four Corners*; 'the Australian Government' and 'calm and quiet', Gregg statement to CMI.
11 *Four Corners*.
12 CDF minute to Reith, 17 Oct. 2001, CDF 760/01.
13 'became hostile', 'the wounds' and 'forced removal', all from Gregg's statement to CMI.
14 Use of force aboard SIEV 5, Chapter VII, *By Invitation Only: Australian Asylum Policy*, Human Rights Watch, 2001.
15 When the authors sought rebuttal material from the Department of Defence covering the Human Rights Watch allegations, the department directed us to Angus Houston's testimony to CMI, 17 April 2002, pp. 1080–3. Human Rights Watch claims in note 186 of its report that the Aziza interview was 'corroborated in every detail by a separate, private interview with her husband, who said he was struck exactly four times and "They must have been electric—otherwise four strokes, even hard jabs, would not have made me completely unconscious". Also corroborated by Human Rights Watch interview No. 22, Mataram, Indonesia, 18 April 2002 and Human Rights Watch interview No. 31, Mataram, Indonesia, 19 April 2002. *Four Corners* report in 'To Deter and Deny'; Iraqi report in their Amnesty Statement; 'I understand', Houston to CMI, p. 1082.
16 Gregg statement.
17 Sheraton Hotel press conference, 19 Oct. 2001.
18 'At this stage', *Sydney Morning Herald*, 16 Oct. 2001, p. 6; 'Minimum of', PST minutes, 19 Oct. 2001.
19 'face difficulties', Max Moore-Wilton to Senate Estimates, 20 Feb. 2002; 'the need to' and 'It is not', *Age*, 27 Oct. 2001.
20 'My secretary', Pundari to Evan Williams, ABC-TV, *Foreign Correspondent*, 15 April 2002; 'I had no', *Age*, 27 Oct. 2001, p. 1.
21 'Navy Force Assignments for Concurrent Operations', CDF 748/2001, received by Reith 15 Oct. 2001.
22 PST minutes, 20 Oct. 2001.
23 Statement of Menhinick to CMI, 30 Oct. 2001.
24 Halton evidence to CMI, 30 July 2002, p. 1955.

CHAPTER 17 THE BOAT THAT SANK

1. Canti is the departure point given by Amal Hassan Basri.
2. This account of the departure is amalgamated from accounts given in interviews with the survivors: Amal Hassan Basri to SS and Sundous Ibramam to MW and SS through translator Kaysar Trad.
3. Unless otherwise stated, the source of all material on Sundous and her family is from an interview Sundous gave to MW and SS.
4. Interview with UNHRC Regional Representative in Jakarta, Choosin Ngaotheppitak.
5. To SS.
6. Amal's interview with SS. Amal's recollection of Abu Quassey on the water is the only account of this.
7. Col. Gallagher's evidence to the CMI, pp. 1750–51, and Admiral Gates' chronology on the SIEV X given to the CMI. Gallagher claims the phone call did not relate to Abu Quassey's vessel. However, the Gates' chronology and the Coastwatch account indicate it does.
8. Admiral Bonser's supplementary submission to CMI, Attachment A, June 17.
9. Target of ASIS, information to DM; DIMA intelligence note 79/2001, 17 October 2001, p. 2, exhibit to the CMI.
10. PST records for October 18, exhibit to CMI. Also note that DIMA testimony to CMI states the intelligence on Abu Quassey's boat was single sourced, not multi-sourced.
11. To MW and DM.
12. Department of Defence intelligence material relating to SIEV X (Gates Report) released to CMI, 4 July 2002.
13. Admiral Bonser's testimony to CMI, p. 1638.
14. SS interview with Mr Adem, brother of Mantaha San Adem, a Mandean survivor who left the boat.
15. SS interview with Amal.
16. This account of the conditions is taken from interviews with both Amal and Sundous.
17. MW interview with Sundous.
18. MW interview with Sundous. See also the transcript of videotape interviews with the survivors recorded in the days after the ordeal by the Muslim Association and translated by Kaysar Trad.
19. Muslim Association videotape interviews.
20. Muslim Association videotape interviews.
21. Interview with Zainaab on Network Nine's *Sunday*, 4 Nov. 2001.
22. Air Commodore Philip Byrne, evidence to CMI, 30 July 2002, p. 2170.
23. Information from the harbourmaster at Sunda Kelapur Port, Nth Jakarta, provided to Geoff Parish of SBS *Dateline* and sighted by the authors. Parish tells the authors these co-ordinateds have not been challenged by military or civilian sources since being broadcast by *Dateline* on 17 May 2002.
24. Byrne to CMI, pp. 2001–2.
25. Report of Rear Admiral Gates on the SIEV X surveillance, exhibit to CMI.
26. 'The tactical priority', Byrne to CMI, p. 2170; 'That is the', Byrne to CMI pp. 1999–20.

27 Amal's interview with SS and the account of the night from the Muslim Association video tape interviews.
28 MW and SS interview with Sundous.
29 Admiral Smith's testimony to CMI.
30 MW interview with Commissioner Mick Keelty.
31 Admiral Bonser's supplementary submission to CMI, 17 June 2001.
32 Col. Gallagher's evidence to CMI, p. 1726.
33 ASTJIC intelligence report 171/01 quoted in CMI Report, p. 210.
34 DIMA's Nelly Siegmund's evidence to CMI, p. 1853.
35 Report of the surveillance flight of October 20 in Admiral Gates' report.
36 Interview with Sundous and Amal.
37 Count of survivors supplied by UNHCR in Jakarta. Some of the discrepancies in these figures are due to different ways of judging who is a child and who is an adult. There is no certain figure for the numbers who embarked on Abu Quassey's boat so final death tolls are all estimates.
38 Admiral Bonser's evidence to CMI, pp. 1655–7.
39 Davidson's evidence to CMI, p. 1706.
40 Davidson's evidence to CMI, p. 1706.
41 Minutes PST, 23 Oct 2001.
42 Ali Hamid in an interview with SBS Arabic Service. The identity of the Australian officials remains a mystery. The survivors did not ask them for 'identification'. The AFP claims no knowledge of these pictures.

CHAPTER 18 THE WORST OF TIMES

1 Beazley's interview on Brisbane radio quoted in Margot Kingston's web diary, 23 Oct. 2001, <smh.com.au>.
2 6PR interview by Paul Murray, 23 Oct. 2001; National Press Club, 8 Nov. 2001.
3 Report to Halton, PST minutes, 23 Oct. 2001; DIMA report, intelligence note 83/01, 23 Oct. 2001; Greenlees' report, 24 Oct. 2001, p. 5; harbourmaster's report, obtained by SBS-TV's *Dateline* in May 2002, puts the point of rescue at 07 40 00S / 105 09 00E. In a report dated 18 Dec. 2002, Matthias Tomczak, Professor of Oceanography at Flinders University, Adelaide, analysed winds and currents to rule out the possibility of the survivors having drifted from some point within Indonesian territorial waters. The reports of both the harbourmaster and Tomczak can be read at >sievx.com<.
4 Halton report to Howard, evidence to CMI, 30 July 2002, p. 2127; 'Our experience', evidence to CMI, p. 2132.
5 *Australian*, 31 Oct. 2001, p. 1.
6 Alie-Mehdi Sobie, quoted in the *Sunday Telegraph*, 28 Oct. 2001, p. 11.
7 *Lateline*, 8 Nov. 2001, a transcript not to be found on the Prime Minister's website.
8 Notes of the speech, DM.
9 'If the Labor', Howard press conference, 26 Oct. 2001; 'because I'll tell', notes, DM.
10 Beazley to DM and MW.

11 Duncan Kerr to MW.
12 'This child', statement of Petty Officer Bosun Christopher Neil Smart, 10 April 2002 to CMI; 'restless and irate', PST minutes, 23 Oct, 2001.
13 Statements of Matthew George Levi. Similar statement covering the incident by Travis Gary Flenley. Both to CMI.
14 Human Rights Watch, *By Invitation Only: Australian Asylum Policy*, 2001, see esp. note 193 in Chapt. VII.
15 *By Invitation Only*, see esp. notes 189–91 in Chapt. VII.
16 'To Deter and Deny', *Four Corners*, ABC-TV, 15 April 2002.
17 *Sydney Morning Herald*, 27 Oct. 2001, p. 4; Minutes PST, 29 Oct. 2001.
18 Statements of Gregg and Menhinick to CMI.
19 Minutes PST, 29 Oct. 2001; Menhinick statement to CMI.
20 Translations from the video, courtesy *Four Corners*.
21 Taylor's statement to CMI.
22 *By Invitation Only*, see esp. note 200 in Chapt. VII.
23 'disproportionate force', *By Invitation Only*, see esp. notes 196 and 197 in Chapt. VII; 'Master appears very', statement of ABCIS Kent Pedersen to CMI; Houston's statement set out in detail on p. 220.
24 They took their', Ali to *Four Corners*.
25 All information, *Four Corners*.
26 Radio 2GB, 31 Oct. 2001.
27 Statement of Lt Commander Wesley Heron to CMI.
28 Heron statement to CMI.
29 Some documents call the boat *Sinar Bontang III*; text of the signs from Titheridge's 'SIEV 9 Event Timeline' dated 6 Nov. 2001, supplied to the authors under FOI; 'removed from AI', statement of Andrew Hawke to CMI; 'Many female PIIs' and 'The TSE de-escalated', statement of Guille Bawden Newham to CMI.
30 'All PIIs', statement of William Taylor to CMI; 'large Middle-Eastern', statement of Kent Scully Pedersen to CMI; 'The mother was', statement of Guille Bawden Newham to CMI; 'This incident', statement of Lt Roy Henry to CMI.
31 'to the vessel's', Hawke's statement to CMI; 'during the riots', joint statement to CMI sworn in April 2002 by RP Henry, S Oben, RII Troughton, WE Bergersen, JR Nimmett and LG Mahalm; Titheridge says in his 'SIEV 9 Event Timeline' of 6 Nov. 2001, 'There is no material evidence to support the observations and perceptions of the on-scene ADF personnel regarding activities of some of the asylum seekers'.
32 Generally drawn from Titheridge's 'SIEV 9 Event Timeline'; 'to allay seasickness', Titheridge; 'The news was', statement of Andrew Hawke to CMI.

CHAPTER 19   THE NAVY LEAKS

1 Walters to MW and DM.
2 Houston to CMI, pp. 1055–65.

3 Houston to CMI, p. 1059.
4 Houston to CMI, p. 1064.
5 Houston to the Senate Committee for Foreign Affairs, Defence and Trade (Estimates), 20 Feb. 2002, p. 76.
6 Silverstone to CMI, pp. 346 and 361.
7 Statement by Peter Reith, 21 Feb. 2002.
8 Howard press conference, 19 Feb. 2002.
9 Sidhu to CMI, p. 1563 and Halton to CMI, p. 1037.
10 Howard press conference, 19 Feb. 2002.
11 Howard press conference, 19 Feb. 2002. Scrafton has never given an account of what he told Howard that night and declined to give evidence to CMI.
12 Howard press conference, 19 Feb. 2002.
13 Jones evidence to Senate Finance and Public Administration (Estimates) Committee, 18 Feb. 2002. Text of ONA report, pp. 136–7; purpose of the report discussed p. 136: 'We were simply listing a series of devices used by asylum seekers to identify the sort of behaviour which had occurred elsewhere.'
14 'the ONA report', Jones to Estimates, p. 138; 'was aware that', p. 141. Jordana declined to give evidence on these matters to CMI.
15 The terrible *New International Version* of Ecclesiastes 3:1–8.
16 See transcript of Howard's Press Club address, PM's website.
17 Smith to CMI, p. 590.
18 Banks to CMI, pp. 207–8.
19 Transcript of Shackleton's doorstop interview.
20 Banks to CMI, p. 32.
21 MW and DM compiled that report, which appeared in the *Sydney Morning Herald*, 8 Nov. 2001, p. 1. Yu had spoken the night before on ABC-Radio National. Sydney's religious leaders—the Catholic Archbishop Dr George Pell, the Anglican Archbishop Dr Peter Jensen and Rabbi Apple of the Great Synagogue—declined to take part.
22 *Australian*, 9 Nov 2001, p. 5.
23 Shackleton's statement to the Powell Inquiry, lodged as an exhibit to CMI; also Shackleton to CMI, p. 101.
24 Halton's and Moore-Wilton's role, Halton to CMI, p. 1037–41; McKenry's and Hawke's role, McKenry to CMI, p. 1131.
25 McKenry's statement to the Powell Inquiry, lodged as an exhibit to CMI.
26 *Australian*, 9 Nov 2001, p. 1.
27 At <www.sbs.com.au/insight>, not available on PM's website.
28 At <www.abc.net.au/lateline/archives>, not available on PM's website.

CHAPTER 20 THE BURNING ISSUE

1 This account of the sighting, boarding and abandoning of the SIEV is based on statements to CMI by Wes Heron, James McLaughlin, Brock Symmons, Matthew Philp, Craig Duff, Malcolm Yeardley, Jason Hillier, Darren Walker, Gregory Hogarth.

2 Sayyed Shahi Husseini's statement on the death of his wife to AFP, 21 Nov. 2001.
 3 Musa Husseini's statement to AFP, 20 Nov. 2001. The life jacket problem is discussed in the AFP report to the WA Coroner.
 4 Ali Reza's statement to AFP, 20 Nov. 2001 and Bradley Mulcahy's statement to AFP, 15 Nov. 2001.
 5 Duff's statement to CMI.
 6 Duff's, Zanker and Mooney's statements to CMI.
 7 Duff's, Zanker and Mooney's statements to CMI.
 8 Duff's statement to CMI.
 9 Yeardley's and Duff's statements to CMI.
10 Statements to AFP; Ali Reza reported *West Australian*, 8 Nov. 2002.
11 Northern Command report on SIEV 10, released by Reith on 9 Nov. 2001; AFP Brief of Evidence to the WA coroner.
12 *Daily Telegraph*, 10 Nov. 2001, p. 28
13 'If there had', to Cathy van Extel on ABC Radio National.
14 *Sydney Morning Herald*, 9 Nov. 2001, p. 6.
15 *Australian*, 10 Nov. 2001, p. 4.
16 Newspoll published in News Ltd papers, 10 Nov. 2001.
17 Sayyed Shahi Husseini's statement to the AFP.
18 Yeardley's statement to CMI.

CHAPTER 21   VICTORY PARTY

 1 Crosby to the National Press Club, 21 Nov. 2001.
 2 *Daily Telegraph*, 10 Nov. 2001, p. 2.
 3 *Sydney Morning Herald*, 7 Nov. 2001, p. 4.
 4 Press conference, 7 Nov. 2001.
 5 *Australian*, 10 Nov. 2001, p. 3.
 6 'white or Japanese', to Glen Milne, Channel 7 *Sunrise*, 9 Nov. 2001; 'I don't find', to Cathy van Extel, ABC Radio National, 9 Nov. 2001; 'self-flagellation', to Leon Byner, 5AA Adelaide, 9 Nov. 2001.
 7 'completely unsurprising' and 'Many of them', press conference, 7 Nov. 2001; Hewson, *Australian Financial Review*, 2 Nov. 2001, p. 74.
 8 *The Bulletin*, dated 13 Nov. 2001 but on the streets 7 Nov., p. 18.
 9 'Australia had no', *Courier-Mail*, 7 Nov. 2001, p. 1; the scene on the plane, Tom Allard, *Sydney Morning Herald*, 16 Nov. 2001, p. 9; for a discussion of this incident, *Howard's Race*, David Solomon (ed.), HarperCollins, Sydney, 2002, pp. 127–8.
10 'Why would people', Hobart *Mercury*, 9 May 2002, p. 1.
11 'We knew once', doorstop interview in Hobart, 1 Nov. 2001; all security precautions taken, doorstop in Launceston, 2 Nov. 2001; 'We have to', to Cook and Moore on Radio HOFM, Hobart, 2 Nov. 2001.
12 *Inside Al Qaeda* by Rohan Gunaratna, preface to the paperback edition, Scribe Publications, Melbourne, 2002, pp. xv–xxiv. Downer was interviewed on

ABC-TV's *Lateline* three days before the Bali bombing disclaiming any specific threat by al-Qaeda.
13 Details from Murray Mottram in *Sunday Age*, 11 Nov. 2001, p. 3; *New York Times*, 9 Nov. 2001, p. 3, quoted accusers and defenders of Howard on the issue of him playing on fears—including racial fears—in the campaign; 'Well that's ridiculous' and 'Here I am', transcript PM's doorstop, Eastwood Public School.
14 Details from Karen Kissane's notebook in *Sunday Age*, 11 Nov. 2001.
15 Exit poll figures supplied by Beazley to DM and MW show swings to Labor from health (2.5%), education (0.5%), jobs (3.9%) and the 'roll back' of GST (8%). Total gains from those policies of 14.9%. The swings against Labor were caused by welfare (1.4%), defence (7.4%), the economy (5.5%) and immigration (6%). Total losses of 20.3%.
16 Beazley conceded Labor lost heavily in the 30–39 year-old bracket (particularly women) and the $40–50 000 income bracket i.e. young families. Lynton Crosby at the National Press Club on 21 Nov. 2001 said Liberal post-election polling also revealed a 14% lift (on a two-party preferred basis) among women 18–34.
17 Rising support for Howard's leadership, 'Commonwealth Election 2001', Parliamentary Library research paper No. 11, 2001–02, pp. 10–1.
18 Halving of One Nation vote, 'Commonwealth Election 2001', p. 19; return of Liberal voters, Geoff Walsh to National Press Club, 3 Dec. 2001. Walsh said, '*Tampa* restored a massive 10 per cent to the Liberal Party primary vote. And the great bulk of these votes came from One Nation and right-wing independents . . . *Tampa* effectively knee-capped One Nation and anointed John Howard. Three-quarters of the One Nation vote loss went straight to the Coalition'.
19 'It was not', doorstop, 11 Nov. 2001; Beazley's resignation, *Sydney Morning Herald*, 12 Nov. p. 7 and *Australian Financial Review*, 12 Nov. 2001, p. 5.
20 *Australian Financial Review*, 12 Nov. 2001, p. 3.
21 Raw footage provided by ABC-TV.
22 Party's thunder and 'I believe', *Daily Telegraph*, 12 Nov. 2001, p. 6; 'It's how', *Sydney Morning Herald*, 12 Nov. 2001, p. 8.
23 *Sunday Age*, 11 Nov. 2001, p. 3.
24 Howard's technique was to aim his rejoinder at those few—and incorrect—commentators who claimed the government's victory was 'entirely' due to border protection, and then point out, correctly, that there were many other factors. In this way, he and his party officers skirted *any* detailed discussion of the role of border protection in the 2001 win. This strategy was already in place the morning after the victory party. At his doorstop, Howard listed as a priority, 'from a political point of view we've got to disabuse some of the mythology that's starting to emerge as to why the Government won. I think the government's victory lies in a campaign and a number of responses that began months ago. The idea that the victory was entirely due to the impact of border protection and the . . . the point I want to make is that the government was clearly in a lot of political difficulty seven or eight months ago and we began to address those concerns'.
25 The shemozzle over the national anthem, Tony Stephens in *Sydney Morning Herald*, 12 Nov. 2001, p. 3; Moore-Wilton entering the private party, *Australian Financial Review*, 12 Nov. 2001, p. 3.

AFTERMATH

1 Full count: *Palapa* plus SIEVs 1–12, essentially taken from Admiral Smith's 'SIEV Event Summary', though there is an error there for the count on SIEV 7 where Smith only counts those asylum seekers returned on the *Arunta* and omits to count approx 160 returned on the SIEV itself; Howard, campaign launch speech, 28 Oct. 2001.
2 Several counts are given for the numbers on SIEV 11. Admiral Smith's 'SIEV Event Summary' says 18 asylum seekers and 4 crew. Senator Ellison when accounting the forced return of the boat said in media release E258/01 on 14 Dec. 2001 that there were 17 asylum seekers and 3 crew. Details of the return of SIEV 12, from statement of Damien Denis Casey to CMI.
3 At p. 327 of its report, the CMI attributed the 'substantive difficulty' of costing the operation to 'the inability fully to identify the cost of the activities of the Australian Defence Force in support of the arrangements'. Costello gave those figures of top-up allocations made to DIMA and other departments post Relex/Pacific Solution on 13 Feb. 2002 at Hansard, H of R, p. 106.
4 'We are not', Howard to Alan Jones, 30 Aug. 2001; figures supplied by DIMIA.
5 Figures as at the time this book went to press, early Feb. 2003. 'We have always', Howard press conference, 1 Sept. 2001; figures of acceptances by NZ supplied by DIMIA.
6 Figures supplied by DIMIA as at early Feb. 2003.
7 Figures supplied by DIMIA as at early Feb. 2003.
8 Ruddock particularly praised Britain for reflecting 'many of the measures, policies and practices already employed in Australian immigration', press release, 8 Feb. 2002.
9 *Australian Financial Review*, 4 Feb. 2002, p. 3.
10 *Australian Financial Review Magazine*, 27 Sept. 2002, p. 64.
11 The enquiries were conducted by Jenny Bryant, Assistant Secretary, Education and Immigration Branch of PM & C, and Major General R. A. Powell. Their conclusions were tabled in parliament on 13 Feb. 2002.
12 *Sydney Morning Herald*, 23 Feb. 2002, p. 27.
13 Doorstop, 17 Dec. 2002.
14 'the wonderful', *Sydney Morning Herald*, 7 May 2002, p. 6 plus other details of the Auckland reception from *New Zealand Herald*, 7 May 2002; 'It is a', *Australian*, 14 May 2002, p. 4; 'It's an unwritten', *Sydney Morning Herald*, 14 May 2002, p. 5.

Glossary and abbreviations

ACS   Australian Customs Service, see *Coastwatch*.
ADF   Australian Defence Force, including the navy, air force and army.
AFP   Australian Federal Police. AFP Commissioner, Mick Keelty.
AGs   Attorney General's Department. Minister, Daryl Williams QC. Employed by the department are the Solicitor General, David Bennett QC, and the Chief General Counsel, Henry Burmester QC.
APEC   Asia Pacific Economic Cooperation Forum.
APS   Australian Protective Services, the specialist protective security service of the Australian Federal Police.
ASTJIC   Australian Theatre Joint Intelligence Centre.
AMSA   Australian Maritime Safety Authority. An independent statutory authority responsible for the delivery of safety and other services to the Australian maritime industry. CEO, Clive Davidson. Umbrella body for *AusSAR*,

	Australian Search and Rescue, which operates a national 24-hour centre, and the *RCC*, Rescue Co-ordination Centre in Canberra with the job of co-ordinating Australia's civil search and rescue activities.
ASEAN	Association of Southeast Asian Nations.
ASIO	Australian Security and Intelligence Organisation, responsible for domestic intelligence.
ASIS	Australian Secret Intelligence Service, operates as Australia's intelligence arm overseas.
ATSIC	Aboriginal and Torres Strait Islander Commission, the national policy-making and service agency for Indigenous people.
Asylum seeker	A person seeking protection as a refugee. See also *SUNC*, *UA*, *UBA* and *PII*.
AusSAR	See *AMSA*.
BASARNAS	Indonesian National Search and Rescue Authority (Badan SAR Nasional).
BP	Boarding party of *RAN* sailors who take control of *SIEV*s.
Coastwatch	A division of the Australian Customs Service (*ACS*) that manages and co-ordinates Australia's civil maritime surveillance and response program using contracted aircraft, Australian Defence Force (*ADF*) patrol boats and aircraft, and sea-going vessels of the Customs Marine Fleet. *Operation Relex* took over some of the surveillance responsibilities in September 2001. Represented on *PST*.
CDF	Chief of Defence Force, Admiral Chris Barrie.
CLP	Country Liberal Party, for many years the ruling right-of-centre party in the Northern Territory.
COMAST	Commander Australian Theatre, Rear Admiral Chris Ritchie.
CZ	Contiguous Zone, the sea between 12 and 24 nautical miles from the Australian coastline.
DFAT	Department of Foreign Affairs and Trade. Minister, Alexander Downer. Represented on *PST*.
DIMA	Department of Immigration and Multicultural Affairs. Minister, Philip Ruddock. Represented on *PST*. Players in turning back the *Tampa* were first deputy secretary, Andrew Metcalfe, and first assistant secretary, Philippa Godwin.

DSD	Defence Signals Directorate, Australia's intelligence agency that is responsible for electronic interception.
Forecastle	Short, raised deck in the front of a ship.
GPS	Global Positioning System, a worldwide radio-navigation system.
GST	Goods and Services Tax.
Habeas corpus	A writ for securing the liberty of the subject, whether from unjustifiable detention in prison, hospital or private custody. It enables the court to enquire into the justification for the detention.
HREOC	Human Rights and Equal Opportunity Commission.
INP	Indonesian National Police (Kepolisian Negara Republik Indonesia), also known as POLRI.
International Convention on Maritime Search and Rescue	Australia became a party to this convention on 22 June 1985. Annex Chapter 2.1.10 provides: 'Parties shall ensure that assistance be provided to any person in distress at sea. They shall do so regardless of the nationality or status of such person or the circumstances in which that person is found.'
IOM	International Organisation for Migration, an international agency working usually under contract with national governments and the *UNHCR* on migration, refugee and people smuggling issues.
JI	Jemaah Islamiyah, radical Islamic group in Southeast Asia with close ties to al-Qaeda.
MAYDAY	A message that a ship, aircraft, etc. is in grave and imminent danger and requires immediate assistance.
NSC	National Security Committee, a sub-committee of the Australian Cabinet that deals with defence and security issues.
Non-refoulement	A fundamental principle of the 1951 Convention Relating to the Status of Refugees, where a country is obligated to protect would-be refugees from the risk of being returned to a country where they may face persecution.
ONA	Office of National Assessments, the intelligence and security agency that analyses international developments and gives direct advice to the Prime Minister.

Operation Cranberry	The military operation assisting Immigration and Customs in the handling of boat people that was in place before Operation Relex.
Operation Relex	The military operation launched by the Australian government on September 3 to block the entry to Australia of asylum seekers arriving by boat.
PACC	The Defence Department's office of Public Affairs and Corporate Communications.
PAN PAN	An urgent message concerning the safety of a ship, aircraft, other vehicle or person/s.
P-3C Orions	RAAF surveillance aircraft used in *Coastwatch* operations and *Operation Relex*.
P & I clubs	Protection and Indemnity clubs, an international network of lawyers, insurers and troubleshooters that handle the legal, immigration and other problems of shipping lines.
PII	Potential Illegal Immigrant.
PILCH	Public Interest Law Clearing House, a Melbourne organisation that finds lawyers willing to work *pro bono* on issues of public importance.
PM & C	Department of Prime Minister and Cabinet. Max Moore-Wilton was head of the department and Jane Halton was PM & C's Executive Co-ordinator.
PST	People Smuggling Taskforce, a high level committee chaired by Jane Halton from *PM & C* with representatives from *AFP*, *AGs*, *AMSA*, *Coastwatch*, the Department of Defence, *DFAT*, *DIMA*. It met continuously from the arrival of the *Tampa* until after the election to supervise the handling of boat people.
PNG	Papua New Guinea. Prime Minister Sir Mekere Morauta was defeated in the subsequent election.
PUA	Possible Unauthorised Arrival, asylum seeker.
RAN	Royal Australian Navy.
Refugee	A person who 'owing to a well-founded fear of being persecuted for reasons of race, religion, nationality, membership of a particular social group or political opinion, is outside the country of his nationality and is unable or, owing to such fear, is unwilling to avail himself of the

	protection of that country'. Article 1A of the *Refugee Convention*.
Refugee Convention	The 1951 Convention Relating to the Status of Refugees and the 1967 Protocol Relating to the Status of Refugees, signed by Australia.
RCC Australia	See *AMSA*.
RHIB	Rigid Hull Inflatable Boat.
RFDS	Royal Flying Doctor Service.
SAS	Special Air Services regiment, Australia's special forces.
SIEV	Suspected Illegal Entry Vessel.
SOLAS	International Convention on Safety of Life at Sea, 1974. Australia became a party to SOLAS on 17 November, 1983.
SUNC	Suspected Unauthorised Non-Citizen, asylum seeker.
TPV	Temporary Protection Visa, introduced in October 1999 grants a three-or five-year stay in Australia to refugees. Holders of TPVs are not eligible for immediate family reunion or a range of resettlement services and social security benefits.
Territorial sea	The sea out to 12 nautical miles from the Australian coast.
TSE	Transit Security Element, specially trained military units assigned to navy commanders to control asylum seekers on the *SIEV*s.
UA	Unauthorised Arrival, asylum seekers.
UBA	Unauthorised boat arrival, asylum seeker.
UNCLOS	United Nations Convention for the Law of the Sea, 1982. Australia became a party to the UNCLOS on 16 November, 1994. It is part of the law of both Australia and Norway. UNCLOS obliges every ship's master: 'in so far as he can do so without serious danger to the ship, the crew or the passengers, to render assistance to any person found at sea in danger of being lost' and 'to proceed with all possible speed to the rescue of persons in distress'.
UNHCR	United Nations High Commissioner for Refugees, mandated to lead and co-ordinate international action to protect refugees and resolve refugee issues worldwide.
Weatherdeck	Exposed top deck of a ship.

Acknowledgements

Sue Spencer was the third hand in this book. She worked on the project for many months in 2002 and even from Phnom Penh, where she was posted late year, she continued to research, plan and advise. We thank her very much. This book is also built on the deep foundations of the work our colleagues published and broadcast at the time of these events. Our debts are acknowledged in many hundreds of footnotes but we especially wish to thank the many journalists for whom the story of the *Tampa* and the SIEVs has been a nagging piece of unfinished business and who have handed us their research and their contacts in the hope that we could take the story further.

Our thanks especially to refugees and their families for helping us with the book: Khodadad Sarwari, Rajab Ali Hossaini, Assadullah Rezaee, Rajab Ali Merzaee; the man who asked to be referred to in the text as a 'scholar' and the young men and boys at Dingwall hostel in Auckland, in particular Wahidullah Akbari, Abdul Halek and Zakaria. Our thanks to our guide and interpreter in Auckland, Siraj Salarzi. Our deep gratitude goes to those who shared their painful experiences of SIEV X, especially Sundous Ibramam and her husband Ahmaed al-Zalimi, and Amal Hassan Basri, Montaha San Adem and her family, and Majid. Thanks also to Kaysar Trad for his translations and advice.

Arne Rinnan had spent the best part of a year answering questions— 'always the same questions'—but gave us three interviews in Oslo and Sydney. Our thanks also to Wilh Wilhelmsen, the owner of the line; Australian manager Peter Dexter; the first mate of the *Tampa*, Christian Maltau; the line's Sydney lawyer James Neill; and Hans Christian Bangsmoen in Oslo, Yvette Farrell and Jannikke Berger in Sydney and many others in the line who assisted this project with Scandinavian caution.

We thank the Prime Minister for responding to a list of written questions. The Deputy Prime Minister, John Anderson, and the Foreign Minister, Alexander Downer, also answered our written questions. Philip Ruddock answered written questions and granted us an interview. Our thanks also to Admiral Chris Barrie, whom we interviewed after his retirement, and to Max Moore-Wilton who, in the end, answered a couple of questions. Thanks to Kim Beazley for a long and frank interview. Also on the Labor side we would like to thank Michael Costello, Geoff Walsh, Duncan Kerr, Laurie Brereton, and John Della Bosca. We are especially grateful to the many high-level participants in these events—politicians, bureaucrats and military officers—who spoke to us off the record.

Our thanks to Thorbjoern Jagland, the former Foreign Minister of Norway; Jonas Gahr Støre, Chief of Staff to Prime Minister Jens Stoltenberg; Hans Wilhelm Longva and Rolf Einar Fife of the Royal Norwegian Foreign Ministry; Ove Thorsheim, the ambassador to Australia; Lars Alsaker, the first secretary at the Canberra embassy; Nils H. Thommessen of Wiersholm, Mellbye and Bech; and Claes Isacson and Christen Guddal of Gard Services.

In Indonesia, thanks to Don Greenlees for his incredible generosity, to Choosin Ngaotheppitak and his staff at UNHCR for all their help and also to the many Indonesian and Australian officials in Jakarta who agreed to speak on background. At UNHCR we also want to thank assistant High Commissioner for Refugees Søren Jessen-Peterson, Jonathan Prentice, Michel Gabaudan, Ellen Hansen and Gabrielle Cullen.

In New Zealand, our particular thanks to the Refugee and Migrant Service—a mostly volunteer NGO—for opening its doors and introducing us to the *Tampa* refugees. Thanks especially to Jenni Broom and Janet Seager in Auckland, and Catherine Comber in Christchurch. Also to Kiri Warburton, Julie Sutherland and Dr Martin Reeve who briefed us at Mangere. Our thanks to the Minister for Immigration, Lianne Dalziel, her

ACKNOWLEDGEMENTS

then press secretary Juli Clausen and current press secretary James Funnell; and to John Tulloch, press secretary to the elusive Minister for Foreign Affairs, Phil Goff. The New Zealand story would have been impossible to tell without the generous help of Ruth Laugesen of Auckland's *Sunday Star Times*.

In Melbourne, thanks to Eric Vadarlis and the PILCH lawyers Emma Hunt and Phil Lynch, to John Manetta and Debbie Mortimer, Julian Burnside QC, Chris Maxwell QC, Dr Gavan Griffith QC, and Kate Eastman; to David Shaw and Andrew Giles at Holding Redlich, Karen Anderson and Christine Rodan at Erskine Rodan, and Bruce Phillips, public affairs officer at the Federal Court.

In Cairns, particular thanks to Dr Peter Schuller of the Royal Flying Doctor Service and the service's PR Stephen Penberthy.

This book is also built on the work of the Senate Select Committee on a Certain Maritime Incident. We are extremely grateful to John Faulkner for all his assistance and for his incisive questioning of witnesses. He made an enormous difference to those who wanted to understand what happened during this extraordinary time. We would like to thank all the senators who sat on the committee and who worked incredibly hard to examine the issues, especially Jacinta Collins, Andrew Bartlett and Peter Cook. For his role in broadening the focus of the committee, special thanks to the deputy chair George Brandis. We were greatly assisted in writing this book by the staff of the committee, especially Brenton Holmes, Dr Sarah Bachelard and Alistair Sands.

Thanks to John Pace who provided us with crucial statements prepared for Amnesty International by asylum seekers on Manus and Nauru. For alerting us to the documents, our thanks to Kate Durham and for discussing the Afghan translations, Sharif Amin. Our thanks to Carolyn Graydon of Amnesty International Australia; Patrick Earle of the Human Rights Council of Australia; Liz Curran of the Catholic Commission for Justice, Development and Peace; Greg Conellan of Liberty Victoria; Marion Le of the Refugee Association; Janine MacDonald of HREOC; Ophelia Field of Human Rights Watch, New York; and Simon Rice of Australian Lawyers for Human Rights.

Books like this can't be written without the help of sympathetic, skilled and very patient librarians. We particularly want to thank the staff of the

Fairfax and ABC libraries in Sydney. We were also very grateful to have occasional help from the Parliamentary Library in Canberra.

We are indebted to many public servants, some of them working to answer our enquiries under strange restrictions. Our thanks particularly to the staff of AMSA, especially PRs David Gray and Ben Mitchell (especially for the time zone converter!), and to AMSA's FOI office. At the Department of Defence, thanks to Jenny McKenry, Brian Eagles, Tina Turner, Andrew Stackpool, Neil Phillips, Tim Bloomfield, Belinda Byrne, and Major Vance Khan and Dr Graeme Hammond of the SAS. From DFAT: Nicole Guihot. From the AFP: Senior AFP officials. From Customs: Leon Bennington. From DIMIA: Steve Ingram in the minister's office, the PR team in the department, and Tania Cutting. In Alexander Downer's office, his media advisers Matt Francis and Chris Kenny. From the Prime Minister's office, the unique Tony O'Leary.

We turned to a number of academic commentators for help. Particular thanks to Dr Des Ball and Dr Greg Fealy at the Australian National University; Robert Manne at La Trobe; Professor Don Rothwell of Sydney University; Professor Sam Bateman of Wollongong University; Derek Woolner of the Australian Defence Force Academy, Canberra; Dr Jean-Pierre Fonteyne at the Australian National University; John Basten (again!) of the Sydney Bar; Professor Ivan Shearer of Sydney University; Dr Michael White QC, of the Centre for Maritime Law, University of Queensland; Simon Evans of Melbourne University; John Macfarlane of the Australian Defence Studies Centre, Australian National University; Ernst Willheim, once of the Attorney General's Department but now of the Research School of Social Sciences, ANU; and Professors Hans Jacob Bull and Erik Rosaeg of Norway's Institute of Maritime Law.

Our thanks to Western Australian lawyers engaged in litigation surrounding these events. In particular to the Perth lawyers acting for the Indonesian crew on the *Palapa*: Marilyn Loveday, Hylton Quail and Graeme Pidco. And to Catherine Crawford representing the families of the SIEV 10 victims.

Public and private organisations very generously gave us information. Our thanks in particular to the Red Cross in Australia and its Secretary General Martine Letts, and public affairs officer Andrew Heslop; to Richard Danziger and Maha Bodemar of the IOM in Jakarta and Denis Nihill of the IOM in Canberra; to Franc Asis, administrator of the Maritime Law

Association of Australia and NZ; Michael Hill of Associated Marine Insurers Agents Pty Ltd; Llew Russell of the Sea Freight Council of NSW; Mark Olsen of the WA Nurses Federation; and John Carroll, Federal Master of the Company of Ships' Masters.

There is a handful of colleagues to whom we are especially grateful: Ginny Stein, Jenni Hewett, Debbie Whitmont, Craig Skehan, Andrew Clennell, Ross Coulthart, Patrick Walters, Geoff Parish, Pilita Clark, Laura Tingle, Sarah Crichton and Phil Cornford (the first to crack the story of the blocking of the *Tampa*), Tony Jones, Jenny Brockie, Fran Kelly, Jim Middleton, Peter McEvoy, Mark Jessop, Catherine McGrath, Michelle Grattan (for her company through long nights at the Senate hearings), Gabrielle Hooton (for fantastic support), Kevin Chinnery of Lloyd's List (for helping teach us the subject), Ghassam Nakhoul of SBS, Robert Wainright, Evan Williams, Mary Anne Jolley, David Weber, Jan Mayman, Peter Charlton, David Solomon, and the *Chaser* team. We spoke several times to the Norwegian television star Terje Svabo while he was writing his book, *Tampa*, the secrets of which remain locked away in Norwegian as we go to press.

An untold number of civilians gave us advice and help along the way, too many to thank. Among them are Virginia Jealous on Christmas Island; in Sydney Andrew Marr for help with the engineering, John Vallentine for navigation and John Sandeman for more excellent theological advice; in Canberra we particularly valued the help of Harold Grant, a former officer of the Department of Immigration. Also thanks to Tony Kevin: we don't go all the way but we're grateful for information, stimulation and the controversy.

Enormous thanks to the *Sydney Morning Herald*'s editor, Robert Whitehead, for letting us work together on the *Tampa* story, and then giving Marian Wilkinson extended leave to go to Norway and Indonesia for this book. David Marr extends embarrassed thanks to Peter McEvoy for carrying so much of the load at *Media Watch* while this book was being written. Champagne is not enough.

Dark Victory is dedicated to our friend John Iremonger who believed the truth was always worth telling. He commissioned this book and was working on drafts of its early chapters in hospital only days before he died. We hope we've done justice to his own hopes for the project. Of course, the book is twice as long as we promised and six months late—but John would have known to expect that. Rebecca Kaiser saw the project through. We thank her for her enthusiasm and stamina. And Bruce Donald for his stern legal advice, sharp eyes and common sense. And Lyn Tranter for taking good care of us.

From David Marr: my thanks to Nick Enright and Rae de Teliga who have been godparents to my books for many years and read the proofs of this one too—not always kindly. My greatest debt is to the man with the sharpest eyes and the patience to live with me through this, Sebastian Tesoriero.

From Marian Wilkinson: to Ray Moynihan who put up with a partner who spent far too many weekends and late nights on the phone or in front of a computer and still was kind enough to give much valued criticism on the many drafts, the debt is too great to repay, much love.

Index

SIEV = Suspect Illegal Entry Vessel

Abbas, Rami, 226, 229, 231
ABC-Radio, 203, 259, 274–5
Aborigines, 286
Aceng (boat) see SIEV 1
Adelaide (ship)
  carries asylum seekers from SIEV 4, 192, 194–5
  chronology constructed from signals of, 200, 204
  crew tell truth about children overboard, 206, 210, 253
  intercepts SIEV 4, 181, 183–5
  leaves for Gulf, 260
  party boards SIEV 4 from, 187
  required for service in Gulf, 198
  rescues passengers from SIEV 4, 190–1
  unloads survivors at Christmas Island, 205
Afghan asylum seekers
  on the SIEV 5, 216–20
  on the *Manoora*, 159–60
  meet to fête Rinnan in Auckland, 292
  in Nauru, 163–5
  in New Zealand, 165
  on the *Palapa*, 3–6
  on the SIEV 2, 147, 149
  returned to Afghanistan, 289
  returned to Indonesia, 223
  on SIEV 12, 287
  on the SIEV 10, 269–72
  on the *Tobruk*, 284
Afghan (ship), 153
Afghanistan, 281
Akbari, Wahidullah, 5–6, 163
Ali, Mohammad, 248
al-Qaeda, 144, 179, 281
Alsaker, Lars, 56–7
Alston, Richard, 253
Al-Zalimi, Ahmaed, 225, 241, 242, 245
AM (radio program), 259, 274–5
Amnesty International, 31, 110, 118, 161, 163, 168–9, 171
AMSA, 9, 63
Anders Wilhelmsen Foundation, 292
Anderson, John, 76
Andren, Peter, 98, 156
ANL, 39
Annan, Kofi, 102, 104, 107, 122, 158, 190

Annus, Susie, 275
Ansett Airlines, 153
ANZUS, 144, 197
Armitage, Peter, 138
Arnhem Bay (boat), 266–7, 269, 271, 272, 276
Arta Kencana 38 (boat), 236
Arunta (ship)
　arrives late at Ashmore Reef, 244
　ban on filming from, 66
　daily running costs, 125
　escorts SIEV 7 back to Indonesia, 247
　intercepts SIEV 6, 231
　intercepts SIEV 9, 250
　sails for Christmas Island, 65, 85, 119
　use of as towing ship hinted at, 87
Ashmore Reef
　Afghan asylum seekers run aground on, 147
　as a destination for asylum seekers, 39, 41, 42
　excised from migration zone, 140, 151
　Indonesia buzzes Australian navy at, 137
　Iraqi asylum seekers towed to, 251
　refugee arrivals at, 30, 43, 44
　Vietnamese asylum seekers taken to, 249–50
ASIO, 85–6, 281
ASIS, 67, 227
Association for Rescue at Sea, 292
Aston by-election, 286
asylum seekers
　assessment of refugee status, 288–9
　Australian intake of refugees, 44
　Australian perception of, 30, 35, 36, 37–8, 92–3, 174, 291–2
　on the boat that sank, 224–6, 227–33
　change from 'boat people' to 'illegals', 176
　forward selection of refugees, 35, 36, 44
　Howard links boat people with terrorists, 280–1
　increasing numbers of (1999–2001), 43–4
　from Indonesia, 39–44
　from Iran, 287, 289
　journalists able to interview, 164
　ONA report on tactics of, 258
　from Pakistan, 6
　temporary protection visas for, 225
　turned back by navy, 247–9
　veto on photography of, 135
　videotaping of, 123, 161, 166, 184, 223, 247
　from Vietnam, 34–7, 249–50, 284
　see also Afghan asylum seekers; Iraqi asylum seekers; *specific SIEVs*; Nauru; Operation Relex
Atkins, Dennis, 178, 280–1
Aus Ship P & I, 23
Australia. Attorney General's Department, 71
Australia. Department of Defence, 134–5
Australia. Department of Foreign Affairs and Trade, 49
Australia. Department of Immigration and Multicultural Affairs
　avoids obligations to bring survivors ashore, 113
　briefs journalists on Bedraie family, 47
　drafts warnings for asylum seekers, 131
　ethos of, 31–2
　first awareness of *Palapa*'s presence, 8
　imposes censorship over detention camps, 135–6
　intervenes in search and rescue of *Palapa*, 13
　keeps arm's distance from *Tampa* operation, 55, 81
　participates in Operation Relex, 129
　receives copy of asylum seekers' letter, 117
　receives intelligence on Abu Quassey, 227
　refuses to give Red Cross access to *Tampa*, 115
　warns *Tampa* not to enter Australian territory, 25
Australia. Department of Prime Minister and Cabinet, 8, 63, 115
Australian, 69, 98, 206, 240–1, 253, 256, 262, 272, 279
Australian Defence Force
　denies use of electric batons, 220, 248
　intelligence for Operation Relex, 227–8
　political use of, 288
　pressure between civilian public servants and, 198
　see also Operation Relex; Royal Australian Air Force; Royal Australian Navy; Special Air Service
Australian Electoral Office, 284
Australian Federal Police, 33, 40–2, 67, 126–7, 129, 236

INDEX | **335**

Australian Joint Intelligence Centre, Sydney, 227, 228, 234
Australian Labor Party
  agrees to pass border protection legislation, 155–6
  criticised for position on asylum seekers, 275
  election prospects (2001), 274
  falls in with new Operation Relex policy, 218
  loses 2001 election, 291
  policy for 2001 election, 213
  position on border control, 90–1, 93–4, 212–13
  refuses to support Border Protection Bill, 88, 152
  strategy for 1996 election, 90
  supports Howard on *Tampa*, 87, 94–5
  underestimates Howard, 93
  see also federal election (2001); Hawke government
Australian Maritime Safety Authority, 9, 63
Australian National Line, 28
Australian National Nature Reserve, 39
Australian Protective Services, 162
Australian Secret Intelligence Service, 67, 227
Australian Security Intelligence Organisation, 85–6, 281
Aziza (Afghan asylum seeker), 219

Bandar Lampung, Indonesia, 5
Bangsmoen, Hans Christian, 113
Banks, Norman, 181, 183–8, 190–2, 194–200, 205, 260–1
Barker, Jason, 191, 193, 195–6
Barratt, Paul, 132
Barrie, Chris
  asked about military options by Howard, 46
  attends meeting to discuss *Tampa* crisis, 49
  begs Reith to give sailors a break, 222–3
  in Children Overboard affair, 205–6, 208, 209, 290
  considers whether he is a dill, 291
  contradicted by Houston, 291
  deference to Howard and Reith, 132
  expresses scepticism about naval blockade, 40
  gagged over Operation Relex, 135
  in Hawaii, 253
  humiliated at press conference, 291
  informed by Reith of intention to release photographs, 201
  insists on conditions for Australian military co-operation, 198
  issues minutes on media attention, 214
  issues order for SAS to board *Tampa*, 79
  makes agreement with Reith, 219
  military career, 132
  on Operation Relex, 131, 178
  outlines military options to Howard, 66
  preoccupied with SIEV 4 survivors, 201
  preoccupied with war in Afghanistan, 197
  questioned by Moore-Wilton, 191
  receives *Tampa* MAYDAY, 76
  refuses to risk lives, 188
  retires, 293
  returns from Washington, 182
  sceptical about feasibility of Operation Relex, 129
  told by Reith not to land survivors, 194
  told by Reith of new information policy, 133–4
  warns Howard and Reith about Operation Relex, 129–30
BASARNAS
  bullied by Canberra, 12
  forbids unloading of survivors in Indonesia, 75–6
  futile call for help made to, 251
  notified by RCC of overdue boat, 237
  poor communications with, 16, 59–60
  RCC tries to pass responsibility to, 10, 13
  rings Rinnan on the *Tampa*, 20
  unrealistic expectations of, 219
Basri, Amal Hassan, 226, 229, 231
Basri, Rami Abbas, 226, 229, 231
Battle of the Pot of Jam, 119
Beaumont, Bryan, 144, 146, 153, 154
Beazley, Kim
  accuses Reith of lying, 262–3
  agrees to pass border protection legislation, 155–6
  asks Howard to waive visa conditions, 242
  attacked for xenophobic refugee policy, 262
  attends fundraiser for shipwreck survivors, 242
  becomes Labor leader, 89

casts doubt on children overboard story, 199
concedes defeat in 2001 election, 284
criticised by Howard for not supporting Bill, 143
crushed by Howard's remarks, 240
debates Howard, 211–13
during 2001 election campaign, 176–8, 186–7, 211–13, 239–43, 261–3, 274–5, 282–3, 284
on election prospects, 92
Howard offers to show ONA document to, 259
Howard questions ability of, 89–90, 173
lack of public support for, 174
likeability of, 212
position on asylum seekers, 91, 92, 274–5
refuses to support Border Protection Bill, 87–8, 95–8, 99–100
retires to backbench, 291
sees September 11 as signal for election defeat, 176–7
speaks in St Paul's Cathedral, 258
supports deployment of SAS, 95
supports Howard on *Tampa*, 94–5
supports legislation to excise territories, 141
taunts Howard for not condemning Hanson, 176
Bedraie, Shayan, 46–7
Belcher, Barbara, 179
Bendigo (ship), 243
Bennett, David, 122–3, 124, 125, 140, 145–6, 151, 155
Black, Michael, 144, 146–7, 153, 154–5
Blick, Bill, 86
Bloomfield, Tim, 195, 196, 201–2
Bonser, Mark, 228
border protection, as an election issue, 277–8, 283
Border Protection Bill, 87–8, 95–100, 106, 140, 143, 145
Borderline (Mares), 44
Bornholt, Gary, 135, 202–4, 206–7, 254, 290, 291
Bosca, John Della *see* Della Bosca, John
Bowdler, Elizabeth, 195
Brennan, Danielle, 111
Britain, naval blockade of Palestine, 106, 130
Brockie, Jenny, 264

Bryant, Jenny, 8, 256
Bulletin, 274
Bunbury (ship), 243
Bungendore, New South Wales, 252
Burmester, Henry, 86, 112
Burnside, Julian, 110–11, 118, 119, 122, 124, 125, 146–7
Bush, George W., 140, 213, 221
Byrne, Belinda, 201, 202
Byrne, Phillip, 233

Cabal, Carlos, 110–11
Cameron, Rod, 175
Campbell, Bill, 86
Canada, 177, 289
Castles, Shane, 223
censorship, of information, 133–6, 195, 209, 214–15
Chaney, Fred, 262
Chifley, Ben, 90
Children Overboard affair, 184–7, 189–90, 195–210, 252–61, 263–5
China, 221–2
Chinese immigrants, 35, 38
Chinese Literary Association, 81
Christmas Island
 Adelaide unloads survivors at, 205
 army arrives in, 80
 considered as destination for SIEV 4, 188–9, 194
 excised from migration zone, 140, 151
 increasing refugee arrivals at, 43
 processing of asylum seekers on, 80
 refugee arrivals at, 30, 47
 Tampa changes course for, 22–3
 Tampa enters Australian waters off, 78–80
 Warramunga unloads survivors at, 247
Christmas Island Women's Association, 81
Chubb Protection Services, 162
City Recital Hall, Sydney, 244–5
Clark, Helen, 104, 107, 108, 109, 164
Clarke, John, 261
Clarke, Phil, 249
Clennell, Andrew, 52–3
Coast Guard (US), 292
Coastwatch
 alerted to SIEV X's departure, 234
 communication with police in Java, 226
 confirms presence of SIEV 1, 137
 Heron calls for assistance from, 269
 learns boat is overdue, 236

notified of *Palapa*'s presence, 8
participates in Operation Relex, 129
reports *Palapa*'s presence to Canberra, 9
tells *Tampa* to await further instructions, 49
Cocos Islands, 151, 188
compass, 162
Cornall, Robert, 86
Cosgrove, Peter, 264
Costello, Michael, 87, 177, 262
Costello, Peter, 76, 288
Costello, Tim, 262
Coulthart, Ross, 42
Courier-Mail, 272
Court, Richard, 45, 46
Crosby, Lynton, 174, 277–8
Curtin detention camp, 44
Cyprus, 106

Daily Telegraph, 275
Dalziel, Lianne, 108
Darwin, 34, 36–7
Davidson, Clive, 10, 20–2, 54, 60, 72, 237
Dawood, Haithem, 249
de Mello, Sergio Vieira, 102, 103, 104
Defence Signals Directorate, 85–6, 103, 109, 113, 117–18
Della Bosca, John, 93
Democrats, 98–9, 143, 199
Denmark, 289
detention camps
    Australia, 35, 44, 46–7
    Beazley's view of, 92
    censorship of information about, 135–6
    Nauru, 150, 162–5, 288, 289
    New Zealand, 107–8, 109, 164
    Papua New Guinea, 178–80, 222, 288, 289
Dexter, Peter, 28–9, 69, 77, 85
Dietz, Walter, 62–3
DIMA *see* Australia. Department of Immigration and Multicultural Affairs
Disun, Bastian, 5, 7
Dixon, Leigh, 33, 34, 40
dog whistle politics, 280
Dowiyogo, Jesaulenko, 221
Downer, Alexander
    asks East Timor to take asylum seekers, 102, 103
    asks New Zealand to take asylum seekers, 104
    calls Nauru prime minister, 105
    contacted by Norwegian Foreign Ministry, 115
    demands Norway takes *Tampa*, 76
    drops hints that *Tampa* will be towed out to sea, 87
    fails to persuade Indonesia to take refugees, 55–6, 64–5
    receives copy of asylum seekers' letter, 117
    receives *Tampa* MAYDAY, 76
    refuses to answer questions on ASIS, 67–8
    rings Norwegian Foreign Minister, 73
    sees no terrorist threat in Australia, 281
    talks of 'illegals' on television, 110
    threatens to tow *Tampa* out to sea, 84–5
    visits Jakarta after *Tampa* confrontation, 136–7
Doyle, Peter, 185
Duff, Craig, 270–1
Dunn, Major, 163–4
Dutton, Peter, 178

East Timor, 40, 102, 132
Edwards, Katrina, 185, 198, 200, 204
Effendi, Arizal, 64–5
Election Chaser (television program), 245, 284–5
Enniss, Kevin John, 41–2, 45, 67, 137
Entalina (ship), 36
Entsch, Warren, 167
Erskine Rodan, 117
Europe, border protection in, 289–90

Faizan (asylum seeker), 248
Fajgenbaum, Jack, 117, 156
Farmer, Bill, 67, 81, 123–4, 185–6, 189, 263–4
Fatama (pregnant Afghan woman), 216
Faulkner, John, 177, 291
Federal Court of Australia, 118–19, 122–6, 142, 144–7
federal election (2001), 175–8, 211–15, 239–43, 245–6, 273–8, 282–6
Fife, Rolf, 58
Fiji, 221
Flying Fish Cove, Christmas Island, 79–80, 84, 112–13
Fonteyne, Jean-Pierre, 141
Fosaas, Marianne, 78
Four Corners (television program), 46–7, 216, 243, 244, 248
Fraser, Malcolm, 262, 279

French Polynesia, 150
French, Robert, 144, 146, 153–4, 155

Gard, 23, 69
Gard News, 69
Gawler (ship), 147
Gelbard, Bob, 144
Georgiou, Petro, 152
Gerrits, Wade, 199
Gibbons, Wayne, 35
Gilmore, Gus, 114
Giuliani, Mayor, 292
Godwin, Philippa, 26, 50, 69, 185
Grant, Bruce, 34
Greenlees, Don, 240
Greens, 45, 98, 199
Gregg, Simon, 149, 218, 219, 246
Griffith, Gavan, 117, 119, 124, 146–7, 155, 156
GST, 177
Guantanamo Bay, Cuba, 106, 141

Haiti, 106, 130
Halton, Jane
  appointed secretary of Health Department, 290
  attends Press Club conference, 259
  attuned to ethos of border protection regime, 40
  awarded Public Service Medal, 290
  in Children Overboard affair, 189, 198, 199, 204–5, 263, 290
  claims not to recall receiving *Adelaide* chronology, 204
  as convener of People Smuggling Taskforce, 54, 65, 151, 162–3, 183, 185, 188, 215, 247
  co-ordinates taskforce for SIEV 4 interception, 182
  directs airlift to Nauru, 162
  discusses prospect of legal proceedings, 103
  hears of misrepresentation of photos, 256–7
  informed of photo release by Reith, 204
  learns of shipwreck, 237
  meets ASIS officials, 67
  meets resistance from bureaucrats, 217
  Moore-Wilton interrupts holiday of, 25–6
  offers UNHCR briefing on Pacific Solution, 121–2
  participates in administration of Operation Relex, 133
  personal style, 40
  persuades Reith to use negotiators, 167
  prepares brief for Howard, 240
  receives news of sunken boat, 223
  receives Shackleton's clarification, 264
  receives update from Silverstone, 186
  shows border protection legislation to Beazley, 155
Hamid (Afghan refugee), 2, 4, 11
Hamid, Ali, 238
Hammer, Brendon, 207
Hammond, Graeme, 68–9, 72–3, 75, 79, 83–4, 127
Hampton, Ross
  asks Bloomfield to email photographs, 201–3
  asks to see navy photographs, 195–6
  attempts to thwart scrutiny of Operation Relex, 136
  briefs press gallery on children overboard, 189
  called by Howard's press secretary, 199
  in Children Overboard affair, 201, 290
  denies receiving call from Bornholt, 204
  forbids taking of humane photographs, 135
  ignores enquiries from journalists, 209
  issues press release on Operation Relex, 139
  military required to clear media releases through, 134
  political power of, 136
  rejects Humphrey's plan, 135
  sent photographs with original captions, 207
Hanson, Pauline, 45, 91, 176, 283, 285, 289
Harapanindah (boat) *see* SIEV 5
Harris, Rene, 105, 162, 166, 167, 289
Haukeland Hospital, Bergen, 59, 68
Hawke, Allan, 133–4, 206, 263–4, 290
Hawke, Andrew, 251
Hawke, Bob, 90, 91, 177
Hawke government, 37, 90–1
Heffernan, Bill, 245
Hendy, Peter, 255, 263, 290
Herald Sun, 100, 189, 206
Heron, Wesley, 249, 266–9, 270
Hewson, John, 262, 279–80
Hill, Dave, 107, 108
Hillier, Jason, 267
Hinch, Derryn, 151
Hogarth, Gregory, 267

INDEX | 339

Holding Redlich, 111
Holloway Beach, Queensland, 38
Holt, Harold, 212
Hosai, Mr (IOM representative), 164
Hossaini, Rajab Ali, 2, 8, 12
Houssein, Karim Jaber, 238
Houston, Angus
  asks for review of information on children overboard, 256
  attends service at St Paul's Cathedral, 258
  contradicts Barrie's statements, 291
  denies use of electric batons by armed forces, 170, 220, 248
  not consulted in investigation, 290
  rings Reith to correct misrepresentation of photos, 253–5, 263
  succeeded by Cosgrove as Chief of Defence, 264
Howard government
  asks about feasibility of towing boat to Cocos, 188
  attacks judiciary, 32
  attempts to bypass judicial review, 91
  authorises ASIS disruption of people smugglers, 67
  authorises unlawful phone taps, 85–6, 113, 117–18
  censors information about Operation Relex, 133–4
  commits troops to Afghanistan, 179, 213
  conducts perfunctory investigation, 290–1
  creates Pacific Solution, 104
  criticises New Zealand government, 104
  cuts contribution to UN High Commission for Refugees, 289
  demolishes One Nation, 283
  does deal with Nauru, 108–9
  does deal with Papua New Guinea, 159, 179–80
  encourages perception of highjacking, 23
  gags officials on Christmas Island, 80
  ignores traditional maritime obligations, 27–8, 73
  informed of misrepresentation in photographs, 207
  lack of legal authorisation to repel boat people, 139–40
  moves to tighten definition of refugee status, 152
  overcomes last obstacle to policy, 156
  in panic about influx of boat people, 30
  places ban on comments by public officials, 65–6
  places embargo on news from Operation Relex, 214–15
  politicises *Tampa* rescue, 28
  rebuffed by United Nations, 103, 104–5
  re-elected at 2001 election, 275–6
  refuses Red Cross access to *Tampa*, 115
  rejects UNHCR solution, 109
  removes Christmas Island and Ashmore Reef from migration zone, 140
  seeks islands for Pacific Solution, 150–1
  supports decision to make *pro bono* lawyers pay, 155
  threatens to tow *Tampa* out to sea, 84–5
  undeterred by imprisonment without trial, 163
  world perception of attitude to refugees of, 141
Howard, Janette, 286
Howard, John
  agrees to inquire into children overboard evidence, 200–1
  alienates Indonesia in press conference, 55
  allows Norwegian ambassador to visit *Tampa*, 115
  announces November election, 173
  announces Operation Relex, 120–1
  announces Pacific Solution, 120–2
  announces plan to speak to Megawati, 65
  announces return of boat from Indonesia, 221
  announces role of *Manoora*, 124
  appears on talkback radio, 100–1, 273–4
  appoints Halton secretary of Health Department, 290
  appoints Moore-Wilton, 38
  approval rating in opinion polls, 174
  asks Barrie about military options, 46
  assures public about Operation Relex, 132
  on asylum seekers' refusal to disembark, 167
  attacked for xenophobic refugee policy, 262
  attacks Beazley for refusing to support Bill, 94, 101
  attempts to use military solution to civil problem, 228

attends ceremonial farewell for soldiers, 258–9
on Australia's share of refugees, 289
backs Reith's use of photographs, 206
boasts of Operation Relex's success, 249
capitalises on *Tampa* in election campaign, 93
champions naval blockade of Indian Ocean, 66
in children overboard affair, 186–7, 189–90, 199, 209, 256–60, 264–5, 290
claims boat sinks in Indonesian waters, 240
co-directs Operation Relex, 133
comes through Pacific Solution unscathed, 291–2
commends Reith at press conference, 260
concerned over re-election prospects, 45–6
conducts first press conference on *Tampa*, 50–1, 52–3
congratulates Ruddock, 245
criticises Beazley's refusal to support Bill, 143
debates Beazley, 211–13
decides where SIEV 4 to be towed, 188
defends Reith in Children Overboard affair, 264–5
dismisses critics as grudge-bearers, 279–80
drops hints that *Tampa* will be towed out to sea, 87
during 2001 election campaign, 173–4, 186–7, 198, 211–13, 239–40, 245–6, 257–60, 273–4, 278, 282, 283–6, 287
on efforts to procure a helicopter, 80
endorsed by newspaper editorials, 272–3
farewells Moore-Wilton, 293
farewells Peter Reith, 172
flies to Washington, 140
fudges medical situation on *Tampa*, 70, 84
fudges situation on *Manoora*, 158
hectors Indonesians on radio, 64
informs joint party meeting of Border Protection Bill, 95–6
insists that *Tampa* not Australia's problem, 51
on the interception of SIEV 10, 273–4
issues new orders for Operation Relex, 217

knowledge of *Tampa* operation, 25
learns of *Tampa*'s entry into Australian waters, 78–9
links boat people with terrorists, 198, 280–1
loses temper at interviews, 264–5
makes political use of Border Protection Bill, 96, 98, 99–100
meets with Morauta in Shanghai, 222
misrepresents position of Kofi Annan, 122
misrepresents reaction of asylum seekers, 123
on Operation Relex, 278–9
organises drafting of law to avoid scrutiny of courts, 86–7
pledges military support for US, 144, 197
policy on Aborigines, 286
on political correctness, 176
as a politician, 50–1
prepares to speak to National Press Club, 255–6
queried about plans for medical assistance, 63–4
questions ability of Beazley, 89–90
on racism in Australia, 279
reacts to Federal Court decision, 142–3
receives Shackleton's clarification, 264
on the refugee problem, 47
refuses to waive visa conditions, 241–2
regains fighting position in election campaign, 93
relationship with Moore-Wilton, 39
releases report from navy, 273
releases *Adelaide* videotape, 259–60
reports on *Tampa* to parliament, 82, 83–4
ridicules claims of health crisis on *Tampa*, 84
rings Kofi Annan, 107
rings Norwegian Prime Minister, 76, 77–8
Ruddock votes against, 31
sent Children Overboard report by Halton, 199
shows Beazley Border Protection Bill, 88, 95
stalls for time regarding SIEV 4 survivors, 198
success with Nauru operation, 171
suggests Indonesian detention camp, 137

suggests Norway supports Pacific Solution, 121
suggests shipping line deceiving government, 70
support for Operation Relex, 217
tables Border Protection Bill, 97–8
thanks Dexter for respite, 77
threatens to blame lawyers for plight of asylum seekers, 122
travels to China during election campaign, 221–2
use of dog whistle politics, 280
vision as prime minister, 212
visits Indonesia, 46
warned of dangers of Operation Relex, 129
whisked away by Secret Service, 143
willingness to use race as an election issue, 175–6
wins 2001 election, 285–6
works to placate electorate over GST, 177
Howard, Melanie, 282
Howard, Richard, 282
Human Rights and Equal Opportunities Commission, 44, 118
Human Rights Watch, 220, 244, 248
Humphreys, Brian, 134–5
Humphries, Greg, 36
Hunt, Emma, 111, 113, 114
Hussein, Musa, 269
Hussein, Samira, 269
Hussein, Thamer, 249
Husseini, Fatima, 269, 270–1, 276, 284
Husseini, Nurjan, 269–70, 276, 284
Husseini, Sayyed Shahi, 269, 276

Ibramam, Emaan, 224, 230
Ibramam, Fatima, 224, 230
Ibramam, Sundous, 224, 230, 234, 237, 245
Ibramam, Zahra, 224, 230
Indah Jayah Makmur (boat), 235–6
Indonesia
    attempts to disrupt people smuggling, 41
    grows hostile to Australian operations in, 44–5
    hectored by Howard on radio, 64
    participates in meeting on people smuggling, 282
    rebuffs plan for detention centre, 46
    refuses to take *Tampa* survivors, 56, 74, 75–6

Ruddock claims *Tampa* responsibility of, 52
visit by Downer to discuss boat people, 136–7
visit by Reith to discuss boat people, 136–7
visits by Ruddock to discuss boat people, 30–1, 33–4, 136–7
see also BASARNAS
Indonesian National Police, 33, 40–2, 67, 137
Insight (television programme), 264
Intelligence Services Act, 86
International Office for Migration, 120, 159, 166, 171, 237
IOM, 120, 159, 166, 171, 237
Iranian asylum seekers, 287, 289
Iraqi asylum seekers
    in Australia, 289
    on the *Manoora*, 160–2
    in Nauru, 166–71, 289
    in New Zealand, 289
    in Papua New Guinea, 289
    on SIEV 1, 138
    on SIEV 3, 147–9
    on SIEV 4, 181–5, 187, 190–1
    on SIEV 7, 243–4
    on SIEV 9, 250–1
    on SIEV 12, 287
    on SIEV X, 225, 229
    on the *Tobruk*, 284
Islamic Council, 81
Iyengar, Ramesh, 22–3

Jackson, Steve, 126–7
Jagland, Thorbjoern, 73–4, 76, 82, 83–4
Jemaah Islamiah, 281
Jessen-Petersen, Soren, 104, 106, 107, 109
Jessop, Mark, 143
Jones, Alan, 100, 178, 189
Jones, Kim, 258
Jones, Tony, 241, 264–5
Jordana, Miles, 54, 182, 183, 188, 256, 257–8
judiciary, attacks on, 32, 91, 119, 145

Kanimbla (ship), 260
Kanton, 150
Keating, Paul, 177, 212
Keelty, Mick, 33, 42, 67
Kein Giang (boat), 34, 35
Kelly, Fran, 259
Kelly, Jim, 151

Kempsey, New South Wales, 38
Kernot, Cheryl, 178
Kerr, Duncan, 177, 243
Khan, Vince, 82–3, 120, 123, 126, 127, 159, 161
Khodadad Sarwari, 1–3, 5, 7, 11, 20, 22, 60
King, Chief Petty Officer, 138
King, Stefan, 207
Kiribati, 150, 221
Krakatau Islands, 229
Kupang, Indonesia, 41

Lalatute, Evoa, 179, 222
Lam Binh, 34
Lapuz, Noel, 58–9
Lateline (television programme), 84, 241, 264
Law of the Sea *see* United Nations, Convention for the Law of the Sea
Laws, John, 273
Leader, Malcolm, 57
Lebanese Muslim Association, 244–5
Lehane, John, 153
Liberal Party, election strategy (2001), 277–8
Liberty Victoria, 118, 125, 145, 152, 155, 156
Licciardello, Chas, 245
Lindstrøm, Bjarne, 57
Lloyds of London, 292
Longva, Hans Wilhellm, 56–7, 58, 76–7, 115
Lynch, Phil, 111

Mackay, Hugh, 92, 176
Macphee, Ian, 31, 262
Malaysia, 36
Maltau, Christian
  asks Hammond for medical report, 127
  assumes Hammond civilian doctor, 72
  on Australia's failure to provide assistance, 60
  boards *Palapa* during rescue, 18
  challenges Hammond, 83
  in command of survivors on *Tampa*, 19
  conversation with Dietz, 62–3
  conversation with Schuller, 71
  counts asylum seekers during transfer, 126
  notes survivors happy to see Christmas Island, 29
  realises soldiers on way to *Tampa*, 81

  responsible for health of survivors, 48, 50, 59, 68
  talks with delegation from survivors, 20
Maltau, Jan Martin, 68
mandatory detention, 37, 43, 91
Manetta, John, 110–11, 118
Mangere detention centre, 107–8, 109, 164
Manoora (ship)
  appears in minutes of taskforce, 104
  arrives in Nauru, 157, 164
  asylum seekers deceived into boarding, 160
  conditions for asylum seekers on, 158–61, 163–4
  en route to Nauru, 139, 149, 153, 159
  forced removal of asylum seekers' from, 166–71, 214
  rendezvous with *Warramunga*, 160
  transfer of asylum seekers to, 124, 125, 126
  violence breaks out on, 169
Manus Island detention centre, 179–80, 222, 288, 289
Mares, Peter, 44
Martin, Ray, 213
Mauritius, 106
Maxwell, Chris, 118
McGrath, Catherine, 259, 274–5
McKenry, Jenny, 135, 206–7, 259, 261, 263–4
McLaughlin, James, 267–8
McMillan, Hec, 36
McPhedran, Ian, 134
media, 214–15, 253, 272–3
Meet the Press (television program), 183
Megawati Sukarnoputri, 46, 55, 74, 137, 221, 281
Menhinick, Richard, 138, 139, 148–9, 223, 246
Merak, 24
Merzaee, Rajab Ali, 2, 3, 6, 12, 50
Metcalfe, Andrew, 26, 27, 185
Migration Act 1958, 54–5, 65, 78, 81, 118, 124, 145–6, 154
Mirnawaty (boat) *see* SIEV 7
Mitchell, Neil, 47
Mooney, Linden, 270–1
Moore, John, 132, 133
Moore-Wilton, Max
  assembles coastal surveillance taskforce, 39
  attends NSC meeting with Howard, 66

INDEX | **343**

on Australia's Westminster system, 284
becomes CEO of Sydney Airport, 293
celebrates election victory with Howard, 286
claims military at fault with children overboard advice, 290
demands answers from taskforce, 151
directs plan to divert *Tampa* from Australia, 25–6, 28–9, 53
discusses policy for SIEV 4 asylum seekers, 188
as head of Department of Prime Minister and Cabinet, 8
low profile of, 215
meets with Morauta in Shanghai, 222
negotiates deal with Papua New Guinea, 178–9, 180
nominates Halton for Public Service Medal, 290
organises meeting to discuss *Tampa* crisis, 49
oversees purging of public service, 38–9
personal characteristics, 39
proposes removing boat from Ashmore Reef, 40
receives Shackleton's clarification, 264
receives *Tampa* MAYDAY, 76
relationship with Howard, 39
rung by Halton re SIEV 4, 182
snarls at comedian, 285
succeeds in mounting Operation Relex, 129
suggests naval blockade of boats, 40, 46, 183, 217
tries to shore up government position, 263
unhappy about rescue of SIEV 4, 191
Morauta, Sir Mekere, 159, 221, 222, 289
Morrison, Bob, 161
Mortimer, Debbie, 117
Moylan, Judy, 98
Mulcahy, Bradley, 266, 270
Mulya Jaya (boat) *see* SIEV 6
Murdoch, Simon, 104
Murphy, Lionel, 31–2

National Press Club, 255
National Security Committee, 46, 65, 133
National Surveillance Centre, 8
Nauru
   Afghans and Iraqis taken to, 284

   agrees to take asylum seekers, 105–6, 108–9, 150
   asylum seekers granted special visas, 163
   Australia wants UN aid for, 107
   blocks entry to lawyers, 163
   considered as destination for asylum seekers, 104
   detention camps, 150, 162–5, 288, 289
   legality of detaining asylum seekers on, 162–3
   transfer of asylum seekers to, 166–71, 247
   UNHCR obliged to carry out processing on, 121
Navigation Act, 131
Neill, James
   assembles legal team in Sydney, 85
   confers with Rinnan, 23–4
   DSD intercepts communications of, 103
   flies to Christmas Island, 114
   on implications of *Tampa* entering Australian waters, 28
   on law versus maritime convention, 27
   negotiates deal with Federal Police, 126–7
   outlines conditions for *Tampa*'s departure, 69
   regrets lack of consultation with Rinnan, 29
   requests to be taken to *Tampa*, 114, 115
   rings Godwin with medical assessment, 50
New Guinea, 104
New Zealand
   Afghan asylum seekers arrive in, 164
   Afghans fête Rinnan in Auckland, 293
   agrees to take *Tampa* asylum seekers, 107–8, 109, 121
   bears brunt of Pacific Solution, 289
   declines to take asylum seekers from SIEV 1, 150
New Zealand Immigration Service, 159
Newcastle (ship), 138
Nixon, Neville, 23–5, 26, 27, 28, 48
Nolte, Kai, 18
non-refoulement, principle of, 113
Nordheim, Frank, 70
North, Tony, 118–19, 122–4, 140, 142–3, 145, 158
Norway
   change of government, 289
   concerned over possible act of piracy, 85

demands Australia assists *Tampa*, 71
impracticality of transporting asylum
  seekers to, 52
protests to Australia, 58
reaction to *Tampa* crisis, 56–8
refuses to support Pacific Solution, 121
Norway. Royal Ministry of Foreign Affairs,
  56, 70
Norway. Royal Ministry of Trade, 292
Norwegian Maritime Directorate, 70
Nutt, Tony, 257

Oakes, Laurie, 280, 291
O'Brien, Natalie, 253
O'Donnell, Don, 79
Office of National Assessment, 39, 258
O'Leary, Tony, 199, 202, 257, 264
Olong (boat) *see* SIEV 4
One Nation, 45, 46, 91, 93, 280, 283, 289
Operation Cranberry, 131
Operation Enduring Freedom, 197, 213
Operation Relex
  attacked by Peek, 278
  as the brainchild of Moore-Wilton, 129
  capsize and sinking of SIEV X, 227–33,
    282, 288
  censorship of information about, 133–4,
    135, 195, 209, 214–15
  cost of, 288
  deflects SIEV 1, 137–9
  discussed by Howard at press
    conference, 120–1
  examined by Select Committee, 291
  failure of, 215–16
  government prepares legislation to
    underpin, 151
  intelligence for, 227–8
  interception of SIEV 2, 147, 149
  interception of SIEV 3, 147–9
  interception of SIEV 4, 181–5, 187,
    190–1, 200–2
  interception of SIEV 5, 216–20
  interception of SIEV 6, 223, 231, 244,
    246
  interception of SIEV 7, 243, 244, 247–9
  interception of SIEV 8, 250–1
  interception of SIEV 9, 250–1
  interception of SIEV 10, 266–9
  interception of SIEV 11 and SIEV 12,
    287
  launch of, 129–32

military perception of during election,
  214
military regrets over reporting
  arrangements, 208–9
navy warns of dangers of, 129–30
NSC orders plan for, 66
perception of boat's failure to arrive, 236
political control of, 132–3
political implications of, 157
pressure on senior Defence leadership,
  198
role of Halton in, 133
takes more aggressive stance, 217–18
as a top priority for Howard, 144
unpopularity of with navy, 178
use of Transit Security Element units,
  161
  see also Tampa (ship)
Operation Trump, 66
opinion polls
  on asylum seekers, 100, 241, 292
  federal election campaign (2001), 274
  Howard's approval rating after *Tampa*,
    174

Pace, John, 111
Pacific Solution
  Annan not interested in, 107
  architects of wait for Federal Court
    decision, 119
  budget for, 160, 162, 167, 288
  circumvention of courts via, 106
  critics of, 279–80
  examined by Select Committee, 291
  Howard misrepresents view of Annan
    on, 122
  journalists barely interested in, 120
  Labor offers no opposition to, 171
  New Zealand agrees to participate in,
    108–9
  New Zealand bears brunt of, 289
  Norway objects to, 121
  Papua New Guinea joins, 205, 222
  political implications of, 157
  portrayal of by Bennett in court, 150
  Reith negotiates with Harris, 105
  shocks UNHCR, 106–7
  vain efforts to find new locations for,
    221–2
  see also Nauru
Page, Sir Earle, 262
Pakistani asylum seekers, 6

INDEX | 345

Palapa (ship)
  appalling conditions on, 18
  composition of passengers, 6, 19
  detected by Surveillance Australia, 8, 9, 12
  embarks from Indonesia, 3–5
  Indonesian crew arrested, 127
  rescued by the *Tampa*, 1–3, 17–20
  stranded when engine fails, 7
  voyage from Indonesia, 5–8, 11–12
Palau, 150
Palestine, 106, 130
Pantau, Indonesia, 4
Papua New Guinea
  approached by Howard government, 151
  asks favour of Australia, 221
  Australia desires detention camp in, 159
  change of government in, 289
  decides not to take asylum seekers, 161–2
  detention camps in, 178–80, 222, 288, 289
  as part of the Pacific Solution, 205, 222
Parliament House, Canberra, 172
Patrick Stevedores, 119
Peek, Sir Richard, 278
Penfold, Hilary, 87
Pentrose, Jeff, 282
People Smuggling Group, 33
People Smuggling Taskforce, 54, 65, 103–4, 112–13, 133, 205, 215
Philp, Matthew, 267, 268
PILCH, 111, 113–14, 118, 125
Playfair, David, 15
political correctness, 176
Port Hedland detention camp, 44, 135
Potts, Michael, 179
Powell, Colin, 151
Pratt, Kylie, 234–5
Prentice, Jonathan, 104
President Warfield (ship), 130
Progressive Conservative Party, Canada, 177
Public Affairs and Communications Office, 136
Public Interest Law Clearing House, 111, 113–14, 118, 125
public service, 38–9, 53–4
Pundari, John, 222
'pushing off', 34, 36

Quassey, Abu, 225–7, 229, 234, 237–8, 288

race, as an election issue, 175–6, 242, 262, 279, 280, 285
Radio 2GB, 249
Ramsay, David, 12
Ratna Mujia see SIEV 2
RCC *see* Rescue Coordination Centre Australia
Red Cross, 110, 115
Refugee Convention, United Nations, 37, 106–7, 112, 121, 221
refugees *see* asylum seekers
Reith, Peter
  appears on *Meet the Press*, 185
  on asylum seekers' refusal to disembark, 166, 167
  attends national prayers, 260
  attends South Pacific Forum, 105
  avoids farewell to *Adelaide*, 260
  Barrie complains to re Moore-Wilton, 191
  becomes defence consultant, 290
  becomes Defence Minister, 132
  begged by Barrie to give sailors a break, 222–3
  brawling skills, 172–3
  briefed by Titheridge, 182–3
  censors information about Operation Relex, 133–4, 135
  in Children Overboard affair, 201, 202–4, 207–8, 254–5, 257, 265, 290–1
  co-directs Operation Relex, 133
  contradicted by Houston, 291
  demands clarifying statement from Shackleton, 263, 264
  demands to see photographs of SIEV 4 rescue, 195
  denies use of force to remove asylum seekers, 168–9
  exonerated in government inquiries, 290
  Howard claims to rely on advice from, 259
  ignores own protocol, 290
  informs Barrie of intention to release photographs, 201
  leaves parliament, 172
  negotiates with Rene Harris, 150, 167
  prepared to use naval blockade of refugees, 46
  rebuked by Beazley over videotape, 262
  receives briefs of Operation Relex, 219
  receives news of burning boat, 272
  receives *Tampa* MAYDAY, 76

refuses to release videotape from
  Adelaide, 209, 253, 255
signs deal with Nauru, 162
stalls for time regarding SIEV 4
  survivors, 198
suggests moving *Tampa* survivors to
  Nauru, 105
suggests terrorists among asylum
  seekers, 151, 213–14
support for Operation Relex, 217
tells Barrie not to land survivors, 194
visits Jakarta after *Tampa* confrontation,
  136–7
warned of dangers of Operation Relex,
  129
Rescue Coordination Centre Australia
  alerted to *Palapa*'s presence, 9
  contact with Flying Doctor Service, 68–9
  contact with Philippa Godwin, 26
  during disappearance of Abu Quassey
    boat, 236–7
  ignores fax from Dr Schuller, 72
  ignores PAN PAN broadcast by Rinnan, 71
  informs *Tampa* that Indonesia is rescue
    co-ordinator, 16
  monitors *Tampa* after rescue, 20–1, 22
  passes Schuller onto Prime Minister's
    Department, 72
  questions Rinnan's judgement, 75
  seeks helicopter to assist *Tampa*, 59
  tries to contact BASARNAS, 10
  tries to pressure Indonesia into taking
    action, 13
  warns Rinnan not to enter Australian
    waters, 78
Reza, Ali, 269–70, 271
Rezaee, Assadullah, 3–4, 11, 60, 81–2, 160
Richardson, Dennis, 281
Rinnan, Arne
  allays fears regarding hijack, 24
  asks for medical assistance for survivors,
    59
  background, 14–15
  on berthing at Christmas Island, 70
  Black's view of predicament of, 153–4
  broadcasts PAN PAN, 71
  changes course for Christmas Island,
    22–3, 28–9
  contacted by PILCH, 111–12
  contradicts Howard, 102–3
  declines offer of help from PILCH, 114
  defended by Norwegian Foreign
    Minister, 73–4
  farewelled from Christmas Island, 127–8
  fêted by Afghans in Auckland, 293
  informs Dr Hammond of situation, 72–3
  informs press of situation, 69–70
  issues MAYDAY, 75–6
  judgement questioned, 75–7
  leaves *Tampa* outside territorial waters,
    29, 48–9
  makes last voyage in *Tampa*, 292–3
  meets delegation from survivors, 20, 21
  meets Norwegian ambassador on *Tampa*,
    115
  meets SAS commander, 82
  moves *Tampa* into Australian waters,
    78–9
  Norway's Foreign Ministry checks
    trustworthiness of, 58
  offered free legal assistance, 112
  pestered by Vadarlis, 117
  presented with map by SAS, 127
  receives backing of Christmas Island
    locals, 81
  receives numerous honours, 292
  reconsiders changing course to Merak,
    26–7
  refused permission to land at Christmas
    Island, 49
  refuses to divert from Christmas Island,
    27, 47
  refuses to leave Australian waters, 82–3,
    84
  in rescue of *Palapa*, 17–20, 154
  responds to MAYDAY for *Palapa*, 14, 16
  rings Neill for assistance, 23, 24
  sets course for Merak after rescue, 20
  talks with Dr Schuller, 71–2
  threatened by DIMA official, 25, 26, 39
  threatened by Rescue Coordination
    Centre, 78
  told to sail for Merak, 56, 59
  worries over survivors' suicide threats,
    78
Riordans (law firm), 117
Ritchie, Chris
  in Children Overboard affair, 200, 201,
    205–6, 208–9
  gagged over Operation Relex, 135
  ordered to prepare plan for Operation
    Relex, 66

INDEX | 347

orders feasibility report for government, 188
Prime Minister's office demands answers from, 195
second-in-command of Operation Relex, 132132
Silverstone reports conversation with Reith to, 255
Smith ordered to report SIEV events to, 133
supports Smith in call for operational safety, 131
Ronnevig, Per, 85
Roti Island, 41, 42, 248–9, 287
Royal Australian Air Force, 231–3
Royal Australian Navy, 217, 259, 272, 279
see also names of specific ships; Operation Relex
Royal Flying Doctor Service, 62, 84
Ruddock, Philip
adds Aboriginal affairs to portfolio, 290
apocalyptic vision of Australia, 33
applause for at campaign opening, 245
asks Federal policeman about pirates, 33
asks RCC to monitor *Tampa*, 20–1
attends NSC meeting with Howard, 66
attends *Tampa* press conference with Howard, 50–1
in Children Overboard affair, 186, 199
claims Europe following Australia's example, 289–90
criticises courts, 32, 152
criticises UNHCR solution, 107
endorses DIMA warnings to *Tampa*, 25
gazettes changes to *Migration Act*, 55
Howard claims to rely on advice from, 259
Ian Macphee on, 31
nicknamed 'Minister with No Ears', 31, 137
on occupation levels of detention centres, 8
personal characteristics, 31, 32
prevaricates over fate of Afghan asylum seekers, 216–17
proposes more vigorous initiatives against refugees, 46
raises possibility of tampering with boats, 33–4
receives *Tampa* MAYDAY, 76
ridicules claims of health crisis on *Tampa*, 84

sent Children Overboard report by Halton, 199
shows border protection legislation to Beazley, 155
support for Operation Relex, 217
visits Jakarta after *Tampa* confrontation, 136–7
visits Jakarta before *Tampa* confrontation, 30–1, 33–4, 44–5
warns of dangers facing boat people, 43

Saatchi and Saatchi, 177
Saddam Hussein, 225, 289
Safety of Life at Sea Convention, 121, 130–1, 217
Salteri, Paul, 290
SAS *see* Special Air Service
Satta, Alya, 230
Satta, Kawthar, 230
Satta, Roukayya, 230
Savoy Tavern, 167
Schuller, Peter, 62–3, 68–9, 70, 71–2
Scotts Head, New South Wales, 38
Scrafton, Mike, 201, 204, 206, 207, 257, 290
Seafarers and International House, 292
Seamen's Church, 292
search and rescue agencies, 10
Secretaries Committee on National Security, 217
Select Committee On a Certain Maritime Incident, 291
Senate Estimates Committee, 291
September 11 attack, 143, 197, 283
The Settlement, Christmas Island, 79, 80
7.30 Report (television program), 205, 259
Shackleton, David, 205, 206, 260–1, 262–5, 274, 290
Shanghai, China, 221–2
Shipowners' Association, Norway, 292
shipwreck survivors, 36–7
Sidhu, Harinder, 207, 256
SIEV 1 (*Aceng*), 137–9, 140, 147, 149, 160
SIEV 2 (*Ratna Mujia*), 147, 149
SIEV 3 (*Sumber Bahagia*), 147–9
SIEV 4 (*Olong*), 181–5, 187, 190–1, 200–2
SIEV 5 (*Harapinindah*), 216–20
SIEV 6 (*Mulya Jaya*), 223, 231, 244, 246
SIEV 7 (*Mirnawaty*), 243, 244, 247–9
SIEV 8, 250–1
SIEV 9 (*Sinar Bontano III*), 250–1
SIEV 10 (*Sumber Lestari*), 266–9, 271, 276

SIEV 11, 287
SIEV 12, 287
SIEV X, 227–33, 282, 288
Silverstone, Mike
  Banks apologises to, 199
  calls Banks in middle of rescue operation, 184–5
  gagged over Operation Relex, 135
  investigates children overboard reports, 196, 197, 200
  place in Operation Relex chain of command, 132–3
  realises no evidence for children overboard claims, 196
  Reith discusses videotape with, 255
  seeks permission for *Adelaide* to tow boat, 187–8
Sinar Bontano III (boat) *see* SIEV 9
Singapore, 52
Sinodinos, Arthur, 87
60 Minutes (television programme), 132, 158
Skehan, Craig, 105, 164
Smart, Christopher, 243
Smith, Geoff
  asks Banks for chronology of SIEV 4 rescue, 200
  assesses likelihood of conflict in Operation Relex, 130, 131
  attends national prayers, 260
  briefs Shackleton on children overboard, 260
  in chain of command of Operation Relex, 132, 133
  gagged over Operation Relex, 135
  on housing of asylum seekers on *Manoora*, 158
  on landing of asylum seekers, 166
  on new Operation Relex policy, 217
  on outbreak of violence on *Manoora*, 169
  plans Operation Relex, 132
  realises no evidence for children overboard reports, 196–7
  on refugee status of asylum seekers, 147
  retires, 291
  stunned by children overboard claims, 205
Smith, Ric, 30, 218
Sojan, Lindsey, 138, 160
SOLAS, 121, 130–1, 217
Solomon Islands, 159
South Pacific Forum, 105

Spain, 292
Special Air Service
  Battle of the Pot of Jam, 119
  Beazley alerted to presence of, 95
  on board the *Tampa*, 80–3, 95, 103, 117, 119, 127
  cleans up after asylum seekers, 127
  commander speaks to Vadarlis anonymously, 117
  dresses lawyer and diplomat in camouflage suits, 115
  government decides to use, 63
  makes videotapes of asylum seekers, 103, 123
  ordered by Barrie to proceed to *Tampa*, 79
  presents Rinnan with map, 127
Spencer, Barry, 8, 9, 12–13
Stoltenberg, Jens, 76–7, 289
Stone, Shane, 174–5
Støre, Jonas Gahr, 76, 77
Stutchbury, Michael, 253
Sukaimi, Johari, 80–1
Sukarnoputri, Megawati *see* Megawati Sukarnoputri
Sumber Bahagia (boat) *see* SIEV 3
Sumber Lestari (boat) *see* SIEV 10
Sunday (television programme), 42
Surveillance Australia, 8
Suspect Illegal Entry Vessels, 8
  see also Operation Relex, *specific SIEVs*
Sweden, 289
Sydney Airport, 293
Sydney Morning Herald, 105, 164, 262, 272

Taliban, 21–2, 214, 281, 287, 289
talkback radio, 100, 145, 151, 178
Tampa (ship)
  asylum seekers endure unsanitary conditions, 103
  asylum seekers give letter to Norwegian ambassador, 115–17
  asylum seekers send pleas for asylum, 112–13
  asylum seekers suffer from food poisoning, 123
  asylum seekers suffer from heat and diarrhoea, 68
  asylum seekers transferred to *Manoora*, 126, 149
  asylum seekers wage hunger strike, 60–1, 70

Battle of the Pot of Jam, 119
boarded by Special Air Service, 80–3, 95, 103, 117, 119, 127
changes course for Christmas Island, 22–3, 24, 28–9
course monitored by RCC after rescue, 20–1, 22
delay in provision of medical assistance, 54
Federal Court forbids moving of, 119
judge convinced of detention of asylum seekers on, 153
lawyers plead case of asylum seekers in court, 111–12, 118–19, 122–6
leaves Christmas Island, 128–9
makes last voyage with Rinnan, 292–3
moves into Australian waters, 78–9
no legislative basis to expel, 65, 71
Norwegian ambassador allowed to visit, 115
political capital made out of, 174, 178, 280, 283
popular opinion on, 100
radio jammed, 68
refused entry into Australian waters, 24, 49–50
rescues *Palapa* survivors, 17–20
responds to *Palapa*'s Mayday, 14–15
spotted by the *Palapa*, 2
threatened with removal from Australian waters, 84–5
waits outside territorial waters, 29, 58–9
Taronga (ship), 15
Taskforce, 39
Taylor, Bill, 49
Taylor, Simon, 247
temporary protection visas, 91
Tenix, 290
Tennessee (ship), 14
terrorism, 143–4
Textor, Mark, 100, 174–5
Thompson, Gordon, 246
Thorsheim, Ove, 58, 114–17
Titheridge, Al, 139–40, 182–3, 184–6, 199, 200–1, 254
Tobruk (ship), 171, 221, 276, 279, 284
Tonga, 150, 221
Trad, Kaysar, 241
Transit Security Element units, 161
Trees, Wal, 38
Trioli, Virginia, 203
Tuvalu, 150, 221

Unauthorised Arrivals Taskforce, 40
UNCLOS, 17, 121
Union of Christmas Island Workers, 81
United Mineworkers Federation Band, 212
United Nations
  Convention for the Law of the Sea, 17, 121
  Convention on the Status of Refugees, 37, 106–7, 112, 121, 221
  fails to establish convention for sea rescue, 27
  High Commission for Refugees, 37, 51, 106–7, 120–2, 141, 166, 169, 171, 180, 199, 221, 289, 292
  peacekeeping force in East Timor, 102
  rebuffs Australian request on asylum seekers, 103, 104–5
  resettlement plans for boat people, 17
United States, 179, 292
Utting, John, 177

Vadarlis, Eric, 117–18, 122, 145, 152, 155, 156
Vienna Convention on Diplomatic Relations, 114
Vietnam War, 17
Vietnamese refugees, 17, 34–7, 249–50, 284
Villawood detention camp, 44, 46–7
The Visionary, 167
voting patterns, 2001 election, 283

Wali, Mohammed, 69, 78, 115, 116
Walker, Darren, 267, 268
Walker, Steve, 186, 189
Wallace, Duncan, 278–9
Wallenius Line, 15
Walsh, Geoff, 93, 177, 275
Walters, Patrick, 252
War Against Terror, 179, 258, 281, 283
Warner, Nick, 159, 179
Warramunga (ship)
  asylum seekers transferred to *Manoora* from, 160
  intercepts SIEV 1, 137, 138, 139
  intercepts SIEV 3, 147–9
  intercepts SIEV 5, 216, 218–19
  intercepts SIEV 6, 223
  lack of respite for crew of, 222–3
  passengers on SIEV 6 evacuated to, 246
  unloads survivors at Christmas Island, 247
wedge politics, 175

West Timor, 41–2, 45
wharfies' dispute (1998), 119
White Australia Policy, 35
Whitlam, Gough, 35, 90
Whitmont, Debbie, 216
Whittle, Laura, 191, 193, 195–6
Wilhelmsen Line
  awarded Nansen Refugee Award, 292
  begins legal proceedings, 109
  concerned over possible act of piracy, 85
  declines to help PILCH, 113
  follows crisis from contingency room in Oslo, 16
  happy to see Indonesian crew arrested, 126
  history of in Australia, 15
  Howard legislates to prevent suit by, 152
  knows Australia not compelled to land survivors, 27
  prepares to take *Tampa* into Christmas Island, 70
  receives assurance from Howard re medical assistance, 84
  rescue of Vietnamese refugees by ships of, 17
  Rinnan joins, 14
  on Rinnan's reaction to being refused entry, 49
  threatened by Canberra, 77

Wilhelmsen, Wilh
  attends meetings with Norwegian government, 57, 58
  background, 16
  concerned over possible act of piracy, 85
  declines to help PILCH, 113–14
  follows crisis from contingency room, 19
  on the politicisation of the *Tampa* crisis, 28
  reaction to boarding of *Tampa*, 83
  reaction to Canberra's behaviour, 27, 69
  on shipping, 17
  threatens legal action against Australia, 102
  worries over safety of *Tampa* crew, 78
Willheim, Ernst, 52
Williams, Daryl, 76, 85–6, 155
Windemeyer, Sir William, 153
Wirajuda, Hassan, 55, 65, 74, 137
Wollongong (ship), 249–50, 266–72, 276
Woomera detention camp, 44, 135
Wran, Neville, 242

Yahia, Hussein, 249
Yeardley, Malcolm, 267, 268, 271, 276
Yu, John, 262

Zaeef, Mullah Abdul Salam, 281
Zainaab (Iraqi shipwreck survivor), 231
Zanker, Dale, 270
Zanker, Mark, 22, 65, 71, 82
Zuhiry, Ibthaj Al, 182, 191